A
History
of
Airlines
in
Canada

by
John Blatherwick

THE UNITRADE PRESS
TORONTO • CANADA

© 1989 THE UNITRADE PRESS

ISBN 0-919801-66-8

Printed and Bound in Canada
Text editing and layout design by W.J. Boynton

THE UNITRADE PRESS
TORONTO

TEL: (416) 787-5658   P.O. BOX 172, STATION A, TORONTO, ONTARIO M5W 1B2   TELEX: 09-969719

F.J. Blatherwick, CD, MD, FRCP(C)

Francis John Blatherwick is currently the Medical Health Officer of the City of Vancouver and Principal Medical Officer of the Naval Reserve Unit, H.M.C.S. Discovery. He is also the current Provincial Commissioner for Saint John Ambulance in British Columbia. John previously served his country in the Royal Canadian Air Force and the Governor General's Foot Guards.

John is married to a physician (a former classmate), Carol, and they have three boys, James, David and Douglas. He is the author of seven previous books including *Canadian Orders Decorations and Medals,* and his latest book *A Thousand Brave Canadians*, which were also published by The Unitrade Press.

Any new information or corrections to this book can be sent to the author at 1060 West 8th Avenue, Vancouver, B.C., V6H 1C4.

A
History
of
Airlines
in
Canada

Contents

Illustrated Aircraft

Abbreviations

ABC	Advanced Booking Charters		MCA	Maritime Central Airways
A/C	Aircraft		Mk	Mark
ACC	Accident		NASARR	Elongated C-47 Nose for CF-104 training
AFC	Air Force Cross		NTU	Not Taken Up
A/L	Airline		NWT	Northwest Territories
A/S	Air Service		OB	Operated By
A/W	Airways		OF	Operated For
BU	Broken Up		OBE	Officer, Order of the British Empire
BOAC	British Overseas Airways Corporation		OO	On Order
C	Current		P	Piston Aircraft
CAF	Canadian Forces		PWA	Pacific Western Airlines
CF	Canadian Forces		RAE	Royal Aircraft Establishment
C/N	Construction Number		RAF	Royal Air Force
CNA	Central Northern Airways		RCAF	Royal Canadian Air Force
CPA	Canadian Pacific Airline		RCN	Royal Canadian Navy
CPR	Canadian Pacific Railway		REG	Re-engined
C/S	Colour Scheme		REG'N	Registration
CTC	Canadian Transportation Commission		RLS	Released
CENT	Central		RR	Re-registered
CVT	Converted To		RT	Returned To
DEW	Distant Early Warning (Line)		RTS	Returned To Service
DBF	Destroyed by Fire		SEBJ	Societe d'Engerie Baie James
DFC	Distinguished Flying Cross		SQD	Squadron
DFM	Distinguished Flying Medal		ST	Sold To
DOT	Department of Transport (Canada)		STOL	Short Take-Off & Landing
DSO	Distinguished Service Order		SVC	Service
EAT	European Air Transport		T	Turbo prop Aircraft
EMR	Energy, Mines & Resources		TCA	Trans Canada Airlines
EPA	Eastern Provincial Airways		TEA	Trans European Airways
EX	Formerly with		TPA	Trans Provincial Airline
F/N	Fleet Number		TT	Total Time
F/S	Flying Service		USAAF	United States Army Air Force
IATA	International Aviation Transport Association		USAF	United States Air Force
IMP	Impounded		WFU	Withdrawn From Use
INV	Investment		W/O	Written Off
IS	In Service		*	C-F registration, formerly CF- registration
J	Jet Aircraft			
LF	Leased From		Dates: written Month/Year or Day/Month/Year.	
LT	Leased To			

Introduction

The railways opened up this vast land, but the history of transportation in Canada has belonged to its airlines. The early history of Canadian aviation has been detailed in such books as *Voyageurs of the Air* and *125 Years of Canadian Aeronautics*; this book details the history of Canadian airlines during the last half century.

In April 1937, when the federal government established *Trans-Canada Airlines* (TCA) as the only national carrier in Canada, all other Canadian airlines were intended to operate merely as regional carriers. This book details the history of TCA and its growth to become the tenth largest airline in the world as *Air Canada*. It also follows the struggle of the regional airlines to compete with the Canadian giant in the trans-continental and overseas markets.

The efforts of Grant McConachie's *Canadian Pacific Airlines* (CPA) to compete with TCA in the Canadian trans-continental market culminates in its amalgamation with *Pacific Western Airlines* and the emergence of the giant *Canadian Airlines International*. The story of *Pacific Western Airlines* is that of a small bush operation which, under the leadership of Frank Baker, became a strong regional operator with continued aspirations to be a trans-continental airline, and culminates in the David and Goliath takeover of CPA to form *Canadian Airlines International*.

Transair, Nordair, Quebecair and *Eastern Provincial Airways* (EPA) along with *Pacific Western Airlines* (PWA) formed the group of regional airlines from the late 1950s to early 1980s. PWA took over *Transair* and CPA absorbed *Nordair, Quebecair* and EPA, effectively eliminating the regional airlines as we knew them.

However, the void was quickly filled by a new group, the commuter airlines, which are rapidly beginning to look like the old regional group. The commuter airlines are all associated with or owned in part by either *Air Canada* or *Canadian Airlines International. Air BC, Time Air, Air Ontario* and *Inter-Canadian* are the largest of this group and each has now entered the jet age. There are now thirteen airlines in the commuter group.

Wardair started the major charter operations and after giving up its northern operations, concentrated on flying jet charters while attempting to become a trans-Canada passenger carrier. After finally succeeding in becoming a scheduled Canadian carrier, the company, with its small fleet of jumbo jets used mainly for inter-national charters, was re-equipping for its Canadian routes. The takeover of *Wardair* by *Canadian* in 1989 will leave the future of *Wardair* in doubt.

Ontario Worldair and *Swiftair Cargo* were two jet operators which only lasted a couple of years. *Worldways Canada* and *Nationair,* however, are companies which purchased older jets (DC-8s) and have made their mark in the Canadian charter market. *Air Transat, Minerve* and *Points of Call* are all new jet charter operations just getting underway. Late 1989 saw the emergence of two Boeing 757 operators, *Odyssey International* and *Air 2000* (to be renamed); DC-8 operators, *Crownair* and *Holidair*; and a Boeing 737 operator, *Vacationair*.

A short section of the book is devoted to the smaller companies which the reader may have seen around the local airports. Some are still flying and may eventually become larger; many others have been absorbed by larger carriers or ceased operations. Another section is devoted to the aircraft flown by the provincial governments and the many organizations which fly aircraft for the Federal Government.

This book brings together in one place for the first time all the fleet lists of Canada's major airlines. *Air Canada* and *Canadian Pacific* have kept detailed histories of their aircraft and both were able to provide details of their early fleets. The other airlines did not keep details of their fleets and these have been put together by researching the *Canadian Civil Aircraft Registry* and the books listed in the bibliography. The *Eastern Provincial* fleet list was only made possible by their senior pilot going through his logbook and giving me dates and registrations. In recent times, the fleets have been maintained by reference to *Aviation Letter, North American Aviation News (NAAN)*, and *Westflight.* These monthly publications were also the source for much of the history of the airlines from 1975 onward. For the real aviation enthusiast, these publications are a must and their addresses are given in the Research Section of the book.

This book is a history of aircraft and routes, not of people. More extensive histories of the individual airlines can be found in the books listed in the bibliography. These books also cover the people in much more detail than this book could undertake to do. Most airline histories do not detail the crashes suffered by the airline but because they are a significant part of any airline's history, I have covered them as best I could. Major accidents to Canadian airlines are fortunately very rare these days; none of the jumbo jets operated by Canadian airlines has ever had a loss of life.

Finally, I would like to thank the publishers for taking on this project which is outside their normal publishing field of philately, numismatics and militaria and giving it the exposure it deserves. For the aviation enthusiast, the fleet lists will be extremely helpful. For the casual traveller, maybe they will look at the paint scheme and registration of the aircraft they next fly in and find it in this book.

Canadian Forces Cosmopolitan, 10954

Canadian Pacific DC-3, CF-CRW
Photo courtesy of CP Air

PART ONE

Major Trans-Canadian and International Airlines

Boeing Stearman CF-ASF – Trans Canada Airlines' first aircraft used for mail service.
Photo courtesy of Air Canada.

TCA started its large fleet of passenger aircraft with Lockheed 10As, like the one above, purchased from *Canadian Airways.*
Photo courtesy of Air Canada.

TCA Bristol Freighter CF-TFY
Photo courtesy of Air Canada.

Air Canada
(Trans-Canada Airlines)

Air Canada Boeing 727 (C-GAAB)
Photo courtesy of Air Canada.

HEADQUARTERS:
1 Place Ville Marie, Montreal, Quebec, H3B 3P7

MAJOR BASES:
Montreal (Dorval), Toronto, Winnipeg, Vancouver

FLEET 1989:
21 - Boeing 767s;
6 - Boeing 747s;
33 - Boeing 727s;
6 - DC-8-73CFs;
35 - DC-9-32s;
2 - L1011-1s;
4 - L1011-100s;
6 - L1011-500s.

COLOURS:
The aircraft is white with a grey lower fuselage and a red tail. A broad, bright red cheat line wraps around the nose and runs the length of the fuselage; with a narrow white cheat line below the red. A large white Air Canada logo is displayed on the tail and the title 'AIR CANADA' appears in red on the upper fuselage. The registration, in black, is aft on the lower edge of the red cheat line. A broad maroon cheat line below the red was added in 1988.

ROUTES:
Canada:
Victoria – Vancouver – Calgary – Edmonton – Saskatoon – Regina – Winnipeg – Thunder Bay – Toronto – Windsor – North Bay – Sudbury – Timmins – Ottawa – Montreal – Rouyn Noranda – Val d'Or – Quebec City – Sept-Iles – Halifax – Sydney – Yarmouth – Fredericton – Saint John – Moncton – Charlottetown – Stephenville – Gander – St. John's – Goose Bay.

U.S.A.:
Boston – Chicago – Fort Lauderdale – Fort Myers – Honolulu – Los Angeles – Miami – New York – Orlando – San Francisco – Tampa/St. Petersburg – West Palm Beach.

Mexico/Caribbean:
Acapulco – Antigua – Barbados – Bermuda – Cancun – Freeport – Ixtapa – Guadeloupe – Kingston – Martinique – Montego Bay – Nassau – Point-a-Pitre – Port-au-Prince – Puerto Plata – Puerto Vallarta – Santo Domingo – St. Lucia – Trinidad – Varadero.

Europe:
Glasgow – Manchester – London – Dusseldorf – Frankfurt – Brussels (cargo hub) – Paris – Zurich – Vienna – Madrid – Lisbon.

East:
Bombay – Singapore

Charters:
Around the world; Cargo trans-Canada and around the world.

HISTORY:

In 1936, the Canadian Government established the Department of Transport under Mr. C.D. Howe. One of Mr. Howe's first endeavours was to establish a naional airline. When he approached the *Canadian National Railway, Canadian Pacific Railway* and *Canadian Airways* to form a consortium to operate the national airline, *Canadian Airways* and the CPR decided not to be a part of the scheme. Thus on 10 April 1937, the Trans-Canada Air Lines Act became law with the airline being a wholly owned subsidiary of the *Canadian National Railway.*

To show his faith in this new airline, Mr. Howe took part in the first dawn to dusk Montreal to Vancouver flight. On 30 July 1937, a *Department of Transport* Lockheed 12A, CF-CCT (now on display in the National Aviation Museum in Ottawa), took off from Montreal (St. Hubert) and 17 hours, 34 minutes later landed in Vancouver. The flight included five stops: Gillies (Ontario), Sioux Lookout (Ontario), Winnipeg (Manitoba), Regina (Saskatchewan), and Lethbridge (Alberta) with 14 hours, 30 minutes of actual flying time.

The new airline acquired its first three planes from *Canadian Airways:* a Boeing Stearman used for mail service, which was sold to *Northern Airways* two years later, and two Lockheed 10As. The first passenger service was operated 1 September 1937 on the Vancouver to Seattle route taken over from *Canadian Airways.* Three more Lockheed 10As were added in October 1937.

The year 1938 was mainly a training year for TCA in preparation for the transcontinental passenger service. Ten Lockheed 14 Super Electras were added and in addition to training flights, these ten-seat aircraft established freight service from Vancouver to Winnipeg and then to Montreal. The airline suffered its first fatal crash on 18 November 1938 when a Lockheed 14 CF-TCL crashed at Regina killing both pilots.

April 1, 1939 saw the first transcontinental passenger revenue service when two aircraft left Vancouver and Montreal respectively to cross the continent. In February 1940, this service was expanded to include Moncton. The five Lockheed 10A aircraft were sold in 1939, four going to the RCAF and one to the *Department of Transport.* Six Lockheed fourteen aircraft were added, resulting in a fleet of fifteen of these planes by the end of 1939. The price of a round-trip ticket from Vancouver to Ottawa was $248.50!

TCA pilots and staff wishing to join the war effort had to have the airline's permission. In 1940, the airline continued to establish its passenger and freight services. On 1 April, 1940, TCA began a second daily transcontinental service.

Six Lockheed 18 Lodestars were added to the TCA fleet in 1941 and two Lockheed 14 aircraft were sold.

On February 6, 1941, a Lockheed 14 crashed at Armstrong, Ontario, with the first loss of passenger life for the airline. Toronto to Halifax service was started in April and Toronto to New York was added in May. The airline began to service BOAC's *Atlantic Return Ferry Service* aircraft at that time.

Six more Lodestars were added in late 1942 and St. John's Newfoundland was added to the airline's route system. Twelve of the Lockheed 14s were converted to model 14-08, increasing their gross weight. Twelve Lodestars were modified in 1942 to increase their carrying capacity.

The Canadian government's Transatlantic Air Service was begun on 22 July 1943 by TCA. Eight modified Lancaster bombers, called Lancastrians, were used to fly mail to the troops overseas and to carry VIP passengers. The first of these aircraft was built in Britain and the remaining seven were built at the Victory Plant in Toronto. The Lancastrians carried ten passengers (not in comfort!) and crossed the Atlantic in twelve and a half hours. These aircraft were cold and noisy but they did the job until retired in 1947.

On 4 November 1943, Lockheed 18 CF-TCX had both engines quit on takeoff from Malton and the pilot settled the plane into a field. The plane was a write-off but there were no serious injuries to the crew or passengers.

The last three Lodestars were added in 1944 bringing the fleet total to fifteen aircraft purchased although only fourteen now remained. TCA also leased a Lockheed 12A from the RCAF during 1944. As the war came to an end, TCA recruited large numbers of ex-RCAF aircrew into the airline. At least two hundred and fifty pilots with wartime flying experience were hired with the seniority list growing from one hundred and one in 1942 to three hundred and nineteen in 1946.

A Lancastrian, CF-CMU, was lost on an eastbound crossing in December 1944 and was never found. Another, CF-CMS, burned after crashing at Dorval on 1 July 1945. The end of the war saw the DC-3 brought into the TCA fleet with three former USAAF aircraft added in 1945. A total of thirty DC-3s eventually served with TCA, most of them former RCAF planes. The DC-3 served with TCA until 1963 and in its twenty-eight year history with the airline, no DC-3s were written-off in crashes.

Two Lockheed 14s were written off at Moncton, New Brunswick in separate incidents, one and a half years apart: CF-TCF in February 1945 and CF-TCJ in September 1946. In 1946, twenty-four DC-3s were acquired, all but four of them being from the RCAF. On 19 November 1946, TCA added a Canadair North Star on loan from the RCAF. Five more of the Mark-1, unpressurized aircraft were loaned to TCA by the RCAF in 1947 and all but one of these was returned in 1949. The one aircraft not returned was CF-TEL which was destroyed by fire when its fuel tanks ruptured on landing at Sydney, Nova Scotia on 12 August 1948. Fortunately, there was no loss of life. These North Stars started trans-Atlantic flights in April 1947, replacing the Lancastrians. The pressurized version of the North Stars, the Mark-2 models, began serving with the airline in October 1947. Twenty were received by TCA by the end of 1948. Three more North Stars were added from *Canadian Pacific* in 1951, these being C-4 models which BOAC referred to as Argonauts.

The North Star was basically a DC-4 with Rolls Royce Merlin engines. The aircraft originally carried forty passengers but in high density seating could carry sixty-two passengers. It was an extremely noisy aircraft, especially the unpressurized model. While many modifications were made to reduce the cabin noise, passengers never came to enjoy quiet trips on the North Star.

aircraft thus giving a boost to the Canadian aircraft industry. However, the plane's small passenger capacity (30-50) and a reluctance to lead the aviation industry into the jet age doomed this Canadian airliner and only one was built. AVRO had wanted to put two 2A.J.65 engines on this aircraft but the British government would not release these engines for civilian use. Thus the company was forced to use four Rolls Royce Derwent engines which used far too much fuel for the small passenger capacity. The AVRO Jetliner flew before either the DC-6B or the Super Constellation!

Early in the 1950's, TCA opened new routes to Europe and the Caribbean. In 1953, to thwart an attempt by *Canadian Pacific* to open a trans-Canada freight service, Trans Canada Airlines purchased three Bristol Freighters to operate its own freight service. These aircraft were too small for the TCA routes and they were quickly retired and replaced by six North Stars, converted to all-cargo configuration. The North Star carried

TCA Lockheed L-1049C Super Constellation CF-TGC.
Photo courtesy of Air Canada.

With the addition of the North Stars, TCA began selling off the Lockheed 14s and Lockheed 18s so that by the end of 1949, the TCA fleet included only twenty North Stars and thirty DC-3s.

In 1948, Group Captain Gordon R. McGregor, OBE, DFC (later OC) became President of TCA and remained at the helm for the next twenty years. He was one of the first Canadian recipients of the Distinguished Flying Cross in WWII, flying in the Battle of Britain. One of his first dilemmas was to decide if TCA should acquire jet aircraft.

On 10 August 1949, the Canadian-built AVRO Jetliner flew for the first time. This was the second jetliner in the world to fly, only two weeks after the de Havilland Comet. AVRO tried to interest TCA in buying this

an eighteen thousand pound payload, compared to the eight thousand pounds carried by the Bristol Freighter. The cargo North Stars remained in service until 1961.

To replace the North Stars for cargo work and meet the increased demand for passenger space, TCA purchased eight Lockheed L-1049 Super Constellations in 1954. This four-engine, piston aircraft carried sixty-three passengers. Six more L-1049s were added during 1956 and 1958, the later models carrying seventy-five passengers.

The year 1954 was not a good one for TCA because of several accidents. On 8 April, North Star CF-TFW, one of the former *Canadian Pacific* aircraft purchased in 1951, was en route Winnipeg to Calgary. At 11:43 AM, it collided with RCAF Harvard #3309 and crashed into the city of Moose Jaw, Saskatchewan. The four crew members and thirty-one passengers aboard the North Star, the pilot of the Harvard and one person in a house on the ground all perished. The Harvard had been at the wrong elevation on a training flight out of RCAF Station Moose Jaw. Newly acquired Super Constellation, CF-TGG, crashed on take-off at Brampton, Ontario on 17 December but fortunately there was no loss of life.

In December 1954, TCA became the first North American airline to add turboprop equipment to its fleet when the first Vickers Viscount was delivered. Fourteen more of the model-724 aircraft were delivered to the airline by February 1956. The aircraft was introduced on the Toronto to New York route and operated with a 97% load factor. This four-engine turboprop was very popular with passengers because of its quiet ride and large oval windows. More than 250 modifications were made to the model-724 for TCA, including redesign of the cockpit for two-man crew operations and use of the Mark 505 Dart engine with a higher cruising power than previous engines. While the 97% load factor did not remain forever, it still levelled out at a very respectable 80% after the first year. Thirty-six of the slightly improved model-757s were delivered between 1956 and 1959 bringing the total number of Viscounts to see service with TCA to fifty-one. The Viscount aircraft carried fifty-four passengers and cruised at 324 mph.

The TCA Viscounts suffered four major accidents resulting in write-offs. The first involved CF-TGL at Idlewild Airport, New York on 10 November 1958. *Seaboard & Western Airlines* L-1049 N6503C went out of control on landing and struck the Viscount. Both aircraft caught fire and were burnt but with no loss of life. The TCA Viscount had only 8,950 hours on its airframe at the time of the accident. On 3 October 1959, CF-TGY struck a water tower on landing at Malton (now Pearson International) Airport, Toronto, and landed short of the runway during a squall. All forty persons on board survived. Another Viscount, CF-THT, also landed short of the runway at Malton and was written-off on 13 June 1964. The final write-off was CF-THK at Sept Iles, Quebec on 7 April 1969. The plane developed a fire in one of the engine nacelles immediately after take-off. It immediately returned for an emergency landing and the Viscount was burnt out on the runway after landing. Sixteen passengers and four crew survived the accident but one passenger was killed when evacuating the still moving aircraft, the only fatality caused by the Viscount in just under twenty years of service.

In 1955, thirteen Viscounts were added, six North Stars were converted to freighters and the three Bristol Freighters were sold. By the end of the year, the fleet consisted of twenty-two North Stars, twenty-five DC-3s, seven L-1049s and fourteen Viscounts.

In 1956, TCA flew refugees to Canada from Hun-

gary. The original three DC-3s acquired from the USAAF in 1945 were sold in 1948 and the first subsequent sale of DC-3s occurred in 1956 when *Quebecair* obtained two from TCA.

On 9 December 1956, North Star CF-TFD reported a fire in one engine near Hope, B.C. and indicated that it was returning to Vancouver. Despite an intense search, the wreckage on Mount Slesse, where the fifty-nine passengers and three crew had lost their lives, was not found until 14 May 1957.

By 1958, the phase-out of the DC-3 had begun in earnest with thirteen having been sold. Another would be sold the following year. TCA greatly expanded its domestic and European routes at this time. Service was begun to Brussels and Zurich and a Montreal to Paris service was started.

On 7 February 1960, TCA took delivery of its first DC-8 jet aircraft. The plane made its first flight for the airline on 1 April 1960. The first eight DC-8s were series 41 and 42 aircraft which were all quickly upgraded to the series 43, giving them each a higher takeoff weight. Three series 43 aircraft were also purchased in 1961. The DC-8 was powered by four Rolls-Royce Conway engines, and had a 127-passenger seating capacity when purchased. The seating capacity was increased over time by using a shorter seat pitch. A $20 million aircraft and engine overhaul plant was built at Montreal's Dorval airport to service the DC-8s.

Another aircraft, the Vickers Vanguard, joined the TCA fleet in December 1960, and first entered service on 1 February 1961. Twenty-three of these four-engine turboprops were purchased. The Vanguard initially carried ninety-six passengers but this was later increased to one hundred and eight. The Vanguards had a great number of problems, in particular excessive noise and vibration in the forward cabin and a large number of engine replacements were necessary. This turboprop was introduced at a time when TCA and the other airlines were phasing in jet equipment and in retrospect probably should not have been purchased. However, this aircraft (whose main passenger feature was very large windows) did serve with the company for twelve years with no major accidents. One of the Vanguards, CF-TKV, encountered severe turbulence over Rocky Mountain House, Alberta, which resulted in one death. After that accident, passengers were encouraged to wear their seatbelts at all times. Vanguard CF-TKK was converted to an all-cargo aircraft in December 1966 and was the last Vanguard to leave the company in March, 1972.

With the arrival of the Vanguards, the North Stars were retired in early 1961. Fifteen of the North Stars were sold to *Overseas Aviation* in the UK but the deal fell through when *Overseas* went bankrupt. Eleven of these then went to Mr. John Gaul and were stored at Baginton in the UK until either scrapped or sold to other airlines. The eighty-four acre Dorval maintenance base was completed in 1961.

TCA began selling it's Super Constellations in 1961 and by the end of 1963 all had been sold. Two DC-3s and one Viscount were sold to *Transair* for $1.00 and the rights to the prairie air route: Winnipeg - Brandon - Yorkton - Regina - Saskatoon - Prince Albert. With the sale of their last two DC-3s and the Constellations, the airline had an all-turbine fleet by the end of 1963, consisting of 14 DC-8s, 45 Viscounts and 22 Vanguards.

Four DC-8-54F cargo jets were purchased in 1963. These aircraft had Pratt & Whitney jet engines and initially operated in a mixed cargo/passenger mode: four pallets plus 117 passengers. On 29 November 1963, DC-8-54F CF-TJN took off from Montreal and crashed shortly after takeoff at Ste. Therese de Blainville, Quebec. All one hundred and eighteen passengers and the crew were killed. This accident remains as the airline's

from London to Ottawa on the first DC-8 painted in the new AIR CANADA titles and paint scheme. The Act changing the name from *Trans-Canada Airlines* to *Air Canada* became law on 1 January 1965. The name change was felt necessary as the airline had extensive routes to Europe, the Caribbean and the United States and was thus much more than a 'trans-Canada' airline. The new name was also bilingual and thus better represented the two official Canadian languages.

TCA had used two major colour schemes since the war. The earlier version was an all silver aircraft with a red cheat line extending the length of the fuselage and covering just above and just below the windows. Two thin white lines ran through the windows. The TCA symbol was on the tail and near the forward door. The title, TRANS-CANADA AIRLINES appeared in red on the upper fuselage. Late in the 1950s, the colour scheme was changed to an all-white aircraft with the same cheat

Air Canada Vickers Viscount CF-THJ
Photo courtesy of Air Canada.

most serious accident. Four more DC-8-54Fs were purchased between 1964 and 1966 and this fleet of seven was used only for cargo after 1966. The DC-8-54F could carry a load of 45,000 pounds. Three all-passenger DC-8-53s were purchased at the end of 1968 to replace the passenger capacity lost when the DC-8-54Fs were converted to all-cargo use.

The 'short' DC-8s suffered two other serious accidents. On 19 May 1967, DC-8-54F CF-TJM crashed on a training flight as it approached the Ottawa International Airport. The three crew members on board were killed. The plane had been practising engine out approaches, a training technique made obsolete by the use of simulators. Corporal John Metka of the RCAF was awarded the British Empire Medal for Gallantry when he entered the burning aircraft to search for survivors. The other accident occurred on 21 June 1973 when CF-TIJ was being refuelled at Toronto and caught on fire. The aircraft was gutted but there were no injuries.

On 13 October 1964, Queen Elizabeth was flown

lines, symbols and titles. The new Air Canada colour scheme had a red cheat line running the length of the fuselage and extending well above and just below the windows. A white band separated the red cheat line from the bare metal (silver) lower fuselage. The tail was all red with a large Air Canada symbol in white. The title AIR CANADA was displayed on the upper fuselage in black and the registration was at the base of the tail in black. The fleet number, in white, appeared on the upper tail. The nose, forward of the cockpit, was all black and a red Air Canada symbol preceded the title on the upper fuselage.

Early 1966 saw six of the seventy-two passenger DC-9-14 jets purchased. These aircraft were quickly proved too small for the Air Canada route structure and were sold to *Southern Airlines* and *Texas Airlines* in 1968. To replace these aircraft and the Viscounts and Vanguards with jet aircraft, a large order for the DC-9-32 was made in 1967. Twelve of these twin-engine jets were delivered in 1967. The DC-9-32 carries one hundred and fifteen passengers, and many of the forty-seven which were purchased by 1974 will continue to serve well into the 1990s. One of the DC-9-32s operated in an all cargo mode for four years during the seventies and carried the title AIR CANADA CARGO.

The stretched versions of the DC-8, the series 61 and 63 aircraft, were bought by Air Canada beginning in 1967. These stretch DC-8 carries up to two hundred and fifty-seven passengers and is thirty-seven feet longer than the short DC-8. The company commenced service to the Soviet Union in 1967.

Gordon R. McGregor stepped down as President of Air Canada on 31 May 1968 and was replaced by Yves Pratte as Chairman and Chief Executive Officer and J.R. Baldwin as President.

Air Canada purchased a 27% interest in *Air Jamaica* in 1969 and immediately loaned them one of their DC-9 aircraft. Service to Prague, Czechoslovakia, was started in 1970.

On 5 July 1970, DC-8-63, CF-TIW, was on a routine approach to the Toronto Airport. The copilot apparently pulled the spoilers too early and the plane lost airspeed rapidly. This resulted in the aircraft hitting the runway very hard and one of the four engines was torn from its mounting. The pilot, not realizing that he had lost an engine, applied full power and tried to go around but the badly damaged aircraft was only able to climb for a short distance before crashing into a field beside the airport. All 109 persons on board were killed.

The jumbo-jet era started for Air Canada in 1971 with the purchase of three Boeing 747s. Initially, these giants could each carry three hundred and sixty-five passengers but in later years, using the all-economy seating, four hundred and twenty-nine passengers could be accommodated. Four additional Boeing 747s were purchased in the seventies, two of them being 'combi' aircraft which could carry ten pallets and two hundred and seventy-five passengers.

The Vanguard passenger service ended in October 1971, but the use of Vanguards for freight lasted for almost another year, ending in May 1972. To replace the Vanguards, eight DC-9-15 aircraft were purchased from *Continental Airlines*. The CD-9-15 carried ninety-four passengers. These aircraft were used on the shorter routes, mainly in Ontario and Quebec.

Rapidair service between Toronto and Montreal commenced in 1972 and a year later between Toronto and Ottawa. The service provides a quick check-in, no reservation feature and operates hourly during peak periods. High density DC-9 and DC-8 aircraft were used initially and Boeing 727s used after 1974.

A second type of jumbo jet was added to the fleet in 1973, three-engine Lockheed L-1011 Tristars. Twelve of the 256-passenger aircraft were purchased

for long haul services within Canada and North America, chiefly replacing the stretch DC-8. Two of these, C-FTNA and C-FTNC, operated with *Eastern Airlines* in the winter and Air Canada in the summer during the 1973 to 1978 period. These aircraft appeared in several colour schemes which were hybrids of the two airlines. The planes bore a wide light blue cheat line with blue Air Canada titles for one summer and operated in full *Eastern Airlines* colours with Air Canada titles for another. With the general decline in passenger service during the late seventies, four of these aircraft were upgraded from series-1 to series-100 aircraft. The major difference was that the series-100 had a much longer range than the series-1 and could thus operate on the trans-Atlantic routes.

With the retirement of the last Viscount in April 1974, Air Canada became an all jet airline. The loss of the Viscount fleet was a blow to employment in the Winnipeg area because the aircraft had been overhauled and serviced in the Air Canada facilities at Winnipeg International Airport. The airline's headquarters had moved from Winnipeg to Montreal in 1949 and now all of the airline's overhaul facilities were also going to be in Montreal. Most of the Viscount fleet was mothballed in Winnipeg and sat there for the better part of the next decade before a few of them were sold in Zaire or were fully scrapped. One Viscount remains on display at the Western Canada Aviation Museum at the Winnipeg Airport and another, without titles, was still sitting outside the museum as late as 1989.

To demonstrate the effectiveness of STOL aircraft for commuter service, Air Canada assisted the Canadian government in setting up a demonstration air service between Montreal and Ottawa. The service operated under the name *Air Transit* and used six DHC-6 Twin Otters. Although Twin Otters usually operate with eighteen to twenty seats, *Air Transit* Twin Otters used only eleven seats to provide greater passenger comfort.

In Ottawa, the Rockcliffe Airport, a former RCAF airfield and now the home of the National Aeronautical Collection, was chosen as the terminal because it was only twelve minutes from downtown Ottawa. In Montreal, the EXPO 67 Victoria parking lot, only five minutes from downtown, was developed as the runway and terminal. Flight time was about forty-five minutes.

STOLmobile taxi service (passenger vans) departed from downtown Montreal fifteen minutes prior to take-off and departed from downtown Ottawa thirty minutes before flight time. This service was included in the airfare with parking at the STOLports also available. Hourly flights operated both ways and there was a surcharge during peak periods.

The service commenced on 24 July 1974 and ceased operations as planned on 30 April 1976. The experiment was deemed very successful although the small capacity of the aircraft used could not have sustained the service. It was hoped that the demonstration project would assist de Havilland Canada in its sale of the Twin Otter and the new DASH-7 aircraft. The six Twin Otters, which had operated in an all-red colour scheme with white titles, were sold to the *Department of Transport* and retained their red paint scheme with the DOT. No other commuter services were started in Canada using de Havilland aircraft until *City Express* began a service between Toronto Island Airport and Ottawa's Uplands Airport using DASH-7 and Saunders ST-27 aircraft in 1984.

Air Canada filled its requirements for a medium sized aircraft in 1974 when it purchased the Boeing 727 (series 200). Thirty-nine of these 132-passenger aircraft were purchased for delivery over the next eight years. Six Boeing 727s were used for Air Canada's *Rapidair* service and operated in a high density 144-passenger configuration.

The early model DC-8-43s were increased in seat density to 161 seats (from 127 initially) for the summer charters of 1975. The short DC-8s were phased out after this when three were leased to *Cubana Airlines* and the others sold, mainly for spare parts. The company made the first change in its colour scheme since adopting the name Air Canada in 1964 by changing the black nose to an all-white nose. Then, in the mid-seventies, the colour scheme included a wide, bright-red cheat line that wrapped around the nose. The AIR CANADA title appeared on the upper fuselage in red but with no company logo ahead of the name. The tail remained all red except for a white Air Canada logo which was much larger than in the previous scheme and the registration was moved to the rear fuselage in black.

Claude Taylor took over as the Chief Executive Officer of Air Canada in 1976. In addition to leasing the DC-8-43s to *Cubana,* Air Canada also provided flight training and ground handling training for *Cubana.* Two of the leased aircraft had serious accidents while with *Cubana.* In March 1976, CF-TJK was destroyed in a mid-air collision and in October 1976, CF-TJI was destroyed on landing. The third DC-8 was returned to Air Canada and sold to International Air Leasing, eventually ending up with *Air Jamaica.*

In the winter of 1976, the first of the L-1011s (C-FTNJ), was sent to Palmdale, California, for conversion to the long range series-100. The conversion consisted of an additional centre fuselage fuel tank, wing tank modifications and tricycle landing gear installation.

Nordair had been rumoured for merger or takeover by several airlines prior to Air Canada's offer of $11.50 per share for all existing *Nordair* stock in 1977. Air Canada was thus able to purchase a majority interest in *Nordair* and in July 1978 the CTC approved the take-over. The plan originally called for the two airlines to merge, with *Nordair* operating many of the Air Canada DC-8s on charter operations and for the seniority of the aircrews to be merged. There was strong opposition from the unions of both companies and from the federal government, and *Nordair* continued to operate as a separate corporate entity from Air Canada until it was finally sold in 1984.

Four of Air Canada's DC-9-15Fs were sold in 1977 to *Air Florida* and the remaining four were sold by 1980. For the summer of 1977, a total of 173,000 charter seats were sold and the L-1011s had their seating capacity increased by thirty-three seats to 289.

The first serious DC-9 accident occurred on 26 June 1978 when CF-TLV tried to abort its takeoff on runway 23L at Toronto International Airport and ran off the end of the runway. The aircraft ended up in a gully where quick evacuation held the casualty list to only two dead although several other passengers were seriously injured. A tire failure on takeoff threw rubber into the right engine causing it to disintegrate. The pilot noticed the loss of power before reaching his rotation point and, except for the gully at the end of the runway, probably could have saved the aircraft.

In May 1978, Air Canada started a small package service called *Airvelope.* By August *Airvelope* linked seventeen Canadian cities and would eventually service all the cities served by Air Canada. The company's highly successful *Courier Service* evolved from *Airvelope.* The former *United Airlines* Boeing 727s (series -100) were bought and operated in an all-cargo configuration, bearing AIR CANADA CARGO titles. Interchange arrangements were made with *Federal Express* the following year with the companies linking their courier services in Chicago. These Boeing 727s were sold via Plymouth Leasing to *Interstate Airlines* in October 1981 when Air Canada found they could not be fully utilized. The *Courier Service* was continued using regular scheduled passenger flights and the DC-8 freighter flights. A close association with *Federal Express* remained, *Federal Express* buying several Boeing 727s from Air Canada and linking up with Air Canada at Vancouver, Winnipeg and Toronto.

In the fall of 1978, Air Canada leased some of their high-density seating DC-8s for use on the *Hadj* flights from Africa to Jeddah, Saudi Arabia. These leases continued each fall for several years and later involved the high-density Boeing 747s as well.

On 17 September 1979, DC-9 C-FTLU was at 25,000 feet on a flight from Boston to Yarmouth when its tail cone separated. The flight returned safely to Boston. Also in 1979, Air Canada was operating two round trips per week Kuala Lumpur – Tokyo – Vancouver – Edmonton or Montreal carrying Vietnamese refugees to

Air Canada Vickers Vanguard CF-TKP
Photo courtesy of Air Canada.

Canada. The high-density (227 seats) DC-8-63s were used for these flights. A profit of $55.4 million was realized in 1979.

In March 1980, the first DC-8-63 was converted to an all-cargo aircraft. A total of six were converted from 1980 to 1982 and two more in 1986. These aircraft replaced the short DC-8s, becoming the mainstay of the company's freight operations during the 1980s. A very extensive summer charter season was undertaken in 1980 with flights to Newcastle, Prestwick, Luton, London, Manchester, Birmingham, Cardiff, Frankfurt and Belfast to name only a few. The Vietnamese refugee flights continued and charter flights to Reno were begun. The first of many leases of the L-1011s to *Air Lanka* occurred in 1980 and Air Canada operated DC-8-54F freighters on flights from Toronto to Caracas for General Motors throughout the year. In the fall of 1980, two stretch DC-8s were leased to *Royal Air Maroc* for the Hadj pilgrimage operating between Morocco and Jeddah. *British Airways* received access to Vancouver, Calgary and Edmonton, thus providing competition to Air Canada between western Canada and England. The last three DC-9-15s were sold in late 1980. Air Canada again showed a profit at the end of the year of $57 million carrying thirteen million passengers.

Connaisseur Service was introduced in early 1981 to compete with *CP Air's* Empress Class Service. Free drinks, free headsets, free meals and a meal selection were some of the features introduced for the full-fare paying economy class passengers. The first of six L-1011-500 Tristars was introduced early in 1981. This aircraft was smaller than the previous L1011s purchased by Air Canada carrying only 214 passengers and was used to replace the DC-8s on domestic and North American routes. A second L1011-1 Tristar was leased to *Air Lanka* when the series-500 Tristars arrived. New life was given to the remaining DC-9 aircraft when 'wide-body' interiors were installed and the engines modified to give 5% more fuel efficiency.

Air Canada continued its aggressive charter operations during the summer of 1981, introducing scheduled charters' from Vancouver to Los Angeles with a Boeing 747 and introducing 'no frills' service Vancouver, Calgary or Edmonton – Toronto, with the 458-seat Boeing 747, C-FTOA. Vancouver to Honolulu Charters were also introduced. The Tristar-500s replaced the Boeing 747s on flights from Western Canada to Europe because of their better load factors. Boeing 747 C-FTOA was leased to *Royal Air Maroc* for the Hadj pilgrimage from September to November 1981.

Air Canada made a profit of $40.1 million in 1981 and also acquired a 30% interest in *Innotech Aviation*. A large part of this profit resulted from the sale of some DC-9s to *Altair* after a previous deal with *Columbia Airlines* had fallen through. Originally five aircraft were to go to *Altair* but only three were delivered with the other two ultimately being sold to *Pacific Southwest Airlines*.

By 1982, the full effects of the recession were being felt by the aviation industry. Air Canada consolidated its routes and eliminated some of the scheduled charter flights where they were not profitable. Two of the Boeing 747s, C-FTOD and C-FTOE were fitted with first class sleeperette seats. The DC-8-61 fleet was withdrawn from use by the end of the year and sent to Marana, Arizona for long term storage and sale. Conversion of the six DC-8-63s to cargo aircraft was completed by the end of the year and a decision was made to re-engine these aircraft with fuel efficient CFM-5 engines. Two DC-9s were sold to *New York Air* early in 1982 with the three DC-9s finally delivered to *Altair* in mid-1982. Air Canada also lost a DC-9 on June 2, 1982, when C-FTLY was destroyed in a hangar fire in Montreal. Connaisseur service was now available on all domestic and international flights except *Rapidair* flights.

The delivery of the 37th to 39th Boeing 727s in 1982 completed the purchase of Boeing 727s.

A second generation, wide-bodied, fuel efficient aircraft were added to the Air Canada fleet in late 1982 when two Boeing 767s were received. Air Canada purchased twelve of these twin-engine, 201-passenger aircraft with this order. The planes carried eighteen first class passengers seated six abreast and one hundred and eighty-three economy class passengers seated seven abreast. The aircraft has a range of 3,100 miles and cruises at 530 mph. When the first two aircraft were delivered, they could not be put into use by Air Canada as the pilots wanted to be paid for flying wide-bodied aircraft while Air Canada wanted to pay the same scale as for the DC-8-63s. The dispute was finally settled and on 17 January 1983, the Boeing 767 flew between Toronto and Montreal. For the year ending 1982, Air Canada lost $32.6 million.

With the arrival of the Boeing 767s, the last passenger DC-8-63s were retired in April 1983. The Boeing 767 did not have an auspicious start in Air Canada service. On 23 July 1983, C-GAUN flew from Edmonton to Montreal despite the fact that its fuel gauges were not functioning. In Montreal, it was refuelled for the return flight to Edmonton but an error was made in converting gallons to litres. The plane next landed in Ottawa where the same conversion error was made and hence it took off for Edmonton with insufficient fuel on board. The aircraft ran out of fuel about 150 miles from Winnipeg and its crew glided the aircraft, weighing more than 100 tons, to a safe landing at the former RCAF Station at Gimili, Manitoba. The plane was landed safely on one of the former runways, which was being used for stock car races, with no serious injuries.The aircraft was only damaged when the nose wheel collapsed because of the short runway, and was returned to service on 30 October 1983.

The DC-9 fleet also had a difficult year. On May 12, C-FTLJ made an approach to Regina but because of a late season snowfall was diverted to Saskatoon. After refuelling in Saskatoon, the pilot made a second attempt at landing in Regina. The plane slid off the side of the runway after landing, with severe damage to the aircraft but no serious injuries to the passengers. The DC-9 was repaired and returned to service the next year. Aircraft C-FTLU, which a few years earlier had lost its tail cone, was not so lucky. On a flight from Houston to Toronto, a fire broke out because of a faulty motor in a rear washroom. The plane began to fill with smoke and the pilot opted to make an emergency landing at Cincinnati. With the aid of a skilled air traffic controller, the pilot brought the smoke filled aircraft to a safe landing. However, when the doors of the aircraft were opened, the plane was engulfed in flames. Twenty-three of the forty-six passengers and crew escaped from the burning aircraft as it was rapidly destroyed by the flames. In September, another DC-9 ran off the runway at Rouyn-Noranda. Because of these accidents, an independent audit of the airline's operations was carried out. Headed by a former *Pan American* pilot, the audit found the airline to have exceptionally high standards of safety and training. It also determined that the incidents were not due to any negligence by the Air Canada operations.

The re-engining of the DC-8-63AF Freighters was started at Dorval in 1983, with the work being done in-house to provide jobs for laid off Air Canada employees and to generate a new source of revenue for the company by re-engining the aircraft of other companies. Air Canada expanded its cargo capabilities by reaching an agreement with *United Airlines* for interline small package services connecting at Chicago. The agreement provided Air Canada customers with small package service over all of North America. In February 1983, *North Cariboo Air* started operating their Convair 440s and Viscount on cargo runs between Edmonton and Vancouver and between Regina, Saskatoon and Edmonton to connect with the Air Canada DC-8 freighter flights.

On 9 September 1983, Air Canada leased DC-8-61 C-FTJX to the Syrian Government. The arrangement was for the aircraft to operate initially for *Syrian Arab Airlines* with Air Canada crews. Then, through *Guiness Peat Aviation,* the aircraft was to acquire Irish registration and be repainted in *Syrian Arab* colours. Just as the Air Canada crews were leaving Damascas on 12 September, however, the Syrian government seized the aircraft. The aircrew were allowed to leave but it took two months of negotiations before the aircraft was returned to Air Canada on 28 November 1983 and again sent to Marana for storage.

Air Canada built a large hangar at Winnipeg to service the Boeing 727 fleet and to rehire many of the company's staff who lost their jobs when the Viscounts were phased out. In September 1983, the company received a contract to overhaul twelve *Alaska Airlines* Boeing 727s at the Winnipeg hangar. The last of the Second World War pilots flying with Air Canada, Gordon Jones and Michael Furgala, retired in 1983. An impressive group of highly decorated WWII pilots served with TCA/Air Canada, including: G/C Davoud, DSO, OBE, DFC; F/L Rames, DFC, AFC; S/L F.E. Smith DFC, AFC, and F/L Yaktes, DFC, DFM to name only a few.

Air Canada stopped all flights into JFK Airport, New York City, in January 1984 with all flights now going to New York's La Guardia Airport. Cargo flights to Brussels began early in 1984. Flights between Toronto – Paris – Munich; Montreal – Geneva; Toronto – Frankfurt – Zurich and Quebec City – Paris were also started. Air Canada also received third freedom rights (the ability to pick up passengers outside of Canada for an onward flight) which would allow the company to fly Toronto – London – Bombay – Singapore.

With increased deregulation in Canada, 1984 was a very busy year for Air Canada. Charter flights to Italy (Rome and Venice), Portugal (Lisbon) and Spain (Malaga) were added. Summer charters from Toronto included flights to Shannon, Belfast, Dublin and Amsterdam. The company was given permission to fly to Belgrade and Zagreb, Yugoslavia.

In March 1984, Air Canada received a contract from *Cammacorp* to re-engine six stretch DC-8s with the possibility of eighteen more. The first three from *United Parcel Service* arrived at Dorval in March and three from *Lineas Aereas Paraguayas* in April.

Air Canada had been negotiating to sell its entire fleet of Boeing 727s to *Federal Express* with an eye to purchasing either the MD-81 (stretch DC-9 from McDonnell) or the Boeing 737-300. The plan did not materialize but two Boeing 727s were sold to *Federal Express* in 1984 and a third in 1985. The last two 767s accepted from Boeing were to be equipped for transatlantic over water flights and were designated ER (Extended Range) aircraft. Later, others in the 767 fleet were also converted.

The DC-8-61 aircraft went back into service from July to September when two were put on the Montreal to Toronto *Rapidair* flights. These aircraft were used to replace the Boeing 727 chartered by the Progressive Conservative Party and the DC-9s chartered by the Liberal and New Democratic Parties during the federal election of 1984. An L-1011-500 was used by Air Canada to fly the Pope back to Rome in September from his Canadian tour. Two L-1011-1 Tristars were leased to *Gulf Air* for three years, with an option for two additional years.

Nordair was sold to Innocan Inc. in mid-1984. It is ironic that Air Canada's chief rival, *Canadian Pacific,* spent a good part of 1985 trying to acquire *Nordair* which Air Canada was forced to give up and would later succeed in making the acquisition. Lockheed 10A CF-TCC was re-acquired by the company in this year and was rebuilt to flying condition in Winnipeg for use in the EXPO 86 promotion and for the 50th anniversary of the airline.

The DC-8 fleet stored at Marana was greatly reduced from late-1984 to mid-1985. One DC8-63 went to *Lineas Aereas Paraguayas* and three were sold to *ATASCO USA Inc.* The two remaining were retained and converted to cargo aircraft, eventually to be re-engined to -73CF standards. Two DC8-61s were sold to *Eagle Air* of Iceland leaving just four of these aircraft still unsold at Marana. The last two DC8-54Fs were disposed of, one going to the RCMP for hijack practice and the other sold to the Loch Ness Corporation.

Air Canada's cargo operations were very busy in

1985. The company wetleased a *Caricagro* Boeing 707 freighter to handle additional domestic service and service to its European hub at Brussels. Air Canada also wetleased one of its own DC8-73CFs to *Air Haiti* for twice weekly flights from New York (JFK) to Port-au-Prince, Haiti. From October to December, a DC8-73CF was wetleased to *Thai International* to fly Brussels to Dhahran and Bangkok once weekly. The company expanded its Brussels cargo hub at this time. To meet the extra demand for cargo flights around Christmas, Air Canada wetleased *Quebecair's* DC8-54F, *Arrow Air's* DC8-63CF and *Caribbean Air Cargo's* 707-351C. Cargo charters included Vancouver to Paris carrying Beaujolais Nouveau wine and cattle charters to China routed Dalian, Shanghai, Beijing, Hong Kong and Adelaide. Late in this year, Air Canada received permission to operate the DC8-73CFs in and out of Toronto International between 0515 and 0615 for a trial period. These flights were the first jets allowed into Toronto in the quiet hours and allowed a Vancouver – Calgary – Toronto – Mirabel night freighter service.

April 28 to May 20, the company was struck by its passenger agents (CALEA) but was able to settle with its pilots, cabin and ground crews.

In April 1985, Air Canada dropped service to Houston and Cleveland. *Air Ontario* picked up the Cleveland flights with Convair 580 aircraft. Air Canada leased the two former PWA Boeing 767s from Citibank for 15 years. The first aircraft went into service on May 20 in the former PWA configuration and the second entered service in July after being converted to the Air Canada 18 First Class/183 Economy Class seating. The Toronto – London – Bombay – Singapore route was proving highly successful by mid-1985.

Air Canada withdrew DC-9 service in July on the Ottawa – Sudbury – Thunder Bay – Winnipeg route when *Nordair* and *Air Ontario* began flying this service. The extra DC-9 freed up was used for additional Vancouver – Winnipeg flights. Five non-stop Toronto – Vancouver and Toronto – Calgary flights were operated per day using mainly the Boeing 767s. The company also began modifying 70 of their 134 engines on the 727 fleet to get a 5 1/2% fuel saving.

Air Canada had begun a DC-9 service between Edmonton Municipal Airport and Calgary International Airport to compete with the PWA Airbus. However, because of PWA's frequency of flights, the venture did not prove successful and was withdrawn in September. The winter saw Boeing 747 charters between Vancouver, Calgary, Edmonton, and Toronto/Winnipeg to Honolulu begin and also flights between Toronto to Port-ou-Spain and St. Lucia were started.

The year 1986 began with rumours of the airline being privatized. These rumours continued throughout the year, but the Conservative government backed away from the issue, having promised in their election campaign not to privatize Air Canada. The company also won the "Passenger Service Award" from *Air Transport World Magazine*. The 'Connaisseur Business Class' section was replaced by 'Executive Class' service, offering more spacious seating room as the major change. Air Canada's rights to Moscow, Prague, Vienna and Copenhagen were formally revoked by the Canadian Transport Commission at this time as Air Canada had not flown these routes for many years. *Time Air* flights operated as Air Canada connector service were shown in the Air Canada *Commuter* with the AC designator. *Air New Zealand* signed an agreement with Air Canada to feed each other at Singapore, Vancouver and Los Angeles. *TOA Domestic* DC-9 pilots from Japan continued to be trained by Air Canada at their training centre in Dorval.

Since the author is a Medical Health Officer, Air

nada, through their Ranger Helicopter Division, began a service between Toronto (Pearson) International Airport and Cherry Beach Heliport (east end of Toronto harbour) with three Aerospatiale AS350B Ecureuil helicopters. Thirty-four flights per day were operated connecting with Air Canada flights. The flights lasted eight minutes and the helicopters were all white with a large Air Canada maple leaf on the side. The service was free of charge for First Class passengers while other classes paid a fee. This service lasted until 27 June 1987 when it was discontinued. Load factors were a problem as was the 15-20 minute drive from the Cherry Beach heliport to downtown, thus negating much of the time saved. A location closer to downtown could not be obtained.

March also saw the return of one of two DC-8-63CFs to service. The aircraft could not be re-engined at this time as there was a shortage of pylons to attach

Air Canada Boeing 747 C-FTOB
Photo courtesy of Air Canada.

Canada's decision, in February 1986, to ban smoking on Toronto/Ottawa/Montreal sector turnaround flights was a major milestone in Canadian aviation history.

On March 19 1986, Lockheed 10A CF-TCC was test flown at Winnipeg for twenty minutes. It was later flown to Montreal and began a cross Canada tour covering fifty cities in Canada and Seattle in the United States on April 10th. The tour ended at Vancouver on May 2nd as part of the EXPO 86 celebrations. This aircraft was also one of the stars of the 1986 Abbottsford Airshow in August. Heavy bookings on all Air Canada flights to Vancouver continued throughout the EXPO 86 show. Another Lockheed 10A was displayed in the Air Canada pavilion at EXPO 86. The show started with the lights dimming, and the Lockheed 10A's engines starting, with smoke and lots of noise and the props spinning. The audience then viewed the runway at the Vancouver Airport as the Lockheed 10A took off on its maiden flight to Seattle.

On August 11, 1986, *Maple Leaf Helicopters Ca-*

the CFM56 engines. Cargo flights from Brussels to Bombay via Bahrain began in January. Cargo flights into Goose Bay were also added. In June and July, the company operated several cargo flights for the Canadian Forces between CFB Trenton and CFB Lahr, West Germany. The last five DC8-61s stored at Marana, Arizona were sold to *United Aviation Services* in April 1986 and two L1011-1s were parked for the summer.

Dallas/Fort Worth was dropped from the Air Canada schedule in the summer while flights to Puerto Plata and Santo Domingo in the Domincan Republic were added. Charter service to Recife, Brazil began in the winter.

Air Nova, a new company set up to provide commuter service in the Maritimes, had 49% of its stock bought by Air Canada to secure the company as a feeder airline in that region. *Air Ontario* took over more flights from Air Canada, providing exclusive service to Sault Ste. Marie and London in October. *Tempus Air* connected Montreal to the Toronto cargo hub with a morning flight between the two cities. Andre Lizette, formerly of *Nordair,* was hired to review Air Canada's need for a commuter airline in Quebec.

To further secure commuter services, Air Canada bought 100% of *Air BC* on November 28, 1986 for between $20 and $30 million. *Air BC* would serve as its British Columbia and Alberta commuter service. The company's agreement with *Time Air* was dropped at this time, *Time Air* becoming associated with *Canadian Pacific.* Air Canada, through a new holding company, also purchased 75% of *Air Ontario* and *Austin Airways,* thus securing their Ontario commuter service. The acquisition was accomplished by buying *Pacific Western's* 24.5% share in *Air Ontario* and the Plaxton family's 25.5% share. The Deluce family of Timmins continued to hold 25% of the two airlines which would be merged into one operation in 1987. *Air Nova* already carried the Air Canada Commuter red/white colour scheme with a large maple leaf on the tail while both *Air Ontario* and *Air BC* began converting to this scheme in 1987. *Air BC* switched to the AC flight designations in early 1987 and *Air Ontario* followed on April 26.

With the signing of a bilateral agreement with Thailand, Air Canada gained access to Bangkok, and immediately began charter cargo flights Toronto – Montreal – Brussels – Dubai – Bangkok in February 1987. The company also followed the lead of *Pacific Western Airlines* in selling twenty-four of their remaining thirty-five DC-9s to Citibank for $200 million and leasing them back for an eight to ten year period. Four Boeing 767-233ER aircraft were then ordered for delivery beginning in April 1988. A former *Qantas* 747 combi aircraft was purchased late in 1987. *Air Nova* had already taken over Halifax to Yarmouth and in mid-1987 also took over the Yarmouth to Boston flights.

Late 1987 also saw *Canadian Airlines* and Air Canada redivide the globe. *Canadian* was confirmed as the Pacific carrier but Air Canada received the rights to all of Asia west of, and including Burma, with Korea, the Phillipines, Malaysia and Singapore being the major new areas served. In addition, Air Canada was designated to serve all of the Middle East, with a Cairo service due in 1988 and former CPAL city Tel Aviv also included. Air Canada also received all of Africa, the Caribbean and Venezuela and retained all of Northern Europe except Russia and Scandinavia which it had held the rights to but not used in more than a decade. In southern Europe, the company gained Portugal, Spain and Greece, the latter two being dormant CPA routes. Air Canada is likely to begin services to Lisbon, Madrid and Athens in the near future as well as scheduled service to Caracas, Venezuela. Air Canada gave up rights to Munich from anywhere in Canada and to Frankfurt from Western Canada. *Canadian Airlines* was reaffirmed as

the carrier to the South Pacific, all of Central and South America with the exception of Venezuela and to the areas of Asia not given to Air Canada.

The airline suffered a shutdown beginning late in November that lasted until mid-December 1987. The heavy bookings over the Christmas holiday were threatened but the airline was able to get back into operations to cover this period.

In 1987, Air Canada's Reserve system and *Canadian's* Pegasus were merged by the two companies to form *Genini Group Automated Distribution Systems, Inc*. Thus all Air Canada, *Canadian Airlines International* and their commuter airlines reservations are on one system, making it easier for travel agents to book Canadians on these airlines.

The company's European charter flights from Toronto in winter 1987 commenced after the strike was resolved and included London, Prestwick, Paris, Shannon, Dublin and Belfast. The company also acquired landing rights in Jeddah, Saudi Arabia on flights operating via Cairo.

A new commuter airline, *Air Alliance* was announced with a start up date of March 27, 1988 to act as a commuter airline for Air Canada in Quebec. The airline began with *Air Ontario* Dash-8s but will eventually get their own Dash-8s. Air Canada held 75% of the shares and the Deluce Family 25%, the same arrangement as for *Air Ontario.*

Air Canada announced that it would replace its fleet of Boeing 727 aircraft with Airbus 320s. Delivery of these 137-passenger aircraft would begin in 1989. The total cost for the purchase of thirty-four aircraft (with an option for 20 more) would be $1.5 billion.

The Progressive Conservative government announced on 12 April 1988 that Air Canada shares would be sold to the public. The plan was to sell off 45% of the shares with foreign investment limited to 25% of these shares, no one individual or group could hold more than 10% of the shares and employees would have the first options to buy the shares. The 55% owned by the government would be in the hands of President Pierre Jeanniot and he would be instructed to vote the 55% share with the majority of the 45%, thus giving the government a hands off approach to the airline. The sale of the shares would permit Air Canada to acquire needed capital for the purchase of new aircraft and would enable them to borrow money on the open market. A decision on the other 55% would be made at a later date. Air Canada had net earnings in 1986 of $40.4 million dollars and increased this by $5.3 million dollars in 1987 with net earnings of $45.7 million on operating income of $103.7 million. Approval for the sale was given by the House of Commons in July 1988. Three Boeing 747-400 aircraft were ordered for 1990-91 delivery.

FLEET LISTING
AIR CANADA

REG'N	C/N	F/N	IS	WFU	NOTES	MODEL	TOTAL TIME
LOCKHEED L-1011 TRISTAR							
C-FTNA*	1019	501	6/73	4/88	ST C-FTNA Air Transat; LT N312EA Eastern	193M-1	
C-FTNB*	1021	502	1/73	8/86	LT 4R-ULT Air Lanka 11/86	193E-1	33,203
C-FTNC*	1023	503	6/73	12/87	ST C-FTNC Air Transat; LT N315EA Eastern	193M-1	
C-FTND*	1025	504	3/73	6/84	LT A40-TP Gulf Air; LT 4R-ALG Air Lanka 1981	193E-1	
C-FTNE*	1027	505	4/73	5/86	LT 4R-ULK Air Lanka 12/86	193E-1	31,667
C-FTNF*	1047	506	11/73	6/84	LT A40-TR Gulf Air; LT 4R-ALE Air Lanka 10/80-4/82	193E-1	
C-FTNG*	1048	507	11/73	C		193E-1	
C-FTNH*	1049	508	12/73	C		193E-1	
C-FTNI*	1058	509	1/74	C		193E-100	
C-FTNJ	1067	510	3/74	C	LT 4R-TNJ Air Lanka 2/82-3/82	193E-100	
C-FTNK	1069	511	4/75	C	LT 4R-TNK Air Lanka 12/81-1/82	193E-100	
C-FTNL	1073	512	4/75	C	LT 4R-TNL Air Lanka 5/82-6/82	193E-100	
C-GAGF	1202	551	2/81	C		500	
C-GAGG	1206	552	9/81	C		500	
C-GAGH	1207	553	4/81	C		500	
C-GAGI	1209	554	5/81	C		500	
C-GAGJ	1212	555	11/81	C		500	
C-GAGK	1218	556	11/81	C		500	
AIRBUS A320**							
C-FDQQ	0059		2/90	OO		211	
C-FDQV	0068		3/90	OO		211	
C-FDRH	0073		4/90	OO		211	
C-FDRK	0084		/90	OO		211	
C-FDRP	0122		/90	OO		211	
C-FDSN	0126			OO		211	
C-FDST	0127			OO		211	
C-FDSU	0141			OO		211	
**A total of 34 aircraft and 20 optional on order.							
BOEING 767							
C-GAUB	22517	601	10/82	C		233	
C-GAUE	22518	602	12/82	C		233	
C-GAUH	22519	603	2/83	C		233	
C-GAUN	22520	604	3/83	C	ACC 23/07/83; ran out of fuel and glided to landing Gimli Manitoba; RTS 12/83	233	
C-GAUP	22521	605	8/83	C		233	
C-GAUS	22522	606	12/83	C		233	
C-GAUU	22523	607	4/84	C	EX N17848 Boeing test registration	233	
C-GAUW	22524	608	4/84	C	EX N6038E Boeing test registration	233	
C-GAUY	22525	609	6/84	C	EX N6055X Boeing test reg'n.; CVT to ER a/c	233ER	
C-GAVA	22526	610	6/84	C	CVT to ER (Extra Range) aircraft	233ER	
C-GAVC	22527	611	10/84	C	EX N1783B Boeing test registration	233	
C-GAVF	22528	612	11/84	C		233	
C-GPWA	22683	671	4/85	C	EX C-GPWA Pacific Western; LF Citibank for 15 years	275ER	
C-GPWB	22684	672	5/85	C	EX C-GPWB Pacific Western;	275ER	
C-GDSP	24142	613	7/88	C	EX N6009F Boeing (maroon cheat)	233ER	
C-GDSS	24143	614	8/88	C	EX N6005C Boeing test registration	233ER	
C-GDSU	24144	615	9/88	C	EX N6018N Boeing test registration	233ER	
C-GDSY	24145	616	10/88	C	EX N6005C Boeing test registration	233ER	
C-FBEF	24323	617	1/89	C	EX N6009F Boeing test registration	233ER	
C-FBEG	24324	618	2/89	C		233ER	
C-FBEM	24325	619	3/89	C		233ER	
BOEING 747							
C-FTOA*	20013	301	3/71	11/82	ST N749R National 7/84	133	33,367
C-FTOB*	20014	302	3/71	5/85	ST EC-DXE; WFU 11/82-7/84; now with Wardair	133	33,426
C-FTOC*	20015	302	6/71	C		133	
C-FTOD*	20767	304	5/73	C		133	
C-FTOE*	20881	305	5/74	C		133	
C-GAGA	20977	306	3/75	C	LT C-GAGA Air National 4/83-11/83; RTS 1/84	233B	
C-GAGB	21627	307	1/79	C		233B	
C-GAGC	21354	308	1/88	C	EX VH-ECA QANTAS	238B	
C-	24	309	12/90	OO	PW4000 engines	433	
C-	24	310	5/91	OO	PW4000 engines	433	
C-	24	311	5/91	OO	PW4000 engines	433	

FLEET LISTING
AIR CANADA

REG'N	C/N	F/N	IS	WFU	NOTES	MODEL
BOEING 727						
C-GAAA	20932	401	9/74	10/86	ST N221FE Federal Express	233
C-GAAB	20933	402	9/74	11/86	ST N222FE Federal Express	233
C-GAAC	20934	403	10/74	3/85	ST N220FE Federal Express	233
C-GAAD	20935	404	10/74	12/86	ST N223FE Federal Express; LT 6Y-JMP 1-2/83	233
C-GAAE	20936	405	10/74	C	LT 6Y-JMH Air Jamaica 1/82 - 2/83	233
C-GAAF	20938	406	3/75	C		233
C-GAAG	20938	407	3/75	C		233
C-GAAH	20939	408	4/75	C	LT PC Party during autumn 1988 election	233
C-GAAI	20940	409	4/75	C		233
C-GAAJ	20941	410	5/75	C		233
C-GAAK	20942	411	5/75	C		233
C-GAAL	21100	412	8/75	C		233
C-GAAM	21101	413	8/75	7/84	ST N218FE Federal Express 9/84	233
C-GAAN	21102	414	9/75	9/84	ST N219FE Federal Express 9/84	233
C-GAAO	21624	415	4/79	C		233
C-GAAP	21625	416	4/79	C		233
C-GAAQ	21626	417	4/79	C		233
C-GAAR	21671	418	11/79	C		233
C-GAAS	21672	419	11/79	C		233
C-GAAT	21673	420	11/79	C		233
C-GAAU	21674	421	11/79	C		233
C-GAAV	21675	422	12/79	C		233
C-GAAW	22035	423	2/80	C		233
C-GAAX	22036	424	3/80	C	LT 6Y-JMG Air Jamaica 10/81 - 12/81	233
C-GAAY	22037	425	4/80	C		233
C-GAAZ	22038	426	5/80	C	EX N57000 Boeing Test Registration	233
C-GYNA	22039	427	5/80	C	EX N57002 Boeing Test Registration	233
C-GYNB	22040	428	5/80	C	EX N57008 Boeing Test Registration	233
C-GYNC	22041	429	6/80	C		233
C-GYND	22042	430	6/80	C		233
C-GYNE	22345	431	12/80	C		233
C-GYNF	22346	432	1/81	C		233
C-GYNG	22347	433	1/81	C	LT 6Y-JMQ Air Jamaica 12/87 - 1/88	233
C-GYNH	22348	434	2/81	C		233
C-GYNI	22349	435	3/81	C	EX N8278V Boeing Test Registration	233
C-GYNJ	22350	436	5/81	C		233
C-GYNK	22621	437	2/82	C	EX N5573E Boeing Test Registration	
C-GYNL	22622	438	3/82	C		233
C-GYNM	22623	439	6/82	C		233
C-GAGX	19191	491	11/78	2/81	ST N725PL Interstate 11/81; CARGO A/C	22C
C-GAGY	19192	492	1/79	4/81	ST N726PL Interstate 11/81; CARGO A/C	22C
C-GAGZ	19193	493	2/79	4/81	ST N727PL Interstate 11/81; CARGO A/C	22C
DOUGLAS DC-9						
CF-TLB	45711	701	4/66	11/68	ST N13699 Douglas; then LT Hawaiian A/L	14
CF-TLC	45712	702	1/66	9/68	ST N1792U Douglas; then LT Trans Texas	14
CF-TLD	45713	703	2/66	9/68	ST N13614 Douglas; then LT Southern Airways	14
CF-TLE	45725	704	2/66	9/68	ST N15335 Douglas; then LT Trans Texas	14
CF-TLF	45726	705	6/66	9/68	ST N5726 Douglas; then LT Trans Texas	14
CF-TLG	45727	706	6/66	9/68	ST N5728 Douglas; then LT Trans Texas	14
C-FBKT	47186	754	5/88	C	LF N8950E Eastern Airlines	31
C-FTLH	45845	707	3/67	C		32
C-FTLI*	45846	708	5/67	11/81	ST N901AK Altair 7/82; Columbia sale NTU	
C-FTLJ*	47019	709	5/67	C	ACC 12/05/83 Regina; RTS 12/83	
C-FTLK*	47020	710	5/67	11/81	ST N902AK Altair 7/82; Columbia sale NTU	32
C-FTLL*	47021	711	7/67	C		32
C-FTLM*	47022	712	7/67	C		32
C-FTLN*	47023	713	8/67	3/83	ST N707PS PSA; N903AK Altair NTU; N557NY New York Air NTU	32
C-FTLO*	47024	714	8/67	C		32
C-FTLP*	47068	715	8/67	11/81	ST M708PS PSA; N904AK Altair NTU; N715CL Columbia NTU	32
C-FTLQ*	47069	716	9/67	C		32
C-FTLR*	47070	717	9/67	7/82	ST N906AK Altair; Columbia sale NTU	32
C-FTLS*	47071	718	11/67	C		32
C-FTLT*	47195	719	3/68	C		32
C-FTLU*	47196	720	4/68	6/83	DBF 02/06/83 at Cincinnati; 23 killed	32
CF-TLV	47197	721	4/68	6/78	W/O at Toronto; ran off end of runway 28; 2 killed	32

FLEET LISTING
AIR CANADA

REG'N	C/N	F/N	IS	WFU	NOTES	MODEL	TOTAL TIME
DOUGLAS DC-9 (Continued)							
C-FTLW*	47198	722	4/68	C		32	
C-FTLX*	47199	723	5/68	C		32	
C-FTLY*	47200	724	7/68	6/82	W/O 02/06/82 in hangar fire in Montreal	32	
C-FTLZ*	47265	725	7/68	C		32	
C-FTMA*	47266	726	7/68	C		32	
C-FTMB*	47289	727	7/68	C			
C-FTMC*	47290	728	8/68	C		32	
C-FTMD*	47292	729	9/68	C		32	
C-FTME*	47293	730	9/68	C		32	
C-FTMF*	47294	731	11/68	C		32	
C-FTMG*	47340	732	11/68	C		32	
C-FTMH*	47341	733	11/68	C		32	
C-FTMI*	47342	734	11/68	C		32	
C-FTMJ*	47348	735	12/68	C		32	
C-FTMK*	47349	736	12/68	C		32	
C-FTML*	47350	737	12/68	C		32	
CF-TMM	47351	738	1/69	3/69	ST 6Y-JGA Air Jamaica	32	
C-FTMM*	47611	752	4/74	C		32	
CF-TMN	47352	739	2/69	3/69	ST 6Y-JGB Air Jamaica	32	
CF-TMN	47041	771	5/73	10/77	ST N59T Southern Airways; CARGO A/C	32F	
C-FTMO*	47353	740	3/69	C		32	
C-FTMP*	47354	741	4/69	C		32	
C-FTMQ*	47422	742	2/70	C		32	
C-FTMR*	47423	743	4/70	1/82	ST N556NY New York Air	32	
C-FTMS*	47424	744	4/70	2/82	ST N557NY New York Air	32	
C-FTMT*	47546	745	3/72	C		32	
C-FTMU*	47554	746	4/72	C		32	
C-FTMV*	47557	747	5/72	C		32	
C-FTMW*	47557	748	6/72	C	LT NDP Party during autumn 1988 election	32	
C-FTMX*	47485	749	7/72	C		32	
C-FTMY*	47592	750	12/73	C		32	
C-FTMZ*	47598	751	2/74	C		32	
CF-TON	45826	761	4/72	6/77	ST N29AF Air Florida; EX N8901 Continental	15F	
CF-TOO	47010	762	4/72	6/77	ST N50AF Air Florida; EX N8902 Continental	15F	
CF-TOP	47011	763	5/72	6/77	ST N60AF Air Florida; EX N8903 Continental	15F	
CF-TOQ	47012	764	6/72	1/78	ST N75AF Air Florida; EX N8904 Continental	15F	
C-FTOR*	47013	765	9/72	10/80	ST N73AF Air Florida 2/81; EX N8905 Continental	15F	
CF-TOS	47014	766	12/72	9/77	ST N70AF Air Florida; EX N8906 Continental	15F	
C-FTOT*	47015	767	4/73	10/80	ST N72AF Air Florida; EX N8907 Continental	15F	
C-FTOU*	47152	768	5/73	10/80	ST N66AF Air Florida 2/81 (N73AF LF AF 1978)	15F	
C-GBWO	47639	753	6/83	NTU	Never in Service; Owned by Guiness Peat	32	
AS350B HELICOPTERS							
C-GATX	1221	---	8/86	6/87	OB Maple Leaf Helicopters Canada, Ranger Helicopter Div.	AS350B	
C-GBBX	1180	---	11/86	6/87	OB Maple Leaf Helicopters Canada, Ranger Helicopter Div.	AS350B	
C-GDUF	1309	---	7/86	6/87	OB Maple Leaf Helicopters Canada, Ranger Helicopter Div.	AS350B	
DOUGLAS DC-8-73CF CARGO EXPRESS							
C-FTIK	46033	867	9/80	C	Re-engined CFMI CFM56-2C5 2/84	73CF	
C-FTIO	46076	871	12/80	C	Re-engined CFMI CFM56-2C5 10/84	73CF	
C-FTIP	46100	872	8/82	C	Re-engined CFMI CFM56-2C5 11/83	73CF	
C-FTIQ	46123	873	4/81	C	Re-engined CFMI CFM56-2C5 8/84	73CF	
C-FTIR	46124	874	8/81	C	Re-engined CFMI CFM56-2C5 4/84	73CF	
C-FTIS	46125	875	4/82	C	Re-engined CFMI CFM56-2C5 6/84	73CF	
C-FTIU	46113	876	5/86	10/88	ST N818EV Evergreen	63C	
C-FTIV	46126	877	8/86	11/88	ST N819EV Evergreen	63C	39,190
DOUGLAS DC-8							
CF-TJA	45442	801	9/60	6/77	ST 6Y-JME Air Jamaica	41	46,292
CF-TJB	45443	802	5/60	6/77	ST CF-TJB Transvalair for spares 1/80	41	
CF-TJC	45444	803	1/60	11/77	ST N72488 International Air Leases	41	
CF-TJD	45445	804	2/60	6/77	ST 4R-ACT Air Ceylon	41	
CF-TJE	45565	805	11/60	9/75	ST CF-TJE FAA for destruction tests	42	
CF-TJF	45566	806	12/60	9/75	ST CF-TJF Cargolux for spares	42	44,154
CF-TJG	45609	807	12/60	9/77	ST N70051 International Air Leases	42	
CF-TJH	45610	808	1/61	9/75	ST N10DC McDonnell Douglas (Zantop)	42	
CF-TJI	45611	809	2/61	2/76	LT CU-T1201 Cubana & W/O 07/10/76	43	45,261

FLEET LISTING
AIR CANADA

REG'N	C/N	F/N	IS	WFU	NOTES	MODEL	TOTAL TIME
DOUGLAS DC-8 (Continued)							
CF-TJJ	45612	810	3/61	2/76	LT CU-T1212 Cubana; ST International Air Leases	43	
CF-TJK	45638	811	12/61	2/76	LT CU-T1200 Cubana & W/0 18/03/76	43	42,192
C-FTJL*	45640	812	4/63	12/84	ST C-FTJL Loch Ness Corp. CARGO a/c	54F	58,620
CF-TJM	45653	813	1/63	5/67	W/O 19/05/67 approach to Ottawa; 3 killed	54F	
CF-TJN	45654	814	2/63	11/63	W/O 29/11/63 Ste Therese, PQ; 118 killed	54F	
C-FTJO*	45655	815	2/63	6/82	ST C-FTJO RCMP hijack practice CARGO	54F	55,800
C-FTJP*	45679	816	3/64	6/82	ST C-FTJP United Air Leasing 3/84	54F	55,068
C-FTJQ*	45686	817	8/64	10/82	ST C-FTJQ United Air Leasing 3/84	54F	54,736
C-FTJR*	45860	818	5/66	5/82	ST C-FTJR United Air Leasing 3/84	54F	45,648
C-FTJS*	45861	819	5/66	5/82	ST YV-128C United Air Leasing 3/84 (VIASA)	54F	
CF-TIH	45933	820	8/68	3/80	WFU & BU summer 1982	53	
CF-TII	45934	821	8/68	6/80	WFU & BU summer 1982	53	
CF-TIJ	45962	822	8/68	6/73	W/O 21/06/73 being refuelled at Toronto	53	
STRETCH DC-8s							
C-FTJT*	45890	860	9/67	9/82	ST N20UA United Aviation Co. 5/86	61	38,714
C-FTJU*	45891	861	10/67	10/67	ST N21UA United Aviation Co. 5/86	61	40,105
C-FTJV*	45892	862	10/67	8/82	ST N22UA United Aviation Co. 5/86	61	38,971
C-FTJW*	45893	863	11/67	10/82	ST N23UA United Aviation Co. 5/86	61	40,392
C-FTJX*	45963	864	4/68	4/83	ST N24UA United Aviation Co. 5/86	61	38,017
C-FTJY*	45964	865	7/68	10/82	ST TF-ISB Eagle Air 8/85	61	38,489
C-FTJZ*	45980	866	7/68	10/82	ST TF-ISA Eagle Air 7/85	61	37,796
C-FTIK*	46033	867	2/69	9/80(C)	CVT CARGO; now -73CF CARGO EXPRESS	63	
C-FTIL*	46034	868	2/69	4/83	ST N868BX ATASCO USA Inc. 6/85	63	39,180
C-FTIM*	46035	869	2/69	4/83	ST N869BX ATASCO USA Inc. 6/85	63	37,832
C-FTIN*	46036	870	3/69	4/83	ST N870BX ATASCO USA Inc. 6/85	63	37,222
C-FTIO*	46076	871	4/69	2/80(C)	CVT CARGO; now -73CF CARGO EXPRESS	63	
C-FTIP*	46100	872	11/69	8/82(C)	CVT CARGO; now -73CF CARGO EXPRESS	63	
C-FTIQ*	46123	873	2/70	4/81(C)	CVT CARGO; now -73CF CARGO EXPRESS	63	
C-FTIR*	46124	874	2/70	8/81(C)	CVT CARGO; now -73CF CARGO EXPRESS	63	
C-FTIS*	46125	875	2/70	4/82(C)	CVT CARGO; now -73CF CARGO EXPRESS	63	
C-FTIU*	46113	876	3/70	4/83(C)	CVT CARGO; now -73CF CARGO EXPRESS	63	35,086
C-FTIV*	46126	877	4/70	4/83(C)	CVT CARGO; now -63CF CARGO EXPRESS	63	35,661
CF-TIW	46114	878	4/70	7/70	W/O 05/07/70 Toronto; 108 killed	63	494
C-FTIX*	46115	879	5/70	4/83	ST ZP-CCH Lineas Aereas Paraguayas 12/84	63	36,854
C-FTJX					LT Syrianair 8/09/83; impounded 12/09/83; Returned to Marana 28/11/83		
VICKERS VISCOUNT							
CF-TGI	40	601	12/54	3/63	ST CF-TGI Transair	724	18,660
CF-TGJ	41	602	1/55	10/63	ST CF-TGJ Maverick Equipment	724	17,757
CF-TGK	42	603	2/55	6/64	WFU and Scrapped July 1970	724	30,946
CF-TGL	43	604	3/55	11/58	W/O 10/11/58 hit by L1049, N.Y	724	8,916
CF-TGM	50	605	3/55	3/64	ST F-BMCH Air Inter	724	18,152
CF-TGN	51	606	4/55	11/63	ST CF-TGN Canadian Schenley	724	18,152
CF-TGO	52	607	5/55	3/64	ST F-BMCG Air Inter	724	17,995
CF-TGP	53	608	5/55	6/64	ST CF-TGP Department of Transport	724	17,872
CF-TGQ	54	609	6/55	3/64	ST F-BMCF Air Inter	724	17,459
CF-TGR	55	610	6/55	1/65	ST F-BNAX Air Inter	724	17,437
CF-TGS	56	611	7/55	4/71	WFU and Scrapped 1973	724	34,356
CF-TGT	57	612	8/55	1/69	WFU and Scrapped 1970	724	30,723
CF-TGU	58	613	8/55	3/70	WFU and Scrapped 1973	724	32,941
CF-TGV	59	614	9/55	5/71	WFU and Scrapped 1973	724	33,569
CF-TGW	60	615	2/56	5/70	WFU and Scrapped 1973	724	31,791
CF-TGX	142	616	3/56	4/73	WFU and Scrapped 1975	757	31,352
CF-TGY	143	617	3/56	10/59	WFU and stored Wpg. ST Mexico 11/82	757	33,577
CF-TGZ	144	618	5/56	3/71	WFU and stored Wpg. ST Mexico 11/82	757	33,577
CF-THA	218	619	2/57	10/62	ST CF-THA Cdn. Inspection & Test Co.**	757	13,820
CF-THB	219	620	1/57	3/74	WFU and stored Wpg. Scrapped 1978	757	35,576
CF-THC	220	621	2/57	3/74	WFU and stored Wpg. Scrapped 1981	757	35,290
CF-THD	221	622	2/57	6/69	WFU and stored Wpg. Scrapped 1981	757	28,355
CF-THE	222	623	2/57	6/69	WFU and stored Wpg. Scrapped 1982	757	28,175
CF-THF	233	624	3/57	2/74	WFU and moved to Teulon, Man. Hwy #7	757	35,062
CF-THG	224	625	3/57	2/74	ST CF-THG Harrison-now PVI YVR airp't	757	35,405
CF-THH	269	626	5/57	9/68	WFU and stored Wpg. Scrapped 1983	757	26,390
CF-THI	270	627	5/57	11/69	WFU and displayed TCA C/S, Ottawa	757	27,771
CF-THJ	301	628	5/57	1/69	WFU and stored Wpg. Scrapped 1981	757	27,142

**Damaged at Bagotville 10/11/62; repaired and sold.

FLEET LISTING
AIR CANADA

REG'N	C/N	F/N	IS	WFU	NOTES	MODEL	TOTAL TIME
VICKERS VISCOUNT (Continued)							
CF-THK	271	629	6/57	4/69	W/O 07/04/69 Sept. Illes, Quebec	757	26,975
CF-THL	272	630	12/57	4/74	WFU and stored Wpg. Scrapped 1981	757	33,014
CF-THM	273	631	12/57	5/71	WFU and stored Wpg. Scrapped 1983	757	29,455
CF-THN	274	632	1/58	10/73	WFU and stored Wpg. Scrapped 1983	757	32,948
CF-THO	275	633	1/58	4/74	WFU and stored Wpg. Scrapped 1981	757	33,151
CF-THP	276	634	1/58	12/73	WFU and stored Wpg. Scrapped 8/84	757	33,053
CF-THQ	277	635	2/58	8/71	ST C-FTHQ Wabush 1977	757	29,363
CF-THR	278	636	2/58	3/71	WFU and stored Wpg. Scrapped 1984	757	28,960
CF-THS	279	637	2/58	4/74	WFU; displayed West. Cdn. Museum Wpg.	757	32,903
CF-THT	302	638	3/58	6/64	W/O 13/06/64 landing at Toronto	757	14,447
CF-THU	303	639	3/58	10/71	ST 9Q-CPD Zaire Aero Service for spares 1978	757	29,759
CF-THV	304	640	3/58	7/73	ST 9Q-CKB Zaire Aero Service 9/78	757	32,380
CF-THW	305	641	4/58	12/71	ST 9Q-CPJ Zaire Aero Service 2/79	757	30,234
CF-THX	306	642	4/58	4/74	WFU and stored Wpg. Scrapped 1981	757	32,581
CF-THY	307	643	5/58	4/74	ST 9Q-CKS Zaire Aero Service 3/79	757	32,191
CF-THZ	308	644	5/58	5/72	ST C-FTHZ Air Caravane 11/79	757	30,533
CF-TIA	309	645	5/58	8/72	WFU and stored Wpg. Scrapped 1983	757	30,351
CF-TIB	310	646	6/58	10/72	ST C-FTIB Air Caravane 11/79	757	30,746
CF-TIC	383	647	6/58	4/73	ST C-FTIC Harrison 1977	757	31,564
CF-TID	384	648	3/59	11/72	ST CF-TID Sarcee-now 5 engine testbed	757	30,453
CF-TIE	385	649	3/59	4/73	ST CF-TIE West. Cdn. Avn. Mus. Wpg	757	29,673
CF-TIF	386	650	3/59	4/73	ST 9Q-CPY Zaire Aero Service 10/78	757	29,441
CF-TIG	387	651	5/59	3/73	WFU; to Summerland Recreation Area	757	28,390
CF-GXK	70	---	3/55	11/55	LF CF-GXK DOT for crew training	737	1,078
VICKERS VANGUARD							
CF-TKA	724	901	11/61	8/69	ST CF-TKA Compania Inter Americana; BU 73	952	20,113
CF-TKB	725	902	4/61	8/69	ST G-AYFN Air Holdings Ltd.	952	15,910
CF-TKC	726	903	12/60	10/71	ST F-BTOX Europe Aero Service	952	20,059
CF-TKD	727	904	12/60	7/69	ST PK-MVW Merpati Nusantara	952	20,738
CF-TKE	728	905	2/61	10/71	ST PK-MVW Merpati Nusantara	952	20,738
CF-TKF	729	906	1/61	10/71	ST G-AZRE Air Holdings Ltd.	952	20,940
CF-TKG	730	907	1/61	6/69	ST G-AYLD Air Holdings Ltd.	952	15,769
CF-TKH	731	908	2/61	10/71	ST F-BTOU Europe Aero Service	952	19,914
CF-TKI	732	909	3/61	12/69	ST CF-TKI Air Holdings Ltd.	952	16,096
CF-TKJ	733	910	5/61	7/72	ST G-AXOO Air Holdings Ltd.	952	16,533
CF-TKK	734	911	5/61	5/72	ST F-BTYB Europe Aero Service; CARGO	952C	20,477
CF-TKL	735	912	5/61	12/69	ST F-OCUA EAS via Air Holdings Ltd.	952	16,045
CF-TKM	736	913	4/61	10/69	ST CF-TKM Compania Inter Americana; BU 73	952	21,057
CF-TKN	737	914	5/61	3/69	ST G-AXNT Air Holdings Ltd.	952	16,593
CF-TKO	738	915	6/61	10/71	ST CF-TKO Air Holdings Ltd.	952	20,386
CF-TKP	739	916	6/61	12/69	ST G-BAFK Air Holdings Ltd./Aviaco	952	15,633
CF-TKQ	740	917	8/61	10/71	ST G-AXUI Air Holdings Ltd.	952	20,600
CF-TKR	741	918	8/61	11/69	ST F-OCUB EAS via Air Holdings Ltd.	952	17,410
CF-TKS	742	919	10/61	9/69	ST CF-TKS Compania Inter Americana; BU 73	952	20,190
CF-TKT	743	920	10/61	10/71	ST F-BYTC Europe Aero Service	952	20,447
CF-TKU	744	921	7/62	11/69	ST G-AZNG Air Holdings Ltd.	952	14,112
CF-TKV	745	922	7/62	6/69	ST G-AXOP Air Holdings Ltd.	952	14,408
CF-TKW	746	923	4/64	10/71	ST F-BTOV Europe Aero Service (EAS)	952	13,786
LOCKHEED L-1049 SUPER CONSTELLATION							
CF-TGA	4540	401	2/54	1/63	ST CF-TGA Douglas Aircraft; BU 1964	C	19,457
CF-TGB	4541	402	3/54	3/62	ST N97392 California Airmotive	C	19,000
CF-TGC	4542	403	4/54	3/62	WFU and BU to rebuild CF-TEZ	C	18,566
CF-TGD	4543	404	5/54	11/63	ST N4715G Capitol Airways	C	19,337
CF-TGE	4544	405	5/54	10/63	ST CF-RNR Montreal Air Service	C	19,993
CF-TGF	4563	406	6/54	5/62	ST N97427 Capitol Airways	E	20,131
CF-TGG	4564	407	7/54	12/54	W/O 17/12/54 at Brampton, Ontario	E	763
CF-TGH	4565	408	8/54	2/62	ST N9639Z Douglas Aircraft	E	19,287
CF-TEU	4641	409	4/56	2/62	ST N9640Z Douglas Aircraft	G	18,183
CF-TEV	4643	410	5/56	2/62	ST N9641Z Douglas Aircraft	G	15,243
CF-TEW	4682	411	11/57	6/62	ST N7772C California Airmotive	G	11,571
CF-TEX	4683	412	12/57	3/62	ST N96422 Douglas Airmotive	G	11,407
CF-TEY	4850	413	1/59	3/61	ST N9752C Lockheed Aircraft Corp	H	6,324
CF-TEZ	4851	414	12/58	2/60	ST N9740Z California Airmotive; ACC 10/02/60 at Toronto; rebuilt & sold	H	4,542

FLEET LISTING
AIR CANADA

REG'N	C/N	F/N	IS	WFU	NOTES	MODEL	TOTAL TIME
BRISTOL FREIGHTER 170							
CF-TFX	13137	501	9/53	12/55	ST CF-TFX Central Northern Airways	31	3,087
CF-TFY	13138	502	10/53	12/55	ST CF-TFY Central Northern Airways	31	2,930
CF-TFZ	13139	503	10/53	12/55	ST CF-TFZ Central Northern Airways	31	2,706

TRANS-CANADA AIRLINES

REG'N	C/N	F/N	IS	WFU	NOTES	RCAF NO.	TOTAL TIME
DOUGLAS DC-3							
CF-TDJ	6261	357	9/45	10/48	ST CF-TDJ Goodyear Tire	USAAF	5,320
CF-TDK	6319	358	11/45	10/48	ST CF-TDK Rimouski; now C-FPQE PQ Gov't.	USAAF	5,118
CF-TDL	6343	359	10/45	11/48	ST CF-TDL Gulf Aviati	USAAF	5,202
CF-TDM	12004	360	6/46	9/61	ST N124R Charlotte Aviation	FL595	37,449
CF-TDN	12007	361	9/46	8/58	ST N4990E Frontier Airlines	FL598	31,719
CF-TDO	12026	362	9/46	1/59	ST CF-TDO Matane Air Service	FL615	30,203
CF-TDP	12027	363	7/46	9/61	ST N9184R Charlotte Aviation	FL616	37,276
CF-TDQ	12039	364	7/46	10/58	ST N4995E Frontier Airlines	FL618	33,526
CF-TDR	12042	365	6/46	1/61	ST CF-TDR Matane Air Service	FL621	32,179
CF-TDS	12092	366	7/46	10/56	ST CF-QBF Quebecair	FZ557	28,596
CF-TDT	12093	367	9/46	9/61	ST CF-TDT Matane Air Service	FZ558	37,818
CF-TDU	12106	368	10/46	9/58	ST N4991E Frontier Airlines	FZ571	31,573
CF-TDV	12110	369	6/46	9/61	ST N9123R Charlotte Aviation	FZ575	33,172
CF-TDW	12139	370	7/46	11/58	ST N4992E Frontier Airlines	FZ584	30,936
CF-TDX	12141	371	6/46	9/58	ST N4996E Frontier Airlines	FZ586	13,101
CF-TDY	12191	372	9/46	11/58	ST N4997E Frontier Airlines	FZ634	13,437
CF-TDZ	12192	373	6/46	11/60	ST CF-DTV Department of Transport	FZ635	31,737
CF-TEA	12412	374	8/46	4/63	ST CF-TEA Transair; not C/N 12502	KG382	41,475
CF-TEB	12591	375	9/46	11/60	ST CF-DTH Department of Transport	KG479	36,564
CF-TEC	12597	376	5/46	3/58	ST CF-DTB Depratment of Transport	KG485	37,695
CF-TED	12930	377	12/46	5/58	ST CF-DXU Air Research Aviation	FG526	30,794
CF-TEE	13559	378	7/46	8/58	ST N5998E Frontier Airlines	KG692	35,804
CF-TEF	13560	379	8/46	3/58	ST N5590A Babb Company	KG693	30,408
CF-TEG	13868	380	5/46	8/57	ST CF-GXW Department of Transport	KG769	31,154
CF-TEH	12440	381	11/46	10/58	ST N4993E Frontier Airlines	KG405†	31,951
CF-TEI	12442	382	12/46	8/58	ST N4994E Frontier Airlines	KG407†	31,932
CF-TEJ	13337	383	12/46	11/56	ST CF-QBG Quebecair	KG606†	28,687
CF-TER	12253	390	4/47	3/58	ST CF-DTD Department of Transport	FZ668†	28,508
CF-TES	11906	391	1/47	4/63	ST CF-TES Transair	FL547†	38,802
CF-TET	13393	392	3/47	11/55	ST CF-TET Transair	KG633	27,485
†RAF							

REG'N	C/N	F/N	IS	WFU	NOTES	MODEL	TOTAL TIME
CANADAIR DC-4M NORTH STAR							
CF-TEK	102	184	11/46	4/49	ST 17518 Royal Canadian Air Force	M-1	4,109
CF-TEL	103	185	6/47	8/48	W/O 12/08/48 at Sydney, N.S	M-1	3,241
CF-TEM	104	186	1/47	3/49	ST 17520 Royal Canadian Air Force	M-1	4,319
CF-TEO	105	187	2/47	10/49	ST 17521 Royal Canadian Air Force	M-1	4,272
CF-TEP	106	188	3/47	8/49	ST 17522 Royal Canadian Air Force	M-1	3,752
CF-TEQ	107	189	3/47	6/49	ST 17523 Royal Canadian Air Force	M-1	3,805
CF-TFA	125	201	10/47	8/61	ST XA-NUM Lineas Aereas Unidas	M-2	39,326
CF-TFB	126	202	10/47	10/61	ST XA-NUU Lineas Aereas Unidas; CARGO	M-2C	35,781
CF-TFC	127	203	10/47	5/61	ST CF-TFC International Air Freighters Cubana	M-2	38,992
CF-TFD	128	204	1/48	12/56	W/O 09/12/56 near Hope, B.C.	M-2	27,196
CF-TFE	129	205	12/47	7/61	ST CF-TFE Overseas Aviation	M-2	39,627
CF-TFF	130	206	12/47	11/61	ST CF-TFF World Wide Airways	M-2	39,627
CF-TFG	131	207	12/47	11/61	ST XA-NUW Lineas Aereas Unidas	M-2	38,529
CF-TFH	132	208	1/48	10/61	ST XA-NUR Lineas Aereas Unidas; CARGO	M-2C	37,190
CF-TFI	133	209	1/48	10/61	ST XA-NUV Lineas Aereas Unidas	M-2	39,112
CF-TFJ	134	210	2/48	7/61	ST CF-TFJ Overseas Aviation; CARGO	M-2C	37,541
CF-TFK	135	211	2/48	7/61	ST CF-TFK Overseas Aviation	M-2	39,048
CF-TFL	136	212	2/48	7/61	ST CF-TFL Overseas Aviation	M-2	39,180
CF-TFM	137	213	2/48	7/61	ST CF-TFM Overseas Aviation	M-2	36,020

FLEET LISTING
TRANS-CANADA AIRLINES

REG'N	C/N	F/N	IS	WFU	NOTES	MODEL	TOTAL TIME
CANADAIR DC-4M NORTH STAR (Continued)							
CF-TFN	138	214	3/48	7/61	ST CF-TFN Overseas Aviation	M-2	35,515
CF-TFO	139	215	3/48	7/61	ST CF-TFO Overseas Aviation	M-2	37,338
CF-TFP	140	216	4/48	11/61	ST CF-TFP World Wide Aviation	M-2	35,827
CF-TFQ	141	217	4/48	1/61	ST CF-TFQ Overseas Aviation	M-2	35,777
CF-TFR	142	218	5/48	12/61	ST CF-TFR International Air Freighters	M-2	37,550
CF-TFS	143	219	5/48	12/61	ST CF-TFS International Air Freighters	M-2	36,070
CF-TFT	144	220	6/48	7/61	ST CF-TFT Overseas Aviation	M-2	36,069
CF-TFU	147	221	11/51	7/61	ST CF-TFU Overseas; EX CF-CPI CPAL	C-4C	31,232
CF-TFV	149	222	2/52	7/61	ST CF-TFV Overseas; EX CF-CPJ CPAL	C-4C	30,059
CF-TFW	150	223	12/51	4/54	W/O 08/04/54 over Moose Jaw EX CF-CPP	C-4	7,763
AIR TRANSIT DHC-6-300 TWIN OTTERS							
CF-CST	351	---	7/73	5/76	ST C-FCST Department of Transport	300	
CF-CSU	352	---	9/73	5/76	ST C-FCSU Department of Transport	300	
CF-CSV	354	---	7/73	5/76	ST C-FCSV Department of Trannsport	300	
CF-CSW	355	---	9/73	5/76	ST C-FCSW Department of Transport	300	
CF-CSX	357	---	11/73	5/76	ST C-FCSX Department of Transport	300	
CF-CSY	358	---	11/73	5/76	ST C-FCSY Department of Transport	300	
LANCASTIANS							
CF-CMS	R5727	100	3/43	6/45	DBF 01/06/45 at Dorval		
CF-CMT	KB702	101	5/43	5/47	WFU; #3 aircraft built at Victory Plant, Toronto		
CF-CMU	KB703	102	5/43	12/44	W/O 28/12/44 on eastbound flight		
CF-CMV	KB729	103	6/43	5/47	WFU; #30 aircraft built at Victory Plant, Toronto		
CF-CMW	KB730	104	6/43	5/47	WFU; #31 aircraft built at Victory Plant, Toronto		
CF-CMX	FM184	105	7/43	5/47	WFU; built at Victory Plant, Toronto		
CF-CMY	FM185	106	7/43	5/47	WFU; built at Victory Plant, Toronto		
CF-CMZ	FM186	107	8/43	5/47	WFU; built at Victory Plant, Toronto		
CF-CNA	FM187	108	8/43	5/47	WFU; built at Victory Plant, Toronto		
BOEING STEARMAN HEM							
CF-ASF	4010	20	9/37	3/39	ST CF-ASF Northern Airways		
LOCKHEED 10A ELECTRA							
CF-AZY	1063	21	9/37	10/39	ST 1529 Royal Canadian Air Force		
CF-BAF	1064	22	9/37	10/39	ST 1528 Royal Canadian Air Force; later CF-HED		
CF-TCA	1112	23	10/37	10/39	ST 1526 Royal Canadian Air Force; later CF-BTD		1,877
CF-TCB	1113	24	10/37	10/39	ST 1527 Royal Canadian Air Force		2,301
CF-TCC	1116	25	10/37	5/39	ST CF-TCC Department of Transport; display Ottawa		1,746
LOCKHEED 14H-2							
CF-TCD	1429	26	5/38	5/47	ST CF-TCD Montreal Air Services		19,339
CF-TCE	1430	27	5/38	10/47	ST CF-TCE Photographic Survey Company		17,978
CF-TCF	1450	28	6/38	2/45	W/O 27/02/45 at Moncton		14,665
CF-TCG	1451	29	6/38	10/47	ST CF-TCG Photographic Survey Company		18,035
CF-TCH	1471	30	8/38	1/48	ST CF-TCH Nickel Belt Airways		18,757
CF-TCI	1472	31	8/38	5/48	ST CF-TCI Jason W. Pike & Company		19,019
CF-TCJ	1473	32	9/38	9/46	W/O 02/09/46 at Moncton		15,928
CF-TCK	1474	33	9/38	11/46	ST CF-TCK Photographic Survey Company		15,556
CF-TCL	1475	34	9/38	11/38	W/O 18/11/38 at Regina		320
CF-TCM	1477	35	9/38	4/47	ST CF-TCM Montreal Air Services		19,019
CF-TCN	1499	36	5/39	4/47	ST CF-TCN Montreal Air Services		17,178
CF-TCO	1500	37	7/39	10/47	ST CF-TCO Photgraphic Survey Company		17,198
CF-TCP	1501	38	7/39	2/41	W/O 06/02/41 while landing at Armstrong, Ontario		3,094
CF-TCQ	1502	39	8/39	1/47	W/O 17/01/47 near Winnipeg, Manitoba		15,178
CF-TCR	1503	40	8/39	8/41	ST CF-TCR Yukon Southern		4,494
CF-TCS	1504	41	8/39	8/41	ST CF-TCS Yukon Southern		4,130
LOCKHEED 12A							
CF-CCT	1219	--	7/37	7/37	LF CF-CCT DOT for cross Canada flight 30/07/37		14
7645	1207	--	6/44	10/44	LF 7645 Royal Canadian Air Force		503
LOCKHEED 18 LOADSTAR							
CF-TCT	----	42	1/41	8/49	ST CF-TCT Magnavox Company Ltd.		17,876
CF-TCU	----	43	1/41	9/49	ST CF-TCU Pacific Petroleum		16,525
CF-TCV	----	44	1/41	10/49	ST CF-TCV I.O.C.O		17,198
CF-TCW	----	45	2/41	10/49	ST CF-TCW Magnavox Company Ltd.		17,899
CF-TCX	----	46	2/41	11/43	W/O 04/11/43 at Toronto		6,029

FLEET LISTING
TRANS-CANADA AIRLINES

REG'N	C/N	F/N	IS	WFU	NOTES	TOTAL TIME
LOCKHEED 18 LOADSTAR (Continued)						
CF-TCY	2064	47	2/41	3/47	ST CF-TCY Department of Transport	15,954
CF-TDA	----	48	8/42	5/48	ST CF-TDA T. Eaton Company	14,482
CF-TDB	2220	49	9/42	11/47	ST CF-TDB Imperial Oil Company	14,800
CF-TDC	----	50	10/42	2/48	ST CF-TDC Department of Transport	15,813
CF-TDD	----	51	10/42	10/49	ST CF-TDD Magnavox Company Ltd.	15,813
CF-TDE	----	52	10/42	4/48	ST CF-TDE Nickel Belt Airways	12,788
CF-TDF	----	53	10/42	4/47	W/O 28/04/47 at Vancouver, B.C.	12,924
CF-TDG	2465	54	8/44	7/48	ST CF-TDG Massey Harris Company; then CF-CPH	11,211
CF-TDH	2403	55	8/44	7/48	ST CF-TDH C.M.C.; later to CPA as CF-CPI	
CF-TDI	2464	56	10/44	6/48	ST CF-TDI F.Mannix & Co. Ltd.; then CF-CPH	11,059

AIRCRAFT
AIR CANADA / TRANS-CANADA AIRLINES

AIRCRAFT	PASSENGERS	CRUISE MPH	RANGE MILES	TOTAL A/C	19 37	19 40	19 45	19 50	19 55	19 60	19 65	19 70	19 75	19 80	19 85	19 90
Boeing Stearman	C	140	440	1	1	0	0	0	0	0	0	0	0	0	0	0
Lockheed 10A	10	185	750	5	5	0	0	0	0	0	0	0	0	0	0	0
Lockheed 12A	6	200	750	2	1	0	0	0	0	0	0	0	0	0	0	0
Lockheed 14	10	200	800	16	0	15	12	0	0	0	0	0	0	0	0	0
Lockheed 18	17	190	800	15	0	14	0	0	0	0	0	0	0	0	0	0
Lancastrians	10	230	3100	9	0	0	9	0	0	0	0	0	0	0	0	0
DC-3s	21	160	1100	30	0	0	3	27	27	9	0	0	0	0	0	0
North Star M-1	40	250	3000	6	0	0	0	6	0	0	0	0	0	0	0	0
North Star M-2	62	260	3000	23	0	0	0	23	22	21	0	0	0	0	0	0
Lockheed L1049	71	310	4820	14	0	0	0	0	7	13	0	0	0	0	0	0
Bristol Freighter	C	165	490	3	0	0	0	0	3	0	0	0	0	0	0	0
Vickers Viscount	54	315	1720	51	0	0	0	0	14	49	39	31	0	0	0	0
Vickers Vanguard	108	415	3130	23	0	0	0	0	0	23	23	9	0	0	0	0
DC-8-41	127	480	4100	4	0	0	0	0	0	4	4	4	4	0	0	0
DC-8-42	127	480	4100	4	0	0	0	0	0	4	4	4	4	0	0	0
DC-8-43	133	480	4100	3	0	0	0	0	0	0	3	3	3	0	0	0
DC-8-53	133	480	4800	3	0	0	0	0	0	0	0	3	2	2	0	0
DC-8-54F	117	470	4800	8	0	0	0	0	0	0	3	6	6	6	1	0
DC-8-61	257	550	4800	7	0	0	0	0	0	0	0	7	7	7	0	0
DC-8-63	269	550	5200	13	0	0	0	0	0	0	0	13	12	12	6	0
DC-8-73CF	C	550	5200	8	0	0	0	0	0	0	0	0	0	2	6	6
DC-9-14	77	520	1750	6	0	0	0	0	0	0	6	0	0	0	0	0
DC-9-15F	94	520	1750	8	0	0	0	0	0	0	0	8	3	0	0	0
DC-9-32	115	520	1500	47	0	0	0	0	0	0	0	36	44	43	34	35
L1011-1	256	580	3000	8	0	0	0	0	0	0	0	0	8	8	8	2
L1011-100	256	580	5600	4	0	0	0	0	0	0	0	0	4	4	4	4
L1011-500	246	580	6000	6	0	0	0	0	0	0	0	0	0	6	6	6
727-233	132	550	2500	39	0	0	0	0	0	0	0	0	14	31	39	33
727-11C	C	540	2800	3	0	0	0	0	0	0	0	0	0	3	0	0
747-133	429	570	5000	5	0	0	0	0	0	0	0	0	5	5	4	3
747-233B	295	555	5000	3	0	0	0	0	0	0	0	0	1	2	2	3
767	201	530	3100	14	0	0	0	0	0	0	0	0	0	0	12	21
A320	137	525	2310	34	0	0	0	0	0	0	0	0	0	0	0	6

Canadian Airlines International

Canadian Boeing 737 (with EPA tail), C-GEPA (Flagship "Labrador")

HEADQUARTERS:
Suite 2800, 700 - 2nd Street S.W.,
Calgary, Alberta, T2P 2W2
(offices of Pacific Western Corporation,
parent company)
1 Grant McConachie Way,
Vancouver International Airport,
Vancouver, B.C. V7B 1V1
(major operating base)

MAJOR BASES:
Vancouver, Calgary, Edmonton, Toronto,
Montreal, Halifax

FLEET 1989:
66 - Boeing 737-200s;
3 - Boeing 737-300s (leased winters);
12 - DC-10-30s; 2 - L-188s;
8 - Boeing 767-375ERs (with 4 on order).

COLOURS:
The white upper body is separated from the dark lower
body by cheat lines of grey, red and thin grey. The dark
blue tail bears five broad grey bands separated by thin
dark blue stripes with the company's red > superimposed on the bands. The company name Canadian appears on the forward upper fuselage in dark blue with
the last 'a' replaced by the symbol '>' to make the name
biligual. The engines are also painted dark blue.

ROUTES:
Canada:
B.C.: Vancouver – Castlegar – Cranbrook – Dawson
Creek – Fort Nelson – Fort St. John – Kamloops –
Kelowna – Penticton – Prince George – Quesnel – Wil-
liams Lake – Prince Rupert – Sandspit – Smithers – Ter-
race.
Yukon: Whitehorse – Watson Lake.
Alberta: Calgary – Edmonton – Grande Prairie – Fort
McMurray— Fort Smith
Saskatchewan: Saskatoon – Regina
Manitoba: Winnipeg – Brandon – Flin Flon – The Pas
– Thompson – Gilliam – Churchill— Lynn Lake.
Ontario: Toronto – Dryden – Thunder Bay – Sault Ste.
Marie – Sudbury – Windsor— Ottawa
Quebec: Montreal – Quebec City – Val d'Or – La
Grande – Kuujjuarapik – Kuujjuaq (Fort Chimo)
New Brunswick: Fredericton – Saint John – Chatham
– Charlo
Nova Scotia: Halifax – Sydney
Prince Edward Island: Charlottetown
Newfoundland/Labrador: St. John's – Gander – Deer
Lake – Goose Bay – Wabush – Churchill Falls
Northwest Territories: Inuvik – Norman Wells – Yel-
lowknife – Hay River – Cambridge Bay – Resolute –
Nanisivik— Hall Beach – Iqaluit (Frobisher Bay)

International:
Pacific: Bangkok – Hong Kong – Shanghai – Beijing –
Tokyo – Nandi – Sydney – Auckland
USA: Honolulu – San Francisco – Los Angeles – Fort
Lauderdale – Pittsburg
South America: Lima – Santiago – Buenos Aires – Rio
de Janeiro – San Paulo
Europe: Amsterdam – Frankfurt – Munich – Milan –
Rome – Lisbon
Charters: Worldwide

35

HISTORY:

Canadian Airlines International resulted from a merger of *Pacific Western Airlines* and *Canadian Pacific Airlines*. The parent company of the new airline is *Pacific Western Airlines Corporation*, based in Calgary. The airline uses the name CANADIAN on its aircraft and advertizing. To make the name bilingual, the last 'A' in CANADIAN is replaced with the company's symbol (five wide Grey lines with a red superimposed). Thus the English Canadian and the French Canadien languages are represented.

Following the December 2, 1986 announcement of the merger for $300 million, the new company emerged on April 26, 1987 with one DC10-30 painted in the new colour scheme. *Canadian Pacific* had taken over *Nordair, Quebecair,* and *Eastern Provincial* previously and *Pacific Western* had taken over *Transair,* so the merger effectively took the five regional airlines plus one of the two large national airlines and merged them into one large airline with routes from coast to coast. Unlike *Air Canada,* Canadian also has many north-south routes as well, reaching into the high arctic and into the Yukon. *The Pacific Western Airlines Corporation* now held 100% of PWA, 100% of *Canadian Pacific,* 46% of *Time Air,* 25% of *Norcanair,* 20% of *Air Atlantic,* 100% of *Nordair,* 35% of *Nordair Metro* which owns 100% of *Quebecair Inter,* and, two of the former *Quebecair's* Boeing 737s and *Quebecair's* jet routes. Chairman and Chief Executive Officer of CANADIAN is Mr. Rhys T. Eyton, formerly of PWA, and President and Chief Operating Officer is Mr. Murray Sigler.

At the time of the merger, Canadian had seventy Boeing 737-200s and had as many as seventy-three of these aircraft during its first year. The company also had nine DC10-30s, quickly adding the three leased from *United Airlines.* Although Canadian briefly operated the three DC10-30s leased from *United Airlines,* they never appeared in Canadian colour scheme. The new company also acquired the two ice patrol Lockheed Electras. It will continue to operate these aircraft and has had their radar and data communication equipment updated by Innotech Aviation for $815,000. These aircraft have retained the *Nordair* colour scheme with the yellow nose and broad red band around the fuselage but bear the CANADIAN title on their forward lower fuselage.

A multitude of colour schemes have appeared on Canadian aircraft. The DC10-30s wore the full Canadian colour scheme; the *Canadian Pacific* colours with CANADIAN titles and the CPA symbol on the tail; partial Canadian colour scheme but with a silver lower fuselage; or the orange *CP Air* colour scheme with CANADIAN titles. The company's Boeing 737s also wore a wide variety of colour schemes. The use of CANADIAN colours increased through 1987, although some aircraft simply wore the blue CPA colours with CANADIAN titles

(these planes retained the CPA tail symbol). In addition, several CPA aircraft still bear the orange *CP Air* colour scheme with CANADIAN titles in 1988. The former *Eastern Provincial* aircraft appeared in two colour schemes: white with CANADIAN titles and EPA on the tail; or white with CANADIAN titles and CANADIAN on the tail. The *Pacific Western* aircraft used four colour schemes: full PWA colours with CANADIAN titles; *American West* all white with three thin blue stripes and plain tail; the former Dome Petroleum 737 with full Canadian tail but aqua bottom; C-FPWP returned to Canada with full Canadian colour scheme minus the five grey stripes on the tail. When the *Monarch* Boeing 737-300 aircraft began operating, they retained the basic *Monarch* colour scheme (a broad orange cheat) with CANADIAN titles. The *Nordair* and *Quebecair* aircraft did not carry partial schemes as most had been repainted in CPA colours. The new airline dropped the names on the aircraft and also dropped the CPA call sign 'Empress' and replaced it with CANADI>N.

Canadian Pacific Airlines carried the International areas of Asia, South America and the Pacific into the merger as well as limited access to Europe through Amsterdam, Portugal and Italy. Canadian continued to serve Los Angeles and San Francisco from Vancouver and added *Nordair's* cities of Pittsburgh and Fort Lauderdale in the USA. In October 1987, *Air Canada* and Canadian traded some routes to give Canadian greater access to Europe and *Air Canada* entry to Asia. Canadian gave up Portugal and the rights to Korea to *Air Canada* in exchange for Munich and Frankfurt from western Canada. CANADIAN also became the designated Canadian carrier for Denmark, Sweden, Norway and the U.S.S.R.

Pacific Western Airline Corporation acquired 25% interest in *GPA Airbus 320 Ltd.* This company, associated with Ireland's *Guiness Peat Aviation,* will acquire and lease out new Airbus 320 aircraft throughout the world. The *PWA Corporation* had acquired a 50% interest in *GPA Jetprop Limited* in May 1986, which at the end of 1987 had fifteen leased aircraft. The company also wholly owns *Treasure Tours (Canada) Ltd.* and *Transpacific Tours (Canada) Ltd.* and shares ownership of *Gemini Group* equally with *Air Canada.* The Gemini system handles all of the company's reservations.

Pacific Western Airlines held a part interest in *Time Air* (a feeder airline for *Air Canada*) and *Air B.C.* (a feeder line for *Canadian Pacific*) at the time of the merger. *Air Canada* purchased *Air B.C.* and thus the two major carriers switched feeder airlines after the merger. Canadian established a series of feeder airlines throughout Canada in 1987 under the title of 'Canadian Partner.' In British Columbia and Alberta, *Time Air* with its Shorts 360, Dash-7s, Dash-8s and Convairs linked all parts of

British Columbia to the company through Vancouver (particularly Victoria, Vancouver Island and the B.C. interior). *Norcanair* became the Canadian Partner in Saskatchewan but was taken over by *Time Air* making *Time Air* a large regional airline. *Time Air* now serves thirty-four communities in the west, including Winnipeg and Minneapolis which it serves with the former *Norcanair* F28 aircraft. The F28 will probably take over some of the former PWA routes in British Columbia freeing up Canadian's Boeing 737s.

Calm Air is the Canadian Partner in Northern Manitoba, flying HS748s, DC3s, Twin Otters, and Piper Chieftains. Serving major centres such as Winnipeg, Flin Flon, Lynn Lake and Churchill, *Calm Air* links twenty-eight centres to Canadian service. In Atlantic Canada, *Air Atlantic* had been established by *Canadian Pacific* as a commuter airline to replace *Air Maritime* and continues as a Canadian Partner. Flying Dash-8s and Dash-7s, it links Yarmouth, Saint John, Fredericton, Moncton, Charlottetown, Iles de la Madeleine, Sydney, Saint-Pierre et Miquelon, and Newfoundland to Halifax. *Air Saint-Pierre* operating HS-748 aircraft is also a maritime partner.

In Ontario, Canadian set up its own partner airline, *Ontario Express.* Beginning services on July 15, 1987, this Toronto-based airline serves nine Ontario communities with 19-seat Jetstream 31 aircraft. Thunder Bay, Kingston, London, Sarnia, Windsor, Sault St. Marie, Sudbury, Ottawa and Toronto are linked to Canadian through this airline.

In Quebec, *Nordair Metro* and *Quebecair* were merged to form a new company, *Inter-Canadian,* which provides commuter services for Canadian although the new company is not a full Canadian partner.

In the fall of 1987, the Attache and Empress class services were dropped on all flights and a new 'Canadian Business Class' was instituted on all international flights to major Canadian cities (the former CPA cities). This featured a separate cabin reserved exclusively for the business traveller and frequent flyer, with the middle seat replaced by a table. Extended leg room, wide seats and extra generous elbow room allows more personal space for each passenger. Excellent in-flight service, exclusive reservation lines, fast check-in and priority baggage handling are also included. Initially, fourteen Canadian cities (mostly former CPA routes), and eighteen international cities will have the service. First class service was dropped on all Boeing 737 flights and the ban on smoking on all Boeing 737 aircraft was made permanent.

The company announced an order for six (later expanded to eight) Boeing 767-375ER aircraft to replace its DC10-30s on Canadian domestic flights leaving the DC10-30s available for more International flights. The first of these aircraft was due in April 1988. These aircraft had the new and more powerful CF6-80C2-B2 General Electric engines. Fuel burned per seat is 35% less for these engines than previous engines. The aircraft will have a 24,050 gallon fuel capacity with a take-off weight of 400,000 pounds carrying 260 passengers in a mixed class configuaration. Each aircraft cost in excess of $100 million.The 767-375ERs entered service on Canadian's trans-Canada routes in May 1988.

Canadian ordered three 421-seat Boeing 747-475s in July 1988 (with options on four more) with delivery expected late in 1990. These aircraft will replace the DC-10-30s currently flown on Vancouver – Asia and Toronto – Asia routes. To begin the phase out of its older Boeing 737s, the company also ordered ten 147-seat A320-200s with delivery expected in 1993, and holds options on thirty-four more of these aircraft. Canadian will lease eight A320-200s from *GPA Airbus 320 Ltd.* in 1991. *PWA Corporation* is a 25% stockholder in *GPA Airbus 320 Ltd.* Thirteen older Boeing 737s were sold to *Polaris Aircraft Leasing* during 1988 and leased back for various periods to coincide with the delivery of the A320s.

In January 1989, *PWA Corporation* continued to shock the Canadian aviation world with a takeover offer for *Wardair Canada.* The offer was approved in April 1989 after *American Airlines* of the United States (with a group of Canadian businessmen who were to own 75% of the shares) failed to submit its expected counter offer. The takeover was still in process as this book was going to press but the immediate impact on *Wardair* was the cancellation of the company's orders for F-100, MD-89 and two A310 aircraft. *Wardair* has also shut down its Winnipeg operations, resulting in more than 600 layoffs. As with previous takeovers by PWA, the promise was made that the two operations would be kept separate, but Canadian began booking blocks of seats on *Wardair* flights in 1989, thus releasing some of their aircraft from the competing Canadian routes. One possible scenario of this takeover would see *Wardair* replacing Canadian for international operations, thus taking advantage of *Wardair*'s familiarity and reputation for quality throughout the world. The name Canadian would be retained on selected international flights and all North American routes.

When Canadian began operating to Chicago's Midway airport in March 1989, it signed a major agreement with *Midway Airlines* providing Canadian with an extensive connecting network out of Chicago's second airport.

Canadian has dropped many of its shorter routes, permitting its commuter partners to expand while making better use of its jet equipment. Late in 1989 the company created a Northern Division and assigned a fleet of Boeing 737s to operate airlifts to Canada's north.

FLEET LISTING
CANADIAN AIRLINES INTERNATIONAL

REG'N	C/N	F/N	IS	WFU	NOTES	MODEL
BOEING 767-375ER						
C-FCAB	24082	631	4/88	C	CF6-80C2B6 Engines	-375ER
C-FCAE	24083	632	5/88	C	CF6-80C2B6 Engines EX N6046P Boeing	-375ER
C-FCAF	24084	633	5/88	C	CF6-80C2B6 Engines EX N6038P Boeing	-375ER
C-FCAG	24085	634	5/88	C	CF6-80C2B6 Engines EX N6009F Boeing	-375ER
C-FCAJ	24086	635	10/88	C	CF6-80C2B6 Engines	-375ER
C-FCAU	24087	636	12/88	C	CF6-80C2B6 Engines	-375ER
C-FPCA	24306	637	5/89	C	CF6-80C2B6 Engines	-375ER
C-FTCA	24307	638	5/89	C	CF6-80C2B6 Engines	-375ER
C-GLAW	24	639	4/90	OO	CF6-80C2B6 Engines	-375ER
C-GLCA	24	640	4/90	OO	CF6-80C2B6 Engines	-375ER
C-FXCA	24574	641	/90	OO	CF6-80C2B6 Engines	-375ER
C-FDCA	24575	642	/90	OO	CF6-80C2B6 Engines	-375ER
BOEING 737-200						
C-FACP	22072	728	4/87	C	EX C-FACP CPAL; EX C2-RN9; EX C-GQBA Quebecair	-2L9
C-FCAV	22906	788	11/87	4/88	LF PH-TVU Transavia	-2K2
C-FCPM	22761	730	4/87	C	EX C-FPWD PWA; EX G-DWHH Monarch	-2T7
C-FCPN	22762	731	4/87	C	EX C-FPWE PWA; EX G-DGDP Monarch	-2T7
C-FCPV	20196	766	4/87	4/88	EX C-FCPV CPAL; ST LN- Braathens Safe	-217
C-FCPZ	20197	767	4/87	C	EX C-FCPZ CPAL; ST AIG LSG 11/87, LB til 11/89	-217
C-FEPL	20396	791	4/87	C	EX C-FEPL EPA	-2E1
C-FEPR	20397	792	4/87	C	EX C-FEPR EPA	-2E1
C-FEPO	20300	793	4/87	10/87	EX C-FEPO EPA; ST N197AL AIG Leasing Corp.	-2E1
C-FEPP	20681	794	4/87	C	EX C-FEPP EPA	-2E1
C-FEPU	20776	795	4/87	C	EX C-FEPU EPA	-2E1
C-FHCP	22024	729	4/87	C	EX C-FHCP CPAL; EX EI-BPV Guinness Peat	-2T5
C-FNAB	19847	701	4/87	C	EX C-FNAB Nordair	-242C
C-FNAH	19848	702	4/87	C	EX C-FNAH Nordair	-242C
C-FNAP	20496	704	4/87	C	EX C-FNAP Nordair	-242C
C-FNAQ	20455	703	4/87	C	EX C-FNAQ Nordair	-242C
C-FPWP	20588	735	5/87	C	LF N381PA ATASCO/Pan Am; EX C-FPWP PWA	-275
C-FPWW	20670	736	6/87	C	LF N380PA ATASCO/Pan Am; EX C-FPWW PWA	-275
C-GAPW	20922	739	7/88	C	EX C-GAPW PWA; EX N127AW American West	-275
C-GBPW	20958	740	4/87	5/89	EX C-GBPW PWA; LT N128AW American West	-275
C-GCAU	22640	789	11/87	4/88	LF G-BJCV Britannia	-204
C-GCPM	21716	708	4/87	C	EX C-GCPM CPAL	-217
C-GCPN	21717	709	4/87	C	EX C-GCPN CPAL	-217
C-GCPO	21718	710	4/87	C	EX C-GCPO CPAL	-217
C-GCPP	22555	711	4/87	C	EX C-GCPP CPAL	-217
C-GCPQ	22256	712	4/87	C	EX C-GCPQ CPAL	-217
C-GCPS	22257	714	4/87	C	EX C-GCPS CPAL	-217
C-GCPT	22258	715	4/87	C	EX C-GCPT CPAL	-217
C-GCPU	22259	716	4/87	C	EX C-GCPU CPAL	-217
C-GCPV	22260	717	4/87	C	EX C-GCPV CPAL	-217
C-GCPW	20959	741	10/87	5/89	LT N126AW American West; EX C-GCPW PWA	-275
C-GCPX	22341	718	4/87	C	EX C-GCPX CPAL	-217
C-GCPY	22342	719	4/87	C	EX C-GCPY CPAL	-217
C-GCPZ	22658	720	4/87	C	EX C-GCPZ CPAL	-217
C-GDPA	21116	784	4/87	C	EX C-GDPA PWA & Dome Petroleum	-2T2C
C-GDPW	21116	742	4/87	C	EX C-GDPW PWA	-275C
C-GEPA	20976	796	4/87	C	EX C-GEPA EPA	-2E1
C-GEPM	22395	797	4/87	5/89	EX C-GEPM EPA; EX G-BHVG Orion; LT 9M-MBO Malaysian	-2T5
C-GEPW	21115	743	4/87	5/89	EX C-GEPW PWA; LT N129AW American West	-275
C-GFCP	22659	721	4/87	C	EX C-GFCP CPAL	-217
C-GFPW	21294	752	4/87	C	EX C-GFPW PWA	-275
C-GGPW	21639	744	4/87	C	EX C-GGPW PWA	-275
C-GIPW	21712	745	4/87	C	EX C-GIPW PWA	-275
C-GJCP	22728	722	4/87	C	EX C-GJCP CPAL	-217
C-GJPW	21713	746	4/87	C	EX C-GJPW PWA	-275
C-GKCP	22729	723	4/87	C	EX C-GKCP PWA	-217
CC-GKPW	21819	748	4/87	C	EX C-GKPW PWA	-275
C-GLPW	22086	749	4/87	C	EX C-GLPW PWA	-275
C-GMCP	22864	724	4/87	C	EX C-GMCP CPAL	-217
-GMPW	22087	750	4/87	C	EX C-GMPW PWA	-217
C-GNDC	21728	761	4/87	C	EX C-GNDC Nordair	-242C
C-GNDL	21186	705	4/87	C	EX C-GNDL Nordair	-242

FLEET LISTING
CANADIAN AIRLINES INTERNATIONAL

REG'N	C/N	F/N	IS	WFU	NOTES	MODEL
BOEING 737-200 (Continued)						
C-GNDM	22074	706	4/87	C	EX C-GNDM Nordair	-242
C-GNDR	22075	707	4/87	C	EX C-GNDR Nordair	-242
C-GNDS	21518	771	4/87	C	EX C-GNDS Nordair; EX B-2611 Far Eastern A.T.	-2Q8
C-GNDU	22877	762	4/87	C	EX C-GNDU Nordair	-242C
C-GNPW	22159	751	4/87	C	EX C-GNPW PWA	-275
C-GOPW	22160	782	4/87	C	EX C-GOPW PWA	-275C
C-GPPW	22264	753	4/87	C	EX C-GPPW PWA	-275
C-GPWC	22416	790	12/87	4/88	LF G-BMON Monarch; EX C-GPWC PWA (12/88-4/89 F/N 397)	-2K9A
C-GQBB	22276	732	4/87	C	EX C-GQBB Quebecair	-296
C-GQBH	22516	734	4/87	C	EX C-GQBH Quebecair	-296
C-GQCA	22415	398	12/88	4/89	LF CS-TET Air Atlantis	-2K9A
C-GQCP	22865	725	4/87	C	EX C-GQCP CPAL	-217
C-GRCP	21397	726	4/87	C	EX C-GRCP CPAL; EX PH-TVP Transavia	-2K2
C-GRPW	22255	755	4/87	C	EX C-GRPW PWA	-275
C-GSPW	22618	783	4/87	C	EX C-GSPW PWA & EPA	-275C
C-GTPW	22807	756	4/87	C	EX C-GTPW PWA	-275
C-GUPW	22873	758	4/87	C	EX C-GUPW PWA	-275
C-GVPW	22874	759	4/87	C	EX C-GVPW PWA	-275
C-GWPW	23283	760	4/87	C	EX C-GWPW PWA	-275
C-GXPW	20521	765	6/87	5/89	EX C-FNAW Nordair; EX N130AW American West	-212
BOEING 737 - 300						
C-FPWD	23495	301	11/87	4/89	LF G-DHSW Monarch (Leased Nov-Mar 87/88 & 88/89)	-3YO
C-FPWE	23497	302	11/87	4/89	LF G-MONF Monarch (Leased Nov-Mar 87/88 & 88/89)	-3YO
C-GPWG	23498	303	11/87	4/89	LF G-MONG Monarch (Leased Nov-Mar 87/88 & 88/89)	-3YO
McDONNELL DOUGLAS DC-10-30						
C-FCRA	46931	909	4/87	C	EX C-FCRA CPAL; EX AP-AXC PIA; $7 million fire, Amsterdam 10/04/89	
C-FCRB	46940	910	4/87	C	EX C-FCRB CPAL; EX AP-AXD Pakistan International	
C-FCRD	47889	912	4/87	C	EX C-FCRD CPAL; EX AP-AYM Pakistan International	
C-FCRE	47868	911	4/87	C	EX C-FCRE CPAL; EX AP-BBL Pakistan International	
C-GCPC	46540	901	4/87	C	EX C-GCPC CPAL; EX PP-VMO Varig	
C-GCPD	46541	902	4/87	C	EX C-GCPD CPAL; EX PP-VMP Varig	
C-GCPE	46542	903	4/87	C	EX C-GCPE CPAL	
C-GCPF	46543	904	6/87	C	EX C-GCPF United	
C-GCPG	48285	905	5/87	C	EX N1850U United	
C-GCPH	48288	906	5/87	C	EX C-GCPH United	
C-GCPI	48296	907	4/87	C	EX C-GCPI CPAL	
C-GCPJ	46991	908	4/87	C	EX C-GCPJ CPAL; EX 9V-SDC Singapore International	
C-GFHX	46990	914	5/88	5/89	EX C-GHFX Wardair; ST F-GGMZ Minerve (France)	
LOCKHEED L188 ELECTRA – ICE PATROL AIRCRAFT						
C-FNAY	1113	113	4/87	C	EX C-FNAY Nordair; major rebuild 6/88; full Canadian c/s 7/88	
C-GNDZ	1111	111	4/87	C	EX C-GNDZ Nordair; planned WFU 9/89	
TURBO PROP EQUIPMENT ACQUIRED FROM NORDAIR/EPA BUT NOT OPERATED IN CANADIAN COLOURS						
FAIRCHILD FH-227						
C-FNAI	505	505	1/87	2/88	ST SE-KBP Malmo Aviation	
C-FNAJ	508	508	1/87	WFU	Stored Montreal	
C-FNAK	519	515	1/87	2/88	ST SE-KBR Malmo Aviation	
C-GNDH	529	529	1/87	WFU	Stored Montreal; ST Malmo Aviation 10/88	
C-GNDI	530	530	1/87	WFU	Stored Montreall; ST Malmo Aviation 10/88	
HAWKER-SIDDLEY HS748						
C-FINE	1611	301	5/86	WFU	Not yet disposed of	
C-GDOP	1745	304	5/86	3/88	ST C-GDOP Calm Air; LT F-ODQQ Air St Pierre 1987	
C-GEPB	1686	303	5/86	9/87	ST C-GEPB Calm Air; LT C-GEPB Austin 7/8	

Canadian Pacific Canso CF-CRV
Photo courtesy of CP Air

Canadian Pacific Lockheed Lodestar CF-CPA
Photo courtesy of CP Air

Canadian Pacific Convair 240, CF-CPD
Photo courtesy of CP Air

Canadian Pacific Airlines

Canadian Pacific Boeing 727-200 C-GCPA
Photo courtesy of CP Air

HEADQUARTERS:
1 Grant McConachie Way,
Vancouver International Airport,
Vancouver, B.C. V7B 1V1

MAJOR BASES:
Vancouver, Toronto.
(Halifax for EPA; Montreal for *Nordair*)

FINAL FLEET:
46 - Boeing 737-200s;
9 - DC10-30s (plus 3 leased out) (April 1987);
2 - L188 Electras;
3 - DC10-10s (leased)

FINAL COLOURS:
CPA: The white upper fuselage is separated from the dark blue lower fuselage by a narrow red cheat line which runs just above the wings. The tail is dark blue with the new company logo on the upper tail. The logo consists of five narrow grey lines (motion mark) separated by thin dark blue lines which form a semi-circle at the back inside of which is a red triangle. The fleet number is in white on the tip of the tail while the registration number appears in white on the rear fuselage with a Canadian flag. The engines are also painted dark blue with a thin red stripe through the middle. The titles are in black on the upper fuselage, with 'Canadian Pacific' on one side (usually but not always the port side) and 'Canadien Pacifique' on the other. All aircraft carried Empress names on the forward fuselage in black lettering with 'Empress of City' on the English side and 'Empress du . . . ' or 'Empress de . . . .' on the French.
Orange CP Air: The upper fuselage and tail were orange with a wide red stripe starting at the top of the aircraft above the pilot's window and wrapping back to the middle of the aircraft where it became a cheat line running to the back of the aircraft. The remainder of the aircraft was silver. A large CP logo in white and red appeared on the tail and the black title 'CP Air' was on the forward lower fuselage. The registration and fleet numbers were displayed in black on the rear fuselage and the tip of the tail respectively.

ROUTES:
British Columbia-Yukon:
Victoria – Vancouver – Prince George – Fort St. John – Fort Nelson – Terrace – Prince Rupert – Whitehorse – Watson Lake.
Canada:
Victoria – Vancouver – Edmonton – Calgary – Winnipeg Grande Prairie – Dryden – Thunder Bay – Sault Ste Marie – Sudbury – Toronto – Windsor – Ottawa – Montreal – Quebec– Val d'Or – La Grande – Fort Chimo – Poste-de-La-Baleine – Fort Chimo – Saint John – Fredericton – Charlo – Chatham – Halifax – Sydney – Charlottetown – St. John's – Gander – Wabush – Churchill Falls – Goose Bay – Frobisher Bay – Hall Beach – Nanisivik – Resolute Bay.
USA:
Honolulu – Los Angeles – San Francisco – Pittsburgh – Fort Lauderdale.
Pacific:
Auckland – Sydney – Nandi – Hong Kong – Shanghai – Tokyo.
South America:
Lima – Santiago – Buenos Aires.
Europe:
Amsterdam – Lisbon – Milan – Rome.

HISTORY:

In 1928, *Inter-Provincial Airlines* was formed in eastern Canada and *Western Canada Airways* was formed in western Canada. In 1930, these two companies merged to form *Canadian Airways Limited*. Although the Canadian Pacific Railway had declined to be a partner in *Trans-Canada Air Lines* in 1936, they purchased a block of stock in *Canadian Airways* in 1930 for $250,000. In 1939, the railway decided to own its own airline and began purchasing companies in all parts of Canada.

During the early part of World War II, the CPR helped organize the *North Atlantic Ferry Service* and operated six Air Observer schools as part of the British Commonwealth Air Training Plan. The CPR also managed five repair plants for the wartime overhaul of aircraft and engines.

Canadian Pacific Airlines was formed 16 May 1942 by the merger of *Canadian Airways* and nine other airlines owned by the CPR: *Yukon Southern Air Transport* (Grant McConachie's airline, serving Alberta and the Yukon); *Mackenzie Air Service* (which served along the Mackenzie River, NWT); *Arrow Airways* (The Pas, Manitoba); *Starratt Airways and Transportation Limited* (Hudson, Ontario); *Prairie Airways* (Regina); *Ginger Coote Airways* (Vancouver); *Quebec Airways* (Quebec City); *Dominion Skyways* (Rouyn, Quebec); and *Wings Limited* (Manitoba). The initial CPA fleet consisted of seventy-eight aircraft of twenty-six different types, located across Canada. The founding companies continued to operate under their own names during most of the war and at least twenty-one of these aircraft were written off in various accidents. Most of these planes were disposed of by 1944 with only a few remaining until 1947.

Grant McConachie became the General Manager of Canadian Pacific Airlines in 1942 and President in 1947. He was awarded the McKee Aviation Trophy in 1945 for his outstanding contribution to aviation. A complete account of this outstanding Canadian can be found in a book titled 'Bush Pilot with a Briefcase' by Ronald Keith.

Canadian Pacific really began taking shape just after the war with the acquisition of Norsemen, Cansos (to serve the B.C. coastal communities), Ansons, and DC-3 aircraft. Seventeen DC-3s were acquired from 1945 to 1947 and served in large numbers until 1959, only one aircraft remaining by 1974. Eleven Lockheed 18 Lodestars were acquired in 1948. These were delivered in USAAF camouflage colours and operated in this colour scheme with Canadian Pacific titles until they were sold in 1950.

The company had a series of accidents between 1949 and 1951. Two Cansos crashed on coastal duties and were written off, one on 11 May 1949 at Prince Rupert and the other on 9 July 1949 at Asisko Lake, B.C. On 9 September 1949, a DC-3 was destroyed in flight near St. Joachim, Quebec, by a timebomb placed on board. Another DC-3 was written off 22 December 1950 at Okanagan Park, B.C. These accidents plus the North Star and CD-4 accidents described later made this a difficult time for the airline.

When TCA declined the Pacific Ocean routes to the Orient, Grant McConachie convinced the Canadian Pacific Directors to operate the routes. Granting of the routes to the orient and Australia was in part conditional on the company buying Canadair North Stars. CPA borrowed a North Star, CF-TEP (#17522), from the RCAF early in 1949 for training and extensive proving flights. In April 1949, one of these proving flights went as far as Shanghai and the aircraft left the Orient just before the Communist takeover. This noisy, unpressurized aircraft was returned to the RCAF when four pressurized and noises reduced C-4-1 models were delivered to the airline. The company operated these on the Orient route but found them to be too small and still too noisy for a comfortable flight to Tokyo, Hong Kong, Honolulu, Nandi (Fiji), New Zealand or Sydney (Australia). Three of these planes were sold to TCA in 1951-52. The fourth aircraft, CF-CPR, was written-off at Tokyo, 2 February 1950, when the North Star landed in poor weather. The Captain did not hear the wave-off by the ground controller and touched down half-way along the runway. The brakes could not hold the plane on the wet concrete it ran off the end of the runway, hit the sea wall and ended up nose down in shallow water in Tokyo Bay. All the passengers and crew were rescued.

To replace the North Stars and fill in on the Pacific routes until the larger DC-6Bs became available, five DC-4s were purchased from *Pan American Airlines* and refurbished by CPA. The Korean War proved beneficial to CPA which was employed by the United States Army to carry large numbers of troops and VIPs to Tokyo. The company airlifted more than thirty-nine thousand military personnel between Canada and Tokyo during the Korean War. The large number of immigrants coming to Canada from Hong Kong also benefited CPA as most of their flights were filled with immigrants paying full first class airfares. These two groups of passengers permitted Canadian Pacific to establish its routes to the Orient and persuaded Canadian Pacific's Board of Directors to persist with the Australian route until it also could be made profitable. Four of the DC-4s were sold by 1957 while the fifth was lost on a flight to the Orient, 21 July 1951. Thirty-seven lives were lost in this crash which occurred in Alaska between Silk and Yahutat.

Five Convair 240 aircraft were purchased from *Continental Airlines* during 1952-1953. This pressurized, twin-engined, piston aircraft could carry forty pas-

Canadian Pacific DC8-43 CF-CPF
Photo courtesy of CP Air

sengers. The planes were used on domestic routes for the next decade until sold in Japan during 1963-64.

Canadian Pacific became the second airline in the world (after BOAC) to place an order for a jet transport when it ordered two Comet 1s late in 1949. When the first of these aircraft was ready for delivery, five Canadian Pacific crew members and six de Havilland technicians were dispatched to deliver the aircraft. Since the Comet did not have the range to fly from Vancouver to Hawaii, it was to be based in Sydney, Australia and operate between there and Honolulu where it would link up with the piston powered aircraft from Vancouver. Thus the delivery flight was not to Canada but to Australia and the airline hoped that the Comet would set an elapsed time record between England and Australia. After leaving England on March 1 and overnighting in Beirut, Comet 1, CF-CUN, "Empress of Hawaii" was taking off from Karachi, Pakistan early in the morning of 3 March 1953, on the final leg of the delivery flight. Captain Charles Pentland, with a crew of four and six technicians aboard, began his takeoff run; the nose lifted as the plane was about to leave the runway but the nose-up attitude was too great for flight. The aircraft crashed and burned beyond the end of the runway and the eleven people on board were killed. The other Comet 1 order was cancelled and despite an order for three Comet 3s in 1953 which were also cancelled, Canadian Pacific did not enter the pure jet age until 1961.

The DC-6B was a pressurized, four piston, 60-passenger aircraft with a range of 3860 miles and a cruise speed of 311 mph. Four were acquired early in 1953 to replace the DC-4s on the Pacific routes. This included service on the Korean airlift, and flights to South America which Canadian Pacific had begun in 1955. These aircraft also permitted Canadian Pacific to expand into Europe when the first over-the-pole flight from Van-

couver to Amsterdam was made in 1957. Flights from Toronto and Montreal to Lisbon and Madrid were also started at this time.

Because Canadian Pacific could not fly passengers completely across Canada, they decided to introduce an all freight service in 1953. Two DC-6A Liftmasters, the cargo version of the DC-6, were purchased to begin this route. *Trans Canada Airlines* opposed the plan on the grounds that Canadian Pacific was not permitted to compete on the trans-Canada route and the federal transport authorities agreed with TCA. Thus the two planes had to be sold within a year. TCA felt that it had to justify its opposition to the CPA plan and so bought three Bristol Freighters to fly a trans-Canada cargo operation. The plan proved uneconomical and TCA sold these aircraft after suffering three years of heavy losses, probably saving Canadian Pacific from incurring these same losses!

Construction of the Distant Early Warning (DEW) Line in 1955 was very beneficial to Canadian Pacific as they were one of the major contractors. Eight Curtiss C-46 aircraft were purchased from *Flying Tigers* and used as cargo aircraft for support of the DEW Line construction. The C-46 offered an increase in gross weight of approximately 45% over the venerable DC-3 and almost twice the cabin volume. These planes were well suited to this type of work and as DEW Line work dropped off, the planes were sold to the regional carriers, *Pacific Western, Northern Wings* and *Quebecair,* during 1957-1959. Two remained in service until 1963.

Two DHC-3 Otters were purchased in 1955 to serve in the Mackenzie District of the Northwest Territories. The planes were operated on skis and on floats, and connected with DC-3 flights from Edmonton (and other points) to Norman Wells. The Otters carried passengers, mail and freight south to Fort Norman and north as far

Canadian Pacific Bristol Britannia CF-CZD
Photo courtesy of CP Air

as Aklavik. Both aircraft were sold to *Pacific Western* in 1959 when PWA acquired the northern Alberta and Mackenzie River routes from Canadian Pacific as part of the new domestic air policy.

The DC-6B became the backbone of the Canadian Pacific fleet when twelve were purchased during the period 1956-1958. One of these crashed at Cold Bay, Alaska, on 29 August 1956 as the plane attempted a go around following a missed landing in foul weather. The long range of these planes allowed Toronto-Mexico City to be added in 1955 and Vancouver-Lime, Santiago, Chile and Buenos Aires to be added in 1957 as Canadian Pacific began its South America service.

The Canadian government introduced a new domestic airline policy in 1958 which allowed limited trans-continental service by Canadian Pacific in return for relinquishing certain regional routes. As noted previously, PWA acquired the Mackenzie River and northern Alberta services, while Canadian Pacific continued to operate its Vancouver – Prince Rupert – Terrace and Vancouver – Prince George – Fort St. John – Grande Prairie – Whitehorse – Edmonton routes. These remained highly profitable routes throughout Canadian Pacific's history. The airline also gave up regional routes in Quebec but in return acquired one flight per day, Vancouver to Montreal via Winnipeg and Toronto .

To operate this trans-Canada route, Canadian Pacific entered the turbo-prop era in 1958 by purchasing six Bristol 175 Britannia aircraft for $2.9 million each. This was the world's first long-range turbine powered aircraft and carried one hundred and fourteen passengers in quiet comfort. These aircraft were supplemented by the lease of two additional Britannias, the last two Britannias built.

The last Canso was sold in 1960 when the British Columbia coastal routes were transferred to *B.C. Airlines*. With the introduction of the Britannias, eight DC-6s were sold in the period 1959 to 1962. About 1960, there was a change in the airline's colour scheme. The previous scheme had consisted of a white upper fuselage separated from the silver lower fuselage by a broad red cheat line running the length of the fuselage and wrapping around the nose. Two white stripes ran

through the middle of the red cheat line and the tail was white with a series of horizontal stripes half way up the tail, of red, white, red, white and red. Canadian Pacific was written in black on the upper fuselage and the registration and fleet number were in black on the tail. The new scheme consisted of a white upper fuselage and silver lower fuselage but the cheat line, running below the windows, was red, white and red. The tail was white with a red vertical line. Half way up the tail a circle containing a goose was surmounted by the letters CPA. The lettering was in black and Canadian Pacific titles appeared in written form on the upper fuselage. Later aircraft in this colour scheme had the Canadian Pacific titles in block letters rather than script. The Empress name was on the left side of the aircraft behind the door.

This new colour scheme was seen on the jet aircraft introduced in 1961. Eight years after the Comet crash, four DC-8-43 aircraft were purchased between February and November 1961, and two more acquired in 1963 and 1965. These early jets originally carried only one hundred and twenty passengers but later, with reduced seat pitches, carried up to one hundred and seventy-one passengers.

The Convair 240s were sold in Japan during 1963-64 and the remaining C-46s were sold in 1963. The Britannias were retired during 1964-65 as the jet aircraft replaced them in the fleet. One Britannia, the "Empress of Vancouver" was attempting an overshoot on three engines at Hickam Field, Honolulu, on 22 July 1962 when it crashed. At a critical point in the landing, the aircraft had lacked sufficient altitude to manoeuvre for the final touchdown.

Grant McConachie's last flight on Canadian Pacific Airlines occurred on 30 June 1965. On that flight, DC-6, CF-CZZ, flew Grant's body back to Vancouver from Los Angeles where he had died of a heart attack a day before. Thus ended the career of this great Canadian aviator who had been president of Canadian Pacific since 7 February 1947. He had modernized the airline and acquired the Pacific, Orient and South American routes. He had convinced the airline that the polar route to Europe from Vancouver was feasible and had fought the federal government bureaucrats to gain permission for his airline to compete with *Trans Canada Airlines* within Canada.

Several key members of the Winnipeg Blue Bombers football team, which had just competed in the CFL Allstar game in Vancouver, were among the passengers aboard the DC-6B, "Empress of Buenos Aires" on a flight from Vancouver to Winnipeg. At 15,000 feet over Dog Creek, 150 miles north of Vancouver, a bomb exploded in the cargo hold and the aircraft, her crew and passengers died in the crash.

Rome was added to the airline's routes in 1965 and this flight was extended to Athens in 1968. Canadian

Pacific finally received a transborder flight into the United States when it began flying from Vancouver to San Francisco in 1967. Two DC-8-50 aircraft were purchased and another was leased during the 1966-67 period. This leased aircraft, CF-CPN, was the prototype DC-8 which had been rolled out on 9 April 1958 and first flew on 30 May 1958. In its one year lease with Canadian Pacific, this aircraft flew 4200 hours.

The only serious accident involving DC-8 aircraft suffered by Canadian Pacific was to CF-CPK, the "Empress of Edmonton," when it undershot on landing at Tokyo, 4 March 1966, killing all sixty-four on board. The plane had logged only 1,775 hours total flying time at the time of the accident.

Early 1968 saw the purchase of four stretch DC-8 Series 63 aircraft. These 269-passenger jets gave a large boost to Canadian Pacific's carrying capacity. While awaiting the delivery of these aircraft, a Boeing 707 was wet leased from *Standard Airlines* in October, 1967, and was operated by *Standard Airline's* pilots with Canadian Pacific cabin crews. On 7 February 1968, the "Empress of Sydney" was landing in a thin ground fog at Vancouver International Airport after a flight from Honolulu. The official report stated:

> "The pilot lost visual reference between the flare-out and the touchdown resulting in the aircraft running off the runway and colliding with a small building near the south terminal."

An airport employee in the building and the Canadian Pacific purser on board were killed and the airplane was destroyed by fire. This was the last fatal accident Canadian Pacific was to suffer, operating for almost two more decades with no further loss of life.

Canadian Pacific Airlines dropped its logo of a Canadian Goose late in 1968 and adopted a modern, simpler name, *CP AIR*. The company introduced the new Canadian Pacific corporate logo and a new colour scheme on the first Boeing 737 jet delivered late in 1968 and the seven delivered early in 1969. The new colour scheme consisted of a silver body with a red stripe beginning on the top of the aircraft at a point just aft of the cockpit and sweeping down and under the fuselage at the rear of the aircraft. To the rear of the red stripe, the remainder of the aircraft, including the tail, was a bright orange. Canadian Pacific's corporate logo, a red triangle with two partial white circles on two sides, filled much of the tail. The title CP AIR appeared in black on the lower forward fuselage, just below the cockpit. The fleet number was just below the title and the registration number appeared on the rear of the fuselage at the level of the windows, both in black. The wings were silver. The DC-8 jets and one remaining DC-3 aircraft were also painted in this colour scheme but the DC-6s, which were phased out completely in 1970, never changed from their white paint scheme. The DC-3, CF-CRX, was

used as a training aircraft until late 1974 when it was sold to *Harrison Airlines* where it continued to operate in its orange colour scheme.

CP Air sold its hangars on the south side of the Vancouver International Airport to *Pacific Western Airlines* in 1971, and moved its operations to a new complex on the north side of the airport, just east of the main terminal. The new complex, on fifty-two acres, provided CP Air with modern hangar and office space.

CP Air purchased four Boeing 727-17s during 1970-1971. This three-engine jet was tried on the company's longer domestic routes but did not fit in well with the rest of the CP Air fleet. With a capacity of one hundred and eighteen, it carried only a few more passengers than the Boeing 737 yet consumed more fuel. Hence the four aircraft were sold in 1977.

The company continued to help employ people in the Seattle area with a further Boeing purchase in 1973-1974. At this time, the company entered the jumbo jet era with the purchase of four Boeing 747 aircraft. One was immediately leased to *Braniff* for a four year period and was the all-orange *Braniff* jumbo jet during this period. The other three planes were striking in the orange, red and silver colours and were quickly put into transcontinental and international service. The normal seating capacity of the Boeing 747 was 442 when they were delivered, with a range of 5,000 nautical miles at a cruise speed of 553 mph. The first revenue flight for these aircraft was on December 16, 1973, from Vancouver to Tokyo and Hong Kong.

Two Boeing 727-217s were added in 1975 for use on the Vancouver to Toronto and Vancouver to San Francisco routes. These aircraft could carry one hundred and thirty-two passengers with a range of 2,200 nautical miles at a cruising speed of 550 mph. These aircraft, like the previous four Boeing 727s (series 100), did not fit the CP Air route system and were leased out in 1981, after six years of service, and finally sold in 1984. In the summer of 1975, DC-8-55, CF-CPT, was converted to an all-economy aircraft for use on ABC Charters. The plane could now carry one hundred and seventy-one passengers, thirty more than previously, and fifty-one more than the Series-41 aircraft. This plane was sold in 1978.

The recession began to hit CP Air as early as 1977, with more than two hundred staff being laid off, while the Boeing 737 fleet began to be converted to all-economy, 112-passenger seating. A new government ruling now allowed the airline in 1978 to increase its share of the transcontinental traffic from 25% to 35% of *Air Canada's* capacity, and to 45% in 1979. The policy also allowed CP Air to overnight their aircraft in any of the cities on their routes. Previously, flights had to overnight in Vancouver, Montreal, Ottawa or Toronto. These were dramatic increases for a company allowed its first daily transcontinental flight in 1958 and a second daily flight in 1967. It had been the 1967 policy which permitted CP Air to have only 25% of the capacity of Air Canada. At this time, DC-8-43, C-FCPF, became the longest serving DC-8 with one company, having flown 58,880 hours, or six and a half calendar years, for the company.

In May 1978, CP Air began a Calgary to Prince George service. It also commenced *Courier Jet Service,* a small package air service between major cities served by the company. Boeing 727s flew across Canada at night in a mixed cargo/passenger arrangement to operate this service. For the Toronto to Winnipeg and back section, CP Air leased *Transair* 737s to fly this route each night.

CP Air was awarded unlimited transcontinental authority in May 1979. A consolidation of their licence permitting them to fly between any two cities in their system without first obtaining CTC permission. SKYBUS service was begun on 1 June 1979, offering a no frills flight (no meals, no headsets, no papers, limited baggage) between Toronto and either Edmonton, Calgary or Vancouver. Boeing 747s were used initially, to be replaced in October 1979 by DC-8-63s (C-FCPP and C-FCPS). These aircraft were fitted out in an all-economy 221-seat arrangement and bore the title SKYBUS / AEROBUS in black on the rear fuselage.

The company returned to McDonnell Douglas for aircraft in 1979 with the purchase of the long range, wide-body DC-10-30s. The first two of these planes were immediately leased to *Varig* of Brazil for a year. However, by the end of 1980, four were in service with the airline and two more were added in 1981 and another two in 1982. With a total of eight of these aircraft in service, the airline was able to sell all of its DC-8s. The short DC-8s were sold in 1980. The departure of DC-8, C-FCPG, ended the career of a remarkable aircraft with CP Air. While still with Douglas as N9604Z, it became

Canadian Pacific DHC-3 Otters CF-CZP and CF-CZO
Photo courtesy of CP Air

the first commercial jet aircraft to exceed the speed of sound on 21 August 1961, while the manufacturer was testing aerodynamic wing improvements. This aircraft also established an airliner altitude record at this time of 15,876 metres and flew more than thirty-nine million miles on CP Air routes. The Super DC-8-63s were sold in 1983, four of them going to *Worldways* of Toronto.

At this time, CP Air decided to standardize its fleet with three basic aircraft: the jumbo Boeing 747, the midsize DC-10 and the smaller Boeing 737. Following the sale of the 727s and DC-8s, considerable savings were realized in the cost for training aircrews, with only three types of aircraft rather than five. Considerable expansion of the Boeing 737 fleet had taken place between 1979 and April 1983, with seventeen jets delivered. Five of the Boeing 737s obtained in 1968 were sold during 1982-1983, leaving nineteen Boeing 737s in service with the airline in 1984.

The Canadian Transport Commission awarded CP Air a Halifax to Toronto route but in an unusual move, the Federal Cabinet on 27 June 1980 overturned the decision and awarded the route to *Eastern Provincial Airways.* CP Air was allowed to fly to Halifax from Montreal or from Ottawa but the company did not pick up these routes at this time. An agreement was reached with *Philippine Airlines* for around-the-world flights using both airlines at a cost of $1999 economy and $2999 first class.

In September 1980, CP Air entered the highly competitive Montreal – Toronto market with an unique service called *The Company Jet.* Boeing 737, C-FCPV, carried the title "Company Jet / PremiAir" and only sixty-eight of the available one hundred and seventeen seats on the aircraft were sold with the middle seats not being used. This service, aimed at the business traveller cost $22.00 more than the normal economy fare and consisted of four flights daily between the two cities. Unfortunately for CP Air, *Air Canada's Rapidair Service,* which was providing hourly non-reservation service, held the businessman's loyalty due to its flexibility and CP Air discontinued the service after one year.

The company introduced "Empress Class Service" in October 1980. This was for full economy paying passengers and offered free drinks, free newspapers and a choice of meals. Empress Class passengers were seated in the forward portion of the aircraft, just behind first class, with the special fare passengers seated in the rear. The end of 1980 showed 3.6 million passengers carried at a 70% load factor and a modest profit of $6.8 million.

The airline did begin a Montreal-Halifax service in March 1981. Two of the Boeing 737s delivered in 1981, C-GCPV and C-GCPX, had extra fuel tanks installed prior to delivery permitting longer-range operations. In an effort to save the *Company Jet* service, regular fare passengers were booked into the back of the aircraft but even this failed to produce adequate load levels. CP Air began flying DC-10 charters into Reno from Vancouver and Alberta, the first wide-bodied jets to fly into Reno. By the summer of 1981, there was *Empress Class Service* on all transcontinental flights and most foreign flights.

Vancouver to Victoria service was begun on 15 June 1981. In 1981 the company decided to purchase six Boeing 767 aircraft but delayed delivery for seventeen months. Former Canadian Pacific DC-3 CF-CPY was placed on a pedestal outside the Whitehorse Airport Terminal in full CPA colours where it acts as a weathervane. During the summer of 1981, sleeper seats were added in the first class section of all Boeing 747 and DC-10 aircraft and the Skybus concept was dropped, with the company switching to ABC charters. For the year 1981, CP Air had a 70.1% system wide load factor, fifth highest among IATA carriers. However, the airline still lost $22.8 million.

CP Air began flying into Saskatchewan again in 1982 with Vancouver – Regina – Toronto service beginning in April and Vancouver – Saskatoon – Toronto in June. The nightly Vancouver – Toronto flights were expanded to include Calgary and Winnipeg, enabling the courier cargo service to be expanded.

In October 1982, CP Air and *Eastern Provincial Airways* integrated their Halifax to Montreal or Ottawa or Toronto flights. The two companies provided joint check-in service with CP Air handling services in Toronto, Ottawa and Montreal, while EPA serviced Halifax. CP Air also began providing passenger reservation service and engine overhauls for EPA under this arrangement. Three older Boeing 737s were sold to *People's Express* late in 1982 for $5.5 million each. Dan Colussy, a former Pan American executive, was named the company's new Chief Executive Officer in 1982.

A new scheduling strategy for CP Air was introduced in 1983, with Toronto and Vancouver acting as hub cities for the airline's flights. Flights to Saskatchewan were again dropped this year because of poor load factors, but with a promise that they would return. At the beginning of the year, CP Air traded three DC-10-30 aircraft to *United Airlines* for three DC-10-10s. The slightly longer DC-10-30 has a third main landing gear unit, almost 68% more fuel tankage, 22% higher take-off load weight and a longer range (4,000 miles) than the Series-10 (2,700 miles). The company planned to use the *United* aircraft on its domestic routes where the extended range of the Series-30 aircraft was not required. CP Air also benefitted financially from the trade agreement which was to run for three years, but was later extended to five years. In addition, *United* planned to modify the DC-10-30s they received in the trade, which will be a benefit to CP Air when they are returned. Because the DC-10-10 aircraft is not certified in Canada,

CPA, rather than going through the expense of having them licenced, operated these aircraft with American registrations during the term of the lease.

Another major aircraft change was announced early in 1983 for CP Air. The order for the Boeing 767s was cancelled and ten Boeing 737-300 aircraft were to be purchased between 1985 and 1988. The Series-300 Boeing 737 has an extended fuselage and can carry twelve passengers more than the Series -200 Boeing 737 then in service with CP Air. This change thus did not introduce a fourth type of aircraft into the CP Air fleet and the mix of 747, DC-10 and 737 was maintained.

In June 1983, after the long *Eastern Provincial* strike, CP Air and EPA began an aircraft interchange. EPA flew from Montreal and Toronto to Halifax with its Boeing 737s which had small CP Air stickers on the fuselage just above the wings. These flights were integrated with the trans-Canada flights of CP Air giving CP Air access to Halifax without using its own aircraft. It also gave CP Air passengers access to all of EPA's routes and freed up two Boeing 737s for CP Air to use elsewhere in its system.

In October 1983, *Air BC* took over all but one Vancouver to Victoria flight using their Dash-7 aircraft with Twin Otters as backup aircraft. The *Air BC* aircraft carried "CP Air Commuter" stickers and their flights tied into the regularly scheduled CP Air flights. All *Air BC* flights were designated as CP Air commuter flights thus linking the large number of British Columbia communities served by *Air BC* with the worldwide flights of CP Air. *Pem Air* of Pembroke, Ontario also began to operate as a CP Air commuter airline between Pembroke and Toronto.

The DC-10-10s were used on the night courier/passenger flights between Vancouver, Calgary and Toronto. *NWT Air* Electras were used for the Winnipeg to Toronto sector of the courier flights and Learjets operated by *Business Flights* connected Edmonton to Calgary for the courier service.

Service resumed to Saskatchewan in November 1983, with a weekly Boeing 747 flight Regina – Vancouver – Honolulu. A wide range of charters operated from Toronto during the winter of 1983-84, including flights to Charleis, Montego Bay, San Jaun, Nassau, Acapulco, Puerto Vallarta, Cancun, Cozumel and St. Petersberg.

All CP Air's Boeing 747s and DC-10s entered service displaying "Empress" names representing cities, usually outside of Canada, serviced by CP Air. Early in 1984, Boeing 737 aircraft began appearing with "Empress" names representing destinations within Canada.

On 17 April 1984, CP Air announced that *Eastern Provincial Airways Ltd.* would be bought by Canadian Pacific Airlines for $20 million. Halifax based EPA and its affiliate *Air Maritime* would continue to operate separately under their current management team headed by Harry Steele, president and chief executive officer of EPA. The purchase was ratified by the CTC in the summer of 1984 and the amalgamation of the two airlines began immediately, although the *Eastern Provincial* aircraft would remain with EPA titles for a couple of years more.

Boeing 747, "Empress of Canada," was painted with a large EXPO title on its tail and an EXPO 86 logo on the side of the plane to honour the 1986 World Exposition to be held in Vancouver. A DC-10-10, "Empress of Canada," was renamed "Empress of EXPO 86;" a DC-10-30 was named "Empress of British Columbia;" and a Boeing 737 was named "Empress of Vancouver." All three also displayed the special EXPO titles.

After negotiating all year, CP Air was finally allowed to add a second weekly flight to Buenos Aires by extending its existing flight to Santiago. The company also resumed flying to Central British Columbia in October 1984, when it inaugurated 'charter' flights between Vancouver and Kelowna. *Attache Class Service*, a premium business class service, was begun at this time using an extended range Boeing 737, with eight first class seats and fifty-four "attache" seats. The "attache" seats were the same concept as used on "The Company Jet" service, with the middle seat being left unsold allowing the business flyer more room to work or relax. This service was first used on flights from Vancouver to Toronto or Montreal.

CP Air began the first Boeing 737 Series-300 service in Canada on 17 April 1985 when C-FCPG flew Vancouver – Winnipeg – Toronto. The aircraft wore the regular orange colour scheme and was named "Empress of Ontario." The Series-300 aircraft is nine feet, seven inches longer than the Series-200 and carries one hundred and thirty-eight passengers. The next two Series-300 Boeing 737s were delivered in the new ATTACHE colour scheme: the cream white upper fuselage and tail isseparated from the grey lower fuselage by a thin maroon cheat line and a wider maroon cheat line. "ATTACHE from CP Air" appears on the left upper fuselage in black lettering and "ATTACHE de CP Air" on the right. On the tail, in black, is the flying horse, Pegasus. The registration, also in black, can be seen on the rear fuselage preceded by the title CANADA. Only these two aircraft wore this special colour scheme.

During July-August, while one of the DC10-30 aircraft was being converted to the extra range version, a DC10-10 was leased from *United* and operated in full *United* colour scheme, titles and registration. Late in October 1985, CP Air announced that it would standardize its fleet on the Boeing 737-200 and DC10-30. The four Boeing 747s in the CP fleet at this time were to be traded one at a time to *Pakistan International* (PIA) for four DC10-30s during 1986. Once the DC10-30s were returned from the *United* lease, the DC10-30s would operate on all long haul international flights. During the winter of 1985, three additional Boeing 737-200s were leased, one each from *Britannia, Transavia Holland* and *Air Nauru*.

CP Air purchased a large block of *Nordair* shares, clearly intending to integrate *Nordair* into the company's operations once the takeover was approved by the Canadian government. However, *Quebecair* also held a large block of *Nordair* stock and both companies pursued the shares held by Innocan. In November 1985, CP Air acquired a further 43.7% of *Nordair* stock for $17 million, giving them more than 60% of all *Nordair* shares. In December, *Nordair,* now majority owned by CP Air, announced the formation of *Nordair Metro* to act as a commuter airline for CP Air and *Nordair* flights and to compete with *Quebecair* in Quebec.

Although the name CP Air was widely recognized in Canada, surveys outside the country had shown that the name was not associated with Canada and thus, late in1985, it was decided to replace the name CP Air with a familiar name, "Canadian Pacific Airlines," and new company logo and colour scheme were adopted. The first aircraft to appear in the new dark blue colour scheme was the first of the DC10-30s acquired in the Boeing 747 trade with PIA and was rolled out in January 1986. The first Boeing 737 was the EPA aircraft C-GEPM which had just been completely overhauled at Luton. The *Eastern Provincial* aircraft had just all been repainted in a new dark blue livery and were now slated to be repainted in the new dark blue CPA scheme. On January 12, 1986, all *Eastern Provincial* flights were switched over to CP flight numbers, effectively ending EPA as a separate entity. However, several of the aircraft retained their EPA colour schemes until late 1987 when the orange CP Air aircraft began to receive their new colours. The *Nordair* fleet had first priority for repainting in the new colours and by the time of the *Canadian* takeover, all *Nordair* aircraft had been repainted.

January 1986 also saw a joint marketing and scheduling agreement with *Nordair* on the Toronto – Ottawa – Montreal sector and *Nordair* joined the CP Air frequent flyer program.

This was a busy time for the airline as it had received a contract to overhaul the *America West Airlines* Boeing 737 fleet for $5 million (through August 1986) and also had gained access to Rio de Janeiro and Sao Paulo, Brazil. In April 1986, the company began its flights from Vancouver to Shanghai, China, a route that Grant McConachie had longed to operate. Canadian Pacific had dropped Regina and Saskatoon from its routes prior to this and decided in April 1986 to withdraw from Saskatchewan for an indefinite period. In addition, jet service to Stephenville, Newfoundland was also dropped. Increased competition on the Vancouver to Kelowna route lead to the discontinuation of these charters during this period as well.

In April 1986, the three Boeing 737-300s were sold to *Guiness Peat Aviation*. Attempts were made to sell the remaining two 737-300s before delivery but the company did take delivery of these aircraft in the new blue colour scheme. These two aircraft would be sold in December 1986.

April 1986 also saw Canadian Pacific file a notice of intent to purchase an interest (20%) in *Air Atlantic Ltd*. This airline was acting as a commuter airline for Canadian Pacific in the Maritimes and Newfoundland. When CPA acquired EPA, it also acquired its subsidiary, *Air Maritime*, which flew HS-748 (propjet) aircraft, but CPA did not wish to operate propjet aircraft and busily transferred *Air Maritime* routes, including Moncton and the Magdalen Islands, to *Air Atlantic*. With an interest in *Air Atlantic*, CPA began its commuter partner network with these airlines, adopting the parent CPA colours but replacing the dark blue with ocean (dark) green. *Air Atlantic's* Dash-7, C-GILE, was the first aircraft in this colour scheme and several others would follow such as *Norcanair's* Convair 640s and F-28s. *Inter-City*, a new airline operating out of Oshawa, had planned to join as a CPA partner but folded when CPA decided not to continue listing them in their reservations system.

Quebecair finally had to admit that CPA had control of *Nordair* and in July 1987, *Quebecair* was bought out by *Nordair Metro*. As a shareholder in *Nordair Metro*, through its holdings in *Nordair*, CPA now had the remaining *Nordair* stock in friendly hands, thus allowing them a full takeover of *Nordair*. By October, *Nordair* aircraft were being repainted in the full blue CPA colour scheme at the rate of one aircraft per week. The two Electras were not repainted and the F-227s were withdrawn from service. *Quebecair* did not disappear at this time, *Nordair Metro* planning to operate the *Quebecair*

Convair 580s and F-28s as a separate entity for a period of time. However, two of the Boeing 737s were bought by CPA and a third sold in Europe, leaving Quebecair with the remaining aircraft until finally sold late in 1987.

On October 25, 1986, the last Boeing 747 was withdrawn from service, marking thirteen years of accident-free service with the airline for this aircraft. In fact, except for the accident involving the only leased 707, Canadian Pacific never had a fatal accident with any of its Boeing aircraft. The DC-10s were also operated without a fatal accident.

Following the termination of *Air Maritime* in November 1986, all of its routes were flown by *Air Atlantic*. *Air Ste Pierre* continued to fly one leased HS-748 on the Halifax-St. Pierre route. *Nordair*, whose takeover was effectively completed when *Nordair Metro* bought out *Quebecair*, flew its last service on 24 January 1987, with all flights after that date having CP designation. By this time, most of the *Nordair* aircraft were already in CPA colour scheme. In February 1987, Canadian Pacific purchased a 25% share of Saskatoon based *Norcanair*. *Norcanair* Convair 640s and F-2828s were painted in the CP Air "Commuter Partner" colour scheme of ocean green.

The big news for Canadian Pacific occurred on December 2, 1986 when *Pacific Western Airlines Corporation*, parent company of PWA, announced the purchase of all assets of Canadian Pacific Airlines for $300 million. The original announcement was that the two airlines, CPA and PWA would continue to operate as separate entities but this of course would not last for long. On April 26, 1987, the two companies integrated as one airline under the name *Canadian Airlines International* and Canadian Pacific Airlines joined *Pacific Western Airlines, Nordair, Transair,* and *Eastern Provincial Airways* as historical names.

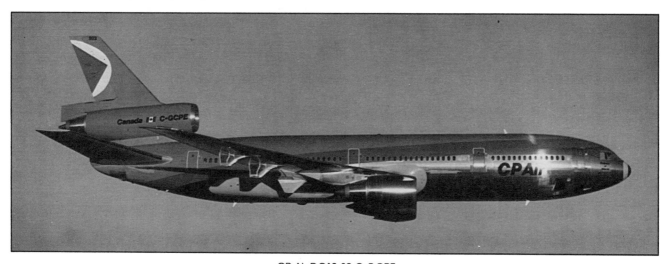

CP Air DC10-30 C-GCPE
Photo courtesy of CP Air

FLEET LISTING
CANADIAN PACIFIC AIRLINES

REG'N	C/N	F/N	IS	WFU	NOTES	MODEL	EMPRESS OF
BOEING 737-317							
C-FCPG	23173	751	4/85	4/86	ST PP-SNQ VASP (full CP Air c/s)		ONTARIO
C-FCPI	23174	752	5/85	4/86	ST PP-SNS VASP (Attache c/s)		
C-FCPJ	23175	753	5/85	7/86	ST PP-SNR VASP (Attache c/s)		
C-FCPK	23176	754	4/86	12/86	ST PP-SNT VASP (CPAL blue c/s)		MANITOBA
C-FCPL	23177	755	4/86	12/86	ST PP-SNU VASP (CPAL blue c/s)		QUEBEC
C-FCPM	23462	756	NTU	NTU	NTU; due 4/87 but cancelled		
C-FCPN	23463	757	NTU	NTU	NTU; due 4/87 but cancelled		
BOEING 737-217							
C-FACP	22072	728	11/85	4/87	To Canadian; LF C2-RN9 Nauru (C-GQBA)	-2L9	ST. JOHN'S
C-FCPB*	19884	701	10/68	11/82	ST N431PE Peoples Express		
C-FCPC*	19855	702	11/68	11/82	ST N432PE Peoples Express		
C-FCPD*	19886	703	12/68	12/82	ST N433PE Peoples Express		
C-FCPE*	19887	704	12/68	3/83	ST N434PE Peoples Express		
C-FCPM	22761	730	12/86	4/87	To Canadian; EX C-FPWD PWA	-2T7	YUKON
C-FCPN	22762	731	10/86	4/87	To Canadian; EX C-FPWE PWA	-2T7	HAMILTON
C-FCPU*	19888	705	12/68	5/83	ST N435PE Peoples Express		
C-FCPV*	20196	706	3/69	4/87	To Canadian; F/N 766 in 1987 (EXPO c/s)		VANCOUVER
C-FCPZ*	20197	707	3/69	4/87	To Canadian; F/N 767 in 1987		LOS ANGELES
C-FHCP	22024	729	4/86	4/87	To Canadian; EX EI-BPV	-2T5	KITIMAT
C-FICP	22025	780	11/86	4/87	LF PH-TRV Transavia	-2K2	
C-GCPM	21716	708	5/79	4/87	To Canadian		SAN FRANCISCO
C-GCPN	21717	709	6/79	4/87	To Canadian		CALGARY
C-GCPO	21718	710	7/79	4/87	To Canadian		EDMONTON
C-GCPP	22255	711	5/80	4/87	To Canadian		WINNIPEG
C-GCPQ	22256	712	6/80	4/87	To Canadian		VICTORIA
C-GCPS	22257	714	4/81	4/87	To Canadian		PRINCE GEORGE
C-GCPT	22258	715	6/81	4/87	To Canadian		FORT ST. JOHN
C-GCPU	22259	716	6/81	4/87	To Canadian		FORT NELSON
C-GCPV	22260	717	7/81	4/87	To Canadian		TORONTO
C-GCPX	22341	718	8/81	4/87	To Canadian		OTTAWA
C-GCPY	22342	719	10/82	4/87	To Canadian		GRANDE PRAIRIE
C-GCPZ	22658	720	4/82	4/87	To Canadian		MONTREAL
C-GFCP	22659	721	5/82	4/87	To Canadian		PRINCE RUPERT
C-GJCP	22728	722	10/82	4/87	To Canadian		TERRACE
C-GKCP	22729	723	11/82	4/87	To Canadian		WATSON LAKE
C-GMCP	22864	724	3/83	4/87	To Canadian		WHITEHORSE
C-GQCP	22865	725	4/83	4/87	To Canadian		RICHMOND
C-GRCP	21397	726	10/85	4/87	To Canadian; EX PH-TVP Transavia	-2K2	GRANDE PRAIRIE
C-GXCP	22640	727	11/85	4/86	LF G-BJCV Britannia	-204	
FORMER EASTERN PROVINCIAL AIRCRAFT							
C-FEPL	20396	201	5/86	4/87	To Canadian (in CPA c/s) 10/86	-2E1	GANDER
C-FEPR	20397	202	5/86	4/87	To Canadian (not in CPA c/s)	-2E1	Flagship SAINT JOHN
C-FEPO	20300	203	5/86	4/87	To Canadian (not in CPA c/s)	-2E1	Flagship CHARLOTTETOWN
C-FEPP	20681	204	5/86	4/87	To Canadian (not in CPA c/s)	-2E1	Flagship FREDERICTON
C-FEPU	20776	205	5/86	4/87	To Canadian (in CPA c/s 10/86	-2E1	CAPE BRETON
C-GEPA	20976	206	5/86	4/87	To Canadian (not in CPA c/s)	-2E1	Flagship CORNER BROOK
C-GEPM	21960	207	5/86	4/87	To Canadian (in CPA c/s 1/86)	-2Q8	LABRADOR
FORMER NORDAIR AIRCRAFT							
C-FNAB	19847	701	1/87	4/87	To Canadian (CPA c/s)	-242C	KUUJJUAQ
C-FNAH	19848	702	1/87	4/87	To Canadian (CPA c/s) 10/86	-242C	BAFFIN ISLAND
C-FNAQ	20455	703	1/87	4/87	To Canadian (CPA c/s)	-242C	RADISSON
C-FNAP	20496	704	1/87	4/87	To Canadian (CPA c/s) 11/86	-242C	RESOLUTE BAY
C-GNDC	21728	761	1/87	4/87	To Canadian (CPA c/s)	-242C	VAL D'OR
C-GNDL	21186	705	1/87	4/87	To Canadian (CPA c/s)	-242	DRYDEN
C-GNDM	22074	706	1/87	4/87	To Canadian (CPA c/s)	-242	THUNDER BAY
C-GNDR	22075	707	1/87	4/87	To Canadian (CPA c/s) 11/86	-242	FLORIDA
C-GNDS	21518	771	1/87	4/87	To Canadian (CPA c/s) 11/86	-2Q8	SAULT STE. MARIE
C-GNDU	22877	762	1/87	4/87	To Canadian (CPA c/s)	-242C	KUUJJUARAPIK
C-GNDX	20911	781	1/87	4/87	LF OO-SDE Sabena (Sabena c/s)	-229	
FORMER QUEBECAIR AIRCRAFT							
C-GQBB	22276	732	10/86	4/87	To Canadian (CPA c/s 10/86)	-296	QUEBEC CITY
C-GQBH	22516	734	8/86	4/87	To Canadian (CPA c/s 12/86)	-296	WABUSH
LN-BRL	22277	733	10/86	3/87	LF LN-BPL Braathens (C-GQBJ)	-296	

FLEET LISTING
CANADIAN PACIFIC AIRLINES

REG'N	C/N	F/N	IS	WFU	NOTES	EMPRESS OF
BOEING 747-217B						
C-FCRA*	20801	941	11/73	9/86	ST AP-BCN Pakistan International	ITALY (Japan, Asia)
C-FCRB*	20802	942	12/73	5/86	ST AP-BCM Pakistan International	JAPAN (Canada)
C-FCRD	20927	943	11/78	11/86	ST AP-BCO PIA (EXPO 86 c/s)	CANADA (Japan, Aust.)
C-FCRE	20929	944	11/74	12/85	ST AP-BCL Pakistan International	AUSTRALIA (Italy)
McDONNELL DOUGLAS DC-10-30						
C-GCPC	46540	901	3/80	4/87	To Canadian; LT PP-VMO Varig 3/79-3/80	AMSTERDAM (Quebec)
C-GCPD	46441	902	6/80	4/87	To Cdn; LT PP-VMP Varig 7/79-6/80; EXPO 86 c/s	BRITISH COLUMBIA (Sydney)
C-GCPE	46542	903	11/79	4/87	To Canadian	ROME
C-GCPF	46543	904	11/80	7/83	LT C-GCPF United Airlines	SANTIAGO (Buenos Aires)
C-GCPG	48285	905	2/81	4/83	LT N1850U United Airlines	FIJI
C-GCPH	48288	906	11/81	3/83	LT C-GCFH United Airlines	LIMA
C-GCPI	48296	907	2/82	4/87	To Canadian	HONOLULU
C-GCPJ	46991	908	3/82	4/87	To Canadian; EX 9V-SDC	ROME
C-FCRA	46931	909	9/86	4/87	To Canadian; EX AP-AXC PIA	
C-FCRB	46940	910	5/86	4/87	To Canadian; EX AP-AXD PIA	TOKYO
C-FCRD	47889	912	11/86	4/87	To Canadian; EX AP-AYM PIA	
C-FCRE	47868	911	2/86	4/87	To Canadian; EX AP-BBL PIA	CANADA
McDONNELL DOUGLAS DC-10-10						
N1816U	46615	---	7/85	8/85	LF United Airlines (full United c/s)	
N1834U	47966	334	3/83	5/87	LF United Airlines (CP Air c/s)	LIMA
N1836U	47968	336	6/83	6/87	LF United Airlines (EXPO 86 c/s)	EXPO 86 (CANADA/SANTIAGO)
N1837U	47969	337	3/83	5/87	LF United Airlines (CP Air c/s)	FIJI
BOEING 727-217						
C-GCPA	21055	711	3/75	11/81	ST G-BKAG Dan Air 4/82	SAN FRANCISCO
C-GCPB	21056	772	4/75	11/81	ST G-BKNG Dan Air (LT Alaska Airlines)	LOS ANGELES
BOEING 727-17						
CF-CPK	20327	721	3/70	4/77	ST N115TA Nigeria Airways	
CF-CPN	20328	722	4/70	4/77	ST XA-GUU Mexicana	
CF-CUR	20512	723	3/71	3/77	ST CP-1339 Lloyd Aero Boliviano	
CF-CUS	20513	724	4/71	6/77	ST XA-GUV Mexicana	
BOEING 707-138B						
N791SA	17698	---	10/67	3/68	LF N791SA Standard; full CPA c/s; W/O 07/02/68 Vancouve	SYDNEY
DC-8-43						
C-FCPF*	45620	601	2/61	11/81	ST ARCA Columbia; BU 1981	SANTIAGO /ROME/VANCOUVER
C-FCPG*	45623	602	11/61	3/80	ST F.B. Ayer; BU 1980	BUENOS AIRES/MONTREAL
C-FCPH*	45621	603	4/61	11/80	ST F.B. Ayer; BU 1982	LIMA/TOKYO/WINNIPEG
C-FCPI*	45622	604	5/61	11/80	ST F.B. Ayer; BU 1982	HONG KONG/AMSTERDAM/CALGARY
C-FCPJ*	45661	605	5/63	12/81	ST ARCA Columbia; BU 1982	MEXICO CITY/TORONTO
CF-CPK	45761	606	10/65	3/66	W/O 04/03/66 Tokoyo	EDMONTON
DC-8-50						
C-FCPM*	45809	607	5/66	8/81	ST ARCA Columbia; BU 1982	LISBON
CF-CPN	45252	600	10/66	10/67	ST N8008D TIA (-51)	SANTIAGO (Prototype DC-8)
CF-CPT	45858	608	11/67	3/78	ST G-BSKY IAS (-55F)	SANTIAGO
DC-8-63						
C-FCPO*	45926	801	1/68	5/83	ST C-FCPO Worldways	QUEBEC/TOKYO/HONOLULU
C-FCPP*	45927	802	1/68	5/83	ST C-FCPP Worldways Skybus	ALBERTA/HONOLULU/MADRID
C-FCPQ*	45928	803	2/68	5/83	ST C-FCPQ Worldways	ONTARIO/HONG KONG/LIMA
C-FCPS*	45929	804	6/68	6/83	ST C-FCPS Worldways	B.C./SYDNEY/MADRID/HONOLULU
C-FCPL	46095	805	9/72	12/81	ST N29180 Cammacorp	MANITOBA /ATHENS
DEHAVILLAND COMET 1A						
CF-CUM	6013	421	NTU	NTU	NTU; ST G-ANAV BOAC	
CF-CUN	6014	422	3/53	3/53	W/O 03/03/53 Karachi, Pakistan	HAWAII
BRISTOL BRITANNIA						
CF-CZA	13393	521	4/58	7/65	ST G-ATGD B.U.I.	HONG KONG/BUENOS AIRES
CF-CZB	13394	522	4/58	7/62	W/O 22/07/62 Honolulu	VANCOUVER
CF-CZC	13395	523	5/58	6/65	ST G-ATLE Air Links	TOKYO/MADRID
CF-CZD	13396	524	6/58	1/66	ST G-ATNZ Caledonia	WINNIPEG/BUENOS AIRES
CF-CZW	13453	525	8/58	5/64	ST G-ASTF British Eagle	TORONTO/ROME/EDMONTON
CF-CZX	13428	526	7/58	12/65	ST G-ATMA Caledonia	CANADA/SANTA MARIA
CF-CPD	13516	527	10/59	2/61	ST G-ARKA Cunard Eagle	AMSTERDAM
CF-CPE	13517	528	11/59	4/61	ST G-ARKB Cunard Eagle	MEXICO CITY

FLEET LISTING
CANADIAN PACIFIC AIRLINES

REG'N	C/N	F/N	IS	WFU	NOTES	EMPRESS OF
CONVAIR 240						
CF-CUU	73	391	12/52	12/63	ST JA5125 Toa Domestic; EX Continental	
CF-CUV	94	392	3/53	2/64	ST JA5126 Toa Domestic; EX Continental	
CF-CUW	95	393	2/53	8/63	ST JA5118 Toa Domestic; EX Continental	
CF-CUX	96	394	3/53	10/64	ST JA5131 Toa Domestic; EX Continental	
CF-CUY	97	395	5/53	6/64	ST JA5130 Toa Domestic; EX Continental	
DC-6B						
CF-CPC	45500	431	9/58	5/61	ST N45500 World; later CF-NWY	
CF-CPB	45499	432	7/58	7/61	ST N11565 World; LT Northwest 1960	
CF-CPB	45322	---	9/60	12/60	LF N93126 Western Airlines	
CF-CUO	43842	433	1/53	6/59	ST F-BHMR UAT	LIMA
CF-CUP	43843	---	2/53	8/56	W/O 29/08/56 Cold Bay, Alaska	MEXICO CITY
CF-CUQ	43844	434	2/53	7/65	W/O 08/07/65 Dog Creek, B.C.	TOKYO
CF-CUR	44062	435	6/53	5/59	ST F-BHMS UAT	AMSTERDAM/RIO DE JANEIRO
CF-CUS	44063	---	9/53	6/54	ST F-BGSK Aigle Azur; a DC6A	
CF-CUS	45178	436	6/65	12/68	LF N93123 Western Airlines	
CF-CUT	44064	---	9/53	6/54	ST F-BGSK Aigle Azur; a DC6A	
CF-CZE	44891	437	1/56	6/61	ST N45502 World	TORONTO
CF-CZF	44892	438	2/56	11/61	ST SE-BDH Transair	AUCKLAND/HONG KONG
CF-CZQ	45078	439	10/56	8/69	ST N122M Concare	HONG KONG/AUCKLAND
CF-CZR	45079	440	11/56	1/62	ST SE-BDI Transair	SYDNEY/AUCKLAND
CF-CZS	45326	441	4/57	3/69	ST CF-CZS Transair (Canada)	EDMONTON/LISBON
CF-CZT	45327	442	6/57	8/69	ST N122A OFC Leasing	LISBON/MONTREAL
CF-CZU	45328	443	7/57	9/70	ST N55CA Concare; LT PWA 1969	HONOLULU
CF-CZV	45329	444	8/57	11/61	ST SE-BDG Transair	SUVA
CF-CZY	45505	445	6/58	6/61	ST N15564 Northwest	
CF-CZZ	45498	446	7/58	3/70	ST CF-CZZ PWA; a DC6AB	
DC-4						
CF-CPC	10327	411	12/50	7/51	W/O 21/07/51 flight to Sitka, Alaska	
CF-CPD	10412	412	12/50	6/52	ST VR-HFF Cathay Pacific	
CF-CUJ	27261	413	11/51	12/57	ST CF-MCI Maritime Central	
CF-CUK	10323	414	12/51	8/54	ST N9940F Transocean	
CF-CUL	10384	415	11/51	8/54	ST N9941F Transocean	
CANADAIR C-4-1 NORTH STAR						
CF-CPI	147	401	5/49	11/51	ST CF-TFU Trans Canada Airlines	SYDNEY
CF-CPJ	149	403	7/49	2/52	ST CF-TFV Trans Canada Airlines	AUCKLAND
CF-CPP	150	404	7/49	12/51	ST CF-TFW Trans Canada Airlines	HONG KONG
CF-CPR	148	402	6/49	2/50	W/O 09/02/50 landing at Tokoyo	VANCOUVER
CURTISS C-46						
CF-CZG	22523	251	1/55	5/63	ST N355W Carolina Aircraft	
CF-CZH	22515	252	2/55	12/58	ST CF-CZH Quebecair	
CF-CZI	22542	253	2/55	7/59	ST CF-CZI Pacific Western Airlines	
CF-CZJ	22574	254	2/55	7/59	ST CF-CZJ Pacific Western Airlines	
CF-CZK	22501	255	2/55	3/63	ST N355K Carolina Aircraft	
CF-CZL	22494	256	3/55	11/57	ST CF-CZL Northern Wings	
CF-CZM	22453	257	5/55	7/59	ST CF-CZM Pacific Western Airlines	
CF-CZN	22445	258	4/55	7/59	ST CF-CZN Pacific Western Airlines	
DC-3						
CF-BZN	13845	171	5/46	10/56	ST CF-BZN Trans Labrador Airlines	
CF-CPV	4594	172	12/45	9/57	ST CF-TAR Transair (Canada)	
CF-CPW	4666	173	6/45	8/57	ST CF-TAS Transair (Canada)	
CF-CPX	6085	174	12/45	6/69	ST CF-CPX Harrison	
CF-CPY	4665	175	12/45	4/60	ST CF-CPY Connelly-Dawson; now on display Whitehorse	
CF-CRW	18958	176	4/47	4/59	ST CF-CRW Quebecair; then to EPA	
CF-CRX	19276	177	6/46	11/74	ST CF-CRX Harrison; only piston a/c in CP Air colours	
CF-CRY	20592	178	6/46	9/58	ST CR-LCY DTA Angola via Stewart-Davis Inc.	
CF-CRZ	20180	179	7/46	5/69	ST CF-CRZ Harrison	
CF-CUA	4518	---	2/47	9/49	W/O 09/09/49 at St. Joachim, Quebec by a timebomb	
CF-CUB	12711	281	4/47	9/58	ST CR-LCZ DTA Angola via Stewart-Davis Inc.	
CF-CUC	19366	282	8/46	4/59	ST CF-CUC Cities Servies Oil	
CF-CUD	6187	283	9/46	5/59	ST CF-QBM Quebecair	
CF-CUE	12983	284	4/47	9/56	ST CF-CUE Department of Transport	
CF-CUF	12855	---	5/47	12/50	W/O 22/12/50 Okanagan Park, B.C.	

FLEET LISTING
CANADIAN PACIFIC AIRLINES

REG'N	C/N	F/N	IS	WFU	NOTES		MODEL
DC-3 (Continued)							
CF-CUG	9891	285	5/47	5/59	ST CF-CUG Eldorado		
CF-DIG	11850	286	10/46	4/59	ST CF-TAT Transair (Canada)		
DEHAVILLAND DHC-3 OTTER							
CF-CZO	071	71	4/55	3/59	ST CF-CZP Pacific Western Airlines		
CF-CZP	069	72	4/55	3/59	ST CF-CZO Pacific Western Airlines		
PBY-5A CANSO							
CF-CRP	CV271	231	11/45	6/58	ST CF-CRP Trans Labrador Airlines;	EX RCAF 9837	
CF-CRQ	CV256	232	3/46	7/49	W/O 09/07/49 Osisko Lake;	EX RCAF 9822	
CF-CRR	-----	233	4/46	3/60	ST CF-CRR Northland Airlines;	EX RCAF 9767	
CF-CRV	-----	234	4/46	5/49	W/O 11/05/49 Prince Rupert, B.C.;	EX RCAF 9755	
AVRO ANSON V							
CF-CRG	MDF180	221	4/46	6/47	ST CF-CRG Central Aircraft of Winnipeg;	EX RCAF 12084	
CF-CRH	MDF330	222	4/46	7/55	ST CF-CRH Northland Fish Ltd.;	EX RCAF 12519	
CF-CRI	MDF169	223	4/46	11/53	ST CF-CRI Central Aircraft of Winnipeg;	EX RCAF 12072	
CF-EFZ	MDF220	224	5/46	7/55	ST CF-EFZ Pacific Western Airline;	EX RCAF 12124	
NOORDUYN NORSEMAN							
CF-BHU	N29-08	61	12/45	11/49	ST CF-BHU Territories Air Service		Mk. V
CF-BHV	N29-10	62	12/45	11/49	ST CF-BHV Territories Air Service		Mk. V
CF-BHW	N29-11	63	12/45	11/55	ST CF-BHW Central Northern Airways		Mk. V
CF-BHX	N29-12	64	12/45	11/55	ST CF-BHX Central Northern Airways		Mk. V
CF-BHZ	N29-13	65	3/46	1/49	ST CF-BHZ F.H. Wheelere		Mk. V
CF-BXL	456	71	3/46	12/46	W/O 09/12/46 Lake Indin, B.C.		Mk. VI
CF-CPL	253	70	3/44	9/44	ST CF-CPL Mont Laurier Aviation		Mk. VI
CF-CPM	254	72	3/44	6/47	ST CF-CPM Mont Laurier Aviation		Mk. VI
CF-CPN	255	73	3/44	9/44	ST CF-CPN Mont Laurier Aviation		Mk. VI
CF-CPO	256	74	3/44	9/44	ST CF-CPO Mont Laurier Aviation		Mk. VI
CF-CPP	436	75	3/44	NTU	NTU		Mk. VI
CF-CPQ	437	76	3/44	NTU	NTU		Mk. VI
CF-CPR	438	77	3/44	NTU	NTU		Mk. VI
CF-CPS	439	78	3/44	9/44	ST CF-CPS Ontario Central Airlines		Mk. VI
CF-CRC	25	43	8/46	9/46	ST CF-CRS Central Northern Airways		Mk. IV
CF-CRD	23	44	2/46	7/46	ST CF-CRD Central Northern Airways		Mk. IV
CF-CRE	26	45	2/46	7/46	ST CF-CRE Central Northern Airways		Mk. IV
CF-CRF	37	46	3/46	7/46	ST CF-CRF Central Northern Airways		Mk. IV
CF-CRS	53	47	9/46	3/47	ST CF-CRS Queen Charlotte Airlines		Mk. IV
CF-CRT	15	48	2/46	7/46	ST CF-CRT Central Northern Airways		Mk. IV
CF-CRU	8	49	2/46	7/46	ST CF-CRU Peace River Northern		Mk. IV
LOCKHEED 18 LOADSTAR							
CF-CPA	2177	261	8/48	6/50	ST CF-CPA Hollinger Ungava Transport Ltd.		
CF-CPB	2179	262	8/48	6/50	ST CF-CPB F.D. Lundy, Vancouver		
CF-CPE	2489	263	8/48	6/50	ST C.H. Babb Inc. California;	EX USAAF 42-56016	
CF-CPF	2466	264	8/48	6/50	ST C.H. Babb Inc. California;	EX USAAF 42-55993	
CF-CPG	2509	265	8/48	6/50	ST C.H. Babb Inc. California;	EX USAAF 42-56036	
CF-CPH	2403	---	8/48	6/50	SOLD; EX CF-TDI Trans Canada Airlines		
CF-CPI	2464	---	8/48	6/50	SOLD; EX CF-TDH Trans Canada Airlines		
CF-CPJ	2465	---	8/48	6/50	SOLD; EX CF-TDG Trans Canada Airlines		
CF-CPK	2534	266	8/48	6/50	ST CF-CPK Canadian Packers		
CF-CPT	2268	267	8/48	6/50	ST Remmert Werner Corp. USA		
CF-CPU	2492	268	7/45	2/51	ST C.H. Babb Inc. California;	EX USAAF	
CF-CPZ	2563	269	8/48	6/50	ST C.H. Babb Inc. California		
LOCKHEED HUDSON							
CF-CRJ	6448	241	5/46	5/49	ST CF-CRJ Photographic Survey		
CF-CRK	7555	242	5/46	5/49	ST CF-CRK Photographic Survey		
CF-CRL	7546	243	6/46	5/49	ST CF-CRL Photographic Survey		
CF-CRM	7550	244	4/47	5/49	ST CF-CRM Photographic Survey		
CF-CRN	7551	245	4/47	5/49	ST CF-CRN Photographic Survey		
CF-CRO	7547	246	5/47	5/49	ST CF-CRO Photographic Survey		
WACO ZQC-6							
CF-BDL	4593	---	7/43	5/44	ST CF-BDL W.E. Brett, Chilliwack, B.C.		
FAIRCHILD 71C							
CF-BXG	FAC-8	---	2/44	3/45	W/O 13/03/45 at Cliff Lake, Manitoba		

FLEET LISTING
CANADIAN PACIFIC AIRLINES

REG'N	C/N	F/N	IS	WFU	NOTES
FLEET 50K FREIGHTER					
CF-BJU	202	---	8/42	10/42	LF 799 Royal Canadian Air Force; now on display Ottawa
CF-BJW	203	---	8/42	11/42	LF 800 Royal Canadian Air Force
D.H.90 DRAGONFLY					
CF-BFF	7543	---	12/42	12/45	ST CF-BFF deHavilland Aircraft of Canada
CURTISS-WRIGHT D-3 KINGBIRD					
CF-BVG	2016	---	8/42	9/43	ST C.H. Babb Inc., California; EX Yukon Southern A/T

CANADIAN PACIFIC AIRLINES
Merger Companies' Aircraft

REG'N	C/N	IS	WFU
ARROW AIRWAYS			
Waco YKC-5			
CF-AYS	4267	5/42	5/44
Norseman IV			
CF-BAW	9	5/42	1/44
MACKENZIE AIR SERVICE			
Fairchild 82D			
CF-AXM	62	6/44	2/47
CF-AXQ	69	5/42	12/46
Bellanca 66-76			
CF-BKV	722	5/42	5/47
Bellanca 66-75			
CF-BTW	721	9/43	5/47
Barkley-Grow T8P			
CF-BQM	8	5/42	3/50
CF-BTX	11	12/43	10/45
PRAIRIE AIRWAYS			
Barkley-Grow T8P			
CF-BVE	1	11/42	2/45
Cessna C-47			
CF-BFE	354	5/42	3/43
Beechcraft 18D			
CF-BKN	177	5/42	3/43
CF-BKO	178	5/42	5/44
DOMINION SKYWAYS LTD.			
Norseman I			
CF-AYO	1	5/42	10/47
Waco ZQC-6			
CF-BBR	4541	5/42	3/44
QUEBEC AIRWAYS			
Dragon Rapide			
CF-AYE	6304	5/42	7/47
Boeing 247D			
CF-BVW	1735	10/43	5/45 now displayed Ottawa
CF-BVX	1699	10/43	1/45
CF-BVZ	1946	10/43	4/45

REG'N	C/N	IS	WFU
YUKON SOUTHERN AIR TRANSPORT			
Boeing 247D			
CF-BVF	1706	11/43	7/45
CF-BVT	1732	10/43	2/45
CF-BVV	1725	10/43	3/45
Lockheed 14			
CF-CPC (CF-TCR)	1503	7/41	3/45
CF-CPD (CF-TCS)	1504	7/41	3/45
Lockheed 18			
CF-BTY	2084	4/41	9/41
CF-BTZ	2085	4/41	9/41
Fairchild 82			
CF-AXA	35	8/42	3/44
Beech D-17S			
CF-BLU	238	5/42	8/42
Barkley-Grow T8P			
CF-BLV	3	12/43	11/49
CF-BMG	4	5/43	2/47
CF-BMW	6	1/43	12/49
Curtiss Condor			
CF-BQN	32	5/42	6/44
American Pilgrim			
CF-BUA	6608	5/42	1/44
GINGER COOTE AIRWAYS			
Waco YKC-5			
CF-AWL	4238	5/42	2/43
DH89 Dragon Rapide			
CF-BNG	6472	5/42	2/43
DH90 Dragonfly			
CF-BPD	7538	5/42	4/43
CANADIAN AIRWAYS			
DH89 Dragon Rapide			
CF-BBH	6370	5/42	3/47
Lockheed Vega 1			
CF-AAL	30	5/42	6/44
Fairchild FC-2W2			
CF-AKT	516	5/42	7/47

FLEET LISTING
CANADIAN PACIFIC AIRLINES
Merger Companies' Aircraft

REG'N	C/N	IS	WFU
CANADIAN AIRWAYS (Continued)			
Fairchild 71C			
CF-ATZ	17	5/44	7/47
CF-AWG	27	5/42	4/43
CF-AWV	31	5/42	7/47
CF-BKP	68	5/42	5/45
Fairchild 71B			
CF-BVS	FAC7	5/42	3/43
CF-BVU	688	12/43	3/44
Fairchild 82A			
CF-AXE	40	10/44	5/47
DH83 Fox Moth			
CF-APG	4038	5/42	9/42
DH84 Dragon			
CF-APJ	6024	5/42	10/42
Junkers Ju W.34			
CF-AMZ	2588	5/42	1/45
CF-AQW	2587	5/42	10/47
CF-ASN	2731	5/42	9/46
Junkers Ju W.24			
CF-ATF	2718	5/42	9/46
Junkers Ju 52			
CF-ARM	4006	5/42	6/43
Bellanca 66-70			
CF-AWR	719	5/42	1/47
Stinson Reliant			
CF-AZV	9733	5/42	8/43
CF-BEB	5222	5/42	8/43
Norseman IV			
CF-BAU	6	5/42	5/87
CF-BDC	10	5/42	5/47
CF-BDD	11	5/42	12/45
CF-BDF	13	5/42	9/47
CF-BDG	14	5/42	2/43
Beech A-18A			
CF-BQG	291	5/42	3/48
CF-BQH	318	5/42	6/48
CF-BQQ	290	5/42	11/46
DH89 Dragon Rapide			
CF-BBH	6370	5/42	3/47

REG'N	C/N	IS	WFU
STARRATT AIRWAYS			
Stinson Reliant			
CF-ANW	9321	5/42	10/42
DH60M Moth			
CF-AGX	DH127	12/43	1/45
Fokker Universal			
CF-AJB	CV137	5/42	11/42
Travel Air SA60000			
CF-AEJ	1040	5/42	5/46
Fairchild 82A			
CF-AXG	42	5/42	11/42
Beech C-17R			
CF-BIF	120	5/42	5/44
WINGS LTD.			
Fairchild 82A			
CF-AXF	41	5/42	9/42
Fairchild 71C			
CF-AWX	33	5/42	7/43
Fairchild 71			
CF-BVI	674	5/42	2/44
CF-BVJ	690	5/42	8/44
Waco ZQC-6			
CF-AYT	4450	5/42	7/43
CF-AZP	4481	5/42	8/44
CF-BBO	4497	5/42	9/44
Waco YKS-6			
CF-BDK	4269	5/42	5/42

Wardair A310-304, C-FSWD

Wardair DeHavilland Dash-7 C-GXVF
Photo courtesy of DeHavilland Canada

WARDAIR

Wardair Boeing 747 CF-DJC
Photo courtesy of Wardair

HEADQUARTERS:
2201 T.D. Towers, Edmonton Centre,
Edmonton, Alberta, T5J 0K4

MAIN BASES:
Edmonton International Airport;
Toronto (Pearson) International Airport

FLEET 1989:
3 - Boeing 747s;
1 - DC-10-30s;
2 - Airbus 300s;
12 - Airbus 310-300s

COLOURS:
A white upper fuselage with a blue cheat line running the length of the aircraft below the windows. WARDAIR appears in blue on the upper fuselage and an widening red cheat line starts behind the name and widens until it sweeps up the tail. WARDAIR CANADA appears on the tail in block letters (previously in stylized letters on the 747s) and a Canadian flag is displayed on nose. On the new A310s, the red cheat line is just above a blue cheat separated by a line of white and widens slightly until it reaches the rear of the aircraft where it sweeps up the tail. A half red/half blue maple leaf appears in the middle of the all white engine.

ROUTES:
Domestic: Vancouver – Edmonton – Calgary – Winnipeg – Toronto – Montreal

U.S.A.:
Toronto/Montreal – Ft. Lauderdale – Tampa

Europe:
Paris (Orly) – Stansted (London) – Birmingham – Leeds /Bradford – Cardiff – Newcastle – London (Gatwick) – Manchester – Prestwick

South:
Barbados – Puerto Plata

CHARTERS:
All over the world

HISTORY:

The history of Wardair is the story of two separate operations: the Northern Wardair and the International Charter Schedule Wardair. Today, the Northern Wardair charter no longer exists and International Wardair has also become a scheduled Domestic and International airline. The story of Wardair is also the story of Maxwell W. Ward. Max Ward started as a bush pilot and has gone on to win such awards as membership in the Order of Icarus, the Aviation Hall of Fame and in June 1975 was made an Officer of the Order of Canada.

Max Ward began his flying in the wartime Royal Canadian Air Force and in 1945 became a bush pilot with Jack Moar's *Northern Flights* at Yellowknife. He formed *Polaris Charter Company* at Yellowknife in 1946 with a single aircraft, the four passenger DH-83C Fox Moth biplane, CF-DJC. From his base at Yellowknife, Max Ward flew passengers and supplies throughout the Northwest Territories. In 1947, the Air Transport Board decided that all air carriers had to have an operating licence which *Polaris Charter* did not have. Ward therefore teamed up with Geoge Pigeon who did have a licence and together they formed *Yellowknife Airways* with Ward's Fox Moth and Pigeon's Stinson 104. The partnership and the company ceased operations in 1949 and Ward went back to bush flying for other companies, including *Associated Airways*. Matt Berry and Max Ward reinstituted *Yellowknife Airways* in late 1950 but were bought out by *Associated Airways* in 1951.

In 1952, Max Ward formed Wardair at Yellowknife and ordered a new deHavilland Canada Otter. The fifth production Otter was delivered on 2 June 1953 and cost $96,000. *Rewarders* operating licence was received on 6 June 1953 and the blue Otter was seen throughout the western Canadian arctic. Wardair's northern operation aircraft are dark blue, with a wide red cheat line through the windows with narrow white cheat lines on either side of the red cheat. The tail, nose and wing tips are trimmed in red and 'WARDAIR LTD' appears white on the red cheat line with 'YELLOWKNIFE, NWT' below it on the blue fuselage in smaller letters.

In 1954, a Beaver was added to the fleet. A second Otter was purchased in 1955 and a third was added in 1956. A second Beaver was bought in 1956 and the first Beaver sold at the end of that year.

Trans-Canada Airlines had started an unsuccessful trans-Canada cargo service with three Bristol Freighters in 1953 and sold these aircraft to *Central Northern Airlines*. Wardair bought one of these planes, CF-TFX for cargo work in the arctic. This plane became the first aircraft to land at the North Pole in 1958 and served the company until 1968, when replacement of its main spar was required. It was cheaper to purchase another aircraft than to repair this one and it was mounted at the entrance to the Yellowknife Airport in full Wardair blue colour scheme where it stands today.

A fourth Otter was purchased in 1958 but was destroyed in an accident in May 1959 at Coral Harbour, Hudson Bay.

A Beech 18 Seaplane was added to the fleet of three Otters, one Beaver and one Bristol Freighter in 1963. The Beech 18 and one of the Otters were sold in 1967 when Wardair bought a DHC-6 (Series 100) Twin Otter. This aircraft was sold in just over a year and replaced by a series 200 Twin Otter. This aircraft was replaced again in less than a year by two series 300 Twin Otters in 1969. The difference between the series 100 and series 200 Twin Otters was the increased baggage space provided by extending the aft baggage compartment into the rear fuselage and by lengthening the nose. The Series 300 was the same as the Series 200 except for its more powerful PT6A-27 Pratt & Whitney (United Aircraft of Canada) engines. When operated on floats, the shorter nose was installed on the aircraft.

Four former RCAF Bristol Freighters were purchased during 1967-1968. These aircraft, RCAF 9698 (CF-WAC); RCAF 9850 (CF-WAD); RCAF 9699 (CF-WAE); and RCAF 9700 (CF-WAG) were converted to civil status by *Western Airways Limited*. They were flown in a silver colour scheme with a red cheat line through the windows, thin white/blue cheat lines above the red cheat and with red trim on the nose, tail and wingtips. The upper fuselage from the wings to the rear of the cockpit was blue and the title WARDAIR CANADA appeared in blue and red on the tail. One of these aircraft was lost on 3 May 1970 when it fell through the ice on Great Slave Lake near Snowdrift, NWT. A salvage attempt proved unsuccessful and the plane was stripped and sunk. Two other Bristol Freighters were sold in 1970, one to *Lambair* and the to *Norcanair*. The final Bristol Freighter was written off in November 1977 at Hay River, Northwest Territories.

The two remaining single Otters were sold during 1971-72 and replaced in 1972 with two more Series 300 Twin Otters. Another two Twin Otters were purchased in 1973 making a fleet of six of these aircraft. A Mitsubishi MU-2 was bought in 1974 for passenger transport. This high wing twin turboprop has a cruise speed of 340 mph and a range of 1600 miles. Wardair operated it on charter and scheduled service out of Yellowknife for four years.

A replica of Max Ward's original DH-83C Fox Moth was build in 1976 and registered CF-DJB. The plane crashed during the Toronto International Airshow that year and was rebuilt for display purposes only.

The company leased a fourteen-passenger Grumman Gulfstream 1, twin turboprop, for a year in 1977-

78. This aircraft was operated on behalf of the Yukon government for executive transport in the north.

Wardair became the first Canadian operator of the de Havilland Dash-7 aircraft when it took possession of C-GXVF on 8 June 1978. This aircraft operated in a blue colour scheme with a broad white cheat on the fuselage and a red tail. WARDAIR CANADA appeared in white on the tail. The plane was named 'Don Braun' after a famous Canadian bush pilot and operated on charter and scheduled services out of Yellowknife. A second Dash-7 was acquired a year later, with a third on order. The first Dash-7 was sold to *Air Pacific* in late 197 and the second aircraft then had the name 'Don Braun' painted on it.

The northern charter and scheduled business was not going well at this time and Max Ward decided to sell his northern operations and concentrate on the international charter business. The second Dash-7 was sold to *Air Wisconsin* and the third one on order was cancelled. The six Twin Otters were sold to various operators in 1979 with two remaining in the north with *Ptarmigan Airlines*.

Max Ward shut down his northern operations but retained his interest in flying bush aircraft, particularly those from de Havilland Canada. He purchased a DHC-4 Caribou for his private use and had it painted in the original dark blue northern colour scheme. Unfortunately, with Max Ward at the controls, the aircraft suffered a double engine failure shortly after takeoff from the Edmonton International Airport on 14 June 1981. The aircraft was skilfully flown into a farmer's field just north of St. Albert, near Morinville, Alberta by this former bush pilot and no serious injuries occured. The plane was repaired and sold to *Kenn Borek Aviation,* still in the dark blue colour scheme. Max Ward then bought a former RCMP single-engine Otter for his personal use. On weekends during the summer, Max and his aviation friends in the Edmonton area would fly up to a cabin that Ward owned in the north. Max would lead the aircraft in his Otter. In 1985, the Otter was traded in for a former Wardair Twin Otter which continues in use by Max Ward.

In 1962, Wardair leased a DC-6AB aircraft from *Canadian Pacific* to begin its international charter operations. Eight charters were flown with this leased aircraft which was returned to *Canadian Pacific* late in the winter of 1963. Wardair bought a DC-6B from *KLM Royal Dutch Airlines* in March 1963. By 1965, seventy charters per year were being flown with this aircraft but it was not big enough for the expanding charter market.

In 1966, *Air Canada* and *Canadian Pacific* were the only Canadian airlines operating pure jet aircraft. Both companies operated Douglas DC-8s as Boeing had not yet penetrated the Canadian market. Max Ward changed that in April 1966 with the purchase from Boeing of a 727 aircraft, series 100, which wasappropriately registered C-FFUN. The plane had 110 seats of which 102 were used on Atlantic flights. Its first flight was Vancouver to London (Gatwick) with a stop for refuelling at Sondre Stromfjord in Greenland. Flights were also made from Canada to Amsterdam, Copenhagen and Dusseldorf, but it was soon apparent that the refuelling stop in Greenland or Iceland and the small capacity of the 727 made a larger type aircraft a necessity. With the introduction of the 727, Wardair began the practice of naming its aircraft after famous Canadian bush pilots and this plane was named after Cy Becker.

In April 1968, a long range, 189-passenger Boeing 707-320C aircraft was bought new for the international charter business. One year later, a second 707 was purchased new from Boeing, this aircraft originally being destined for *Quebecair*. These two aircraft operated to Europe but also opened the lucrative Hawaiian market to Wardair. With the delivery of the second 707, the 727

Wardair Boeing 707 CF-FAN
Photo courtesy of Wardair

was leased to *Braniff* as N302BN for the winter 1969-70 and used sparingly after that until finally sold to *Cruzerio* of Brazil in May 1973.

The two 707s were named after Punch Dickens and Wop May. Wardair carried more stewardesses than the scheduled airlines and quickly became noted for its excellent in-flight service. These two aircraft served with Wardair for almost ten years before giving way to the wide-bodied jumbo jets.

A quantum leap forward in charter operations in Canada was made in 1973 when Wardair purchased a 455-passenger Boeing 747 from *Braniff* and purchased a second 747 from *Continental* a year later. The first 747 carried the same registration as Max Ward's first Fox Moth, CF-DJC and the second 747 recycled the Boeing 727 registration of C-FFUN. By now, all major carriers and regional carriers were also into charter operations, but Wardair had the greatest capacity in the charter field. Max Ward began a campaign to allow his airline to operate charters within Canada but the Canadian Transport Commission refused to permit such charters. Wardair also campaigned for fewer restrictions on charter flights but regulations such as having to book so many number of days in advance, stay a fixed number of days and include hotels in the package continued to hamper the growth of Wardair.

The corporate name was changed to *Wardair Canada (1975) Limited* on 1 January 1975 and *Wardair International Limited* was incorporated 1 June 1976 as the parent company to the airline and also to *International Vacations Limited.*

Early in 1978, a Boeing 747 (series 200) aircraft was purchased new from Boeing and another followed in early 1979 making a fleet of four 747s. The charter market was not large enough for all destinations to fill an aircraft the size of the 747 and with the sale of the Boeing 707s in 1978, a smaller aircraft was needed. Wardair decided to become an all jumbo jet operator and ordered three-engine, long range McDonnell-Douglas DC-10 (series 30) aircraft.

This aircraft has a cruising speed of 564 mph and a range of 7,500 miles. Two aircraft were due for delivery in the summer of 1978 but a strike at McDonnell-Douglas delayed the delivery until late 1978 and greatly disrupted Wardair's planned summer charters for that year. In May 1979, an *American Airlines* DC-10 lost an engine on take-off from O'Hare Airport in Chicago resulting in all on board being killed. The subsequent investigation into this accident grounded Wardair's DC-10s for a period during the summer of 1979, again disrupting its summer charter schedule. The subsequent follow-up reports on this accident also discouraged passengers from flying on DC-10s despite the final report showing that improper maintenance was the major factor in the accident. With the additional checks required

on the DC-10s, they probably became the safest aircraft in the air. Wardair stuck by this aircraft and in 1981 purchased a third DC-10, this one from *Singapore Airlines*.

Wardair flew several charters in 1980 on Viet Nam refugee contracts with the federal government. In May 1980, the first domestic charters with full frills were flown between Vancouver and Toronto using the DC-10s. A mixed flight of full frills and no frills ($20 off) sections was introduced the next month on domestic services. In December 1980, Wardair became the first Canadian operator to fly a Boeing 747 jumbo jet into Saskatoon as part of a Saskatoon to Calgary and Honolulu charter.

Canadian domestic charters were cancelled in the winter of 1980-81 but began again in the summer of 1981. Wardair was named the official flag carrier to St. Lucia. This meant that Wardair passengers could interline with St. Lucia carriers such as *Prinair, Air BVI* and *LIAT.* In summer 1981, flights were made all over the world from Ottawa, London, Winnipeg, Toronto, Montreal, Calgary, Edmonton and Vancouver. Wardair's profit in 1981 was $1.04 million with 1,251,000 passengers carried.

Wardair placed an order in late 1981 for six Airbus A310 aircraft with options for six more. In April 1982, the delivery date for these aircraft was postponed until 1985 and the order was finally cancelled in 1983.

Interline agreements with various Canadian airlines were established in 1982. Passengers from London (Ontario) and Ottawa could connect with Wardair flights out of Toronto on an interline agreement with *Air Ontario,* while passengers in Victoria could connect with Wardair's Vancouver flights via an interline agreement with *Pacific Western Airlines.* This service was extended to all *Pacific Western* cities the following year.

The airline was caught by the recession in 1982 and lost $13.5 million. Wardair's fleet of jumbo jets had an overcapacity for the available passengers and the competition for charter passengers from the scheduled airlines was very great. In 1983 domestic and international charters improved somewhat, but the airline dropped domestic charters in the winter of 1983.

During the first three months of 1984, the company made a $2.31 million profit compared to a $1.29 million loss for the same period in 1983. Domestic charter service Toronto to Calgary, Toronto to Edmonton, Toronto to Vancouver, Vancouver to Montreal, Calgary to Montreal, Toronto to Halifax and Toronto to Regina and Saskatoon was resumed in the spring of 1984 with Toronto to Winnipeg and Vancouver to Calgary being added in June.

During the summer of 1984, Wardair operated the above noted domestic charters but still could not get permission to operate scheduled flights. In June, the company reached an agreement with the *Canadian Airline*

Flight Attendants on a contract allowing new flight attendants to be paid $15.00 to $19.15 per hour, which was 36.5% less than current flight attendants would be paid. Wardair had hired four hundred potential new attendants and trained them at *Pan Am's* base in Miami in preparation for a possible strike.

Wardair obtained its first scheduled route in January 1985 but did not begin operating Toronto or Montreal to San Juan, Puerto Rico until October 1985. Scheduled service to Manchester and London began in December 1985 when Wardair was named as the second Canadian carrier into Britain.

President George Curley continued to request permission to fly trans-Canadian routes as 1986 began. The company dropped Amsterdam flights and made London and other locations in Great Britain their major destinations for summer flights. Finally on May 4, 1986, Wardair was given permission to operate scheduled domestic service and began Toronto – Calgary – Edmonton – Vancouver schedules with DC10 aircraft, configured in a First Class and Economy service at this time.

In August 1986, Wardair received the first of three Airbus A300 aircraft from *South African Airways* and operated this aircraft on its domestic service between Toronto and Vancouver. When the other two aircraft arrived in October, Montreal was added to the domestic schedule. A plan was drafted at the end of 1986 to operate a commuter service with *Inter City Airways* both in Ontario and British Columbia but this service never began.

The airline sold two Boeing 747s to *British Caledonian* at the end of 1986 and acquired a former *Air Canada* Boeing 747 at the same time.

With their domestic schedule secure, Wardair, in February 1987 announced an order for twelve Airbus Industries A310-300 aircraft for $920 million with delivery due between November 1987 and December 1988. This aircraft would carry one hundred and ninety-six passengers in a two-class configuration. Once delivery of these aircraft commenced, the DC-10s would begin to be phased out.

The company added Toronto – Winnipeg flights to its domestic schedule in May 1987 and continued its extensive scheduled and chartered international flights. Prestwick was added as a scheduled service at this time. July saw a reduction in domestic flights with Toronto – Winnipeg dropped and Toronto – Vancouver decreased when *South Africa Airways* recalled one of the three A300s. Montreal/Toronto flights to San Juan also had to be briefly halted due to the loss of this aircraft. The lease of these three aircraft from *South Africa Airways* also became a political incident at the Commonwealth Conference held in Vancouver at this time as it significantly increased Canada's overall trade with South Africa over the previous year.

Scheduled flights between Toronto/Montreal and Puerto Plata began late in 1987 and a 224-seat *Nationair* DC-8 was wet leased to allow this and Toronto–Winnipeg flights to start.

The first of the A310-300 aircraft arrived shortly after. These aircraft had thirty "Big Seat" (businessman) and one hundred and sixty-six regular economy seats. The purchase terms for these aircraft was 25% cash and 75% financed over fifteen years. The cash portion would come from the floating of a share issue which would increase public ownership in the airline to 49% and increase the debt/equity ratio from 1:1 to 2:1. Some of the cash portion would also come from the sale of the 747s, DC10s (to *Guiness Peat Aviation* between April and October 1988) and the two A300s. The A310-300 is a long range aircraft with a range of 3,700 nm, long enough to make the Vancouver to London flight non-stop.

Wardair was awarded scheduled flights to France and was to add Ottawa and Halifax to its domestic routes during 1988 as the A310s arrive. An order for smaller aircraft such as the MD88 is expected to be announced in 1988, permitting Wardair to operate each of its domestic flights on a two-a-day basis to attract the business customer while continuing to be attractive to the economy traveller.

The 1988 summer schedule saw weekly Toronto to Hamburg flights as well as service to Paris from Toronto, Montreal and Quebec City. Vancouver to Frankfurt flights were planned to compete with *Canadian Airlines* service and charters between Toronto and Los Angeles were to operate three times weekly. The company's planned Vancouver to Calgary domestic flights continue to be delayed.

In June, 1988, Wardair introduced domestic Vancouver – Ottawa and Montreal – Ottawa service. Toronto to San Francisco twice weekly and Toronto to San Diego weekly flights also were introduced in June. Wardair sold one of its DC-10s to *Guiness Peat Aviation* who immediately sold it to *Canadian Airlines International* in March 1988.

Wardair announced the purchase of eight McDonnell Douglas MD-88s, a version of the DC-9, in March 1988, with an option for eight more. The planes will operate as 128-passenger aircraft with four-abreast seating in business class and five-abreast in economy. The aircraft has a range of 4,800 kilometres. Delivery of the aircraft was to begin in June 1989 and continue through June 1991. These will be used primarily on Canadian domestic flights with Wardair also hoping to acquire scheduled service to the United States. The Airbus 310s would then be freed up to use on longer scheduled and chartered flights.

While the MD-88s were intended for service on a Canada-wide network, Wardair also planned to build a small feeder network to Vancouver and Toronto along the lines of *Air Canada*'s Connector airlines and *Canadian*'s Commuter network. To do this, 12 Fokker F-100s were ordered with delivery expected early in 1990. Wardair had also planned to complete a major maintenance base at the Vancouver International Airport by the summer of 1990.

All of this planned expansion came to an abrupt halt in January 1989 when the company was purchased by PWA. The MD-88 and F-100 orders were cancelled, as was the maintenance base in Vancouver. Indications were that up to a third of the present staff would be released, beginning with more than 600 personnel in Winnipeg with the closing of Wardair's domestic service in that city in March 1989.

Initial reports indicated that Wardair, scaled down in size, would continue to operate in competition with *Canadian*. A complete merger of the two companies was considered difficult because *Canadian* and Wardair pilots were members of different unions. It has been speculated that Wardair will again become an all-charter airline, taking over many of *Canadian*'s overseas charters while *Canadian* handles Wardair's domestic services. Indeed, by May 1989 Wardair's domestic flights had been assigned *Canadian* flight numbers and the Canadian Plus mileage bonus program now applies to Wardair flights.

It is clear that the Wardair headed by Max Ward ceased to exist early in 1989 but only time will tell if the Wardair name will continue to be seen in Canadian skies during the 1990s.

Beginning with its Boeing 727, Wardair aircraft have carried the names of famous Canadian bush pilots. The first person so honoured was Cy Becker, whose name is now carried on one of the A300s. The following is a list of the names used to date with a brief history of each person:

CY BECKER:
A Canadian ace with thirty-eight enemy aircraft to his credit, he became a bush pilot following WWI, and was instrumental in amalgamating ten airlines to form *Canadian Pacific* in 1940 .

PUNCH DICKENS:
The first person to cross the Arctic Circle in Canada by air and the first pilot to fly from upper Hudson's Bay, across the unmapped barren lands to Lake Athabaska. He was the first to stand on the radium-rich shelf of Great Bear Lake and the first to log over a milliion miles flying across the unchartered north without a radio. During WWI he was awarded the Distinguish Flying Cross and founded the *Atlantic Ferry Command* in WWII.

WOP MAY:
He was rescued during WWI by Captain Roy Brown as the Red Baron was about to add Wop to his list of victories. He established one of Canada's first commericial aviation services after WWI.

PHIL GARRATT:
He began flying in 1915 and won the Air Force Cross during WWI. As the General Manager of de Havilland, Canada, Phil guided the company from a small assembly plant to become a world leader in STOL aircraft design.

HERBERT HOLLICK-KENYON:
He is best remembered for his part in the 1937 search for the Russian pilot Sigmund Levaneffsky and five companions, who went missing on a trans-polar flight from Moscow to Fairbanks, Alaska.

ROMEO VACHON:
He made flying history on Christmas Day 1927 when he set out from St. Agnes, Quebec to provide mail service to twenty-eight small villages on the north shore of the St. Lawrence River.

S.R. "STAN" McMILLAN:
He was one of the eight members of the MacAlpine Expedition.

H.A. "DOC" OAKS:
One of the first pilot-geologists, he was insturmental in the formation of *Western Canada Airways, the forerunner of Canadian Pacific Airlines*.

G/C ZEBULON LEWIS LEIGH:
He was awarded an OBE for his work with the RCAF in establishing the overseas mail service during WWII.

DON C. BRAUN:
A Wardair Captain who was in command of Bristol Freighter CF-TFX when it made the first wheel-equipped aircraft landing at the North Pole. He earned the Air Force Cross during WWII and flew with Wardair from 1955 to 1969.

JACK MOAR:
He flew with *Western Canada Airways* and in 1938 selected landing fields between Fort St. John and Whitehorse which were used during WWII as the Northwest Staging Route.

ARTHUS MASSEY "MATT" BERRY:
After flying in WWI, he became a bush pilot in the 1930s. In 1936 he piloted an aircraft farther north during the winter than anyone before with a flight to the Arctic Ocean to rescue five persons.

H.W. HARRY HAYTER:
A bush pilot with over 20,000 flying hours, he once searched for eleven days before finding nine crew members of a freighter lost on Great Slave Lake.

C.C. CARL AGAR:
He won an Air Force Cross during WWII and after the war flew the first commercial helicopter in Canada.

FLEET LISTING
WARDAIR

REG'N	C/N	F/N	IS	WFU	NOTES	MODEL	AIRCRAFT NAME

International Operations

747-100

REG'N	C/N	F/N	IS	WFU	NOTES	MODEL	AIRCRAFT NAME
C-FDJC*	20208	399	4/73	C	EX N602BN Braniff	747-1D1	PHIL GARRATT
C-FFUN	20305	398	12/74	C	EX N26864 Continental	747-1D1	ROMEO VACHON
C-FTOB	20014	395	12/86	C	EX CF-TOB Air Canada	747-133	H.A. "DOC" OAKS

747-200

C-GXRA	21516	397	6/78	10/86	ST G-GLYN British Cal'd	747-211B	H. HOLLICK-KENYON
C-GXRD	21517	396	4/79	10/86	ST G-NIGB British Cal'd	747-211B	H.A. "DOC" OAKS

DC-10-30

C-GXRB	46976	101	12/78	4/88	ST EI-BZD Garuda		W.R. WOP MAY
C-GXRC	46978	102	11/78	9/88	ST OH-LHE Finnair		PUNCH DICKENS
C-GFHX	46990	103	10/81	3/88	ST C-GFHX Canadian EX 9V-SDA Singapore		STAN McMILLAN

A300B4

C-GIZJ	138	501	10/86	C	LF ZS-SDE South Africa		CY BECKER
C-GIZL	192	502	8/86	C	LF ZS-SDF South Africa		H. HOLLICK-KENYON

A300C4

C-GIZN	212	503	10/86	8/87	LF ZS-SDG South Africa		H. HOLLICK-KENYON

A310-304

C-FGWD	438	803	11/87	C	EX F-WWCE test reg'n		G. LEVINE LEIGH
C-FHWD	441	804	11/87	C	EX F-WWCQ test reg'n		DON C. BRAUN
C-FNWD	444	805	12/87	C	EX F-WWCR test reg'n		JACK MOAR
C-FSWD	418	801	1/88	C	EX F-WWCL test reg'n		A.M. MATT BERRY
C-FWDX	425	802	2/88	C	EX F-WWCP test reg'n		H.W. HARRY HAYTER
C-GBWD	446	806	2/88	C	EX F-WWCM test reg'n		C.C. CARL AGAR
C-GCWD	447	807	3/88	C	EX F-WWCN test reg'n		S.R. STAN MCMILLAN
C-GDWD	448	808	3/88	C	EX F-WWCO test reg'n		T. "RUSTY" BLAKEY
C-GIWD	472	809	5/88	C	EX F-WWCB test reg'n.		GW GRANT MCCONACHIE
C-GJWD	475	810	8/88	C	EX F-WWCL test reg'n.		SHELDON LUCK
C-GKWD	481	811	8/88	C	EX F-WWCQ test reg'n.		W.R. WOP MAY
C-GLWD	482	812	10/88	C	EX F-WWCR test reg'n.		C.H. "PUNCH" DICKENS
C-GPWD	502	813	8/89	NTU	Not accepted; due 8/89		(CY BECKER)
C-FZWD	504	814	8/89	NTU	Not accepted; due 8/89		(H. HOLLICK KENYON)

MD-88

C-	43759	---	6/89	NTU	Order cancelled 1989		
C-	43760	---	6/89	NTU	Order cancelled 1989		
C-	43761	---	6/89	NTU	Order cancelled 1989		
C-	43762	---	6/89	NTU	Order cancelled 1989		
C-	43763	---	7/89	NTU	Order cancelled 1989		
C-	43764	---	7/89	NTU	Order cancelled 1989		
C-	53765	---	7/89	NTU	Order cancelled 1989		
C-	43765	---	7/89	NTU	Order cancelled 1989		

707-300

C-FZYP*	20043	---	3/69	12/78	ST OE-IDA Montana	707-396C	W.R. WOP MAY
C-FFAN*	19789	---	4/68	10/78	ST 9K-ACK Kuwait	707-311C	PUNCH DICKENS

727-11

CF-FUN	19242	---	4/66	5/73	ST PP-CJI Cruzeiro		CY BECKER

DC-6A

CF-PCI	43555	---	3/63	11/66	LT CF-PCI PWA; became C-FCKJ LINA Congo		

DC-6AB

CF-CZZ	45498	---	5/62	12/63	LF CF-CZZ CPAL; later with PWA & NWT Air		

F28-0100 (F100)

C-	11307	---	3/90	NTU	Order cancelled 1989		
C-	11316	---	3/90	NTU	Order cancelled 1989		
C-	11318	---	3/90	NTU	Order cancelled 1989		
C-	11324	---	3/90	NTU	Order cancelled 1989		
C-	11326	---	3/90	NTU	Order cancelled 1989		
C-	11327	---	3/90	NTU	Order cancelled 1989		
C-	11333	---	3/90	NTU	Order cancelled 1989		
C-	11335	---	3/90	NTU	Order cancelled 1989		

FLEET LISTING
WARDAIR

REG'N	C/N	F/N	IS	WFU	NOTES	AIRCRAFT NAME
					Northern Operations	
DeHavilland Dash-7						
C-GXVF	007		6/78	10/79	ST N27AP Air Pacific	DON BRAUN
C-GXVG	011		6/79	1/80	ST N791S Air Wisconsin	DON BRAUN
C-GXVH	015		NTU	NTU	NTU: ST 70-ACK Alyemda 11/79	
DHC-4 Caribou						
C-GVYX	292		6/79	6/81	ACC 14/06/81 near Morinville.	
DHC-6 Twin Otter-300						
CF-TFX	340		1/72	11/79	ST C-FTFX Ptarmigan	
C-FWAA*	238		5/69	11/79	ST N5584H UNICEP	
C-FWAB*	349		2/73	11/79	ST C-FWAB Ptarmigan	
CF-WAC	350		2/73	3/79	ST N90503 Atlantis Airlines	
CF-WAF	122		5/68	2/69	ST CF-WAF Great Northern A/L	
C-FWAG*	343		6/72	9/72	ST C-FWAG Southern Frontier	
C-FWAH*	240		5/69	11/79	ST C-FWAH Chevron	
CF-VOG	035		4/67	5/68	ST CF-VOG La Ronge Aviation	
C-FWAH	240		6/85	C	Max Ward's personal aircraft	
DHC-3 Otter						
CF-GBY	005		6/53	5/67	ST CF-GBY La Ronge Aviation	
CF-IFP	073		6/55	11/72	ST CF-IFP South Peace Air Service	
CF-ITF	089		2/56	7/71	ST CF-ITF Kyro's Albany River AW	
CF-JRS	110		4/58	5/59	W/O 5/59 Coral Harbour, Hudson Bay	
C-FMPY	324		12/79	6/85	Max Ward's personal plane; ex RCMP; ST C-FMPY Loon Air	
DHC-2 Beaver						
CF-HNN	618		2/54	8/56		
CF-IFJ	831		2/56	10/68	ST CF-IFJ La Ronge Aviation	
MU-2B						
C-GWID	557		4/74	9/78	ST N192MA	
Grumman Gulfstream 1						
CF-COL	064		8/77	9/78	LF G-1 Leasing; OF Yukon Gov't.	
Beech D-18S Seaplane						
CF-PCL	AF-80		1/63	8/67	ST CF-PCL La Ronge Aviation	
Bristol 170 Freighter						
CF-TFX	13137		3/58	2/68	ON display at Yellowknife Airport	
CF-WAC	13079		12/67	11/70	ST CF-WAC Lambair	
CF-WAD	13253		3/68	11/77	W/O 20/11/77 Hay River, N.W.T.	
CF-WAE	13219		7/68	3/70	ST CF-WAE Norcanair	
CF-WAG	13249		4/69	5/70	W/O 03/05/70 near Snowdrift, NWT.	
DH83C Fox Moth						
CF-DJC	-----		6/46	4/55	OB Polaris Charter Company	
CF-DJB	FM-28		5/76	9/76	W/O 9/76 Toronto Airshow	

PART 2

Regional
Airlines

Pacific Western

Pacific Western Boeing 737, C-GPPW

HEADQUARTERS:
Suite 2800, 700 - 2nd Street S.W.,
Calgary, Alberta, T2P 2W2

MAJOR BASES:
Vancouver International, Calgary International,
Edmonton International,
Toronto International (Pearson).

FINAL FLEET:
20 Boeing 737-200s and 1 leased Boeing 737-200;
2 - Boeing 737-300 (leased).
(April 1987)

COLOURS:
Upper white fuselage separated from a lower silver
fuselage by two thin blue cheat lines. At mid-aircraft,
the upper cheat line (light blue) sweeps up over the top
of the fuselage giving a light blue wraparound stripe.
The lower dark blue cheat leaves a small white stripe
between it and the light blue wraparound and then it too
sweeps up over the top of the fuselage leaving a solid
dark blue rear upper fuselage. The tail is all white with
a stylized PWA symbol (flying wing) in red. PACIFIC
WESTERN titles are in red on the upper fuselage and the
registration is in white on the rear blue fuselage.

ROUTES:
British Columbia:
Victoria – Vancouver – Kamloops – Kelowna – Penticton – Castlegar – Cranbrook – Williams Lake – Prince George – Quesnel – Terrace – Dawson Creek – Sandspit – Smithers – Port Hardy.
Alberta:
Calgary – Edmonton Municipal & International – Fort McMurray.
Northwest Territories:
Fort Smith – Hay River – Yellowknife – Cambridge Bay – Resolute – Norman Wells – Inuvik.
Yukon: Whitehorse.
Saskatchewan: Regina – Saskatoon.
Manitoba:
Brandon – Winnipeg – The Pas – Flin Flon – Thompson – Gillam – Churchill.
Ontario:
Thunder Bay – Toronto – Ottawa
U.S.A.:
Seattle, and extensive charters to Reno, Las Vagas, Los Angeles.

HISTORY:

On 1 July 1945, Russ Baker of Fort St. James, B.C., a bush pilot, and Karl Springer, a mining executive, established *Central British Columbia Airways*. Their first plane was a leased Beech 17 biplane and their major customer in the early years was the B.C. Forest Service. A Junkers was added in 1946 and in 1948, the first production de Havilland Canada Beaver, CF-FHB was purchased. Alcan's large project at Kitimat in 1949 provided rapid expansion of the airlines. This immense hydro-electric project for the production of aluminium required the construction of the town of Kitimat and the port of Kemano and 95% of the heavy airlift was carried out by *Central British Columbia Airways*.

Baker and company started buying up smaller operators and purchased *Kamloops Air Service* in 1950, *Skeena Air Transport* in 1951 and *Associated Air Taxi* in 1953. With the purchase of the last company, a scheduled flight Vancouver to Kitimat was awarded on 15 May 1953. The amalgamated companies took the name 'Pacific Western Airlines Ltd.,' at this time with it headquarters in Vancouver. The fleet in 1953 consisted of one DC-3, four Beavers, two Cansos, four Norsemen, one Grumman Widgeon, two Fairchild 71s, one Beech 17 and a Beech 18.

Pacific Western obtained *Whitehorse Flying Services* in 1954 and *Queen Charlotte Airlines* in July 1956.

Queen Charlotte Airlines had been started in May 1946 and provided scheduled and charter routes along the British Columbia coast. It had also benefited by the Kitimat project and carried the cargo and passengers that *Central British Columbia Airways* did not. Obtaining *Queen Charlotte Airlines* added a DC-4 (CF-HYV), two Stanraers, seven Norsemen and a few smaller aircraft to the PWA fleet.

Associated Airways was formed in 1945 by Tommy Fox and David Dyck with a Tiger Moth (CF-BEN) and a former RCMP Dragonfly (CF-BZA). The Tiger Moth was operated until 1946 and the Dragonfly until 1949. Tommy Fox's famous Anson CF-EKO clipped its right wing on a landing at Lake Chiewyan. In the Arctic cold, Tommy cut nine and a half feet off the left wing to balance the aircraft and using full power was able to get the aircraft airborne and fly back to Edmonton for full repairs.

Associated Helicopters was begun in 1950 with a Bell 47 CF-GSL operating out of the Lesser Slave Lake area. Associated took over *Territories Air Services* in 1951. Also in that year, *Associated* bought *Yellowknife Airways* which was jointly owned by Matt Berry and Max Ward. *Associated* purchased the first Canadian operated Bristol Freighter 170 in February 1952 and used it extensively on the uranium development at Beaver Lodge on Lake Athabasca. The Mark 31 version operated by *Associated* was the same type as flown by the RCAF in Europe. Its nose opened to allow large loads to be accommodated and it could carry more than thirteen thousand pounds of cargo almost five hundred miles at a speed of 165 mph. A second Bristol Freighter was bought in January 1953 but was sold to *Maritime Central Airways* in March 1953.

Associated obtained many of the DEW Line contracts in 1955, using its extensive fleet of Beavers, Norsemen, Skyrocket, Barkley-Grow, Lockheed 14, Anson, DC-3, DC-4, Avro York and Bristol Freighter to operate these flights. However, several accidents at this time, including two Yorks and the Lockheed 14, put the company in financial difficulties.

Bristol Freighter CF-GBT was written off 17 September 1955, on a flight from Yellowknife to Edmonton. After the right engine failed, the crew jettisoned more than a half a ton of cargo. The plane still had to make a forced landing 10 miles north of Thorhild, Alberta, resulting in two deaths and injuries to four others.

Pacific Western bought the financially troubled airline in November 1956 and thus obtained the rights to most of the DEW Line contracts in the west and to *Associated's* scheduled services in the north. *Associated Helicopters* was not involved in the sale and operated independently until it was sold to *Okanagan Helicopters* in 1977.

Pacific Western bought two Grumman Mallards for their coastal operations in 1954. These planes remained with the company until 1960 when they were sold to *B.C. Airlines*. One of these was re-acquired when *B.C. Airlines* was purchased by PWA in 1970. Three Beaver aircraft were added in 1954 with PWA ultimately operating 22 Beavers, the largest DHC-2 fleet in the world.

In 1955, Pacific Western purchased two Curtiss C-46s to service their DEW Line contracts. The colour scheme on these aircraft was a white upper fuselage and a silver lower fuselage, separated by a dark blue cheat line running the length of the fuselage. This cheat line covered from just above to just below the windows. The tail was white except for the top portion which was all red. A red stripe appeared at the root of the tail. The registration was in black, in the white portion of the tail, with 'Pacific Western' in black stylized letters on the upper fuselage.

Eleven Ansons were added in 1955-56 while two Fairchild 71s were lost in accidents during this period. The first, CF-BVK, was lost on 13 November 1955 at Ocean Falls, B.C., when the Fairchild's float hit a dead-head on takeoff. The aircraft overturned while being towed back to the floats and was written off. The second accident occurred on 8 August 1956 when CF-BXI hit a sandbar during a landing at Kitimat. The plane overturned and was also a write-off.

Pacific Western Convair 640, CF-PWS

In the mid-1950s, eight Cessna 180s were acquired and operated on floats and skis mainly. Pacific Western also entered the helicopter business, buying two Bell 47Gs in 1956 and five more in 1958. The company remained in the helicopter business only until 1960, when the fleet of seven Bell 47s was sold to *Pacific Helicopters Ltd.*

The PWA takeovers of *Queen Charlotte Airlines* and *Associated Airways* in 1956, plus other aircraft purchases, added four DC-3s, one DC-4 and two Avro Yorks to the company's heavy lift capabilities. Otter aircraft were added to assist in the DEW Line contract work.

The transition from bush operations and charter work to a regional carrier began in 1957 when Pacific Western took over *Canadian Pacific's* Edmonton to Regina route. Two DC-4 aircraft were acquired for this route. The company lost a DC-3 at Port Hardy on 23 May 1957, but still had five of these aircraft for their scheduled routes and charter work.

The airline adopted the registration series CF-PW, converting all DC-3s and C-46s from their former PWA registrations to the new series. Pacific Western also applied to operate deHavilland Comet jets on a trans-Canada jet service at this time but was turned down by the government. The company would apply many more times to become a trans-Canada airline before finally succeeding.

In 1959, in exchange for *Canadian Pacific* obtain-

ing limited return flights between Vancouver and Montreal, Pacific Western received domestic routes in northern Alberta and the Mackenzie River from CPA. PWA gained two DHC-3 Otters in the exchange and purchased four Curtiss C-46s from *Canadian Pacific* at this time. PWA now had an extensive network of scheduled services in the North, Alberta and British Columbia. The routes obtained from *Canadian Pacific* added eighteen stops north of Edmonton to PWA's route structure.

In 1960-1962, Pacific Western sold their Norsemen, Yorks, Ansons, two Cansos, the Bell 47s and the Mallards while acquiring smaller Grumman Goose aircraft to service the British Columbia coastal communities.

Curtiss C-46 CF-PWD was written off in 1960. It had been damaged in an accident on 29 November 1957 and was damaged again on 23 October 1958 in an overrun at Cambridge Bay, NWT. Finally, on 29 January 1960, it was making a single engine landing at Port Hardy, B.C. and overran the runway by about eight hundred feet, coming to rest in a swamp. There were no casualties. Another aircraft written off during this period was DC-3 CF-PWF, which crashed on 24 May 1961 at Snowdrift, NWT.

Pacific Western adopted a new colour scheme with the addition of the DC-6 aircraft. The white upper fuselage was separated from the lower fuselage of natural metal by a narrow, medium-blue cheat line running the length of the fuselage, just below the windows. The cheat line began as a small PWA symbol below, and slightly forward of the cockpit window. A large, red and blue PWA symbol appeared on the all-white tail. The fleet number was in blue near the top of the tail, with the registration and fleet number in blue, on the rear fuselage just above the cheat line. The title PACIFIC WESTERN was in stylized, medium-blue letters, on the upper fuselage.

The DC-6 bought in 1962, and another acquired in 1963, allowed the airline to begin long range charters and to add pressurized aircraft on their extensive domestic routes. PWA dropped Edmonton to Regina in 1962 when the federal subsidy on the route was discontinued and did not fly that route again until after the *Transair* takeover.

The highly successful 'Chieftan Airbus' service was started in 1963 operating DC-4 aircraft. This was a no-reservation scheduled commuter service between the Calgary International Airport and the Edmonton Municipal Airport. By 1969, a quarter of a million passengers were being carried on this service with the DC-6, then Convair 640 and finally the Boeing 737 aircraft being used. There were thirteen flights per weekday in 1978 and fifteen Boeing 737 flights per weekday in 1984.

In 1964, PWA started Inclusive Tour Packages to the Grand Cayman Islands and then to the United Kingdom with the DC-6s. Two DC-7 aircraft were added in 1964 (replaced by two others in 1965), to give the airline added passenger capacity for their charter operations. The DC-7 could carry nineteen passengers more than the DC-6 (105 total) and were approximately 15 mph faster (344 mph), with a 4600nm range (1600 nm more than the DC-6).

In the mid-sixties, Pacific Western began selling off its light aircraft fleet, turning these services over to *Northward Aviation, West Coast Air, BC Airlines* and *Trans Provincial Airlines*. Six Otters were disposed of, along with the twenty-two Beavers. The Cessna 180s and Grumman Goose were sold just after the de Havilland aircraft.

Because many of the DEW Line resupply contracts were running out, the C-46s were sold, leaving Pacific Western, in 1966, with a modern fleet of two DC-7s, five DC-6s, three DC-4s, five DC-3s, five Grumman Goose, five Cessna 180s, eight Beavers and one Beech 18. The last four types were all sold by 1970.

Early in 1967, Pacific Western bought its first turbine equipment, four Convair 640s which had been recently converted from Convair 440 piston aircraft by General Dynamics. Two of these had previously been operated by Arabian American Oil Company and the other two with *All Nippon Airlines* of Japan. The piston engines of the Convair 440s (converted 340s) were replaced with Rolls Royce Dart engines, producing a cruising speed of 300 mph and a range of 1230 miles. The aircraft carried fifty-two passengers.

One of the original four aircraft crashed on 18 September 1969, near Elk Island Park, B.C., and was replaced by a former *Hawaiian Airlines* aircraft the same year. A fifth Convair 640 was purchased in 1971.

Pacific Western bought another turboprop aircraft, the Lockheed 100-10 Hercules, in 1967. This cargo aircraft provided additional capacity for the annual spring airlift to the northern communities in Canada. It was also used to carry large cargo for the northern oil and mining developments which began in the Canadian north at that time.

The Hercules could transport forty-six thousand pounds of cargo and can carry a drill rig without breaking it down into small pieces. Being turbine powered, it is much easier to start in the northern cold than a piston aircraft.

Following its work in the north in 1967, this aircraft was leased to *Trans Mediterranean Airways* from July to September and operated with TMA titles but in PWA's colour scheme, complete with the PWA tail symbol and a Canadian flag just behind the cockpit.

Each year after completing its northern work, the Hercules would tramp around the world carrying whatever was available. During the first three years, it flew into fifty-two different countries without maintenance problems, carrying such diverse cargos as sheep from Finland to Canada, grapes from Nicosia, bullion from London to the Far East and oil well equipment to the Middle East. Unfortunately, this Hercules crashed near Cayaya, Peru on 16 July 1969 with the loss of the crew.

The value of the 'flying truck' had been demonstrated by the first Hercules and thus, in 1969, PWA purchased three more Hercules and added a fourth in 1973. These four aircraft were the series-20 Hercules, longer than the first aircraft (106' versus 98'), capable of carrying 48,600 pounds and able to cruise 20 mph faster at 377 mph. These aircraft also roamed the world in the summer and supplied the Arctic in the winter.

Large bladders were fitted inside the cargo hold for hauling fuel to the north. When livestock were carried, the cattle were dehydrated before handling and the aircraft had a wooden floor installed over the metal floor. Polyetheylene sheeting was placed over the wooden floor, tentest placed over the plastic and sawdust over the tentest. The whole envelope was disposed of after each flight.

Canada's Centennial year also saw the airline enter the pure jet era with the purchase of a Boeing 707. This original 707 replaced the DC-7s on international charters, operating in a high density seating of one hundred and eighty-nine passengers. In 1969, a second 707 was leased from *Qantas* for charter work and remained in service for two years.

In 1968, PWA took over *Canadian Pacific's* Calgary to Kamloops to Vancouver route. To service this route and other interior B.C. cities, the airlines purchased Boeing 737 jets, with the first of 40 of these aircraft delivered in November 1968. Two further 737s were delivered in 1969 and another in 1970 to complete the first order of four aircraft. The last DC-7 was sold in 1969 and the DC-4s and DC-6s were restricted to Northern cargo routes until all were sold by the end of 1972. Pacific Western thus made the Boeing 737 the major aircraft in its fleet.

Before the DC-4s left, they looked very old and out of date to the Boeing 737 Captains. One of the author's friends was flying a DC-4 and pulled up to the terminal at one of the northern stops. A Boeing 737 landed behind the DC-4 and was blocked from pulling right up to the ramp by the DC-4. The Captain of the 737 demanded that the DC-4 be moved as "he had paying customers on board." The DC-4 was moved but placed in such a posi-

B.C. Airlines was incorporated in 1943, but did not become operational until 1946 because of the wartime shortage of planes and crews. The airline started with two Luscombes on floats and in the next ten years acquired a variety of aircraft including a Gobe Swift, a Fairchild 71, a Stinson 108, a Piper Clipper, a Piper Super Cruiser, six SeaBees, a Waco, four Luscombes and two Beavers. During this period, they operated along the entire British Columbia coast. By the early 1960s, larger passenger aircraft such as the Grumman Mallard (from PWA) and the Grumman Goose were added. Entirely a sea plane operation with ten major bases between Vancouver and Prince Rupert, the airline's smaller aircraft were mostly Cessna 170s, Cessna 180s and Beavers. Wheel Equipped aircraft were added in 1967 and the company began to sell its small float planes and concentrate on scheduled service, mainly out

Pacific Western Hercules, C-FPWK

tion that the 737 could not taxi out after a brief stop. The 737 Captain stormed into the small cafeteria to confront the upstart DC-4 Captain who was eating his lunch. After listening to the tirade, the DC-4 Captain agreed to move his aircraft, which pleased the 737 Captain, who left to get into his shiny new aircraft. However, the DC-4 Captain did not appear and the 737 Captain stormed back into the briefing room to find the former filing his flight plan. This was all the fellow could take and he phoned the company's headquarters to explain his situation. When put on the telephone, the DC-4 Captain told headquarters that he was just about to go out and move the DC-4 and didn't know what the other fellow was getting his shirt in a knot about. The DC-4 Captain was ultimately suspended for two months which suited him fine as he had another job to do during that time!

of Vancouver to coastal communities.

To service their coastal routes and newly acquired British Columbia interior flights, four Nord 262 aircraft were acquired from *Allegheny Airlines* and a new Twin Otter (CF-WZH) was purchased. The company's routes in 1970 included Vancouver – Tofino – Tahsis – Bella Bella – Namu – Ocean Falls – Bella Coola, operated mainly with the Mallards and the B.C. interior routes of Vancouver – Penticton – Castlegar – Cranbrook – Kelowna – Kamloops – Williams Lake Quesnel – Prince George – Smithers – Terrace, operated by the Nord 262s and Twin Otter.

Pacific Western reversed its position of giving up smaller routes and aircraft in 1970, when it bought out *B.C. Airlines*. They acquired the four Nord 262s but the Twin Otter was sold prior to the takeover.

B.C. Airlines. They acquired the four Nord 262s but the Twin Otter was sold prior to the takeover.

The Nord 262 is a French built twin turboprop high wing aircraft that carries twenty-nine passengers at a cruising speed of 255 mph. The aircraft were used to operate the Vancouver – Penticton, Castlegar, Cranbrook to Calgary route acquired in the takeover. The company also acquired two Grumman Mallards in the takeover, one of them, CF-HPU, an original PWA aircraft. These were used to operate the coastal services from Vancouver to Tofino, Tahsis, Bella Bella, Namu, Ocean Falls and Bella Coola. The Northern Interior routes to the Okanagan (Prince Rupert, Terrace, Smithers, Prince George, Quesnel and Williams Lake) were not operated by PWA, but were leased to *Trans Provincial Airlines, Northern Thunderbird Air* and *Arrow Aviation*. When the Nord 262s were sold in 1972, Convair 640 aircraft replaced them.

In March 1971, Pacific Western leased two Lockheed Electras to replace the DC-6s on Northern supply routes and as interim passenger aircraft until more Boeing 737s were delivered.

One of these aircraft (CF-ZSR) was unable to lower its landing gear during a flight on 14 September 1972. The plane was diverted to Canadian Forces Base Namao, just north of Edmonton, which has the longest runways in Canada. The runway was foamed and the plane made a wheels-up landing with no injuries to the crew. The plane was repaired and sold to Panarctic Oils Ltd. as CF-PAK.

Two more Electras were acquired in 1972. One replaced the damaged aircraft and the other, operating in an all silver colour scheme with PWA titles, operated as a bulk tanker for northern resupply. After one winter of operating this aircraft, PWA decided that the Hercules could do a better job than the Electra and the lease of this aircraft was terminated. The other two Electras remained with PWA until 1976, when nine additional Boeing 737s made the Electras redundant. The Electra, which could carry sixty-six passengers in pressurized turboporp comfort, ended its career with PWA on the Vancouver to Victoria run.

A second (the airline's third) Boeing 707 was acquired from *Continental Airlines* in 1972. This aircraft was also used for cargo work. On 2 January 1973, this plane, carrying a load of cattle, was on final approach to the Edmonton International Airport. There was a blinding snowstorm and the plane crashed a few miles short of the airport at Nisku killing the crew.

A replacement 707 was quickly acquired (from *Northwest Orient*) in 1973, again for use as a cargo aircraft, and carried the title PACIFIC WESTERN WORLD AIR CARGO on its upper fuselage .

A Boeing 727 was added in 1972 and another in 1974, for use on the northern routes in a combined cargo/passenger arrangement. PWA also used these aircraft on its initial trans-Canada charters. To circumvent the Canadian Transportation Commission's restrictions on such flights, PWA flew Vancouver to Buffalo (with the passengers bused to Toronto) and Toronto to Seattle (with the passengers bused to Vancouver). The Boeing 727 never did fit into the Pacific Western route system and one was disposed of in 1977. The remaining aircraft found a second life, operating on charter to Panarctic Oils after the company sold its Electras. The plane remained on these charters until sold in 1984 to Echo Bay Mines, which had also bought a Convair 640 from PWA in 1976.

The DC-3 aircraft had operated only as backup and training aircraft in the late 60's and early 70's, the last being sold to *Gateway Aviation* in mid-1973. Pacific Western sold the Mallards to *West Coast Air* in 1974, ending the piston era for PWA and once again ending the operation of the B.C. coastal service.

On 1 August 1974, Premier Peter Lougheed, on behalf of the Conservative Alberta Government, made an offer to buy 100% of Pacific Western's common and preferred shares. The deal cost $37 million with the Alberta Government acquiring 99.5% of all the shares. The official reason given for the acquisition was that 80% of SPWA's flights originated or terminated in Alberta and the government needed to protect this vital Alberta transportation link. Another reason may have been that the New Democratic Government in British Columbia was also considering buying the airline and Alberta wanted to block this purchase. Winnipeg based Federal Industries White Pass and Yukon Corp. was also bidding to acquire up to 60% of the stock at this time.

The Alberta Government allowed President Don Watson to continue to operate the airline without government interference and the growth in the subsequent years is a credit to this non-interference.

Following numerous reports indicating the headquarters of PWA should be moved from Vancouver to Edmonton, the Alberta Government decided to move the company headquarters to Calgary because of the tremendous growth in oil business in that city. When the move was made, in September 1976, Donald Watson decided not to leave Vancouver and resigned as President of PWA.

The 1974 fleet consisted of seven Boeing 737s (four more in 1975); two Boeing 707s; four Lockheed L100-20 Hercules; two Boeing 727s and five Convair 640s. The net earnings for the year came to $1.3 million; 1,858,396 passengers were carried on scheduled routes; 65,950 passengers carried on international charters and 31,840 on domestic charters (total 1,956,186). The company retained the rights to some shorter routes and leased them out to small operators.

In June 1975, Pacific Western began operating Van-

Pacific Western DC-3, CF-PWI

couver to Seattle, a route it took over from *Air Canada*. From June to September it operated the flight with a "technical" stop in Victoria. The plane would touch down at Victoria and immediately take off again for Seattle until the Canadian and American Government paperwork was completed.

Two Convair 640s were removed from service in 1975 and sold the next year to *Echo Bay Mines* and *Worldways*. The two Electras were put into storage in 1975 and also sold the following year. The cargo 707 was converted back to passenger service in late 1976 due to the high cost of fuel.

Prior to the conversion, the 707 made the second cargo flight into Red China (Shanghai) in October. The first Canadian flight into Red China had been made by a PWA Hercules in 1973.

In the summer of 1976, Pacific Western began Toronto to either Vancouver or Calgary charters for $199.00 round trip. They also operated some Toronto to Halifax charters to give the airline a cross-Canada presence. The remaining Boeing 727 was started on a $4.2 million contract to operate a charter service, from Calgary to Edmonton and the north, for Panarctic Oils. The contract included the Hercules aircraft doing rig movements for Panarctic. By the winter of 1976, Inclusive Tour Charters (ITC) were allowed to be as short as three days, and PWA began flights from western Canadian cities to Reno and Las Vegas.

A second Hercules was lost in a distant country when CF-PWX crashed on 21 November 1976 near Eastville, Zaire, and the crew killed.

In February 1977, Pacific Western bought 70% of the stock of financially troubled *Transair*. Over the next two years, the *Transair* Boeing 737s were painted in the new paint scheme first seen on Pacific Western's aircraft in 1973. This scheme had a white upper fuselage and a bare metal lower fuselage. A thin dark blue cheat line began near the front of the aircraft, below the windows.

This gradually widened as it went aft, ending in an all dark blue tail with a white leading edge. A large PWA symbol, in red and light blue, was outlined in white on the tail. The registration and the words BOEING 737-200 were white in the blue cheat area of the rear fuselage . The title PACIFIC WESTERN appeared in red leters on the upper fuselage of the aircraft.

Transair remained a separate operating entity during the period 1977 to 1979. The YS-11A and F-28 aircraft were disposed of and the routes slowly amalgamated into PWA routes. As the Boeing 737 aircraft were painted in the PWA colours, they bore TRANSAIR titles in red on their upper fuselage. The takeover was completed in November 1979 and the last Boeing 737 in *Transair* titles disappeared on 21 March 1980.

In 1977, PWA was operating one of its Hercules in Canada, a second was based in the U.K. and the third in Angola until September. A *Southern Airlines* Hercules flew from Edmonton on lease. This aircraft remained in *Southern's* colour scheme and with American registration but had Pacific Western titles.

On 11 February 1978, Pacific Western suffered its only crash with loss of life while operating Boeing 737 aircraft when C-FPWC crashed at Cranbrook, B.C. It was snowing at Cranbrook and the airport's snowplow operator was making one final run to clear the runway, believing he had another five minutes before the 737 was due in from Calgary. The Boeing 737 had shortened its approach and touched down with the snowplow still on the runway. When Captain Chris Miles and First Officer Peter Van Gort saw the snowplow, they applied full power in an attempt to go around the plow. As they lifted off, one of the spoilers failed to retract, preventing lift on one wing, and the plane crashed at the side of the runway. Six people in the rear of the plane survived but the other forty-two, including the pilot and copilot, were killed, making it Canada's third worst air crash.

Pacific Western dropped their long range charters in

1978 but operated ninety Advanced Booking Charters (ABC), with the one hundred and seventeen seat Boeing 737s, in the summer of 1978. The company obtained a contract to transport CF-104s from Europe to Edmonton for overhaul and bought a Hercules Series-30 aircraft for this task. This Hercules is six and one-half feet longer than the series-20 and can carry 52,500 pounds of cargo, 4,000 pounds more than the series-20. The last three Convair 640s were sold in 1978 to *Gateway Aviation, Aero Trades Western* and *Worldways*.

The company's original 707 was sold late in 1978 and its last remaining 707 in May 1979, although it would return to Canada as C-GRYO of *Ontario Worldair* in December 1979. PWA operated extensive ABC charters between Vancouver and Toronto and between Toronto and the major Alberta cities in the summer of 1979. One of the Hercules was based in Tuktoyaktuk for the winter flying for Canmar Dome and later at Churchill, flying for the NWT Government. An *Aer Lingus* 737 was leased at the end of the year and flew in the colourful green-blue-white colour scheme of *Aer Lingus* with PWA titles in red and a PWA symbol on the tail. In October 1979, PWA started a direct Vancouver to Prince George service and established a Toronto base for Inclusive Tariff Charters (ITC) to Florida, Mexico, Las Vegas and the Bahamas.

As part of the *Transair* takeover, Pacific Western had to drop any scheduled flights east of Winnipeg. *Transair* had started operating Winnipeg – Regina/Saskatoon – Calgary/Edmonton flights in February 1979 to link with Pacific Western's Alberta flights. *Nordair* took over the Winnipeg – Northern Ontario – Toronto route from *Transair* at this time. PWA's 1979 profit was a healthy $12.8 million (of which $3.8 million was from the sale of the Boeing 707).

Early in 1980, with the *Transair* turboprop equipment sold, *Calm Air* was permitted to take over some northern Manitoba routes formerly operated by *Transair*.

With the delivery of Boeing 737 C-GLPW, the final livery of light blue/dark blue wraparound stripes was introduced, with the slightly altered PWA tail symbol changed from two colours to red only. Five new Boeing 737s were acquired in 1980, another five in 1981, and another two in 1982. Three older 737s were sold in 1980. Pacific Western carried four million passengers in 1980 on scheduled and charter flights, with charters accounting for 35% of the total.

Hercules C-FPWK was to be sold to *Cargolux* in 1980, but remained in Canada without titles, operating the odd charter before finally being sold to *NWT Air* in 1981. In April 1981, PWA began service from Vancouver to Edmonton International direct and in June began Vancouver to Calgary direct, competing head-on with *Air Canada* and *CP Air*. They also began Vancouver to Cal-

gary, Brandon to Toronto to get back into the Toronto market and make it easier to position aircraft in Toronto for weekend charters. They dropped their flights to Powell River. These had been operated by *West Coast Air,* using a Twin Otter in blue *West Coast* colour scheme but with a red PWA symbol on the tail. *Powell Air* picked up the Vancouver to Powell River route and operated this using a former *Kelowna Flightcraft* Convair 440. One route that PWA did not get was Winnipeg to Prince Albert to Calgary which *Aero Trades Western* of Winnipeg obtained and used their former PWA Convair 640 to operate. Pacific Western's net profit for 1981 was $17.9 million.

In 1982, PWA was all set to operate Vancouver to Lethbridge when the Federal Cabinet overturned the Canadian Transportation Commission and allowed only *Time Air* to fly the route, with a stop in Kelowna. PWA very much wanted to link Vancouver to Lethbridge direct as Lethbridge has a large Japanese community and many passengers coming in on *Japan Airlines* and *CP Air* flights from Tokyo continue on to Lethbridge.

Four Boeing 737s were sold in 1982, three to *Pan Am* and one to *American West Airlines*. PWA dropped service to Uranium City, Saskatchewan in November 1982. The net profit for the company in 1982 was $6.2 million.

In 1983, three Boeing 737s were leased or sold to *American West Airlines*. As part of the deal, PWA provided flight crew training, technical support and aircraft maintenance for five years. An interline agreement was signed with *Wardair* to allow passengers to connect with *Wardair's* charter flights from any PWA city. Two 239-seat Boeing 767s were purchased in early 1983 and put into use on weekdays flying Vancouver – Calgary – Regina – Winnipeg and back, and Vancouver – Edmonton – Saskatoon and back. On weekends they were used for charter flights. An interchange agreement was made with *Monarch Airlines* in the U.K. to supply two Boeing 737s in the winter. Both of these aircraft were based in Toronto and used mainly on southern charter.

Late in 1983, Pacific Western purchased 40% of the stock of *Time Air*. This indirectly allowed them access to the Lethbridge market and also allowed PWA to transfer some of their routes which were better served by turboprops to *Time Air*. *Time Air* initially took over Calgary – Castlegar and later Edmonton – Peace River – High River and Edmonton – Fort McMurray – Fort Chipewyan. The Alberta Government began to privatize Pacific Western again late in 1983 (reducing its share of PWA from 99.9% to 14.9%), with the stock selling very well. PWA's 1983 profit was $10,763,000.

Early in 1984, PWA dropped Victoria – Seattle and put Boeing 767s on the Vancouver – Seattle route. The 767 was used because of the heavy cargo demand on this route, and because the planes could fill up with

Vancouver to Edmonton route and so were replaced by Boeing 737s, with increased use of the 767s on the Vancouver – Calgary – Saskatoon – Winnipeg route.

PWA sold a Hercules to St. Lucia in May 1984. Early in 1985, the company sold the Hercules it had been leasing to *NWT Air* since October 1983, thus ending the Hercules era completely.

In March 1984, at the Calgary airport, a Boeing 737 had its left engine disintegrate during the take-off roll. The pilots quickly aborted the take-off and, suspecting a blowout of the left main landing gear tire, taxied off runway 34 to taxiway C-4. The cabin crew, and later the control tower, informed the pilot of a fire on the wing. The plane was stopped and all one hundred and nineteen passengers quickly evacuated, with no loss of life. The plane was totally engulfed in fire and destroyed.

To replace this aircraft PWA took over the flying operations of Dome Petroleum in June 1984, including

DEW Line contract from Winnipeg to Hall Beach and Cambridge Bay was extended through September 1985. Seating capacity on Boeing 737s was increased from one hundred and seventeen to one hundred and twenty-two.

The Boeing 767s continued to prove uneconomical on most of the company's routes and thus were sold to Citibank in May 1985, which immediately leased these aircraft to *Air Canada*. PWA now had only one type of aircraft in its fleet, the Boeing 737-200.

In April 1985, PWA began operating Toronto – Thunder Bay – Brandon – Calgary – Kelowna – Vancouver. By the end of the year, four flights per day departed Toronto for the west, two direct to Winnipeg, another direct to Thunder Bay and one to Regina. Other changes to its routes in 1985 included dropping Fort Simpson and dropping Whitehorse during winter months. Trans-Canada charters were continued during 1985 and trans-

Pacific Western Nord 262, CF-BCT

Dome's Boeing 737 and its hangar at the Calgary airport. The Dome 737 was used on 'Dome Petroleum Charters' to the north and other PWA flights. Throughout its time with PWA, the aircraft flew in a hybrid colour scheme, with an aqua lower fuselage and *Dome* cheat line, but with PWA titles and tail symbol. The remaining Boeing 727, which had been on lease to Panarctic Oils, was sold to Echo Bay Mines at this time. PWA continued to contract with Panarctic for northern charters but now used Boeing 737s.

In the fall of 1984, Pacific Western again leased the two Monarch 737s and based them in Toronto for flights to southern points such as Cuba and Mexico. The company consolidated its routes, allowing it to fly between any two points and also added Thunder Bay to its list of destinations. Rights were also acquired for Windsor, but never used by PWA. The company received a contract to overhaul the five Canadian Forces Boeing 707s. The

border charters (Kelowna – Reno and Vancouver – San Francisco) were expanded. Mid-1985 net income was $10 million, while the same period in 1983 produced a net income of only $5.76 million. Three *Monarch* Boeing 737s were chartered for winter 1985, two based in Toronto and one in Winnipeg.

CP Air dropped its flights between Victoria and Vancouver because the short hop was uneconomical for the Boeing 737. These operations were transferred to *Air BC,* which used a DASH-7 on this route. Pacific Western also decided to drop its Vancouver-Vancouver Island flights, transferring them all (Victoria, Comox, Campbell River) to *Time Air.* From April to October 1986, *Time Air* operated a DASH-7 on these routes and in October 1986, put two Shorts SD-360 aircraft exclusively on the Vancouver – Victoria route and operated a feeder service called 'Connector Service' for PWA and *Air Canada.*

In addition to the agreement with *Air Canada* noted above, PWA also developed a joint marketing agreement with *Quebecair*. This agreement would make connections between the two airlines easier and connect over one hundred centres in Canada. While it was not considered as being preliminary to a merger, both airlines were looking for expansion possibilities. It was not possible to implement the agreement immediately, as PWA was struck by CALFAA flight attendants and CALEA/UAW groundworkers in December 1985.

Ottawa was finally added to the PWA route system in June 1986. In the fall of 1986, PWA entered into a major agreement with *Time Air* and *Calm Air,* for joint coordination and marketing. This new agreement was called 'Pacific Western Spirit' and the idea was that the two airlines would operate many of the smaller routes for PWA, adopting a modified PWA colour scheme. This incorporated the double blue cheat lines, with the title PWA SPIRIT displayed on the aircraft. *Time Air's* DASH-7 (C-GTAJ) appeared in this colour scheme and operated the Vancouver – Comox/Campbell River route. *Calm Air's* HS-748s were also flown with these colours.

PWA sold sixteen of its Boeing 737s to the Guiness Peat organization and leased them back. This provided the company with a more favourable tax write-off position and provided a large amount of capital ($350 million plus) for expansion. A major rumour at this time was that money realized would be used by PWA to buy out *Air Canada* once the Canadian government decided to privatize the airline.

However, on December 2, 1986, PWA made the ultimate takeover when it purchased *Canadian Pacific Airlines* from the parent Canadian Pacific Group for $300 million. While the original announcement stated that the two airlines would continue as separate entities, it clearly did not make sense to continue that arrangement for long. The purchase gave the Pacific Western

Airlines Corporation, based in Calgary, 100% of *Pacific Western Airlines,* 100% of *Canadian Pacific Airlines* (which now included *Eastern Provincial, Nordair* and *Quebecair*), 25% of *Norcanair,* 20% of *Air Atlantic,* 35% of *Nordair Metro* (which owned *Quebecair Inter*), and 46% of *Time Air*. The company held no equity in *Calm Air*, but had the above noted arrangement. *Air Canada* had just bought out *Air BC,* so *Air Canada's* Connector arrangement with *Time Air* would cease and *Canadian Pacific's* arrangement with *Air BC* would cease, *Air Canada* now having *Air BC* as their connector service and *Canadian Pacific* sharing *Time Air* with PWA.

PWA Corporation also purchased a 50% interest in GPA Jetprop Ltd., an Irish based group to lease jet, turbo and helicopter aircraft of less than 50 seats. It also bought a 25% share of *GPA Airbus 320 Ltd.* to acquire and lease Airbus 320 aircraft.

In January 1987, *Time Air* took over the Vancouver – Quesnel – Williams Lake route and the Ottawa – Toronto flights were dropped. On April 26, 1987, all PWA flights ceased and all flights adopted the CP designator under the new title: CANADIAN AIRLINE INTERNATIONAL. Pacific Western planes had *Canadian* titles applied to their blue colour scheme until such time as the aircraft could be painted in full *Canadian* colours. For the rest of 1987, CPA and Pacific Western continued the integration process, but it was not until 1988 that full integration was achieved.

Thus Russ Baker's dream of an airline from coast to coast flying jets (Comets) was now a complete reality. For a more complete story on Russ Baker and PWA, the book *Wings over the West* by John Condit (Harbour Publishing) should be read. Pacific Western Airlines Corporation remains the parent company of *Canadian* but the name Pacific Western Airlines no longer flies in Canadian skies.

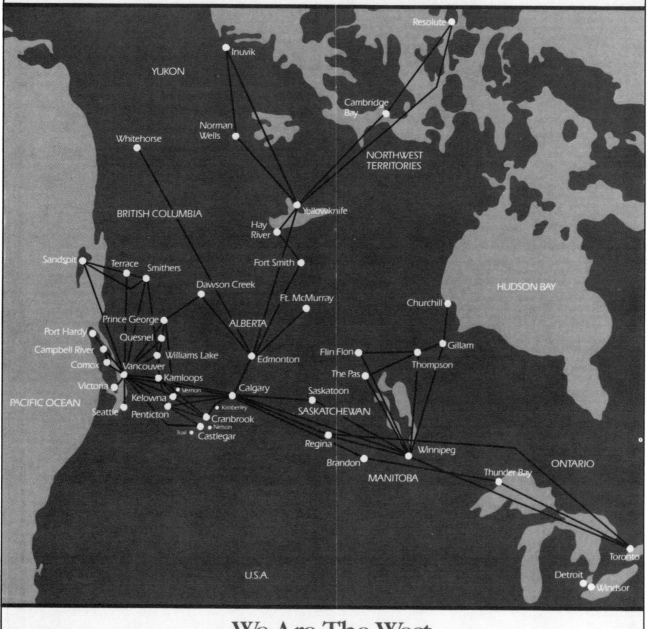

From Victoria across the West to Toronto, Pacific Western flies to over 40 destinations.

Pacific Western

We Are The West

Route map for PWA as it appeared on the back of a 1985 timetable.

FLEET LISTING
PACIFIC WESTERN AIRLINES

REG'N	C/N	F/N	IS	WFU	NOTES	MODEL
BOEING 767-275						
C-GPWA	22683	761	3/83	4/85	ST C-GPWA Air Canada	
C-GPWB	22684	762	3/83	4/85	ST C-GPWB Air Canada	
C-GPWC	22685	763	NTU	NTU	ORDER CANCELLED	
C-GPWD	22686	764	NTU	NTU	ORDER CANCELLED	
BOEING 737-275						
C-FPWB*	20785	738	12/73	2/83	ST N4529W ATASCO for N382PA Pan Am	
C-FPWC*	20142	734	5/70	2/78	W/O 11/02/78 at Cranbrook, B.C.	
C-FPWD*	19742	731	11/68	5/80	ST EI-BJE Guiness Peat for Nigeria	
C-FPWD	22761	788	11/83	4/86	LF G-DWWH Monarch winters 83/84 to 85/86; later C-FCPM Canadian	-2T7
C-FPWE	22762	789	11/83	4/86	LF G-DGDP Monarch winters 83/84 to 85/86; later C-FCPN Canadian	-2T7
C-FPWE*	19743	732	3/69	9/80	ST EI-BJP Guiness Peat for Nigeria	275C
C-FPWM*	19921	733	6/69	3/82	ST N362PA Pan Am; LT C6-BES 3/82-9/82; EX N381PS PSA	-214
C-FPWP*	20588	735	4/72	6/82	ST N381PA Pan Am; NOW C-FPWP Canadian	
C-FPWW*	20670	736	12/72	5/82	ST N380PA Pan Am; NOW C-FPWW Canadian	
C-FTAN	20206	762	4/78	1/87	ST N803AL Aloha; EX C-FTAN Transair	-2A9C
C-FTAO	20205	772	4/78	8/82	ST N383PA Pan Am; EX C-FTAO Transair	-2A9C
C-GAPW	20922	739	8/74	7/83	ST N127AW American West	
C-GBPW	20958	740	1/75	4/87	To CDN; LT N128AW American West 7/83-4/85; 2/86-6/86	
C-GCPW	20959	741	2/75	6/83	ST N125AW American West	
C-GDPA	22057	784	6/84	4/87	To C-GDPA CANADIAN; EX C-GDPA Dome Petroleum	-2T2C
C-GDPW	21116	742	10/75	4/87	To Canadian; LT C-GDPW Alaska International 5/84-8/84	
C-GEPW	21115	743	12/75	4/87	To Canadian; LT N129AW American West 9/83 - 2/85	
C-GFPW	21294	752	12/76	4/87	To Canadian; LT C-GFPW Markair 5/84 - 4/84	
C-GGPW	21639	744	11/78	4/87	To C-GGPW Canadian	
C-GIPW	21712	745	2/79	4/87	To C-GIPW Canadian	
C-GJPW	21713	746	9/79	4/87	To C-GJPW Canadian	
C-GKPW	21819	748	1/80	4/87	To C-GKPW Canadian	
C-GLPW	22086	749	5/80	4/87	To C-GLPW Canadian	
C-GMPW	22087	750	6/80	4/87	To C-GMPW Canadian	
C-GNPW	22159	751	7/80	4/87	To C-GNPW Canadian	
C-GOPW	22160	782	9/80	4/87	To C-GOPW Canadian	
C-GPPW	22264	753	4/81	4/87	To C-GPPW Canadian	
C-GPWC	22416	790	12/85	4/87	LF G-BMON Monarch winters 85/86 & 86/87	-2K9
C-GQPW	22265	754	4/81	3/84	DBF 22/03/84 at Calgary; no fatalities	
C-GRPW	22266	755	5/81	4/87	To C-GRPW Canadian	
C-GSPW	22618	783	11/81	4/87	To C-GSPW CANADIAN; LT C-GSPW EPA 4/82 - 4/83	-275C
C-GTAQ	20956	761	4/78	4/82	ST N131AW American West; EX C-FTAQ Transair	-A9C
C-GTAR	20223	730	10/79	4/80	LF EI-ASH Aer Lingus; EX C-FTAR Transair	-248
C-GTPW	22807	756	12/81	4/87	To C-GTPW Canadian; (c/n 22619 was to be C-GTPW, NTU)	
C-GUPW	22873	758	7/82	4/87	To C-GUPW Canadian	
C-GVPW	22874	759	8/82	4/87	To C-GVPW Canadian	
C-GWPW	23283	760	5/85	4/87	To C-GWPW Canadian	
N131AW	20956	761	12/86	12/86	LF N131AW American West; EX C-GTAQ PWA	-2A9
BOEING 737-3Y0						
C-FPWD	23495	301	11/86	4/87	LF G-DHSW Monarch winter 1986-1987	3Y0
C-FPWE	23497	302	11/86	4/87	LF G-MONF Monarch winter 1986-1987	3Y0
BOEING 737 AIRCRAFT NOT TAKEN UP AT THE TIME OF THE TAKEOVER BY CANADIAN						
C-GYPW	23707	---	NTU	NTU	NTU; ST EC-ECS Air Europa (GPA Group) 5/87	375
C-GZPW	23708	---	NTU	NTU	NTU; ST PT-TEC Transbrazil (GPA Group) 5/87	375
C-G---	23808	---	NTU	NTU	NTU	375
C-GYPW	23284	---	NTU	NTU	NTU; series 200 a/c replaced by series 300 a/c	275
C-GZPW	23285	---	NTU	NTU	NTU; series 200 a/c replaced by series 300 a/c	275
BOEING 727-100						
C-FPXB *	19174	721	10/72	7/77	ST N18479 Continental	-92C
C-FPXD	19859	722	2/74	8/84	ST C-FPXD Echo Bay Mines- LT C-FPXD Panarctic Oil 2/76 - 8/84	-171C
BOEING 707						
C-FPWJ*	18746	776	3/73	5/79	ST OO-ABA Abelag; then C-GRYO Ontario Worldair	-351C
C-FPWV*	17696	773	11/67	11/78	ST N138TA Tigerair	-138B
CF-PWW	17700	774	7/69	3/71	ST N793SA Standard	-138B
CF-PWZ	18826	775	7/72	1/73	W/O 01/01/73 while landing at Edmonton	-321C

FLEET LISTING
PACIFIC WESTERN AIRLINES

REG'N	C/N	F/N	IS	WFU	NOTES	MODEL
LOCKHEED HERCULES						
C-FPWK *	4170	386	11/73	1/81	ST C-FPWK Northest Territorial Air	-20
C-FPWN *	4129	383	3/69	9/82	ST J6-SLO St. Lucia 5/84; LT N109AK Alaska	-20
CF-PWO	4197	382	4/67	7/69	W/O 16/07/69 Cayaya, Peru / International	-10
C-FPWR *	4355	385	11/69	12/80	ST 5A-DHI United African Airlines	-20
CF-PWX	4361	384	12/69	11/76	W/O 21/11/76 Eastville, Zaire	-20
C-GHPW	4799	387	6/78	12/83	ST C-GHPW Northwest Territorial Air	-30
N7984S	4362	---	3/77	10/77	LF N7984S Southern Airline	-20
CONVAIR 640						
CF-PWO	463	645	11/71	6/76	ST C-FPWO Echo Bay Mines; then North Cariboo	
CF-PWR	440	643	3/67	9/69	W/O 18/09/69 at Elk Island Park, B.C.	
C-FPWS *	441	641	2/67	5/78	ST C-FPWS Gateway Aviation; now Time Air	
C-FPWT *	9	640	4/67	5/76	ST C-FPWT Worldways	
C-FPWU *	10	642	4/67	8/78	ST C-FPWU Worldways	
C-FPWY *	108	644	12/69	5/78	ST C-FPWY Aero Trades; now Time Air	
L-188 Electra						
CF-PWG	1035	183	4/72	4/76	ST N415MA MCA Leasing	
CF-PWQ	1064	184	4/72	6/73	LF N5003K North American A/C Leasing. Bulk Tanker in silver c/s	
CF-ZSR	1127	181	3/71	9/72	ACC CFB Namao 14/09/72; ST CF-PAK Pan Arctic	
CF-ZST	1128	182	3/71	4/76	ST N417MA MCA Leasing	
Nord 262A						
CF-BCR	16	201	9/70	2/72	ST N26210 Ransome; EX BC Airline	
CF-BCS	23	202	9/70	2/72	ST N26215 Ransome; EX BC Airline	
CF-BCT	24	203	9/70	2/72	ST N26217 Ransome; EX BC Airline	
CF-BCU	9	204	9/70	2/72	ST N26201 Ransome; EX BC Airline	
DC-7B						
CF-PWD	44136	---	2/64	2/65	ST OY-DMT Flying Enterprise	
DC-7						
CF-PWK	44135	---	5/64	2/65	ST N314A Liberty Air	
DC-7C						
CF-PWM	45181	771	2/65	5/69	ST N22CA Concare Leasing	
CF-NAI	45129	---	2/65	12/67	WFU & BU 1970; EX CF-NAI Nordair.	
DC-6B						
CF-PCI	43555	---	11/66	10/67	LF CF-PCI Wardair	
CF-PWA	44698	601	8/62	4/72	ST CF-PWA Conair Aviation	
CF-PWF	43537	602	12/63	11/71	ST CF-PWF Golden Voyageurs	
DC-6						
CF-PWP	43127	603	3/65	1/71	ST N80MA Mercer Airline	
CF-PWQ	43128	604	5/65	1/71	ST N90MA Mercer Airline	
DC-6B						
CF-CZU	45328	---	2/69	9/70	LF CF-CZU Canadian Pacific	
DC-6AB						
CF-CZZ	45498	607	2/69	6/72	ST CF-CZZ NWT Air; EX CPAL	
DC-4						
CF-PWA	18356	401	10/57	4/61	ST CF-TAM Transair; then CF-KAD Kanting.	
CF-PWB	10314	402	10/57	11/72	ST N74183 Cryderman	
CF-PWJ	10746	403	7/59	11/72	ST N74182 Cryderman; EX CF-LTI Loram Ltd.	
CF-PWK	27236	404	12/69	12/72	ST N74181 Cryderman	
CF-HYV	18364	---	6/55	6/57	OB Queen Charlotte Airlines	
DC-3						
CF-PWC	9397	---	5/56	8/68	ST N3345A; RR from CF-INE 8/57; EX CF-INE	
CF-PWF	9089	---	5/56	5/61	W/O 24/05/61 Snowdrift; EX CF-INB	
CF-PWG	20439	---	5/56	7/68	ST N2082A; RR from CF-IQV 9/57; EX CF-IQV	
CF-PWH	2198	---	6/53	5/73	ST CF-PWH Gateway; EX CF-HCF	
CF-PWI	4880	---	2/56	3/72	ST CF-PWI TPA; EX CF-IHO	
CF-ONH	12857	---	4/62	4/69	LF N44587 Air West A/L	
CF-EPI	7408	---	2/53	6/57	W/O 23/05/57 at Port Hardy, B.C.	
Bristol 170						
CF-GBT	12831	---	2/52	6/57	W/O 17/09/55 Thorhild, Alberta; OB Associated Airways	

FLEET LISTING
PACIFIC WESTERN AIRLINES

REG'N	C/N	F/N	IS	WFU	NOTES
Curtiss C-46					
CF-CZI	22542	---	7/59	4/63	ST N9761Z Intermountain
CF-CZJ	22574	---	7/59	4/63	ST N9760Z Birds & Sons
CF-CZM	22453	---	7/59	5/67	ST CF-CZM Nordair
CF-CZN	22455	---	7/59	5/67	ST CF-CZN Nordair
CF-HYU	22579	---	3/55	10/55	ST N67854 Flying Tiger
CF-PWD	2940	---	2/55	1/60	W/O 29/01/60 Port Hardy; EX CF-HYH
CF-PWE	2934	501	2/55	11/67	WAS CF-HYI from 1955-1959
Grumman Goose					
CF-MSK	B- 32	---	4/61	9/67	Sold
CF-NIF	B-129	---	4/61	8/68	ST CF-NIF Trans Provincial
CF-UMG	B-145	---	8/66	8/68	ST CF-UMG Trans Provincial
CF-UVJ	B- 6	---	8/66	8/68	ST CF-UVJ Trans Provincial
CF-VAK	B-142	---	1/67	8/68	ST CF-VAK Trans Provincial
Grumman Mallard					
CF-MHG	J-21	---	9/70	4/74	ST CF-MHG West Coast Air
CF-HPQ	J -7	---	8/54	6/60	ST CF-HPA BC Airlines
CF-HPU	J -9	---	8/54	6/60	ST CF-HPU BC Airlines
CF-HPU	J -9	---	9/70	4/74	ST CF-HPU West Coast Air
Grumman Widgeon					
CF-GYZ	1309	---	5/53	10/57	Sold
DHC-2 Beaver					
CF-DJM	65	---	3/57	8/63	EX Queen Charlotte Airlines
CF-EYS	484	---	4/61	6/67	ST CF-EYS West Coast Air
CF-FHB	1	---	5/48	1/66	ST CF-FHB Northward
CF-FHN	47	---	5/49	10/65	ST CF-FHN Island Leasing Ltd.
CF-FHZ	66	---	9/56	10/65	ST CF-FHZ Yukon Flying Services
CF-GCY	216	---	4/59	1/66	ST CF-GCY Northward
CF-GIX	16	---	8/48	3/59	EX CF-GIX Associated Airways Ltd.
CF-GQC	75	---	5/50	8/68	ST CF-GQC Harrison Airways
CF-GQN	96	---	10/56	1/66	ST CF-GQN Northward
CF-GQV	105	---	1/51	1/66	ST CF-GQV Northward; EX Associated Airways
CF-GYM	130	---	6/51	4/67	ST CF-GYM Northern Mountain
CF-GYO	143	---	8/51	4/67	ST CF-GYO West Coast Air
CF-HEP	69	---	6/53	3/66	ST CF-HEP Timberland Development
CF-ICK	796	---	4/55	2/62	ST CF-ICK Central Aircraft Lease
CF-ICL	799	---	4/55	2/70	ST CF-ICL W.J. Leboe
CF-IFG	805	---	4/62	7/69	ST CF-IFG Gateway Aviation
CF-JHE	15R	---	4/56	7/68	ST CF-JHE Trans Provincial
CF-JOF	1053	---	5/57	2/70	ST CF-JOF Gateway Aviation
CF-JOM	1024	---	11/57	4/67	ST CF-JOM West Coast Air
CF-JOS	1030	---	4/58	6/65	ST CF-JOS Omineca Air Service
CF-JXO	1036	---	6/58	1/66	ST CF-JXO Northward
CF-JXP	1041	---	6/58	1/66	ST CF-JXP Northward
Barkley Grow					
CF-BLV	3	---	4/56	1/60	DBF 12/01/60 Peace River
F-BMW	6	---	4/56	1/64	ST CF-BMW Northland Assoc'd 49-56
CF-BQM	8	---	11/56	6/59	ST CF-BQM Sioux Narrows Airways
DHC-3 Otter					
CF-CZO	71	---	3/59	1/66	ST CF-CZO Northward; EX CPAL
CF-CZP	72	---	3/59	1/66	ST CF-CZP Northward; EX CPAL
CF-GCV	2	---	4/65	9/66	ST CF-GCV Thunderbird Air; EX EPA
CF-IKK	80	---	1/56	1/66	ST CF-IKK Northward; EX Associated Airways
CF-JAO	129	---	6/56	1/66	ST CF-JAO Northward
CF-RNO	21	---	6/64	12/68	ST CF-RNO TPA: ACC 13/12/68 Schaft Lake, B.C.; EX Royal Norwegian AF
Beech A-18A					
CF-BQH	318	---	8/53	9/58	ST CF-BQH R.H. Laidman
Beech C-18S					
CF-KIA	8385	---	4/62	1/66	ST CF-KIA Northward
Beech D-18S					
CF-PJD	A380	---	2/66	5/69	ST CF-PJD Hooker Air

FLEET LISTING
PACIFIC WESTERN AIRLINES

REG'N	C/N	F/N	IS	WFU	NOTES
Beech SD-17S					
CF-HSK	3186	---	6/54	10/56	ST CF-HSK Trio Tyro Syndicate
Beech D-17S					
CF-GPO	1013	---	9/51	10/56	ST CF-GPO H.O. Thomas; EX QCA
PBY-5A Canso					
CF-FOQ	9738	---	4/51	3/69	EX CF-FOQ Queen Charlotte A/L
CF-GHU	21232	---	12/51	6/58	WFU
CF-GLX	560	---	8/51	8/60	ST CF-GLX Northland Aviation
CF-IDS	11629	---	4/56	8/60	ST CF-IDS Ontario Central A/L
285ACF Canso					
CF-IIW	013	---	6/55	5/62	ST CF-IIW Northern Wings
Avro 685 York					
CF-HFP	MW233	---	6/56	4/60	EX CF-HFP Associated Airways; WFU
CF-HIP	MW287	---	12/56	4/60	EX CF-HIP Maritime Central; WFU
Anson V					
CF-DHX	1587	---	5/55	1/56	WFU
CF-DTU	12468	---	8/55	3/57	WFU; EX CF-DTU DOT
CF-EFZ	220	---	7/55	4/59	WFU; EX CF-EFZ D.T. Hamilton
CF-FJL	1559	---	6/55	4/59	WFU
CF-FQZ	4163	---	7/55	3/57	WFU; EX CF-FQZ Halls Air Service
CF-GDV	3713	---	9/55	4/58	WFU; EX CF-GDV Central Northern
CF-INT	1642	---	8/52	5/63	ST CF-INT Northland
CF-INU	1646	---	8/56	3/61	WFU
CF-INV	1651	---	8/56	3/62	ST CF-INV Northland
CF-PAC	1357	---	7/55	3/62	ST CF-PAC Chiupka Airways
CF-SAR	1337	---	8/56	3/62	ST CF-SAR D. Hornby
Bellanca 31-55B					
CF-EQQ	15	---	4/56	9/59	ST CF-EQQ F.M. Clark
CF-EQR	13	---	4/56	9/59	ST CF-EQR Basco Aircraft Supplies
Junkers W34F					
CF-AQB	2586	---	10/54	4/59	ST CF-AQB Skyway Air Service
Junkers W33/34					
CF-AQW	2587	---	10/47	5/59	ST CF-AQW Skyway Air Service
Junkers H34F/34					
CF-ATF	2718	---	9/46	7/60	ST CF-ATF Pacific Wings Ltd.
Fairchild 71C					
CF-BVK	625	---	10/49	11/55	W/O 13/11/55 Ocean Falls, B.C.
CF-BXI	662	---	11/50	8/56	W/O 08/08/56 Kitimat, B.C.
Norseman UC64					
CF-GOB	421	---	3/58	8/60	ST CF-GOB Ontario Central A/L
Norseman V					
CF-BHU	N29-08	---	8/51	12/50	ST CF-BHU Central Airlines
CF-BHZ	N29-13	---	6/51	6/59	ST CF-BHZ BC Air
CF-OBG	N29-01	---	7/51	8/60	ST CF-OBG Ontario Central A/L
CF-OBM	N29-18	---	6/51	4/59	EX CF-OBM Ontario Provincial A/S
CF-OBR	N29-35	---	12/52	8/60	ST CF-OBR Ontario Central A/L
Norseman IV					
CF-CRS	53	---	3/47	5/63	ALL Norseman IV reg' to Queen Charlotte Airways.
CF-DFU	31	---	5/50	5/63	SOLD
F-DFV	42	---	8/50	5/63	ST CF-DFV BC Air
F-FAA	281	---	9/53	10/59	ST CF-FAA Uranium Corp. B.C. Ltd.
CF-GHH	61	---	5/48	8/60	ST CF-GHH Celgar Ltd.
F-GUE	542	---	12/50	8/60	ST CF-GUE BC Air
F-GUM	279	---	5/52	8/60	ST CF-GUM Bullock Wings & Rotors
Fleet 80					
CF-DPM	039	---	4/56	11/59	ST CF-DPM L.O. Romfo
Stinson 108-2					
CF-FYJ	3103	---	4/56	11/59	Reg'd. To Queen Charlotte Airways

FLEET LISTING
PACIFIC WESTERN AIRLINES

REG'N	C/N	F/N	IS	WFU	NOTES
Stranraer					
CF-BXO	209	---	5/47	2/52	Reg'd. To Queen Charlotte Airways
CF-BYM	1042	---	8/49	10/57	Reg'd. To Queen Charlotte Airways
Cessna 120					
CF-FLK	14332	---	4/56	11/59	ST CF-FLK L.O. Romf
Cessna 170A					
CF-GUV	19909	---	1/55	7/56	ST CF-GUV Pool Barge Ltd.
Cessna 180					
CF-EOO	30157	---	9/57	4/60	EX Whitehorse Flying Service
CF-HIW	30904	---	4/54	5/56	SOLD
CF-HLA	30918	---	4/54	5/69	ST CF-HLA Belliveau Enterprises; EX QCA
CF-HLT	31033	---	6/54	5/56	SOLD
CF-HYE	31527	---	4/57	4/64	ST CF-HYE McMullen & Patterson; EX QCA
CF-HYP	31670	---	5/55	7/68	ST CF-HYP G. Mohr; EX QCA
CF-IDL	31775	---	5/55	4/60	SOLD
CF-JCQ	32505	---	10/56	5/66	ST CF-JCQ J.K. Sloan
CF-PVH	51374	---	8/66	9/68	ST CF-PVH Trans Provincial
Cessna 182A					
CF-JHW	33926	---	4/57	9/62	ST CF-JHW Sawrite Lumber Co. Ltd.
Cessna 185					
CF-SZV	0997	---	5/68	6/69	ST CF-SZV Midwest
Piper Apache					
CF-PWL	272116	---	8/64	9/69	ST CF-PWL David Jones Music Ltd.
Bell 47G					
CF-ISG	1518	---	2/56	5/60	ST CF-ISG Pacific Helicopters Ltd
CF-ISH	1522	---	2/56	5/60	ST CF-ISH Pacific Helicopters Ltd
CF-JSI	1693	---	4/58	5/60	ST CF-JSI Pacific Helicopters Ltd
CF-JSJ	1694	---	4/58	5/60	ST CF-JSJ Pacific Helicopters Ltd
CF-JSK	1695	---	4/58	5/60	ST CF-JSK Pacific Helicopters Ltd
CF-JSL	1696	---	4/58	5/60	ST CF-JSL Pacific Helicopters Ltd
CF-JSM	1697	---	4/58	5/60	ST CF-JSM Pacific Helicopters Ltd

transair

Transair 737, C-GTAQ

HEADQUARTERS:
Winnipeg International Airport,
Winnipeg, Manitoba, R3J 0H7

MAJOR BASE:
Winnipeg International Airport

FLEET 1989:
3 - Boeing 737s;
2 - F-28s;
2 - YS-111As

COLOURS:
A window-wide cheat line of Tangier gold (brown), wraps around the cockpit window and extends to the back of the plane, turning up to cover the back quarter of the tail. A thin white cheat line separates the Tangier gold cheat from the upper fuselage and the front three-quarters of the tail, which are harvest gold. A similar white cheat line separates the Tangier gold from the lower fuselage of natural metal. The title TRANSAIR appears on the upper fuselage in Tangier gold. During the changeover phase of the Boeing 737 aircraft to *Pacific Western Airlines,* these aircraft were painted in the PWA dark blue colour scheme but wore TRANSAIR titles.

ROUTES:
Winnipeg – Dryden – Thunder Bay – Sault Ste. Marie – Toronto.
Winnipeg – Churchill – Yellowknife – Whitehorse.
Winnipeg – Saskatoon/Regina – Calgary/Edmonton.
Winnipeg – The Pas – Flin Flon – Lynn Lake – Norway House – Thompson – Gillam.
Churchill – Resolute Bay – Eskimo Point – Whale Cove – Rankin Inslet – Coral Harbour – Repulse Bay – Baker Lake.
International Charters.

HISTORY:

TransAir was formed in 1956 through a merger of two companies, *Central Northern Airways* and *Arctic Wings*. The large 'A' was later changed to a small 'a' and the name *Transair* used.

Arctic Wings, formed in July 1947, operated out of Churchill, Manitoba for the Roman Catholic Church, in support of the Church's Arctic missions. It operated scheduled services south to Port Severn and north to Baker Lake.

Two World War I flyers, Milt Ashton and Roy Brown, entered the airlines business with *Wings Ltd.,* which was acquired by *Canadian Pacific* in 1941. Following World War II, Ashton and Brown again combined to form *Central Northern Airways*. CNA acquired several of *Canadian Pacific's* routes in northern Manitoba and northwestern Ontario, including Sherridon, Norway House, Ilford, Lac du Bonnet, Flin Flon, Gods Lake, Pickle Lake and Sioux Lookout. When formed on 8 April 1946, CNA acquired three former *Canadian Pacific* Norseman aircraft. Seven more Norsemen, nine Ansons, two Dragon Rapides, three Fairchild 82s, two Bellanca Air Cruisers and three Stinson 108s had been added by the end of 1947.

Central Northern Airways acquired a former TCA Lockheed 14, in May 1951, to operate a Class 1 service between Winnipeg and Red Lake, Ontario. This route had been operated by *Canadian Pacific*. Contracts for air supply to the DEW Line construction sites in 1955 allowed CNA to expand into larger aircraft such as the Avro York, Curtiss C-46 and Bristol Freighter. PBY Cansos were also acquired at this time, while most of their earlier bush aircraft were disposed of to other operators and replaced with Beavers and Cessna 180s.

Following its inception in 1956, Transair acquired additional DEW Line construction contracts and, on 1 September 1957, took over services between Winnipeg, Dauphin, the Pas, Flin Flon, Lynn Lake and Churchill from *Canadian Pacific*. Four DC-3 aircraft were acquired in that year to operate these routes, three of them from *Canadian Pacific*. A DC-4 was also acquired to fly Montreal – Ottawa – Churchill. This route was continued until 1966, supplying the Mid-Canada Line bases.

In 1956 two Bristol Freighters were written off in unusual accidents. On 30 May 1956, CF-TFZ had its left undercarriage break through the ice at the end of its landing run at Beaver Lodge Lake, NWT. The airplane fell onto its port wing, bending the spars and crushing the fuselage sides. On 18 June 1956, CF-TFY was waiting to be unloaded at Povungnituk, on the eastern edge of Hudson Bay. It broke through the ice and was submerged in 40 feet of water and declared unsalvageable.

The third former TCA Bristol Freighter was sold to *Wardair* in 1958.

Transair suffered additional losses through accidents in 1956, when two Curtiss C-46s were lost. An Avro York was burned at Rankin Inlet on 8 January 1957, giving the airline five major accidents in less than a year. These accidents, combined with its failure to obtain any of the DEW Line resupply contracts in 1957, placed Transair in financial difficulties.

The company survived between 1957 and 1961 on their scheduled routes and charters and in 1961, Transair won the largest DEW Line resupply contract from the USAF, to operate out of Winnipeg and Churchill. They also acquired a scheduled service to Thompson, Manitoba. Four DC-4s were added in 1961 and a fifth in 1962 to operate these new services.

Trans-Canada Airlines 'sold' the 'Prairie Air Service,' Winnipeg – Brandon – Yorkton – Regina and Regina – Saskatoon – Prince Albert, to Transair for $1.00 in 1963. The purchase price included two DC-3s and a Vickers Viscount. Transair's fleet in 1963 now consisted of one Viscount, six DC-4s, eight DC-3s, four Cansos, one Avro York and several small bush aircraft. The company's route structure ranged from Montreal in the east to Regina in the west and from Winnipeg and Churchill to the far reaches of northern Canada.

Transair purchased a DC-7 and a DC-6 aircraft in 1965 to operate its trans-Atlantic charters. The DC-7 could carry ninety-five passengers and the DC-6 eighty passengers. The planes operated from 1965 to 1967 before both were sold. A former *Canadian Pacific* DC-6B was acquired in 1969 for cargo work.

Up to this time, Transair operated with a simple colour scheme of white upper and silver lower fuselage, with a narrow red cheat line through the windows separating the two. The titles were in red and blue, (TRANS in red, AIR in blue), with the company's logo (a circle with a flying wing coming out of it), on the tail. The registration was in black at the top of the tail. The DC-7 had an all-red tail in contrast with the all-white tail of the DC-4s. The Viscount and DC-3s had blue cheat lines rather than red cheat lines.

An interim colour scheme was introduced with the former *Canadian Pacific* DC-6B in 1969. The cheat line was metallic gold, titles were in black and on the tail was a red ellipse with a stylized 'T' in the centre. The tail and upper fuselage were all white. On the Viscount and DC-3s, the tail was gold on top and red on the bottom with a large white stylized 'T' in the red area.

In 1968, Transair purchased their second turbo-prop aircraft, the Japanese built Nihon YS-11A. There was an initial dispute with the manufacturer over the purchase and they were almost returned to Japan. The difficulties were resolved and these 46 passenger/cargo aircraft continued in service until mid-March 1979. The only other operator of this aircraft in Canada was *Norcanair,* who leased a Piedmont aircraft in 1983. A Short

Transair Fokker F-28, CF-TAV

Skyvan was bought for northern operations in 1969 but was sold within a year. The smaller bush aircraft were all phased out as Transair entered the seventies.

Midwest Aviation had been formed in 1957 and in April 1969 merged with *Northland Airlines* to form *Midwest Airlines.* The new company leased three HS-748s from *Philippine Airlines* and one from Hawker Siddley in 1969. *Midwest* already owned one HS-748 and bought a second one in 1969. It had few scheduled routes. In addition to the HS-748s, the company operated four Cansos, two DC-3s, two Grumman Geese, a Grumman Mallard, a Twin Otter and several smaller aircraft and helicopters. In November 1969, Transair took over *Midwest Airlines.*

The four leased HS-748s were returned when Transair took over the company, but *Midwest* continued to operate its own HS-748s under its own name, providing scheduled services on the following routes: Norway House – Jenpeg – Cross Lake; Winnipeg – Berens River; and Winnipeg – Garden Hill – Gods Narrows – Gods River – Norway House. It also continued to provide charter Transair work in northern Manitoba with fixed wing and helicopters, including several Jet Rangers. The airline adopted the new Transair colour scheme of gold and brown but retained its own titles on these aircraft.

Transair entered the jet era in March 1970 when two Boeing 737s were added to its fleet. The 'Golden Bird' colour scheme (harvest gold and Tangier gold) was first seen on these aircraft, which Transair used to operate its newly acquired routes: Winnipeg to Dryden, Thunder Bay, Sault Ste. Marie and Toronto; and from Winnipeg to Churchill and on to Resolute Bay.

Four Hawker Siddley Argosy cargo aircraft were purchased from *British European Airlines* in 1970, in the recurring hope of establishing a trans-Canada freight service. These aircraft operated in joint *Transair/Mid-*

west titles, but spent considerable amounts of time on the ground in Winnipeg. When active, they carried cargo to northern Canada. The Argosy had four Rolls Royce Dart engines, 42,000 pound cargo capacity and could fly for 2,000 miles at a cruise speed of 280 mph. Their high tails with rear swing-open door made them an excellent cargo aircraft, but the work never materialized to fully utilize them. They were sold in Australia and New Zealand in 1975.

The Viscount was painted in the Golden Bird colour scheme but was withdrawn from use in 1971, replaced by the Boeing 737s. The last two DC-4s were withdrawn from service in the summer of 1972 and the DC-6B sold at the same time. The DC-3s were also retired in 1972. Thus, in early 1973, Transair operated two Boeing 737s, two YS-11s, four Argosies and had just purchased two Fokker F-28 jets. Transair was the first North American airline to fly this Dutch built, sixty-five passenger, twin jet aircraft. The purchase of this aircraft allowed Transair to provide jet service where the larger Boeing 737s would be uneconomical.

Rosella Bjornson was hired as a First Officer on the F-28s and thus became Canada's first woman airline pilot and the first woman in North America to fly a commercial jet on a scheduled airline.

A third Boeing 737 was leased in the winter of 1973 from *Aer Lingus* and this lease was renewed for five months each winter in 1974 and 1975. The company purchased a third Boeing 737 in 1974. Transair also leased a Boeing 707 for five months in 1973 from *Aer Lingus* to begin long haul charters. The following winter a Boeing 707 was purchased from *Northwest Orient.* However, with PWA and *Nordair* already in the long haul charter business, *Wardair* offering Boeing 747 charters and both *Air Canada* and *CP Air* heavily into charters, the 707 proved to be a poor investment, sitting for long periods of time at Toronto International Airport. It was sold in 1975 to *Bangladesh Biman* and Transair from then on concentrated on the short haul charters to the warm southern climates, using their Boeing 737s.

Transair began disposing of its smaller routes to third level carriers in 1976. *On Air* took over Winnipeg to Red Lake via Kenora, using a Saunders ST-27 aircraft. *Calm Air* of Lynn Lake, Manitoba, and *Perimeter Aviation* of Winnipeg purchased the *Transair/Midwest* Twin Otters and took over many of the shorter Manitoba routes. Despite the sale of aircraft and routes, Transair continued to be in financial difficulty.

In February 1977, *Pacific Western Airlines* bought 70% of the Transair stock. When the takeover was finally approved by the Canadian Transportation Commission, Transair was allowed to operate from Winnipeg to Regina or Saskatoon to Calgary or Edmonton, making connections with *Pacific Western* flights. Transair, however, had to drop its route east of Winnipeg to Toronto.

While the takeover was being approved, Transair dropped all its routes except the Winnipeg – Churchill – Yellowknife – Whitehorse and from Winnipeg – Resolute Bay – Hall Beach – Gillam – Lynn Lake – Flin Flon – Thompson – Norway House – The Pas. It operated the route east from Winnipeg to Toronto until 1 February 1979, when *Nordair* took it over. On this date, it also began its flights from Winnipeg through Saskatchewan to Alberta. The three Boeing 737s were painted in the dark blue *Pacific Western* colour scheme with TRANSAIR titles. In mid-March 1979, the YS-11s made the last scheduled Winnipeg – Norway House – Thompson flight and were sold to *Pinehurst Aviation* early in 1980. The F-28s were sold to *Air Niugini* in mid-1979. The takeover was officially completed in November 1979 and the last Boeing 737 had the TRANSAIR titles removed 21 March 1980. *Calm Air* acquired several other Transair routes at this time.

Transair thus became part of *Pacific Western Airlines* and eventually part of the *Canadian Airlines International* amalgamation.

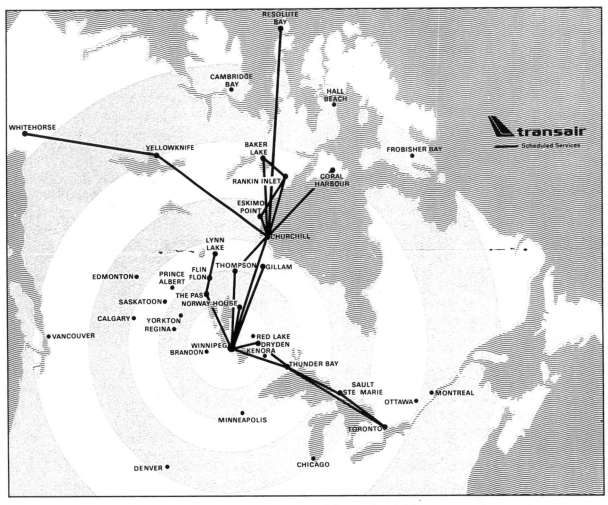

Route Map as shown in 1977 Transair Timetable.

FLEET LISTING
TRANSAIR

REG'N	C/N	IS	WFU	NOTES	Aircraft Name
737-2A9C					
CF-TAN	20206	4/70	4/78	ST C-FTAN PWA	Fort Williams
CF-TAO	20205	3/70	4/78	ST C-FTAO PWA	Fort York
C-GTAQ	20956	11/74	4/78	ST C-GTAQ PWA	Fort Rouge
737-248					
CF-TAR	20223	11/73	5/74	LF EI-ASH Aer Lingus	Fort Rouge
C-GTAR	20223	11/74	4/75	LF EI-ASH Aer Lingus	
C-GTAR	20223	12/75	4/76	LF EI-ASH Aer Lingus	
707-348C					
CF-TAI	19410	12/73	4/74	LF EI-APG Aer Lingus	Fort Garry
707-351C					
C-GTAI	19434	10/74	4/75	ST S2-ACA Bangladesh;	
				EX N373US Northwest Orient	Fort Garry
Fokker F-28					
C-FTAV*	11033	10/72	6/79	ST P2-ANE Air Niugini	Fort Resolution
C-FTAY*	11038	4/73	2/79	ST P2-ANF Air Niugini	Fort Prince of Wales
Nihon YS-11A					
C-FTAK*	2072	8/68	1/80	ST N4989S Pinehurst	Norway House
C-FTAM*	2073	8/68	2/80	ST N5592M Pinehurst	Cumberland House
Viscount 724					
CF-TGI	40	3/63	1/71	ST CF-TGI E.Nold, Houston 1973; EX TCA	
Short Skyvan					
CF-TAI	1864	6/69	7/70	ST 9M-AQG Malaysian Air	
HS-748					
CF-MAK	1668	7/69	4/71	ST CF-MAK Gateway; OB Midwest	
CF-MAL	1587	12/67	2/75	ST TG-MAL Aviateca; OB Midwest/Transair	
CF-TAG	1664	5/69	11/69	LF PI-C-1025 PAL; OB Transair	
CF-TAX	1586	5/69	2/70	LF PI-C-1029 PAL; OB Transair	
CF-TAZ	1663	5/69	11/69	LF PI-C-1026 PAL; OB Transair	
CF-YQD	1635	5/69	6/69	ST C-GEPH EPA (leased); OB Transair	
HS Argosy					
CF-TAG	6801	6/70	10/73	ST ZK-SAF Safeair; OB Midwest/Transair	
CF-TAJ	6802	7/70	7/74	ST ZK-SAE Safeair; OB Midwest/Transair	
CF-TAX	6803	4/70	11/76	ST TR-LWO SOACO; OB Midwest/Transair	
CF-TAZ	6805	4/70	11/76	ST TR-LWR SOACO; OB Midwest/Transair	
DHC-6					
CF-AIV	215	7/71	2/74	ST CF-AIV Norcanair; OB Midwest	
CF-AIY	188	7/71	6/76	ST C-FAIY Perimeter; OB Midwest	
CF-GJK	213	7/73	6/76	ST C-FGJK Perimeter; OB Transair	
CF-QBV	103	7/73	11/76	ST C-FQBV Calm Air; OB Transair	
CF-VMD	21	11/67	4/68	ST N1370T TransEast; OB Midwest	
CF-VTL	26	2/67	2/74	ST CF-VTL Calm Air; OB Midwest	
Bristol 170					
CF-TFX	13137	12/55	3/58	ST CF-TFX Wardair; EX TCA	
CF-TFY	13138	12/55	6/56	W/O 18/06/56 Povungnituk; EX TCA	
CF-TFZ	13139	12/55	5/56	W/O 30/05/56 Beaver Lodge Lake, NWT; EX TCA	
DC-7C					
CF-TAY	45210	9/65	1/67	ST N8852 Airline Components	
DC-6					
CF-TAX	36326	6/65	6/67	ST N901MA Mercer; prototype DC-6	
DC-6B					
CF-CZS	45326	3/69	6/72	ST OY-DRM Gronlandsfly	
DC-4					
CF-TAK	18369	4/61	3/66	ST ZS-EKU Marine Diamond	
CF-TAL	18375	5/61	9/69	ST N401AD Air Distributors 11/73	
CF-TAM	18356	4/61	6/66	ST CF-KAD Kenting; EX CF-PWA Pacific Western	
CF-TAO	10330	3/61	4/68	ST CF-NAG Nordair; EX CF-WAL	
CF-TAP	10494	2/62	9/69	EX CF-LOG Yukon Construction; BU 4/74	
CF-TAQ	7481	6/56	8/72	EX CF-JEA; BU 4/74	
CF-TAW	42914	5/65	8/72	ST N31356 California National Air Service	

FLEET LISTING
TRANSAIR

REG'N	C/N	IS	WFU	NOTES
DC-3				
CF-TAR	4594	9/57	10/70	W/O 07/10/70; EX CF-CPV; RR 11/61
CF-TAS	4666	8/57	7/72	ST CF-TAS Air Caravane; EX CF-CPW; RR 10/61
CF-TAT	11850	4/59	11/69	ST CF-TAT Lambair; EX CF-DIG; RR 10/61
CF-TAU	11877	8/57	3/73	ST CF-TAU Lambair; EX CF-LJS; RR 12/61
CF-TEA	12502	4/63	5/69	ST N3262 Acft. Mod. Inc.; EX CF-TEA TCA
CF-TES	11906	4/63	4/67	ST CF-TES Lambair; Now West Cdn. Avn. Museum
CF-TET	13393	11/55	9/68	W/O 25/09/68 Coral Harbour
CF-IHH	48797	8/69	8/72	ST N57800 East Coast Aviation; OB Midwest
CF-WCM	9053	12/66	3/74	ST N90765 Galcon Owning Co.; OB Midwest
Curtiss C-46				
CF-HZI	22387	2/55	4/56	W/O 03/04/56 Fox, Manitoba
CF-HZL	22394	2/55	7/56	W/O 06/07/56 Coral Harbour, NWT
G-73 Mallard				
CF-YQC	J-55	4/69	3/71	Sold; OB Midwest
G-21A Goose				
CF-GEC	B098	4/69	7/73	ST CF-GEC West Coast Air; OB Midwest
CF-PVE	1200	4/69	7/73	ST CF-PVE West Coast Air; OB Midwest
PBY-5A Canso				
CF-HHR	300	10/53	11/66	ST CF-HHR Field Aviation; OB Transair
CF-HTN	48275	3/57	3/66	ST CF-HTN Field Aviation; OB Transair
CF-IEE	1566	9/55	9/65	ST CF-IEE Austin Airways; OB Transair
CF-SAT	9757	9/55	9/65	ST CF-SAT P. Lazarenko; OB Transair
N68746	----	8/56	10/56	LF N68746 J. Routh; OB Transair
285ACF Canso				
CF-CRR	9767	5/69	4/75	ST CF-CRR Avalon Aviation; OB Midwest
CF-PIU	64092	5/69	5/73	ST CF-PIU St. Felicien; OB Midwest
PBY-5A Canso				
CF-GLX	560	5/69	4/75	ST CF-GLX Avalon Aviation; OB Midwest
CF-NJE	CV437	5/69	7/73	ST CF-NJE St. Felicien; OB Midwest
Avro York				
CF-HAS	MW290	9/56	12/62	WFU 31/12/62 ; c/n is RAF reg'n
CF-HFQ	MW291	9/56	2/58	W/O 02/58 at Fox; EX Arctic Wings a/c
CF-HIQ	MW294	9/56	1/57	W/O 08/01/57 at Rankin Inlet
DHC-2 Beaver				
CF-DIN	68	9/51	10/51	Leased
CF-FHQ	42	3/49	6/67	ST CF-FHQ P. Lazarenko
CF-JEH	1017	6/56	6/65	W/O 06/65 while landing
CF-JEI	1020	8/56	9/64	W/O 09/64 at Fort Severn
Beech D-18S				
CF-TAV	CA194	2/65	8/67	ST CF-TAV Northland Airways; OB Transair
Lockheed 12A				
CF-EPF	1269	11/53	11/59	ST CF-EPF Superior Airways
Lockheed 14-08				
CF-TCN	1939	5/51	7/56	ST CF-TCN Argosy Gas and Oil Ltd.; EX TCA

Central Northern Fleet

REG'N	C/N	IS	WFU	NOTES
Norseman Mk.III				
CF-BAU	6	5/47	9/48	ST CF-BQAU Arctic Wings; scrapped 4/51
Norseman Mk.IV				
CF-BDC	10	5/47	8/47	W/O 05/08/47 at Hudson by a cyclone
CF-BTC	29	1/48	8/58	ST CF-BTC Northland Fish
CF-CRC	25	9/46	6/54	ST CF-CRC P. Lazarenko; EX CPAL
CF-CRD	23	7/46	1/57	ST CF-CRD Northland Fish; EX CPAL
CF-CRF	37	7/46	3/61	ST CF-CRF Slate Falls Trading Co.; EX CPAL
CF-CRT	15	7/46	1/49	W/O 01/49 at Bissett; EX CPAL
Norseman Mk. V				
CF-BHW	N29-11	11/55	1/63	W/O 22/01/63 near Pickle Lake
CF-BHX	N29-12	11/55	6/59	W/O 12/06/59 at SAndy Bank Lake
CF-BSL	N29-28	5/52	1/58	W/O 31/01/58 at Chesterfield Inlet
CF-OBI	N29-?	7/55	1/59	W/O 18/01/59 at Fox Channel

FLEET LISTING
TRANSAIR

REG'N	C/N	IS	WFU	NOTES	
Norseman Mk. V (Continued)					
CF-OBL	N29-16	7/55	6/67	ST CF-OBL P. Lazarenko	
Norseman Mk.VI					
CF-CPN	255	7/55	10/57	W/O 20/10/57 sunk at Wabowden Lake	EX CPAL
CF-FQX	625	6/47	11/65	W/O 11/65 while landing	
CF-GBI	541	7/55	7/67	ST CF-GBI Hooker Air Service	
CF-GSS	561	6/47	12/52	W/O 03/12/52 at Sioux Lookout	
CF-GTP	424	6/47	6/62	ST CF-GTP Canadian Fish Producers	
CF-IRE	635	6/47	7/58	DBF 28/07/58 at Eskimo Point	
CF-OBE	480	7/55	9/65	ST CF-OBE P.Lazarenko	
CF-OBF	587	7/55	1/65	ST CF-OBF P.Lazarenko	
Norseman UC64A					
CF-ENB	324	5/53	7/67	ST CF-ENB Hooker Air Service	
Avro Anson V					
CF-ESA	431	8/46	12/54	W/O 10/12/54 through ice at God's River	
CF-GDV	3713	5/46	9/55	ST CF-GDV Pacific Western Airlines	
CF-GFP	M989	10/47	4/48	W/O 04/48 through ice at Favourable Lake	
CF-GHI	M980	10/47	4/50	W/O 04/04/50 at Bissett	
CF-GIU	MDF365	10/47	5/65	WFU and scrapped	
CF-GJV	RC1602	10/47	4/51	W/O 13/04/51 at Lynn Lake	
CF-GMV	MDF289	10/47	6/52	DBF 06/52	
CF-GMW	8282	2/47	2/58	WFU and scrapped	
CF-GSB	RC1504	3/60	4/60	LF CF-GSB Spartan Air Service	
CF-HQZ	12477	10/47	9/65	WFU and scrapped	
Dragon Rapide					
CF-AYE	6304	7/47	4/49	ST CF-AYE Queen Charlotte Airlines	
CF-BND	6375	6/47	5/49	W/O 09/07/49 when LT Queen Charlotte A/L	
Fairchild 82					
CF-AXE	40	5/47	11/51	ST CF-AXE Associated Air Taxi Ltd.	
CF-MAI	37	8/47	10/52	ST CF-MAI Associated Air Taxi Ltd.	
Fairchild M62A					
CF-CVD	FV733	6/47	1/52	ST CF-CVD Mr. Angus	
DC-3					
CF-ICU	19721	4/56	11/56	LF CF-ICU Arctic Wings Limited	
Republic RC3					
CF-FLU	1013	4/48	8/58	ST CF-FLU Holiday Enterprises	
CF-FOC	542	4/47	8/55	ST CF-FOC M.G. Holden	
CF-FUB	868	6/47	7/52	ST CF-FUB C.A. Robinson	
Waco YKC-S					
CF-AYS	4267	5/47	5/53	ST CF-AYS W. Dzogan	
Waco AQC-6					
CF-BDU	4640	6/49	7/58	W/O 06/07/58 at Sachigo Lake, Manitoba	
Aeronca 11AC					
CF-DUB	AC325	5/50	5/50	LF CF-DUB F. Gartner May 1950	
Stinson 108-2					
CF-EDJ	2929	7/47	8/56	ST CF-EDJ C.J Jeffs	
CF-ELS	683	7/47	3/56	ST CF-ELS Joe Alis	
CF-EXO	2659	7/47	11/56	ST CF-EXO A.E. Margetts	
Cessna 195A					
CF-GRT	7400	4/50	8/52	ST CF-GRT Argosy Oil & Gas Ltd.	
Cessna 170A					
CF-GRW	19227	6/49	6/54	ST CF-GRW Ivan Casselman	
Cessna 180					
CF-HPW	31324	11/54	5/61	ST CF-HPW Northern Canadian Evangelical	
CF-IEF	31881	2/55	6/61	ST CF-IEF Selkirk Airways	
CF-IFE	-----	2/55	5/61	ST CF-IFE Lac Seul Airways	
CF-IRQ	30550	1/56	6/61	ST CF-IRQ North Coast Air	
CF-JFW	32574	7/57	8/57	LF CF-JFW Georgian Bay Airways	
Bellanca Air Cruiser					
CF-BKV	722	5/47	10/49	W/O 06/49 at Smoky Lake, Manitoba	
CF-BTW	721	5/47	7/67	ST CF-BTW Hooker Air Services	

NORDAIR

Nordair F227, C-GNDH

HEADQUARTERS:
1320, boulevard Graham,
Ville Mont-Royal, Quebec, H3P 3C8

MAJOR BASES:
Montreal (Dorval);
Toronto International (Pearson) Airport.

FINAL FLEET:
10 - Boeing 737-200s, plus 1 leased;
5 - Fairchild F227s;
2 - Lockheed Electras
Jan. 1987.

COLOURS:
Three cheat lines separate the white upper fuselage from the silver lower fuselage. The wide top cheat line is light blue and extends from just above the windows to just above the bottom of the doors. A narrow dark blue cheat line below is separated from the light blue by a narrower white cheat line. The tail is white with a large NORDAIR

symbol in light and dark blue. NORDAIR titles are dark blue on the upper forward fuselage. A highly distinctive yellow patch covers the forward 20% of the upper fuselage and angles towards the nose, covering the cockpit and merging with the light blue cheat line. The dark blue fleet number is on the top of the tail and the dark blue registration appears on the lower rear fuselage. A Canadian flag is above the cheat line just forward of the rear door.

ROUTES:
Winnipeg – Dryden – Thunder Bay – Sault Ste Marie – Toronto – Windsor – Ottawa – Montreal (Dorval) – Quebec City – Val d'Or – La Grande – Chibougamau – Poste-de-la-Baleine (Kuujjuarapik) – Arctic Bay (Nanisivik) – Fort Chimo (Kuujjuaq) – Frobisher Bay – Resolute.
USA: Toronto – Pittsburg; Montreal (Mirabel) – Fort Lauderdale.

91

HISTORY:

On 26 May 1947 Mr. Francois 'Frank' Ross, a general contractor from Montreal, incorporated *Boreal Airways Limited*. Its first aircraft was a single motor Norseman V, equipped with skis in winter and pontoons in summer. *Boreal's* clientele was made up of mining company workers, outfitters, hunters, fishermen, trappers, prospectors and surveyors who worked in the general area of St. Felicien. In 1949, *Boreal Airways* acquired its second aircraft, a Fairchild Husky (CF-EIO). That same year a young Montreal lawyer, Roland G. Lefrancois, joined the company and in the 1980s was to become Chairman of the Board of Nordair.

The first major expansion project in *Boreal's* history occurred in 1953. The two principal shareholders in *Maritime Central Airways Ltd.*, Fred T. Briggs and Carl F. Burke, joined with the owners of *Boreal* to form *Boreal Air Services. Maritime Central* remained a separate company. The goal of this venture was the acquisition, during the summer of that year, of *Mont-Laurier Aviation,* an airline company incorporated in 1946 and established in Roberval since 1947. As well as adding a Canso and several Norsemen and Cessnas to its fleet, *Boreal* also was able to obtain the rights to the regular service between Roberval and Fort Chimo which *Mont-Laurier* had operated since 1952. The new company opened several other routes to the far north of Quebec City, notably at Nitchequon, in the heart of New Quebec.

By this time *Boreal Airways* had taken on the look of an airline, with more than twenty employees and a regular flight to Fort Chimo every Tuesday (in summer a Canso and in winter a Norseman equipped with skis). The company formally established its headquarters at Roberval and, in 1954, received permission to provide service between Bagotville and Chibougamau, with a stop at St. Methot, where it constructed a landing strip. It was at this time that *Boreal* acquired its first DC-3 and, from 1953 to 1957, it participated in the establishment of the radar networks of the Mid-Canada Line (crossing the country at the latitude of Schefferville and Poste-de-la-Baleine in Quebec) and the Distant Early Warning (DEW) Line, north of the Arctic Circle.

On 27 November 1956, *Boreal* adopted its new corporate identity: 'Nordair,' thus consecrating its dedication to the North. At the same time company headquarters were shifted to Montreal and services were initiated to such cities as Montreal, La Tuque, Roberval and Chibougamau.

In January 1957, soon after the complete integration of *Mont-Laurier Aviation,* Nordair was authorized to extend its Montreal – Fort Chimo route to Frobisher Bay on Baffin Island and acquired larger cargo aircraft, including the four-engine DC-4 which was assigned to this service. This was the first step in the expansion of Nordair's network outside of Quebec.

Nordair's initial colour scheme was a white upper fuselage with the lower fuselage and wings natural metal. A thin red cheat line ran the length of the fuselage above the windows with a wide blue cheat line running the length of the fuselage. The blue cheat line began with a circular symbol NORDAIR CANADA just behind the cockpit. A large white 'N' was displayed on the all blue tail. The registration, in white, appeared in the rear portion of the blue cheat line, and NORDAIR was in black on the upper forward fuselage. By 1959, the Nordair fleet was made up of one Curtiss C-46, one DC-4, three DC-3s and a few smaller aircraft.

The year 1960 was an important one in the expansion of Nordair. In April, the company acquired the heavy transport section of *Wheeler Airlines* of Montreal and Saint-Jovite, which also controlled Canadian Aircraft Renters Ltd. of Toronto. To the regular Montreal to Chibougamau, Fort Chimo, Frobisher Bay and Cape Dyer routes that Nordair already operated were added *Wheeler's* Montreal to Val d'Or and Poste-de-la-Beleine routes. In addition, Nordair obtained the transport and supply contract for all DEW Line bases from Alaska to Greenland. Nordair's remaining light aircraft were sold to a new company, *Wheeler Airlines (1960)* which at that time operated light and medium sized aircraft. The acquisition of *Wheeler* brought three DC-4s under Nordair's control. Four Curtiss C-46s were also acquired in the deal and Nordair now was a heavy transport regional airline operating mainly vertical airlifts and flights from Montreal to the north.

To expand its routes, Nordair started the 'Seaway' route (Montreal – Kingston – Oshawa – Hamilton – London – Sarnia – Windsor) in 1961, using DC-3 aircraft. Early in 1962, two Handley Page Heralds were purchased to operate on this route. This thirty-six passenger, pressurized aircraft did not improve the patronage, and late in 1962 the route was discontinued. One Herald was sold to *Eastern Provincial*, the other to *Maritime Central*.

Nordair was excluded from the takeover of *Maritime Central* by *Eastern Provincial* in 1963 and was designated by the Federal Government as one of the five regional carriers at that time.

By the summer of 1962, Nordair had inaugurated its commercial service to Resolute Bay on Cornwallis Island, the most northerly air route on the planet at the time.

Nordair entered the charter business in 1963 with trips to such exotic destinations as Africa, the Middle East and Europe. A DC-6 was used that year and a DC-7 purchased in 1964. Both of these aircraft were sold in

1964 when Nordair bought four L-1049H Super Constellations. This four piston engine aircraft could accommodate a maximum of one hundred and nine passengers and the model that Nordair operated could be converted from all-cargo to all-passenger and back very easily. Nordair leased an L-1049 from Montreal Air Services while awaiting delivery of their four Super Constellations from *National Airlines*. These planes served on scheduled and charter work until early in 1969. They were sold to Canairelief, a Canadian charity foundation, and were used to fly food into Biafra. Two of the planes were destroyed on flights into Biafra.

Between 1960 and 1970, the main aircraft used for cargo and passenger service on the Nordair routes were the DC-3, DC-4, C-46 and L-1049. All but one DC-4 were phased out in 1970, with the last one remaining until 1973. The C-46 remained in service until 1974 and the last DC-3 saw service until 1976.

In April 1969, *Nordair Arctic Ltd.* was formed to operate short haul routes from Frobisher Bay as a subsidiary of Nordair. Charters also carried government workers, hunters, students, mining equipment and tourists to Pangnurtung Eskimo settle- ment and Cape Dorset. A Skyvan and a Twin Otter were purchased for this service and painted in the Nordair's new colour scheme but with NORDAIR ARCTIC titles. Two additional Twin Otters were bought for this service in 1974. Two Cansos, a Beaver and a Turbo Mallard also saw service with *Nordair Arctic*. Nordair sold its three Twin Otters to *Survair* in January 1976, and closed down *Nordair Arctic*. The Turbo Mallard and Skyvan were used for charters out of Montreal and sold a few years later when Nordair again got out of the small aircraft business. *Survair* ultimately sold the Twin Otters and the routes to *Bradley Air Service* which operates the old *Nordair Arctic* today under the name *First Air*.

Nordair was the first regional airline into the jet age when it leased four Convair 990s from Modern Air Transport in February 1968. Only two of these aircraft were actually flown by Nordair and both were painted in Nordair colours but retained their American registrations, as the type was not certified in Canada. The two aircraft were leased for eight months, flying on charters between Montreal and Europe.

With the phase-out of the Super Constellations, Nordair entered the jet age permanently in November 1968, when it purchased its first Boeing 737. This aircraft was delivered in Nordair's new paint scheme: an white upper fuselage and a grey lower fuselage, separated by a wide blue cheat line running through the windows . The tail was all blue with a large 'N.' The name NORDAIR was in black on the upper fuselage with the registration appearing on the lower rear fuselage in black.

A second Boeing 737 was purchased in early 1969, but was immediately leased to *Eastern Provincial Airways* and painted in full EPA colours. Three Boeing 737s were leased from *United Airlines,* two operating with Nordair under Canadian registration, the third 737 with *Eastern Provincial* retained its American registration. Nordair and *Eastern Provincial* were planning to merge their jet operations, but the Canadian Government blocked this move. The Nordair 737 was returned from EPA in 1970 and the 737s leased from *United Airlines* were returned when an additional Boeing 737 was delivered that same year. In 1970, Nordair had three Boeing 737s and added one per year in 1971, 1973, and 1975 to give it a fleet of six.

The Canadian Government established its regional airline policy in 1969 and designated Nordair as the carrier for western Quebec, eastern and southern Ontario, and the adjacent Arctic points. At that time, Nordair's northern operations were very strong but it did not have good routes in the south. Thus merger talks with *Quebecair* and EPA continued over the next decade.

In 1971, Nordair decided to reopen the 'Seaway' route (Montreal to Ottawa, Hamilton, Windsor and later Pittsburgh). Three Fairchild FH-227s were bought in 1971-72 for use on this route and for shorter flights in the north. This twin-engine, Rolls-Royce Dart turboprop with the high wing could carry fifty-two passengers, twelve more than the smaller F-27s operated by *Quebecair*. Two additional FH-227s were purchased from the French operator *Touraine Air Transport* in 1982.

Icebergs have always constituted one of the worst menaces to navigation in the world and especially in Canadian waters. One does not have to ponder long to recall the drama of the Titanic incident. The 'unsinkable' ship of the fledgling twentieth century steamed full speed into an iceberg on that fateful night in 1912 with the loss of fifteen hundred lives. The ice banks that form in winter in Canadian sea lanes and the icebergs that are born during the summer in the Arctic Ocean cause considerable problems for navigation on the sea, often threatening supply lanes to towns in the far north during the short sea shipping period. As well as assuring air transport to these areas, Nordair has played a role in sea transportation since 1972, working with Environment Canada and operating Ice Patrol aircraft which relay information to assist navigation in Canadian waters.

Aerial Ice Patrol was first used in 1927, when airplanes were flown to observe ice formations in the waters of Hudson Bay and Hudson Strait. At the time, it was the job of the Royal Canadian Air Force to carry out these reconnaissance flights, an operation the RCAF shared with the United States Navy during refuelling operations at sea in 1951.

In 1954, with the increase of maritime navigation predicated for the coming years (especially with the anticipated opening of the St. Lawrence Seaway), an integrated ice reconnaissance program was inaugurated, coming under the aegis of the Department of Transport. As the program developed, civilian observers became involved, including meteorologists and specialists in ice formation, flying in old Lancaster bombers of the RCAF.

The Ice Patrol service began using commercial aircraft in 1957. Nordair first operated a Beech 18 for the Ice Patrol. An Aero Commander 560 and a Cessna 310, along with larger aircraft such as the DC-3, C-46 and DC-4.were also used on Ice Patrol

In 1967, Nordair lost the Ice Patrol contract to *Kenting Aviation. Kenting* had two DC-4 aircraft fitted with F-86 Sabre canopies on the top of the fuselage for better viewing, and kept the contract until 1973. However, in 1972, Nordair purchased two Lockheed Electras from *Northwest Orient* and made $5 million worth of modification to each. These modifications extended the aircrafts' range and fitted them with special electronic equipment. A plexiglass observation dome was installed above the cockpit and a special radar dome added below. Some of the electronics added to the planes' normal instrumentation were high resolution radar, laser profilometers, auxiliary radar, thermal mappers, special photographic equipment, an onboard computer as well as sophisticated communication devices.

Information gleaned from these patrolling aircraft can be transmitted directly to ships in the area, but most of the time information is passed along immediately to the Atmospheric Environment Service in Ottawa where special maps are prepared daily. This information is continually relayed to all shipping companies and to Transport Canada icebreakers and helicopters. (Ice patrol story condensed from Nordair's publication 'Airmag.')

Since 1973 Nordair (and now Canadian), has operated these two special Electras on the Ice Patrols, logging more than 500,000 nautical miles per year. In winter, they are based at either Gander, Newfoundland or Summerside, P.E.I. From these bases they regularly patrol the Labrador coast, the Gulf of St. Lawrence and the Seaway, as well as the Great Lakes all the way west to Thunder Bay. In summer, the aircraft patrol the Arctic Ocean from Greenland to Alaska, James Bay, Hudson Bay, ranging from Frobisher Bay to Resolute and Inuvik. Flights usually last about ten hours, with six specially-trained observers manning the observation stations in two-hour shifts.

The two Electras are the same basic airframes as the Lockheed Auroras purchased by the Canadian Forces to replace the Canadair Argus aircraft, for fifty million dollars each . On 31 March 1977, Electra C-FNAY was parked at Canadian Forces Base Summerside. A Canadian Forces Argus aircraft (10737), returning from pa-

trol, crashed while landing on three engines in poor weather and struck the Electra. Three members of the 415 Squadron Argus crew were killed and both the Argus and Electra were written off. The nose cone of the Electra was saved and used as part of Electra C-GNDZ which now serves as the second Ice Patrol aircraft.

A third Electra was bought from *Air New Zealand* in September 1972 for cargo and passenger work, to be used until another Boeing 737 could be added. It was sold in 1977.

Nordair, like the other regional airlines, used its Boeing 737 aircraft for charter operations to warmer destinations in the southernUnited States and the Caribbean. To increase the airline's capacity on these charters and to obtain longer range charters, Nordair purchased a DC-8-61 from *Trans International Airlines* in 1974. This aircraft operated charters from Toronto to Cuba and Mirabel to London and Paris, and was used for the Hadj flights for several years. It was sold, finally, in 1978 and replaced by two DC-8-52 aircraft purchased from *Aviaco* of Spain. These aircraft could carry one hundred and seventy-six passengers in high density seating, versus two hundred and fifty-nine for the stretch-eight. These two aircraft were operated for only two years before being sold to *Air Fleets International.* One was delivered to this company in April of 1980 but was repossessed the following month. The two planes then sat, without titles, at Dorval airport until finally sold to Onyx in the United States, in October 1983.

Nordair's Boeing 737s allowed expansion of their northern service, adding flights from Montreal to Quebec City to Fort Chimo in 1977. No passengers could be carried on the Montreal to Quebec City portion.

Nordair continued to struggle as an airline because of the lack of strong southern routes and the merger talks became loud in 1977, *Quebecair* and *Great Lakes Airlines* being the primary suitors. Late in 1977, James Tooley, then Chairman of Nordair, put the company up for sale. *Air Canada* made an offer of $11.50 per share, $4.50 over market quotation, and purchased the airline. The final approval of the takeover occurred on 28 July 1978. Originally Air Canada planned to merge the two airlines, with Nordair operating most of the charter business for the national airline. A threatened *Air Canada* pilots' strike, plus strong opposition from the Conservative Party, persuaded the Liberal Trudeau government to keep Nordair as a separate operation, with the intent of eventually divesting itself of interest in Nordair.

One of the conditions when *Pacific Western Airlines* took over Transair in 1978, was that *Pacific Western*

Opposite: Nordair Arctic Skyvan, CF-NAS.
Photo courtesy of Nordair

would discontinue service east of Winnipeg. The Toronto to Sault Ste. Marie, Thunder Bay, Dryden to Winnipeg route was awarded to Nordair. At the same time, Nordair was allowed Montreal to Ottawa and Toronto and Montreal to Toronto direct flights. Nordair now had the southern routes it desparately needed to become a truly regional airline. Four Boeing 737s were bought and two were leased in 1979-1980, with Nordair starting the Toronto to Winnipeg route on 1 February 1979.

Takeovers again became the main topic in 1980 with the Quebec Government buying 11% of the shares of Nordair and later selling them to the Regionair group. *Air Ontario* continued to make offers for Nordair. With *Quebecair* in financial difficulty and Nordair showing strong profits because of the new routes, it was understandable that Nordair continued as the focal point of takeovers in the Canadian airline industry.

Nordair showed a profit of $2.7 million in 1980, $2.5 million in 1981 and a loss of $2.4 million in 1982. The loss in 1982 was due to a strike from 25 July 1982 to 24 January 1983, which shut down the Toronto to Winnipeg flights and all charter operations. With the strike settled, net profit for the first half of 1983 was $2.4 million. The Ice Patrol contract was extended to March 1987 at this time.

Nordair operated extensive charter operations from Winnipeg, Toronto, London, Windsor, Hamilton, Montreal, Ottawa and Halifax to Ft. Lauderdale, St. Petersburg, Orlando and other southern destinations. Montreal to Ft. Lauderdale became a scheduled route late in 1984 and Montreal to Orlando was scheduled twice weekly in 1985. Nordair also operated extensive trans-Canada flights (mainly in summer), between the above eastern cities and Calgary, Edmonton and Vancouver. Toronto to Charlottetown and St. John's charters were started in 1984, giving the company national exposure. Nordair never had a major accident with its jet aircraft, except for a nose wheel which collapsed during a landing at Sault Ste. Marie, in January 1982.

In the north, *Bradley Air Services* (*First Air*) bought *Survair* in May 1978, thus taking over the former *Nordair Arctic* services in the Frobisher Bay and Hall Beach areas. *Air Inuit* provided interline services with Nordair at Fort Chimo and provided service to the Ungava Bay

Nordair DHC-6 Twin Otter, CF-NAN
Photo courtesy of DeHavilland Canada.

region. *Torontair* and *NorOntair* interlined with Nordair on their Toronto to Winnipeg routes, providing a large feeder network to the airline.

Nordair has operated the DEW Line lateral resupply contract for the United States Air Force since 1960. Two FH-227s (C-FNAI and C-FNAK) operate from Hall Beach in the northern east and from Cape Parry in the northern west area of the DEW Line, in a combined passenger/cargo mode. The planes travel as far east as Cape Dyer on Baffin Island to Barter Island, Alaska in the west.

Late in 1983, Nordair began operating a *Sabena* 737 between Montreal and Detroit as an extension of *Sabena's* Brussels service to Montreal. This arrangement was renewed for the winters of 1984 to 1987. When not operating on this route, the aircraft was integrated into the Nordair service, operating under full *Sabena* colours with small 'Operated by Nordair' titles. The company also operated a weekly Montreal to Miami flight, using Nordair aircraft, on behalf of *El Al* in the mid-1980s.

In December 1983, Boeing 737 C-GNDU was rolled out in the new yellow/light blue/dark blue colour scheme, with the new company logo (a stylized compass) on the tail. The FH-227s and Electras were painted in mid-1984. Nordair leased a *Dan Air* Boeing 737 late in 1984 and replaced it with a 737 leased from *Britannia* in May 1985.

The FH-227s, when not at work on the DEW Line, were used in the south on *Rapidair* flights between Montreal, Ottawa, Toronto and Pittsburgh and between Montreal and Chibougamau in 1984. In 1985 Nordair used a Boeing 737 for service to Hamilton, but by September of that year all operation to Hamilton had ceased. Late in 1985, a plan was developed with *Torontair* to form a new company called 'Commutair' using two FH-227s and *Torontair's* Beech 99s. However, because of the potential takeover by CP Air, this plan was put on hold. Most of the *Rapidair* services were deleted in 1985 and one FH-227 was leased to *Torontair* at the beginning of 1986. Service between Montreal and Chibougamau and Dolbeau were suspended at this time.

In July 1985, Ottawa to Sudbury, Thunder Bay and Winnipeg service was started. Service between Toronto and Windsor was reintroduced in 1985. Nordair applied to consolidate its licences so that service between any two points in their system would be possible. This would allow passengers to be carried on the Montreal to Quebec City route. The summer saw Toronto to Los Angeles charters (with a fuel stop in Kansas City) operated. An extensive winter charter program was operated again during 1985, with Toronto to Grand Cayman charters and charters from Winnipeg, Toronto and Montreal to Miami, Fort Lauderdale, Orlando, St. Petersburg, West Palm Beach, Sarasota and Daytona Beach in Florida and Santiago (Cuba), Port au Prince, Cancun, Nassau, Free-

port as well as Grand Cayman in the Caribbean. Nordair again operated Montreal to Detroit flights on behalf of *Sabena* using a *Sabena* Boeing 737, but this year under Canadian registration. This arrangement was used for both the 1985-86 and 1986-87 winters.

Air Canada finally sold Nordair to Innocan Inc. and Participation Nordair (an employee organization), in the summer of 1984. Nordair had made a profit in thirty-seven of its thirty-nine years ($4 million in 1983 and $2.5 million in 1984). However, late 1985 saw the takeover signs out again. *Quebecair* offered to purchase 100% of Nordair common stock. The Quebec government already owned 22% of Nordair and planned to buy out the remaining shares, combine the money-making Nordair with the money-losing *Quebecair*, then privatize the merged companies. Nordair President, Jean Douville, was against this takeover. *CP Air* then entered the picture, offering to buy out Innocan and the employees' shares. This offer was strongly supported by the employees but the Quebec government did not want to lose control of a Quebec-based airline to British Columbia.

In November 1985, *CP Air* was successful in purchasing the Innocan Inc. and employees' shares in Nordair (44% of common stock) for $17 million ($16.25 per share plus a share purchase warrant entitling the investors to buy three common shares of Canadian Pacific at $7.00 each, with the warrants being exercised if the airline were to go public with an equity issue). The Quebec government still refused to sell their shares to *CP Air* and although *CP Air* now controlled the bulk (60%) of the common shares, Nordair could not be merged completely into *CP Air*. However, beginning in January 1986, Nordair flights appeared in all *CP Air* schedules and their flights were planned to coincide with *CP Air* flights, effectively integrating the two airlines. Nordair joined the CP 'frequent flyer' program and also contracted to complete 'D' checks on the EPA Boeing 737s in the *CP Air* fleet.

Torontair leased an FH-227 (C-GNDI), for use on its Toronto to Trenton and Kingston route, as the start of the 'Commutair' plan. The aircraft was leased from January to June 1986 and returned when *Torontair* folded in June 1986. The 'Commutair' plan was jeopardized by the formation of *Nordair Metro* in December 1985. This was a company formed by *Nordair* (35%), *Conifair* (35%), *Avitair* (20%), plus minor investors to operate a commuter airline in Quebec. *Nordair Metro* would feed Nordair and *CP Air* routes, using Convair 580 aircraft. Cities served by the new company included Quebec City, Montreal, Ottawa/Gatineau, Bagotville, Rouyn, Baie Comeau, Mont Joli/Rimouski, Gaspe, Val d'Or, Iles des Madeleine and later Wabush and Sept Illes. Start up date was March 31, 1986 for the Montreal to Quebec City route, April for Montreal to Saguenay/Bagotville and May for Quebec City to Rimouski, using three ex-*Avensa* Convair 580s purchased via *US Air.*

In July 1986, *Nordair Metro* bought out *Quebecair* at the purchase price of $21 million, plus an agreement that *Nordair Metro* would assume *Quebecair's* long-term debt of $64 million. This price was offset by the sale of the four Boeing 737s for $50 million. The aircraft sale was originally planned to be to *Canadian Pacific*, but in fact only two 737s went to CPA, a third being sold in Norway while the fourth remained with the revamped *Quebecair* for another year.

Nationair bought the two DC-8-63s for $10 million, while the company's consulting division went to Lavalin Inc. (Montreal), which was owned by *Nordair Metro*. The maintenance of the Quebec government's CL-215 fleet went to *Conifair* in St. Jean. *Quebecair* would continue as a separate entity, with its two Convair 580s plus the three operated on behalf of S.E.B.J. but would immediately drop the Toronto – Montreal flights. *Quebecair's* stock was finally in friendly hands and included the 22% of Nordair stock owned by the Quebec government. This now paved the way for *Canadian Pacific* to complete its takeover of Nordair. In the fall of 1986, Nordair switched from the *Air Canada* reservation system to the *Canadian Pacific* system.

In the fall of 1987, Nordair aircraft were repainted, in the new *Canadian Pacific* colours, at the rate of one per week. Finally, on 24 January 1987, the last Nordair flight took off using the ND designator and from January 25, 1987 on, Nordair ceased to exist as a separate entity,

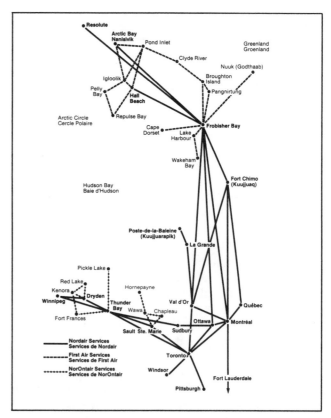

Route map for Nordair as shown in 1985 timetable.

having been completely merged into *Canadian Pacific Airlines.*

Nordair Metro would remain for another year and its history can be seen under *Inter-Canadian.*

FLEET LISTING

NORDAIR

REG'N	C/N	F/N	IS	WFU	NOTES	MODEL
BOEING 737-200						
C-FNAB*	19847	701	11/68	1/87	To C-FNAB CPA	242C
C-FNAH*	19848	702	10/69	1/87	To C-FNAH CPAL; LT C-FNAH EPA 4-10/69 full EPA /c/s	242C
CF-NAI	19945	----	6/69	5/70	LF N9064U United Airline	222
CF-NAP	19946	----	6/69	5/70	LF N9065U United Airlines	222
C-FNAP*	20496	704	5/71	1/87	To C-FNAP CPA	242C
C-FNAQ*	20455	703	5/70	1/87	To C-FNAQ CPA; LT EI-BOC WIEN 5/83-11/83	242C
C-FNAW*	20521	751	3/73	4/83	ST EI-BNS Air Tara; EX 9M-AQC Singapore; now C-GXPW	212
C-GNDC	21728	761	6/79	1/87	To C-GNDC CPA	242C
C-GNDD	21112	DD	8/79	3/82	ST EI-BDY Aer Lingus; EX C-GEPB EPA	2E1
C-GNDG	22054	799	11/85	4/86	LF G-BJXL GATX (see listing for G-BJXL)	2T4
C-GNDG	21719	NDG	1/79	6/79	LF OO-TEK TEA; TO C-GQBT Quebecair	209
C-GNDL	21186	705	11/75	1/87	To C-GNDL CPA; ST N131AW American West 11/83 /to 10/85	242
C-GNDM	22074	706	11/79	1/87	To C-GNDM CPA	242
C-GNDR	22075	707	1/80	1/87	To C-GNDR CPA; named 'TERRY FOX'	242
C-GNDS	21518	771	10/80	1/87	To C-GNDS CPA; EX B-2611 Far Eastern Air Transport	2Q8
C-GNDU	22877	762	6/82	1/87	To C-GNDU CPA	242C
C-GNDW	21694	----	5/85	4/86	LF G-BFVB Britannia	204
C-GNDX	20911	798	10/85	4/87	OF Sabena winters 85/86 & 86/87 full Sabena c/s	209
OO-SDE	20911	798	10/83	4/85	OF Sabena winters 83/84 & 84/85 full Sabena c/'s'	209
G-BJXL	22054	799	10/84	4/85	LF G-BJXL GATX (in Dan Air c/s); 10/85 C-GNDG	2T4

FLEET LISTING
NORDAIR

REG'N	C/N	F/N	IS	WFU	NOTES	MODEL
BOEING 737-200 (Continued)						
N72717	20345	----	1/79	ι/79	LF N72717 Southwest (in Southwest c/s)	2H4
N9057U	19938	----	5/69	10/69	LF N9057U United Airlines; shared with EPA	222
C-GQBH	22516	734	8/86	1/87	To C-GQBH CPA (full CPAL c/s 12/86)	296
					OB Nordair 9-12/86 in Quebecair c/s, Nordair titles	
FAIRCHILD HILLER FH-227						
C-FNAI *	505	505	8/71	1/86	WFU 6/86; LT C-FNAI Toronto Airways 1/86-6/86	227E
C-FNAJ *	508	508	4/72	1/87	WFU 1/87 \C-FNAI ST SE-KBP 2/88	227E
C-FNAK *	515	519	11/72	1/87	WFU 1/87; ST SE-KBR Malmo Aviation 2/88	227E
C-GNDH	529	529	11/82	3/87	WFU 3/87; EX F-GDAH Touraine Air Transport	227B
C-GNDI	530	530	11/82	3/87	WFU 3/87; EX F-GLCP Touraine Air Transport	227B
LOCKHEED L188 ELECTRA						
C-FNAX	2010	----	9/72	11/77	ST N178RV Reeve Aleutian; now C-GNWC NWT AIR	
C-FNAY *	1113	113	3/72	1/87	To C-FNAY CPA; EX N130US Northwest; ICE PATROL a/c	
CF-NAZ	1132	----	5/72	3/77	W/O 31/03/77 Summerside by Argus 10737; ICE PATROL a/c	
C-GNDZ	1111	111	1/78	1/87	To C-GNDZ CPA; used nose of CF-NAX; ICE PATROL a/c	
DC-8-52						
C-GNDE	45618		11/78	4/80	ST N4489M Onyx 10/83	892
C-GNDF	45619		1/79	4/80	ST N893AF Onyx 10/83	893
DC-8-61CF						
C-GNDA	45902		11/74	12/78	ST N810EV Evergreen International	
Convair 990A						
N5607	16		2/68	NTU	LF N5607 Modern Air Transport but NTU	
N5609	21		2/68	10/68	LF N5609 Modern Air Transport; full Nordair c/s	
N5615	27		2/68	10/68	LF N5615 Modern Air Transport; full Nordair c/s	
N5617	29		2/68	NTU	LF N5617 Modern Air Transport but NTU	
Short Skyvan						
C-FNAS *	1872		10/69	2/78	ST D2-EOH Diamond Trading Co.	
Turbo Mallard						
CF-UOT	J-34		5/72	9/76	ST C-FUOT Business Flights; then Canadair	
Dart Herald						
CF-NAC	159	AC	2/62	11/62	ST CF-NAC Eastern Provincial	
CF-NAF	160	AF	3/62	11/62	ST CF-NAF Maritime Central	
DC-7C						
CF-NAI	45129		4/64	12/64	ST CF-NAI Pacific Western Airlines	
DC-6A						
CF-NAB	44577		10/63	12/64	ST N620NA Aaxico	
DHC-6						
CF-NAN	242		5/69	1/76	ST C-FNAN Survair; OB Nordair Arctic	
C-GNDN	427		8/74	1/76	ST C-GNDN Survair; OB Nordair Arctic	
C-GNDO	430		10/74	1/76	ST C-GNDO Survair; OB Nordair Arctic	
DC-4						
CF-IQM	36088	IQM	4/60	11/73	ST CF-IQM Pelly Bay Cooperative	
CF-JIR	10362	JIR	4/60	3/69	LT CF-JIR EPA 1965; EX Wheeler; BU	
CF-MCI	27261	MCI	10/72	10/73	EX CF-MCI Eastern Provincial; BU	
CF-NAA	10457	NAA	3/59	7/68	ST CF-NAA Arabian Marine; EX CF-MCA	
CF-NAB	10478	NAB	3/60	2/63	ST PP-BIT Paraense; EX CF-MCB	
CF-NAG	10330	NAG	4/60	12/69	LT CF-TAO Transair 61-68; EX CF-WAL; BU	
DC-3						
CF-AOH	13860		5/73	9/74	ST CF-AOH Reindeer Air Service	
CF-CSC	6183		3/75	11/75	DBF 15/11/75 La Grande, Quebec	
CF-GKZ	9395		2/59	9/74	ST CF-GKZ Pem Air	
CF-HGD	13041		5/62	2/68	ST N341W Concare Aircraft Leasing	
CF-HTH	27000		6/61	2/73	W/O 06/02/73 Dorval when hit by a truck	
CF-IHH	26058		8/55	5/68	ST CF-IHH Northland; OB Mount Laurier	
CF-IQD	20427		8/60	1/69	ST N625E Continental Avn. Co.\55-61	
CF-IQF	6101		7/61	1/62	W/O 15/01/62 Arctic Bay, NWT	
CF-IQK	25944		1/56	4/68	ST N349W Concare; OB Mount Laurier 55-61	
CF-IQR	11876		6/61	2/76	ST CF-IQR Bradley Air Service	
CF-MCC	13399		6/61	11/73	ST N14636 Air New England	
CF-NAG	12458		10/70	12/70	ST CF-NAG Northern Wings	

FLEET LISTING
NORDAIR

REG'N	C/N	F/N	IS	WFU	NOTES
DC-3 (Continued)					
CF-NAH	10052		7/62	11/64	ST OB-R-774 Cia Aera Trans America Peru
CF-NAO	12332		2/72	6/74	ST CF-NAO Pem Air
CF-NAR	13154		5/71	7/76	ST CF-NAR Survair
Curtiss C-46					
CF-CZL	22494		3/63	5/74	EX CF-CZL Maritime Central; BU Montreal
CF-CZM	22453		5/67	5/74	ST N802FA Fairbanks Air; Now C-GIXZ
CF-CZN	22445		5/67	9/68	ST N94549 Islands of the Bahamas
CF-FBJ	2941		6/60	6/66	W/O 20/06/66 Lake Peribonca, Quebec
CF-HEI	22419		4/60	8/61	W/O 09/08/61 Scapa Lake, NWT
CF-HTJ	22475		2/56	3/66	ST N7560U Channel Airlift; EX Mount Laurier
CF-IHU	22476		4/62	2/64	ST HI-80 Aerovias Quisqueyanas
CF-IHV	22551		4/60	12/72	W/O 20/12/72 Lake Randall, Quebec
CF-ILJ	22417		4/60	5/66	ST N300046 Channel Airlift; EX Wheeler
CF-NAD	30200		3/62	5/67	W/O 15/05/67 Cape Dyer, Baffin Island
CF-NAE	27063		8/61	6/71	DBF 05/06/71 Hall Beach, NWT in hangar fire
CF-NAO	22600		9/66	2/70	ST N18974C Rich International; then CF-NAU
CF-NAU	22600		6/72	5/74	ST N801FA Fairbanks Air
CF-ZQX	22595		6/72	5/74	ST N800FA Fairbanks Air
N9891F	30279		NTU	NTU	NTU; bought for spares in 4/68
L-1049H					
CF-NAJ	4828		12/64	1/69	ST CF-NAJ Canairelief; W/O 03/08/69 Biafra
CF-NAK	4829		12/64	1/69	ST CF-NAK Canairelief; W/O 17/12/69 Biafra
CF-NAL	4831		12/64	1/69	ST CF-NAL Canairelief
CF-NAM	4832		12/64	1/69	ST CF-NAM Canairelief
CF-WWH	4820		8/64	12/64	LF CF-WWH Montreal Air Service
Cessna 310C					
CF-FTB	35908		6/63	9/65	Sold; Ice Patrol Aircraft
CF-CFB	39063		6/63	10/65	Sold; Ice Patrol Aircraft
Aero Commander 560					
CF-CFB	976-3		12/65	2/68	Sold; Ice Patrol Aircraft
Beech C18S					
CF-MCE	35892		4/58	7/59	ST CF-MCE Mordain Ltd.; Ice Patrol Aircraft
PBY-5A Canso					
CF-DIL	427		6/58	8/73	ST CF-DIL Wheeler; OB Mount Laurier 1958-62
CF-FKV	332		4/57	9/63	ST CF-FKV Wheeler; OB Mount Laurier 1957-62
CF-FVE	11052		3/59	9/63	ST CF-FVE Wheeler; EX Maritime Central
CF-NJE	134		6/71	8/73	ST CF-NJE Ste. Felician; Nordair Arctic a/c
Republic RC3					
CF-DLU	746		7/57	2/59	Sold; Ice Patrol Aircraft
Norseman V					
CF-GSJ	N2946		4/57	4/60	ST CF-GSJ Wheeler
CF-GOP	N2948		1/55	10/59	Sold; OB Boreal 1955-1959
Norseman UC64					
CF-HAU	398		8/53	9/63	ST CF-HAU Wheeler; OB Boreal 1953-1957
CF-ILH	326		1/55	10/59	Sold; OB Boreal 1955-1959
DHC-2 Beaver					
CF-GYN	134		3/71	7/73	ST CF-GYN Nipawin Air; Nordair Arctic a/c
CF-DJI	27		6/49	8/62	ST CF-DJI Wheeler; OB Boreal
CF-GCX	196		4/52	4/60	ST CF-GCX Wheeler; OB Boreal
CF-HGU	577		3/53	4/60	ST CF-HGU Wheeler; OB Boreal
Cessna 180					
CF-HCL	30358		6/53	4/60	ST CF-HCL Bolbeau Air; OB Boreal
F-11 Husky					
CF-EIL	2		4/56	9/58	Sold; OB Boreal
CF-EIO	5		9/49	4/60	Sold; OB Boreal
CF-EIP	6		7/55	4/60	ST CF-EIP Wheeler; OB Boreal

≡ QUEBECAIR

Quebecair Boeing 737, C-GQBA

HEADQUARTERS:
100 Boulevard Alexis Nihon, Ste 700,
Ville St. Laurent, Quebec H4L 5C3.

MAJOR BASE:
Montreal (Dorval)

FINAL FLEET:
4 - Boeing 737-200s;
2 - DC-8-63s;
5 - Convair 580s;
4 - HS748s;
3 - Convair 580s (OF SEBJ)
July 1986

COLOURS:
The white upper fuseage is separated from the grey lower fuselage by a wide red cheat line covering above and below the windows. Below this is a thin white cheat line with a wider dark blue cheat line below. All three cheats curve up the tail so that the tail is white, red, thin white and blue. QUEBECAIR is on the lower fuselage in white (inside the blue cheat) and on the tail. QUEBECAIR also appears in blue (on an angle) on the forward white portion. On the original DC-8s, there was only a 'Q' in white on the blue portion of the tail, but this was later changed to QUEBECAIR. A Canadian flag is on the upper rear fuselage. The registration, in white, is on the blue cheat line on the lower rear fuselage, except on the 737s where it was in blue on the lower grey fuselage.

ROUTES:
Toronto – Montreal (Dorval) – Quebec City – Sept Illes – Schefferville – Gagnon – Labrador City/Wabush – James Bay – Val d'Or – Hull/Gatineau – Rouyn/Noranda – Saguenay/Bagotville – Rimouski/Mont Joli – Baie Comeau/Hauterive – Bonaventure – Gaspe – Iles-de-la-Madeleine.

Regionair Routes:
Port Menier – Kegaska – Natashquan – Baie Johan Beetz – Gethsemanie/La Romaine – Harrington Harbour/ Chevery – Tete-a-la-Baleine – La Tabatiere – St. Augustine – Blanc Sablon.

HISTORY:

L e Sydnicate d' Aviation de Rimouski was formed in 1947 to provide charter flights and flying lessons in the Gaspe Peninsula. The following year the name was changed to *Rimouski Airlines* and the company acquired local and cross-St. Lawrence air services in the Rimouski and Sept-Iles area from *Canadian Pacific Airlines*. The north-south route across the St. Lawrence River linked Matane, Mont-Joli and Rimouski with Baie Comeau, Sept-Iles and Forestville. Another small airline operating in this region at this time was *Gulf Aviation*.

In 1953, *Rimouski Airlines* and *Gulf Aviation* merged to form Quebecair. At that time, the combined fleet consisted of three Beavers and five DC-3s. One of the DC-3s was sold in 1954 and a Beech 18 added. The company's first major expansion came in 1955 with the addition of Schefferville in the north and Quebec City to the west. Along with the other regional airlines, DEW Line contracts in 1955 allowed the airline to purchase larger aircraft. Two DC-4s, three DC-3s and two Cansos were purchased. Four additional DC-3s were added in 1956 (one was sold), leaving the airline with a fleet of nine DC-3s, two DC-4s, two Cansos, three Beavers and a Beech 18 at the end of 1956.

Montreal was added to the route system in 1957 and, along with Quebec City, would become the hub of the Quebecair route system. The two DC-4s were sold to *Maritime Central* at the end of the year and the first of two Curtiss C-46s was bought that year.

In 1958 Quebecair became the first turbine equipped regional carrier with the purchase of two F-27s. A third aircraft was bought the next year. These three aircraft were purchased new from the Fairchild Aircraft Company who built the aircraft under contract to the Dutch Fokker company. These aircraft carried forty passengers in a high-wing monoplane configuration and were powered by two Rolls Royce Dart turboprops. The two delivered in 1958 were urgently needed to replace the five DC-3s lost in a hangar fire at the Rimouski Airport on 13 July 1958. The last Beaver was sold in 1958.

Gagnon and Riviere-du-Loup were added in 1959; Wabush added in 1960; Manicouagan (of Brian Mulroney fame) and Saguenay were added in 1961, and Murray Bay added in 1962, to the company's route structure.

On 24 August 1960, two Convair 540s were leased from Canadair. These were Convair 440 airframes that Canadair converted to the Eland Convair 540 configuration. However, for financial reasons, Quebecair decided to operate only one type of turboprop equipment, the F-27, and returned these two aircraft to Canadair the next year. Both planes eventually went to the Royal Canadian Air Force as CC-109 Cosmopolitans. The RCAF re-engined their Cosmopolitans in 1966 with Allison engines (making them Convair 580 equivalents), but these two aircraft were sold before that time and thus stayed in commercial service as Convair 540s.

The three F-27s, five DC-3s, Beech 18, C-46 and Cansos served the airline in the early 1960s. Rouyn/Noranda was added to the route system during this period. The airline's colour scheme during this period consisted of a white aircraft with an aqua green cheat running the length of the fuselage through the windows, with a flying 'Fleur de Lis' at the start of the cheat line. QUEBECAIR was on the upper fuselage in black and the company's logo appeared on the tail. The colour scheme changed in the mid-sixties to a white aircraft with a wide red cheat line running two-thirds of the length of the aircraft, where it became five thin red cheat lines with white between. A large white circle started the wide red cheat line. The titles and registration were in red and the tail was all white. This scheme was first seen on the fourth F-27 bought from Yale University, via F.B. Ayer, in February 1966.

Matane Air Services was a small Gaspe Peninsula carrier founded in 1947. In April 1965, Quebecair took it over, along with two DC-3s and three Lockheed 10As. *Northern Wings* and its subsidiary *Northern Wings Helicopters Limited,* were also acquired in 1965. *Les Ailes du Nord* and *Les Ailese du Nord Helicopters* were purchased in 1965. Quebecair operated all of the scheduled services obtained in these takeovers but left the companies to operate charter and contract work under their own names, using light aircraft and helicopters.

Service to Labrador City (Churchill Falls) began in 1967. Quebecair now had extensively scheduled services on both sides of the St. Lawrence River, Western Labrador and Central and Northern Quebec, Montreal, Quebec City, Murray Bay (Charlevoix), Riviere-du-Loup, Rimouski, Mont-Joli, Matane, Saguenay, Forestville, Baie Comeau (Hauterive), Manicouagan, Sept-Iles, Gagnon, Wabush, Schefferville, Riviere-au-Tonnere, Mingan, Havre St. Pierre, Port Menier, Gaspe, Natashquan, Harrigton Harbour and Blanc Sablon saw the Quebecair aircraft on a regular basis. A fifth F-27, a former *Aloha Airlines* aircraft, was leased from 1967 to 1969 at which time jet aircraft were introduced.

Quebecair continued its takeovers in 1968, acquiring *A. Fecteau Transport Aerien*. This airline began in 1936 as a bush operation engaged in contract and charter air services at Senneterre, north of Val d'Or. At the time of the takeover it operated DC-3, Beaver and Cessna aircraft in the Abitibi region. Again the company continued under its own name and in 1978, *A. Fecteau* took over the aircraft of *Northern Wings* which made it the largest Otter aircraft operator in the world with eleven.

Quebecair (S.E.B.J.) Convair 580, C-GFHB

Quebecair bought three DHC-6 Twin Otter aircraft in 1968 to operate on the smaller routes acquired in the various takeovers.

Again in 1969, Quebecair acquired a small operator, this time *Royalair,* which flew a DC-3 and a Lockheed 18 aircraft between Pembroke, Peterborough, Toronto and St. Catharines. Quebecair operated this route only briefly, using *Royalair* aircraft, before abandoning it.

While the other Canadian regional airlines introduced the Boeing 737 as their first jet equipment, Quebecair bought the BAC 1-11. Quebecair had an order in for a Boeing 707 in 1968 and cancelled the order (the plane went to *Wardair* as CF-ZYP). They also had an order for two Boeing 737s but also cancelled this order. Two BAC 1-11s were purchased from *British Eagle International Airlines* in April 1969 and a third was bought from *Philippine Airlines* in 1973. The main reason for selecting the seventy-nine seat twin jet was economics. The used aircraft were much cheaper than new planes and the smaller seating capacity better suited Quebecair's route system. The first two were series 300 aircraft of which only nine were built; the third was a Series 400 which incorporated modifications to meet American requirements. The aircraft entered service in a white colour scheme with a single thin blue cheat line above the windows and a wider blue cheat through the windows. The company's logo, a 'Q' with an airplane in it, was in blue on the tail.

The introduction of the BAC 1-11 jets allowed Quebecair to sell off its DC-3 and Twin Otter aircraft in the early 1970s. In this period, mergers or takeovers by *Nordair, Eastern Provincial* and *Transair* were rumoured almost every year but none occurred. Quebecair services were started to Val d'Or in northwestern Quebec and La Grande 2 at the James Bay Project. The company received a contract to operate a single Lockheed Hercules aircraft, for the James Bay Hydro Project, under the name *Societe d'Energie de la Baie James* (SEBJ). In 1976, SEBJ bought five Convair 580s from *North Central Airlines* to fly workers and equipment to the massive James Bay Project. Quebecair received the contract to operate these aircraft as well as continuing to operate the Hercules until it was sold in 1981.

Quebecair acquired one more small airline in May 1974 when it purchased *Air Gaspe* of Sept-Illes, Quebec. *Air Gaspe* served the Gaspe Peninsula and continued to operate under its own name after the merger. The company had a single HS-748, a DC-3 and a Beech 99 for its scheduled routes. The HS-748 was sold in 1976 and *Air Gaspe* became part of *Regionair.*

Quebecair hoped to obtain the Quebec City to New York City route in 1974 and purchased a Boeing 727 from *Eastern Airlines* for this purpose. However, Quebecair along with *CP Air* and the other four regional airlines saw almost all of the Canada-USA routes go to *Air Canada,* including Quebec City to New York City. The

727 was fitted into Quebecair's regular schedule and on charter work but was really too large for Quebecair's needs.

The BAC 1-11s were used for weekend charter work out of Quebec City, Montreal and Toronto. With the boom in charter travel, Quebecair purchased two Boeing 707-124s from *Amercan Airlines* in the winter of 1974. These planes flew south to the warmer destinations in winter and to Europe in the summer. The addition of the 727 and 707s saw a new colour scheme introduced. The F-27s and BAC 1-11s adopted this colour scheme as well. The aircraft were white with a blue cheat above and below the windows running the length of the fuselage. The top cheat line continued up the middle of the tail as a wide blue stripe and in the centre was the Quebecair 'Q'. The bottom cheat line widened down at the nose and the lower fuselage was grey. QUEBECAIR appeared in blue on the upper fuselage. The registration, in blue, was on the rear of the upper fuselage, with a Canadian flag behind it.

About this time, Quebecair introduced *Regionair,* which operated the subsidiary companies belonging to Quebecair: *Northern Wings Ltd.; Air Fecteau Ltd.; Air Gaspe Ltd.; Les Ailes du Nord,* and *Northern Wings Helicopters Ltd.* At that time, these companies operated aircraft as large as the HS-748, Beech 99, and DC-3 as well as numerous smaller aircraft and helicopters. *Regionair* services were expanded in 1977 to an 'Air Plus' concept, linking all *Regionair* services to scheduled Quebecair flights. *Air Fecteau* operated two Beech 99 aircraft between Mont-Joli, Charlo, Saguenay/ Bagotville, Roberval, Chibougamau and Val d'Or.

Air Gaspe had sold its HS-748 in 1976 and flew two Beech 99s between Mont-Joli, Charlo, Bonaventure, St. Annes des Monts, Sept-Iles, Port Menier and Gaspe. *Northern Wings* operated a HS-748, DC-3s, Beavers, Otters and Piper Navajos between Sept-Iles, Minagan, Havre St. Pierre, Baie-Johan-Beetz, Natashquan, Kegaska, Gethsemanie (Romaine), Chevery (Harrington), Teta-a-la-Balleine, La Tabaterie, St. Augustine, Old Fort Bay, Riviere St. Paul and Blanc Sablon.

The year 1979 was difficult for Quebecair. On 19 February, Boeing 707 C-GQBH had its nose gear break on a heavy landing at St. Lucia, damaging the fuselage. While the aircraft was probably repairable, it was left and scrapped later that year. The other Boeing 707 was sold later in the year. Then, on 29 March, F-27 C-FQBL had an engine catch fire on take-off from Quebec City. The plane tried to return to the airport but crashed into a hill 3300 feet from take-off and all 17 on board were killed.

The company planned to phase out its BAC 1-11s in 1979, but still adopted a modified paint scheme on these aircraft that year. The white portions of the aircraft were changed to bare metal similar to *Eastern Airlines* in the United States. The blue cheat lines and titles remained as before. Two Boeing 737s were leased from *Trans European Airways* (TEA) in 1979 for use on the scheduled routes and for ITC charters on weekends. These aircraft operated in TEA colours with Quebecair titles. In November, the Boeing 727 was removed from service and sold the next year to an Alberta operator.

Four Boeing 737s were ordered, with two delivered in 1980 and two more in 1981. These aircraft arrived in a new colour scheme. The aircraft had a dark blue upper fuselage which was separated from the lower silver fuselage by a thin light blue cheat line below the windows and a white cheat line below that. The QUEBECAIR title appeared in white on the upper fuselage, with a narrow white cheat line running back from the titles to the registration. The leading edge of the tail was bare metal with the remainder of the tail dark blue. At the base of the tail was a horizontal light blue stripe and a white stripe. A large white 'Q' was in the middle of the tail.

The 737s replaced the BAC 1-11s on most scheduled services and operated Sunflight tours out of Toronto on weekends and during the week. By September 1980, Quebecair operated Montreal to Ft. Lauderdale once weekly and by November had increased this to six times per week, hence it was almost a scheduled service. Quebec City to Ft. Lauderdale or Miami was also almost a regular service.

Quebecair was awarded Montreal to Toronto in January 1981, provided the flights originated or terminated east of Montreal. *Air Canada* continued to operate Toronto to Quebec City direct, a route which Quebecair desperately needed. The service between Toronto and Montreal was begun in June 1981, with Quebecair offering special services to entice passengers away from *Air Canada, CP Air* and *Nordair.* The F-27s were all sold in 1981 and on 31 October 1981, the BAC 1-11s were withdrawn from service and stored at Dorval. *Les Ailes du Nord* acquired four HS-748s from *Austin Airways* to operate Quebecair's former F-27 routes, and Quebec City to Hull was subcontracted to *Quebec Aviation.*

With the introduction of the Boeing 737s, Quebecair found itself in great financial difficulty. The airline industry was being hard hit by the recession at a time when Quebecair was spending large dollars to modernize its fleet. In mid-July 1981, the Quebec Government bought $15 million of non-voting shares in the company to block a takeover bid by *Nordair.* During 1981 and 1982, passengers carried dropped from 695,000 to 520,000.

In January 1982, the aircraft operating for *Regionair* were painted in the dark blue colour scheme with *Regionair* titles. *Regionair* began a Quebec City to Boston flight with a Beech 99 aircraft in May 1982. SEBJ Con-

Quebecair BAC 1-11, C-FQBO

vair 580 (C-GFHA) had small Quebecair titles put on it and operated charters and weekend scheduled routes for Quebecair for a short time.

The Boeing 737s were becoming a heavy financial burden to the airline and their seating capacity was too great for most of Quebecair's routes. The leased aircraft were returned to TEA and two of Quebecair's Boeing 737s were leased to *Britannia* for a year, with another being sold later in the year to *Air Nauru.* The three retired BAC 1-11s were refurbished inside and painted in the new blue colour scheme. They were returned to service on 25 April 1982. A *US Air* BAC 1-11 (N117J) was leased late in 1982. Quebecair bought a former *Maersk* Boeing 737 in October 1982 and it sat at Dorval in basic *Arabia* colour scheme (to which it had recently been leased by *Maersk*) until activated as C-GQBA in May 1983.

In December 1982, the Federal Government proposed a bail-out scheme which would see a new company, *Quebecair II,* formed. The plan called for Quebecair to declare bankruptcy, with *Air Canada* taking over the new company. The new company would get some *Air Canada* DC-9 aircraft as well as some *Air Canada* routes (Toronto to Quebec City?). *Nordair* and *Quebecair II* would eventually be merged to form a strong Quebec-Ontario Regional airline. The Quebec Government rejected this proposal and arranged for two loans of $4 million and $8 million to tide Quebecair over.

Two former *Austral* (Argentina) BAC 1-11s were purchased late in 1982 and the leased BAC 1-11 returned to *US Air.* Long term leases for three of the company's Boeing 737s were arranged with *Pan Am* in May 1983, after the two leased to *Britannia* had been returned. The former *Maersk/ Arabia* 737 was painted in full Quebecair colours and put into service in May 1983, but was sold in September 1983 to *Air Nauru.* at which time Quebecair leased a Boeing 737 from TEA to replace it.

In April 1984, Quebecair re-entered the long haul charter market with the lease of a DC-8-63. Transatlantic charters including Toronto to Belfast, London, Lisbon, Paris, Rome, Copenhagen and various Yugoslavian cities; Vancouver to London and Calgary/Edmonton to London were operated. The aircraft was operated by Quebecair on behalf of Fiesta Travel, and appeared in a new colour scheme of red, white and blue, with the title FIESTA on the rear of the aircraft. Minerve, together with a French tour operator, Nouvelles Frontieres, be gan offering non-commissionable charter flights directly to the public (from a newly opened Montreal office), from Montreal (Mirabel) to Paris, in June 1984. To meet the demand for seats created by this company, a second DC-8-63 was obtained late in the year.

Quebecair again started to phase out the BAC 1-11s in 1984, selling two of its older aircraft to *Airways International* in the United Kingdom. One Boeing 737 had remained in service with the company and a second joined it in late 1984. Initially, these aircraft were used on the Toronto-Montreal route. Two HS-748s flew in full blue Quebecair colours but with an 'R' on the tail (R = *Regionair*) and began operating some of the shorter routes as part of the Quebecair timetable rather than as *Regionair.* Eventually, four HS-748s were painted in the blue Quebecair colour scheme, two carrying 'R' on the tail and two with 'Q' on the tail.

Montreal to Boston and Quebec City to Boston, two dormant *Air Canada* routes, were started in March 1985. In mid-1985, the three Boeing 737s leased to *Pan Am* were returned to Quebecair, adopting the new red, white and blue colour scheme and the last three BAC 1-11s were withdrawn from use and eventually sold. The second DC-8-63 flew from Vancouver to Manchester and London, and from Calgary/Edmonton to Manchester & London in the spring of 1985. The collapse of Jetlink Holidays in mid-September 1985 eliminated many transatlantic DC-8 flights and cost the company considerable money.

Service was discontinued to Gagnon when the Quebec Cartier Mining Company closed its operations in June 1985, but a Montreal – Val d'Or – Rouyn route was started. The company was also awarded rights to Winnipeg in 1985 and planned to operate from Winnipeg via Toronto to Montreal and Quebec City in early 1986. *Regionair* sold both its Beech 99s and two of its HS-748s in 1985. Quebecair branched out into the cargo field in June 1985 by leasing an *Arrow Air* DC-8-54F for cargo flights between Mirabel and Santo Domingo. This plane eventually appeared in a colour scheme featuring a white aircraft with a wide dark-blue cheat line and tail. The title QUEBECAIR CARGO appeared in dark blue on the upper fuselage and QUEBECAIR, in white, was displayed on the leading edge of the tail.

Despite the expanded routes, the re-introduction of the Boeing 737s, the transatlantic charter routes and the cargo flights, the airline continued to be a chronic money loser. It lost $22 million in 1982, $16 million in 1983 and $5 million in 1984. Since the Quebec government took it over in 1981, the airline had received more than $100 million. Thus, in a move to stem the losses, Quebecair offered to buy out money-making *Nordair* and form one strong Quebec/Ontario regional airline based in Quebec. However, in December 1985, *CP Air* was successful in purchasing an additional 44% of *Nordair* stock, giving them 60% ownership of *Nordair*. The Quebec government continued to hold 22% of *Nordair* stock, effectively blocking the complete takeover of *Nordair* by *CP Air,* but not enough to allow Quebecair to merge with *Nordair*.

A pact was signed with *Pacific Western Airlines* late in 1985 to coordinate their schedules in Toronto, allowing western PWA passengers access to Quebecair's Quebec routes and Quebecair passengers access to western Canada. Unfortunately, *Pacific Western* was hit by a strike just before the integration was to take place, dealing another blow to Quebecair's hopes of becoming profitable.

Charter operations continued during the winter of 1985-86 with Toronto to Panama City or Cartagena

(Colombia) or Palomar (Venezuela) or Cumana (Venezuela) being some of the DC8 charters. Charters from Montreal to Providenciales (Turks & Caicos) used Boeing 737s. In March, 1986, the airline signed a $100 million deal with Conquest Tours of Toronto to operated trans-Atlantic charters (Toronto to London, Prestwick, Frankfurt, Amsterdam, Paris) and to southern localities for five years. Quebecair also operated Toronto to Brussels flights for *Sabena* with its cargo DC8. Sept Illes to Port Menier flights were given to *Quebec Aviation.* The flights between Quebec City and Newark were dropped and the Montreal to Boston service was reduced.

Quebec Aviation Ltee was bought out by *Propair*, 50% owned by Quebecair, and the two companies were merged. The plan was to use Fairchild Metro aircraft on flights between Montreal, Chibougamau, Bagotville, Ottawa/Gatineau, Rouyn/Noranda, and Val d'Or. A service from Quebec City to Sherbrooke and Montreal was begun in December but dropped in April, 1986. Quebec City to Murray Bay was subcontracted to *Les Ailes de Charlevoix Inc*. Ownership of *Propair* was transferred to 100366 Canada Ltee in April, 1986, and its commercial air services were transferred to *Quebec Aviation Ltd.,* thus ending *Propair* as a Canadian carrier. All of these moves resulted in a new airline titled *Quebecair Inter* which operated Fairchild Metro equipment in red, white and blue Quebecair colours but with INTER in white on the tail where QUEBECAIR appeared on the larger aircraft. *Quebecair Inter* would feed Quebecair at Montreal and Quebec City.

The Boeing 737s continued to prove too large for economical use on many of Quebecair's routes, so two Convair 580s were purchased in mid-1986 to substitute on some of these routes and to compete with *Nordair Metro*. In May, Jacques Leger resigned as President of Quebecair and was replaced by Andre Lizotte.

Quebecair, one of the original five regional airlines, effectively ended on July 31, 1986, when it was purchased by *Nordair Metro*. The purchase price was $21 million with *Nordair Metro* also absorbing the long term Quebecair debt of $64 million dollars. *Nordair Metro*, however, acquired all the Quebecair jets, selling the two DC-8-63s to *Nationair* for $10 million and the four Boeing 737s to *Canadian Pacific* for $50 million. *Canadian Pacific* took possession of only two of the Boeing 737s, selling one to *Braathens* of Norway and leaving one with Quebecair. The DC8-54F was returned to International Air Leases, four HS-748s having already been withdrawn. As part of the package, the shares in *Nordair* held by the Quebec Government (through the Societe Quebecoise des Transports) were sold to *Canadian Pacific Airlines* for $13.5 million, giving CPA complete control of *Nordair* and allowing *Nordair* to be fully merged into *Canadian Pacific*.

The name Quebecair continued to fly following the

takeover with *Nordair Metro* operating Quebecair as a separate entity for the better part of the next two years. The remaining company known as Quebecair still had two Convair 580s and two Boeing 737s. One Boeing 737 was sold in March 1987 (*Braathens*), but the other was withdrawn from use at Montreal and sold in October 1987. For a time, this aircraft operated Montreal to Chicago and Montreal to Boston for *El Al Israel Airlines*.

The plan now was for *Nordair* to be integrated completely into *Canadian Pacific* and disappear as a separate entity; and for *Nordair Metro,* Quebecair and *Quebecair Inter* to continue to operate as separate entities, feeding *Canadian Pacific* at Montreal and Quebec City. *Nordair Metro* and Quebec- air would operate up to fourteen flights per day between Montreal and Quebec City, and divide the rest of the Quebec routes between the two airlines.

Quebecair acquired a former *Kelowna Flightcraft* Convair 580 freighter in November 1986, to serve the Quebec north shore region from Sept Iles. Mont Joli and Iles de Madeleine would be major centres served with this aircraft. In addition, two more Convair 580s were acquired late in 1986 from *Republic* to operate passenger routes. Quebecair continued to operate three Convair 580s for *Societe d' Energie de la Baie James* (SEBJ) and one of these aircraft was a spare which could be used by Quebecair or *Nordair Metro*. Michel Leblanc, *Nordair Metro's* President, became the new Quebecair President and Chief Executive Officer.

Quebecair was able to sell one of its Boeing 737s and retired the other early in 1987 after purchasing two sixty-five-passenger Fokker 28 jet aircraft in March. These replaced the one hundred and nineteen seat 737s on longer Quebecair routes, including Montreal to Quebec City, and brought back the BAC 1-11 size jet to

Quebec skies. The success of the two F28s lead to an order for four Fokker F.100s late in 1987, for 1988 delivery. These aircraft can carry one hundred and nine passengers and have the lowest cost per plane/mile of any jet transport. With these aircraft, Quebecair planned to expand its network and operate charter flights to the south.

Six months after its purchase by *Nordair Metro,* Quebecair reached a breakeven point, a turnaround of close to $1.5 million a month. More than two hundred staff had been cut following the takeover, however, the replacing of the Boeing 737s (which had been operating at only 40% capacity), with Convair 580 and F28 aircraft was also a major factor. Pilots also took a paycut during a three year agreement which saw the salary of Convair 580 pilots drop from $75,000 to $58,000 (5th year captains). Sixth year captains (flying F28 aircraft) were receiving $67,000 per year, while first year F28 captains received only $52,000.

In September 1987, Quebecair announced a new name and livery for its fleet of aircraft. The company's new name is *Inter-Canadian* (spelling Canadian with the last 'A' replaced by a '>' to make it bilingual). Quebecair will remain the name of the corporation operating *Inter-Canadian.* and will operate in full *Canadian* colour scheme except for the title INTER-CAN-ADI>N on the upper fuselage. Nordair Metro and Quebecair will combine their Convair 580 operations, but jet operations will remain separate. Passengers will see only one airline, with one schedule, feeding *Canadian Airlines,* and that will be *Inter-Canadi>n.*

Thus in 1988, Quebecair is an airline no longer flying in Canada. *Quebecair Inter* continues to operate the Metros. *Inter-Canadian* is not a full *Canadian* partner, but operates on a commercial agreement with *Canadian,* despite being 35% owned by *Canadian.*

Quebecair Inter SA226TC Metroliner, C-GQAL

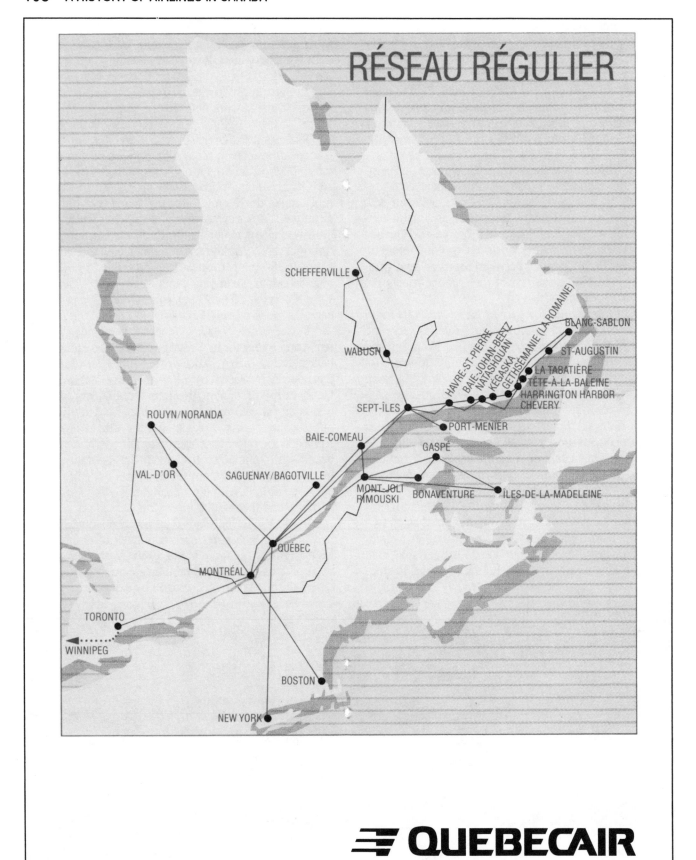

RÉSEAU RÉGULIER

SCHEFFERVILLE

WABUSH

BLANC-SABLON

ST-AUGUSTIN

HAVRE-ST-PIERRE
BAIE-JOHAN-BEETZ
NATASHQUAN
KEGASKA
GETHSEMANIE (LA ROMAINE)

LA TABATIÈRE
TÊTE-À-LA-BALEINE
HARRINGTON HARBOR
CHEVERY

ROUYN/NORANDA

SEPT-ÎLES

PORT-MENIER

BAIE-COMEAU

GASPÉ

VAL-D'OR

SAGUENAY/BAGOTVILLE

MONT-JOLI
RIMOUSKI

BONAVENTURE

ÎLES-DE-LA-MADELEINE

QUÉBEC

MONTRÉAL

TORONTO

WINNIPEG

BOSTON

NEW YORK

QUEBECAIR

Route map as it appeared in 1985 Quebecair timetable

FLEET LISTING
QUEBECAIR

REG'N	C/N	IS	WFU	NOTES	MODEL
F-28-1000					
C-GQBR	11012	3/87	9/87	To C-GQBR Inter-Canadian; EX LN-SUN Braathens	
C-GQBS	11013	3/87	9/87	To C-GQBS Inter-Canadian; EX LN-SUO Braathens	
CONVAIR 580					
C-GKFR	454	11/86	9/87	To C-GKFR Inter-Canadian; EX C-GKFR Kelowna	
C-GQBM	49	4/86	9/87	To C-GQBM Inter-Canadian; EX N26KA Key Airlines	
C-GQBN	50	5/86	9/87	To C-GQBN Inter-Canadian; EX N90855 Republic	
C-GQBO	30	10/86	9/87	To C-GQBO Inter-Canadian; EX N4801C Republic	
C-GQBP	137	11/86	9/87	To C-GQBP Inter-Canadian; EX N7528U Republic	
DC-8-63					
C-GQBA	46155	4/84	9/86	ST C-GQBA Nationair; EX EC-BSE Aviaco; EX N940JW	
C-GQBF	46116	12/84	9/86	ST C-GQBF Nationair; EX EC-BSD Aviaco; EX N457AP	
DC-8-54F					
C-GQBG	45860	7/85	5/86	LF N888B Intern'l Air Leases (Aero Air c/s) CARGO	
737-296					
C-GQBB	22276	5/80	10/86	ST C-GQBB CPAL; LT N387PA Pan Am 5/83 - 5/85	
C-GQBJ	22277	6/80	3/87	ST LN-BRL Braathens; LT N388PA Pan Am 4/83-4/85	
737-2L9					
C-GQBA	22072	5/83	9/83	ST C2-RN9 Air Nauru; EX OY-APO Maersk/Arabia	
C-GQBD	19594	11/84	10/87	ST N728JE Express One; EX N4907 Wien Airline	
C-GQBH	22616	4/81	10/86	ST C-GQBH CPA; LT N389PA Pan Am 4/83-4/85	
C-GQBQ	22070	12/81	9/82	ST C2-RN8 Air Nauru; EX OY-APL Maersk	
737-202C					
C-GQBC	19426	3/85	2/86	ST N801AL Aloha Airlines; EX N2711R Wien Air	
737-2Q8					
C-GQBS	21735	11/79	6/80	LF OO-TEM Trans European Airways (TEA)	
737-2M8					
C-GQBS	21231	12/80	4/81	LF OO-TEH Trans European Airways (TEA)	
C-GQBS	21231	8/83	4/85	LF OO-TEH Trans European Airways (TEA)	
737-2Q9					
C-GQBT	21719	11/79	4/82	LF 00-TEK TEA winters 79/80; 80/81; 81/82; EX C-GNDG	
727-25					
C-GQBE	18970	7/74	1/80	ST C-GQBE Westburn; EX N8146N Eastern	
707-123B					
C-GQBG	17647	12/74	11/79	ST 5A-DHO United African Airlines; EX N752A AA	
C-GQBH	17650	11/74	2/79	ACC 19/02/79 St. Lucia; scrapped 6/79	
BAC 1-11					
C-FQBM*	110	4/69	3/84	ST G-YMRU Airways Intern'l; WFU 10/81-4/82	-304AX
C-FQBO*	112	4/69	11/84	ST G-WLAD Airways Intern'l; WFU 10/81-4/82	-304AX
C-FQBR*	94	3/73	5/85	ST 5N-ACW Okada Air 2/86; EX PI-C-1141 PAL	-402AP
C-GQBP	122	12/82	5/85	ST 5N-ACM Okada Air 2/86; EX LV-IZR Austral	-420EL
C-GQPV	123	10/85	5/85	ST 5N-AC- Okada Air 2/86; EX LV-IZS Austral	-420EL
N117J	99	8/82	11/82	LF N117J US Air	-204AF
F-27					
C-FQBA*	11	8/58	10/81	ST N273PH Horizon Air	
C-FQBD*	27	2/66	6/81	ST N272PH Horizon Air	
CF-QBE	40	12/67	12/69	ST N3225 F.B. Ayer; EX N5095A Aloha Airlines	
C-FQBL*	47	7/59	3/79	W/O 29/03/79 near Quebec City	
C-FQBZ*	14	10/58	5/81	ST N271PH Horizon Air	
BEECH 99					
C-GQFD	U-40	5/81	3/85	ST C-GQFD North Cariboo	Regionair
C-GYNQ	U-67	5/81	3/85	ST N24BH	Regionair
HS-748					
C-FAGI	1699	5/81	4/86	ST C-FAGI Northland Air Manitoba 8/88; EX CF-AGI Air Gaspe	Regionair
C-GAPC	1599	5/81	4/86	Scrapped 6/87; EX XA-SAY Aero Caribe	Regionair
C-GDOV	1582	5/81	3/85	ST C-GDOV Bradley Air Service	Quebecair
C-GDUI	1577	5/81	4/86	ST C-GDUI Bradley Air Service 12/87	Regionair
C-GDUL	1578	5/81	4/86	ST C-GDUL Bradley Air Service 12/87	Quebecair
C-GDUN	1581	5/81	3/85	ST C-GDUN Bradley Air Service	Regionair

FLEET LISTING
QUEBECAIR

REG'N	C/N	IS	WFU	NOTES
CURTISS C-46				
CF-CZH	22515	12/58	6/75	ST CF-CZH Northcoast; EX Canadian Pacific
CF-CZL	22494	11/57	1/60	ST CF-CZL Maritime Central; OB Northern Wings
CONVAIR 540				
CF-LMA	454	11/60	10/61	LF CF-LMA Canadair; ST RCAF 11106/11162
CF-MKO	462	11/60	10/61	LF CF MKO Canadair; ST RCAF 11107/11163
DHC-6 TWIN OTTER				
CF-QBT	95	3/68	4/71	ST CF-QBT Amoco
CF-QBU	99	3/68	6/70	ST CF-QBU Northward Aviation
CF-QBV	103	4/68	5/70	ST CF-QBV Northward Aviation; OB Royalair 3/69
DHC-2 BEAVER				
CF-EYR	497	8/53	9/58	ST CF-EYR Northern Wings
CF-GCO	167	8/53	5/57	Sold
CF-GQF	81	5/53	5/57	ST CF-GQF Eastern Provincial
CANSO PBY-5A				
CF-IHA	CV365	5/55	2/62	ST CF-IHA Eastern Provincial
CANSO 385-ACF				
CF-IHD	48448	5/55	7/65	Sold
BEECH D-18S				
CF-HVZ	A325	6/54	9/57	RR CF-QBL
CF-QBL	A325	9/57	6/59	RR CF-LTB (RR so that an F-27 could have CF-QBL)
CF-LTB	A325	6/59	4/69	Sold
DC-4				
CF-QBA	10512	3/55	5/57	ST CF-MCD Maritime Central Airways
CF-HVL	18374	3/55	5/57	ST CF-MCF Maritime Central Airways
DC-3				
CF-CRW	18958	8/59	6/61	ST CF-CRW Eastern Provincial
CF-GVZ	26997	9/51	1/56	W/O 17/01/56 Oreway Lake, PQ; EX Gulf Avn. 2/51
CF-HVM	26184	3/55	12/55	ACC 09/12/55; rebuilt, ST N714C; OB-PBI-516
CF-QBB	10081	10/55	9/69	ST CF-QBB Air Gaspe; OB Royalair 3/69-9/69
CF-QBC	27026	10/55	9/71	ST CF-QBC Northern Wings; OB Royalair 11/81-7/82
CF-QBD	3256	2/56	7/58	DBF 13/07/58 in hangar, Rimouski Airport
CF-QBE	9649	5/56	7/58	DBF 13/07/58 in hangar, Rimouski Airport
CF-QBF	12092	10/56	7/58	DBF 13/07/58 in hangar, Rimouski Apt.; EX CF-TDS
CF-QBG	13337	10/56	7/58	DBF 13/07/58 in hangar, Rimouski Apt.; EX CF-TEJ
CF-QBH	20219	8/53	7/58	DBF 13/07/58 in hangar, Rimouski Apt.; EX CF-FSP
CF-QBI	6179	8/53	1/70	ST CF-QBI A. Fecteau Transport Aerien; EX CF-GEH
CF-QBM	6187	5/59	5/69	ST N6187 H. Rich; EX CF-CUD
CF-TDK	6319	8/53	3/55	ST CF-ICF, CF-ORD, CF-RBC, CF-CBL & now CF-PQE
CF-TDL	6343	8/53	10/54	ST N37F Remmert Werner; EX TCA & Gulf Avn. a/c

FLEET LISTING
SOCIETE d'ENERGIE BAIE JAMES

REG'N	C/N	IS	WFU	NOTES	Aircraft Name
CONVAIR 580					
C-GFHA	51	9/76	5/83	ST N5810 Sea Airmotive; EX N4804C	EASTMAIN
C-GFHB	38	10/76	C	EX 4802C North Central Airline	SAKAMI
C-GFHC	352	5/77	7/83	ST N5812 Sea Airmotive; EX N2044	CANIAPISCAU
C-GFHD	100	6/77	4/84	ST N5807 Sea Airmotive; EXN4810C	
C-GFHF	176	4/77	C	EX N4634S North Central Airline	OPINACA
C-GFHH	109	7/78	C	EX N5803 North Central Airline	RUPERT
L-382E					
CF-DSX	4303	10/73	5/81	ST C-FDSX Echo Bay Mines L-382E Hercules a/c	

EASTERN PROVINCIAL

Eastern Provincial 737, C-GEPA "LABRADOR"

HEADQUARTERS:
P.O. Box 178, Halifax International Airport,
Elmsdale, Nova Scotia, B0N 1M0

MAIN BASES:
Gander, Newfoundland; Halifax, Nova Scotia

FINAL FLEET:
7 - Boeing 737-200s;
5 - HS-748s (Air Maritime)
January, 1986

COLOURS:
The final colour scheme, introduced in 1985, featured an all-white fuselage and dark blue tail. A large EPA 'Atlantic Gull' symbol appears in white on the tail. On the fuselage, two windows aft of the front door and to the height of the door are the letters 'EPA' in dark blue. On the rear fuselage is a large Canadian flag. The registration number is in blue on the lower rear fuselage, and the fleet number is in blue on the front nose wheel, and 'Flagship Halifax' (or one of six other city names) on the fuselage below the pilot's window.

ROUTES:
Toronto – Ottawa – Montreal – Charlo – Chatham – Saint John – Fredericton – Moncton – Sydney – Charlottetown – Goose Bay – Wabush – Churchill Falls – Stephenville – Gander – Deer Lake – St. John's.

AIR MARITIME:
The colour scheme was all white with a narrow dark-blue cheat line just below the bottom of the windows, then a white line, then a thin dark blue cheat, another white line, and finally a thin red line. All three cheat lines begin just aft of the cockpit, ending forward of the tail. Air Maritime appears in dark blue, beginning in the middle of the upper fuselage. The registration, in dark blue, is on the rear of the fuselage above the cheat line and the fleet number, also in dark blue, can be seen on the nose wheel. The tail is all white except for a large company symbol in a lighter blue.

ROUTES:
Halifax – Charlottetown – Magdalen Islands – Fredericton – Moncton – Sydney – St. Pierre – Stephenville – St. John's – Deer Lake – Gander.

HISTORY:

Eastern Provincial Airways was formed at Torby (St. John's), Newfoundland, in March 1949, the year Newfoundland entered Confederation. The airline was financed by Ches Crosbie, a Newfoundlander, to provide air ambulance services, fire patrols, geological survey work, winter air mail, relief to the outports and passenger services within Newfoundland. A Norseman, Piper Cub, Seabee, Cessna Crane and Stinson 108 made up the initial fleet. In 1953, the company moved its headquarters to Gander and bought a PBY Canso for fire suppression work. A Bell 47 helicopter, Cessna 180, Anson and two more Norsemen had also been added to the fleet by that time, as well as two Beavers and an Otter. The Otter was the second production aircraft from deHavilland.

For most of the regional airlines, the building of the three radar defence lines (the Pine Tree Line, Distant Early Warning Line, and Mid-Canada Line) provided the opportunity for expansion into large cargo aircraft. *Maritime Central,* however, was the largest airline in the Maritimes at that time and received the bulk of the heavy cargo work for these projects. Eastern Provincial did obtain many contracts to fly men and equipment to remote sites in Newfoundland and Labrador, thus continuing to expand as a bush operator. Two Lockheed 10As and seven DHC-2 Beavers were purchased in 1955 to support these contracts. Two more Otters were bought in 1958 and another four in 1960. Nine PBY Cansos were operated by the airline in the late fifties.

One of these Cansos recently took to the air again after 29 years. Canso CF-HFL delivered fuel to Sona Lake, 235 km from Goose Bay, on 1 October 1957. On the return flight, as dusk settled over the rugged Labrador landscape, both engines of the aircraft began to lose power. A mayday signal was sent out as the port engine quit. The pilot opted for a forced landing at a large lake nearby and began his decent, but when the powerplant gave out, the trees greeted the Canso. The plane sliced through the trees and spun around as it came to a halt. The crew, although badly shaken, were unhurt and were rescued the next day. The Canso was stripped of her engines and instruments and left to decay. Twenty-nine years and twenty-nine days later, a Canadian Forces Chinook helicopter lifted her out of the woods and the aircraft completed the journey back to Goose Bay. There it will be reconstructed and placed on permanent display by the Atlantic Canada Aviation Museum, in Halifax. (from *AirForce* Nov/Dec 1987).

In 1958, Eastern Provincial received a contract from the Danish Government to provide ice patrols and photographic surveys in Greenland. Cansos were used for this service. In 1960, the contract was expanded to include a regular passenger service in Greenland. Cansos were used between Sondrestrom and Godthaab, the capital of Greenland, but single-engine Otters provided service to the smaller communities such as Holsteinsborg, Egedesminde, Christianshab, Umanaq, Upernavik, Jakobshavn, Qutdligssat, Disco Bay, Egedesminde and Godavn. The aircraft were operated under lease to *Gronlandsfly Air Service* but were flown and maintained by EPA staff. More than thirteen thousand passengers per year were carried on this service. The Greenland contract lasted until 1965.

On 29 August 1961, Otter CF-MEX crashed, with its engine ablaze, at a small lake just north of Sondrestrom. Although the passengers escaped unharmed, the pilot, James Roe, later died from severe burns, and was awarded the 'Queen's Commendation for Valuable Service in the Air' for his actions in saving the lives of his passengers.The citation from the Canada Gazette reads:

> "On August 29, 1961, a fire broke out in an aircraft piloted by James Roe while in flight over Greenland. Despite reduced visibility because of smoke and flames and intense suffering from burns about the hands and legs, Pilot Roe gallantly remained at the controls until he had brought the aircraft to a safe landing. Four passengers and a crew man escaped unharmed. Unfortunately the pilot was trapped beneath the port float of the burning aircraft and sustained further injuries from which he succumbed a few days later."

In 1960, Eastern Provincial started a service from Newfoundland to Wabush and Twin Falls in central Labrador. The company's fleet during the early 1960s was still chiefly comprised of single-engine bush planes, the twin-engine Cansos and a couple of Sikorsky 55 helicopters.

In 1962, the company leased two Curtiss C-46s from *Nordair.* It also bought one of the *Nordair* Heralds in November 1962. and in February 1963, purchased two additional Heralds from the manufacturer. Another Herald was purchased from *Maritime Central* in May 1963, bringing the EPA Herald fleet to four. This thirty-six-passenger, high wing, twin turbo-prop aircraft provided EPA with a modern passenger aircraft.

A David and Goliath situation took place in September 1963, when this small bush airline took over the much larger *Maritimes Central Airways*. It had long been realized that the Maritimes and Newfoundland could only support one regional airline at that time, and the government of Newfoundland (desiring the regional airline to be based in Newfoundland), strongly supported Eastern Provincial in the takeover. Carl Burke, owner of *Maritime Central,* thus sold his larger airline to the smaller company. The new company was called *Eastern Provincial Airways (1963) Ltd.,* with a fleet of four Dart Heralds, two Curtiss C-46s, seven DC-3s, one

Eastern Provincial DHC-2 Beaver, CF-EYQ
Photo courtesy of Eastern Provincial Airways

DC-4, seven Cansos, seven Otters, five Beavers, two Sikorsky 55 helicopters and a few smaller single-engine aircraft. *Nordair* was not involved in the MCA sale to EPA.

Eastern Provincial now had many scheduled routes in the Maritimes and Newfoundland including service from Sydney, N.S. to the French Islands, St. Pierre and Miquelon. Halifax was the hub of its operations, with service to Charlottetown, Moncton, Fredericton, Saint John, Iles de Lake, Gander and St. John's. Also, service from Newfoundland to Goose Bay, Churchill Falls and Wabush linked Labrador to this regional route system.

Although the airline had suffered accidents to several of its small aircraft and its Cansos, most of these could be attributed to the difficult weather conditions and the terrain encountered on its routes and charters. However, on 17 March 1965, Herald CF-NAF was on a flight from Halifax to Sydney. It disintegrated in flight near Upper Musquodoboit, N.S. and all eight persons on board were killed. The cause of the accident remained a mystery until a second Herald crashed in the Middle East a year later. Investigation found the cause of both crashes to be skin corrosion behind the galley, because of the constant spills in that area. This problem was corrected on the remaining Heralds flown around the world.

The National Air Policy of 1966 officially classified Eastern Provincial as a regional carrier. At that time, the company was restricted to the Maritimes and Newfoundland but, in 1968, it gained access to Montreal and inaugurated a service beginning in Charlottetown and flying through Charlo to Montreal. A Lockheed Super Constellation was leased from *Nordair* that year and used on this route and on charters. Three ATL-98 Carvairs were bought in 1968. These aircraft were modified DC-4s, having a hinged nose for loading and the flight deck raised above the freight hold. The conversion enabled up to six cars and twenty-two passengers to be carried. The aircraft were used to carry cars and cargo between the mainland and Newfoundland and for flights into Labrador. On 28 September 1968, one of the Carvairs crashed at Churchill Falls. It was sold for spare parts to *British Air Ferries*, which also purchased the other two in 1973.

In 1969, EPA operated Twin Otters, CF-BEL and CF-DMR, on behalf of the Government of Newfoundland. Eastern Provincial also operated Turbo Beavers and Cansos for Newfoundland. The Cansos were turned over to the provincial government in 1967, and two of the Turbo Beavers in 1970.

Eastern Provincial decided to drop the bush side of

its operations in 1970, selling all of its Otters and Beavers to a group of EPA employees who adopted the name *Labrador Airways Limited.*

Eastern Provincial entered the jet age in April 1969, when it leased CF-NAH from *Nordair*. This aircraft was acquired directly from Boeing in full EPA colours. In May of that year, a *United Airlines* 737 was jointly leased and operated with *Nordair*. The plan at that time was for *Nordair* and EPA to jointly operate their fleet of Boeing 737s, with a merger planned for the near future. This merger was opposed by the federal government and the two planes were returned to *Nordair* and *United Airlines* at the end of 1969. Eastern Provincial received its own Boeing 737s in November and December 1969 adding a third in 1970.

The Boeing 737s were delivered in the colours that EPA had used since the Heralds were introduced. The upper fuselage and tail was all white and the lower fuselage natural metal. The two were separated by a red cheat line running the length of the fuselage, with thin black cheat lines above and below. The tips of the tail and wings were red. The title EASTERN PROVINCIAL AIRWAYS appeared on the upper fuselage in black, with a Canadian flag on the rear upper fuselage at the same level as the title. The tail symbol has varied: the original Heralds had large EPA letters; the later aircraft and first Boeing 737s had the company logo (a goose within a circle), with EPA behind the circle. In 1975, the circle and EPA were dropped and a large red flying goose appeared on the tail. Then, in 1983, the titles were changed to EASTERN PROVINCIAL, omitting the word 'AIRWAYS'.

As well as the proposed EPA merger with *Nordair* in 1969, *Quebecair* had also proposed a merger with Eastern Provincial. Merger talks among these three airlines continued over the next fifteen years, until they were ultimately merged through *Canadian Pacific*.

When *Air Canada* phased out its Viscounts in 1973, many of the routes flown by these were turned over to EPA. The company also acquired exclusive rights between St. John's, Gander and Stephenville/Deer Lake at this time. In order to carry out this expanded network, more Boeing 737s were ordered. Two were delivered in 1973, and an *Aer Lingus* 737 was also leased for two months. One each were delivered in 1974 and 1975.

Thus by 1975, EPA had seven Boeing 737s. The Carvairs had been sold in 1973 and the DC-4 in 1972. The three Heralds were sold in early 1975, leaving three DC-3s as the only non-jet equipment operated by the company. These aircraft were operated by EPA, in association with *Air St. Pierre*, on the daily service between Sydney, N.S. and the French Islands of St. Pierre and Miquelon. The last DC-3 on this service, CF-GHL, operated with a blue cheat line below a smaller red cheat line, ending in a circle containing the title ASP. The title on the

upper fuselage read AIR ST. PIERRE above EASTERN PROVINCIAL AIRWAYS.

Eastern Provincial had hoped to obtain Toronto to Charlottetown direct in 1975, but *Air Canada* took this route so that it could operate to all the Canadian capital cities.. Eastern Provincial was able to break out of its region again in April of that year when it was awarded Halifax to Montreal, with stops in Moncton, Fredericton or Saint John, New Brunswick. In the winter of 1975, the company became heavily involved in Inclusive Tour Charters (ITC), using their surplus jet capacity on weekends to fly Maritimers to warmer southern climates.

After selling the Heralds, EPA needed more modern equipment than the DC-3s to operate its smaller routes. The company planned to purchase the Twin Otter until the DASH-7 was available. As an interim measure, Eastern Provincial purchased the forty-eight passenger, twin-engine turboprop Hawker-Siddeley 748. This aircraft proved to be excellent for EPA's shorter routes, flying at 280 mph with a range of eight hundred miles. The Twin Otters were never purchased nor was the order for the DASH-7s ever taken up. After the initial HS-748 was bought in 1975, two more were obtained in 1978. This aircraft replaced the DC-3 on the Sydney to St. Pierre and Miquelon flights, operating with standard EPA colour scheme, but with the title AIR ST. PIERRE appearing immediately forward of the rear door. The DC-3s were disposed of in 1977, leaving the company with only HS-748 and 737 aircraft. Six Boeing 737s remained in the fleet, one having been leased (and later sold) to *Nordair*.

Eastern Provincial often had at least one of its Boeing 737s out on lease after the HS-748s arrived. From June to December 1977, C-GEPB was leased to *Aloha Airlines,* and from April 1978 to April 1979, this same aircraft was leased to *Aer Lingus*. The 737 on lease to *Nordair* was sold to them in 1978. In December 1977, Eastern Provincial joined with *Air Canada* in a joint route and fare program. *Air Canada* took over EPA's reservation system and serviced EPA aircraft in Montreal. In the winter of 1979, EPA was awarded Montreal to Halifax direct.

In June 1980, *CP Air* was awarded Toronto to Halifax by the Canadian Transportation Commission, but the Federal Cabinet, pressured by a strong lobby from the Maritimes, reversed that decision and awarded the route to Eastern Provincial. On 7 July 1980, EPA began flying into the lucrative Toronto market with one flight per day, which was increased to two flights per day in September of that year. The company had to drop their direct Montreal to Halifax flight when they acquired the

---

Eastern Provincial Handley Page Herald, CF-EPI
Photo courtesy of Eastern Provincial Airways

Toronto route, but continued to fly it until March 1981, when it was picked up by *CP Air*. The new Toronto route proved to be very beneficial to the company which showed a profit of one million dollars in 1980.

A new corporate structure for the airline was formed in December 1980, when *Eastern Provincial Airways (1963) Ltd.* became a subsidiary of the Newfoundland Capital Corporation, thus assuring the company would continue its headquarters in Gander, Newfoundland, for the present.

Eastern Provincial leased a HS-748 from *Dan Air* in 1981 for several months before purchasing its fourth such aircraft. This new HS-748 had the stylized EASTERN PROVINCIAL titles.

On 29 December 1981, at Sydney, N.S., HS-748 C-GEPH crashed into the terminal building while taxiing. Although there were no serious injuries, the aircraft was written off. The airline then leased another HS-748 from *Regionair* for much of 1982, and bought another HS-748 the same year.

Eastern Provincial decided to operate only jet aircraft and, in January 1982, formed a new company called *Air Maritime*. This was a subsidiary of EPA and took over the operation of the HS-748 aircraft. The routes of the two airlines were fully integrated, with *Air Maritime* using the *Air Canada* reservation system. *Air Maritime's* colour scheme was an all white aircraft with a blue cheat line below the windows and a thin red cheat line below that. The title AIR MARITIME appeared on the upper fuselage in blue, with the company symbol on the tail in blue.

In April 1982, a third 737 flight per day was added between Toronto and Halifax, with a fourth daily flight operated on Thursday, Friday and Saturday. A 737 was leased from *Pacific Western* for a year to provide the extra capacity.

In October 1982, Eastern Provincial dropped its association with *Air Canada* and began integrating its services with *CP Air* at Toronto, Ottawa, Montreal and Halifax. *CP Air* provided check-in service in Toronto, Ottawa and Montreal, while EPA provided the service in Halifax. *CP Air* took over engine overhauls and passenger reservations for EPA.

On 7 January 1983, the company locked out its mechanics and clerical staff. The pilots followed one week later and supervisory staff with non-union crews were used to maintain essential services. *Air Ontario* Convair 580s, which arrived in Montreal early in the day from London and then sat idle all day until returning to London in the evening, flew EPA's flights during the week on the Montreal to Charlo and Chatham route during the strike. *Austin Airways* HS-748s operated the flights on weekends. *Air Maritime* continued to function using supervisory staff and some *Austin* aircrews, but the strike was not settled until early June 1983.

The bitterness created by the strike remained and some pilots had to go to court to win back their jobs from the non-union crews used during the strike. The strike lead to a $2.9 million loss for EPA in 1983.

On 12 June 1983, *CP Air* finally commenced their interchange flights with EPA. Eastern Provincial 737s operated the Toronto to Halifax and Montreal to Halifax routes, bearing small *CP Air* symbols on the forward lower fuselage. This arrangement allowed *CP Air* to free up two Boeing 737 jets, while providing *CP Air* passengers connecting services throughout the Maritimes and Newfoundland. For EPA, the agreement eliminated a competitor on these routes.

Eastern Provincial seemed to be recovering from the bitterness of the long strike when, early in 1984, the airline's owner, Mr. Harry Steele, announced that the company was moving its headquarters from Gander to Halifax. While people in the aviation industry could see that this made good business sense, both the federal and Newfoundland governments were concerned about the damage this would do to the Gander and Newfoundland economy.

The biggest surprise was still to come, because on 17 April 1984, Harry Steele announced that he would be selling Eastern Provincial Airways and *Air Maritime* to *Canadian Pacific Airlines* (*CP Air*) for $20 million. Eastern Provincial and *Air Maritime* would continue to operate as separate entities, and Harry Steele would continue as President and Chief Executive Officer. Thus control of the airlines shifted not just from Newfoundland to Nova Scotia, but all the way across the country to Vancouver, British Columbia.

Eastern Provincial had made a profit of $5 million in 1981/82, but the bitter labour dispute continued to cause Mr. Steele problems. The company also needed to buy new equipment, as the Boeing 737s were growing old, and the much larger *CP Air* would be better able to assist in this area.

During 1984, Eastern Provincial consolidated its licence to allow flights between any two points. EPA thus entered the Toronto - Montreal sector with one flight per day which continued on to Fredericton and Halifax. EPA could now fly from Toronto or Montreal to any other cities in their route structure, and vice versa.

In 1984, *Air Maritime* became the first completely non-smoking airline – a bold move in the mid-1980s. *Torontair* also had a non-smoking policy at that time, but was not operating aircraft the size of the HS-748.

A former *Orion Airways* Boeing 737-200 was put into service in March 1985, and introduced the new dark blue colour scheme of the airline. It was also the first aircraft to copy the *CP Air* policy of naming aircraft after Canadian cities, carrying the title 'Flagship St. John's.' Halifax to Ottawa flights were started in June 1985, with a stop at Montreal introduced in October. EPA aircraft in the old colour scheme carried small *CP Air* stickers on their fuselage and when EPA Boeing 737 aircraft were being overhauled, *CP Air* Boeing 737 C-GCPY replaced them, this plane being appropriately called 'Empress of Halifax.'

January 12, 1987, saw the official end of Eastern Provincial Airways. On that date, all EPA flights began operating under CP designators. Eastern Provincial aircraft continued to fly in the Maritimes, but the company's operations were now fully amalgamated with *CP Air.* All Eastern Provincial aircraft, however, had been painted in the new blue EPA colour scheme and continued to operate this way throughout 1986. *Canadian Pacific* did not intend to operate propeller-driven equipment, planning to phase out Air *Maritime.* CPA bought a share of *Air Atlantic*, making it their partner maritime airline. As DASH-7s became available for *Air Atlantic,* the HS-748s were retired, until finally, all *Air Maritime* flights were shut down in November 1986. *Air St. Pierre*

took over one HS-748 to continue flights between Nova Scotia and St. Pierre.

In January 1987, with the announcement of the new name for the merged *Pacific Western* and *Canadian Pacific* airlines, a DC-10-30 was rolled out in the new *Canadian* colour scheme. Shortly afterwards, the first Boeing 737 appeared in the new *Canadian* colours, this aircraft was C-GEPM and bore the title 'Empress of Labrador'. Other EPA Boeing 737s began to be painted, with C-FEPL, 'Empress of Halifax' and C-FEPP soon appearing in *Canadian* colours. By May 1987, all EPA aircraft had had the title EPA removed and by June 1987, only three remained in hybrid colours, carring *Canadian* titles. (C-GEPA, still with title 'Flagship Labrador,' C-FEPU still had the EPA gull on the tail and C-FEPO was still a white aircraft with a full *Canadian* tail.) By July 1988, all had been repainted in the full *Canadian* colour scheme and the last remnants of EPA had disappeared from the Canadian airline scene.

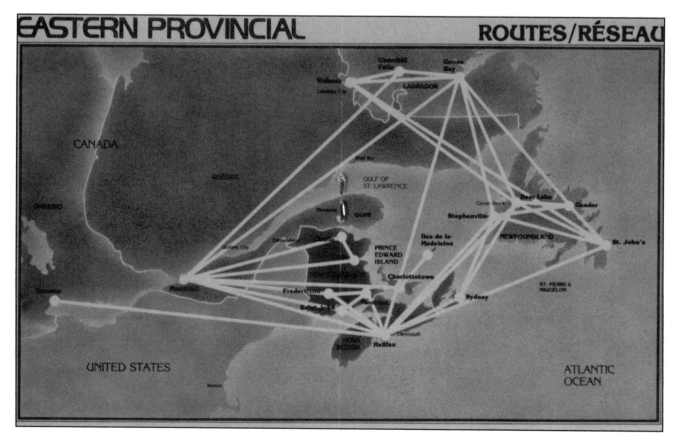

Eastern Provincial Route map as shown in 1980 Timetable

FLEET LISTING
EASTERN PROVINCIAL AIRLINES

REG'N	C/N	F/N	IS	WFU	NOTES	MODEL	FLAGSHIP
737-2E1							
C-FEPL*	20396	201	11/69	5/86	ST C-FEPL CPA		HALIFAX
C-FEPO*	20300	203	7/70	5/86	ST C-FEPO CPA		CHARLOTTETOWN
C-FEPP*	20681	204	3/73	5/86	ST C-FEPP CPA		FREDERICTON
C-FEPR*	20397	202	12/69	5/86	ST C-FEPR CPA		SAINT JOHN
C-FEPU*	20776	205	10/73	5/86	ST C-FEPU CPA		SYDNEY
C-GEPA	20976	206	12/74	5/86	ST C-GEPA CPA		LABRADOR
C-GEPB	21112		10/75	5/76	ST C-GNDD Nordair		
C-GEPM	22395	207	4/82	5/86	ST C-GEPM CPA	-2T5	ST. JOHN'S
737-275C							
C-GSPW	22618		4/82	4/83	LF C-GSPW PWA		
737-248							
CF-ASF	20221		10/73	12/73	LF EI-ASF Aer Lingus		
737-242C							
CF-NAH	19848		4/69	10/69	LF CF-NAH Nordair (full EPA c/s)		
737-222							
N9057U	19938		5/69	1/70	LF N9057U United Airlines		
HS-748							
C-FINE	1611	301	5/78	9/86	ST F-OSPM Air St. Pierre; OB Air Maritime 1/82		
C-GDOP	1745	304	4/82	5/86	LT F-ODQQ Air St. Pierre; OB Air Maritime		
C-GDUN	1581		2/82	10/82	LF C-GDUN Regionair; OB Air Maritime		
C-GEPB	1589		5/81	7/81	LF G-AXVG Dan Air; OB EPA		
C-GEPB	1686	303	7/81	3/86	LT C-GEPB Austin 7/86; OB EPA		
C-GEPH	1635		3/76	12/81	W/O 29/12/81 Sydney N.S.; OB EPA		
C-GEPI	1594	302	5/78	5/86	ST C-BNJK McAvia Int'l; OB Air Maritime 1/82		
C-GQTG	1619		9/84	5/85	LF C-GQTG Austin Airways; OB Air Maritime 1/82		
C-GRXE	1783		3/85	4/85	ST C-GRXE Bradley A/S; OB Air Maritime 1/82		
G-BEBA	1613		7/81	12/81	LF G-GEBA Dan Air; OB EPA		
DART HERALD							
CF-EPC	167		3/63	3/75	ST G-BDFE British Air Ferries		
CF-EPI	166		3/63	1/75	ST G-BCWE British Air Ferries		
CF-NAC	159		11/62	3/75	ST G-BCZG British Air Ferries; EX Nordair/MCA		
CF-NAF	160		5/63	3/65	W/O 17/03/65 near Musquodoboit EX Nordair/MCA		
DC-3							
CF-CRW	18958		6/61	9/63	ST CF-CRW Reindeer Air		
CF-FAJ	12099		10/63	4/65	W/O 03/04/65 at St. Pierre		
CF-GHX	11780		7/65	10/71	ST trade school in Gander		
CF-GOX	7362		10/63	11/64	W/O 21/11/64 at Blanc Sablon, Quebec		
CF-HBX	13854		4/75	9/76	ST CF-HBX Wright Enterprises Ltd.		
CF-HGL	12712		10/63	4/78	ST N37906 Southern Flyer; OB Air Ste Pierre		
CF-ILW	4352		11/61	8/64	ST CF-ILW Canadian Marconi		
CF-JNR	4595		12/59	4/61	W/O 04/04/61 at St. Pierre		
CF-RTB	13803		4/65	6/76	ST CF-RTB Gateway Aviation		
CF-RTY	27078		6/66	12/76	ST 8P-CAW Tropical Air Service		
DC-4							
CF-JIR	10362		1/65	8/65	LF CF-JIR Nordair		
CF-MCI	27261		9/63	10/72	WFU EX CF-MCI Maritime Central		
ATL-98							
CF-EPU	7480		5/68	9/68	W/O 28/09/68 Churchill Falls; Carvair (EX DC-4)		
CF-EPV	10448		5/68	9/73	ST CF-EPV British Air Ferries for spares; Carvair (EX DC-4)		
CF-EPW	10458		2/68	9/73	ST G-ASKD British Air Ferries; Carvair (EX DC-4)		
DHC-6							
CF-BEL	275		11/69	1/74	ST CF-BEL Labrador Airways; OF Newfoundland gov't.		
CF-DMR	36		7/67	5/72	ST CF-DMR Calm Air; OF Newfoundland gov't.		
L-1049H							
CF-NAL	4831		3/68	4/69	LF CF-NAL Nordair		
Curtiss C-46							
CF-HTL	22535		9/63	4/65	ST CP-760 Bolivian Airways		
CF-HTK	22530		9/63	5/65	ST OB-M-764 Cia Anglo "Bartola"		
CF-NAD	30200		4/62	1/64	LF CF-NAD Nordair		
CF-NAE	27063		4/62	12/63	LF CF-NAE Nordair		

FLEET LISTING
EASTERN PROVINCIAL AIRLINES

REG'N	C/N	IS	WFU	NOTES
PBY-5A Canso				
CF-CRP	9837	4/57	4/67	ST CF-CRP Newfoundland Government
CF-HFL	CV110	5/52	10/57	W/O 01/10/57 80 km from Goose Bay: for display
CF-IGJ	48429	6/55	4/67	ST CF-IGJ Newfoundland Government
CF-IHA	CV365	2/62	5/62	W/O 12/05/62 at Godthaab, Greenland
CF-IHN	CV441	5/58	9/59	Leased
CF-IZU	46655	4/56	4/67	ST CF-IZU Newfoundland Government
CF-NJC	CV430	4/57	4/67	ST CF-NJC Newfoundland Government
CF-NWY	48304	5/61	7/67	W/O 7/67 at Geoffrey, Newfoundland
CF-OFI	CV343	4/57	4/67	ST CF-OFI Newfoundland Government
CF-OFJ	CV315	2/62	7/65	W/O 7/65 at Catlina, Newfoundland
DHC-3 Otter				
CF-AGM	400	5/60	6/70	ST CF-AGM Labrador Airways Limited
CF-EYO	16	6/60	6/70	ST CF-EYO Labrador Airways Limited
CF-GCV	2	12/53	6/70	ST CF-GCV Labrador Airways Limited
CF-HXY	67	9/66	6/70	ST CF-HXY Labrador Airways Limited
CF-LEA	286	11/58	6/70	ST CF-LEA Labrador Airways Limited
CF-MEX	332	4/60	8/61	W/O 21/08/61 at Dondre, Stramfjord, Greenland
CF-MIT	273	7/60	5/70	ACC 22/05/70 Goose Bay; ST Austin Airways
CF-PMQ	197	10/58	6/70	ST CF-PMQ Labrador Airways Limited
DHC-2 Beaver				
CF-EYQ	465	4/52	6/70	ST CF-EYQ Labrador Airways Limited
CF-EYW	475	5/52	6/70	ST CF-EYW Lambair
CF-GQF	81	5/57	6/70	ST CF-GQF Labrador Airways Limited
CF-GQU	107	5/56	4/58	W/O 4/58 Musgrave Harbour
CF-IHK	53	4/56	8/57	W/O 8/57 St. Anthony
CF-IVA	515	5/56	6/70	ST CF-IVA Labrador Airways Limited
CF-JAT	925	5/56	6/70	ST CF-JAT Labrador Airways Limited
DHC-2 Turbo				
CF-GFX	TB19	6/67	6/70	ST CF-GFS Newfoundland Government
CF-UKK	TB18	6/67	6/70	ST CF-UKK Labrador Airways Lilmited
CF-VPV	TB37	8/67	6/70	ST CF-VPV Newfoundland Government
Found Brothers				
CF-SVB	24	5/65	7/67	W/O 7/67 Williamsport
Piper Cub				
CF-GPD	8319	6/49	8/55	ST CF-GPD F. Ledrew, Newfoundland
CF-NVM	187749	1/61	6/70	OF Newfoundland Government
CF-NVN	187761	1/61	6/70	OF Newfoundland Governement
Lockheed 10A				
CF-BXE	1936	12/55	1/58	ST CF-BXE Trans Gaspesian Air Lines
CF-HTV	1005	12/55	12/57	ST CF-HTV Trans Gaspesian Air Lines
Cessna 185				
CF-NBL	0119	4/61	8/63	ST CF-NBL Gander Aviation
CF-NBM	0169	4/61	8/63	ST CF-NBM Gander Aviation
CF-NNR	0097	4/61	8/63	ST CF-NNR Gander Aviation
CF-NYF	0282	4/61	8/63	ST CF-NYF Gander Aviation
CF-MYM	0072	3/61	3/61	W/O 3/61 west of Buchans, Newfoundland
Cessna 180				
CF-HCJ	30420	7/53	6/55	ST CF-HCJ Canadian Aircraft Renters
CF-HDK	30559	4/61	8/61	Sold
CF-LFH	50454	4/61	8/61	ACC 08/61; repaired and sold.
Piaggio				
CF-ILU	199	5/57	4/62	EX CF-ILU Timmins Aviation Limited
Seabee				
CF-DLS	627	6/55	12/56	Sold
CF-GPF	---	8/59	11/50	CR 11/50 St. Anthony; EX VO-GPF
Norseman				
CF-GPI	---	12/51	4/52	W/O 25/04/52. Broke through ice Burlington
CF-GPM	162	12/49	1/56	W/O 01/56. Broke through ice at St. Anthony
CF-HAD	628	9/55	12/55	LEASED
CF-QAA	19	11/51	9/56	Sold

FLEET LISTING
EASTERN PROVINCIAL AIRLINES

REG'N	C/N	IS	WFU	NOTES
Stinson 108-3				
CF-FQJ	---	10/51	7/53	Sold; replaced by Cessna 180
CF-GPH	---	9/49	7/53	Sold; replaced by Cessna 180
Anson				
CF-GSA	4178	5/50	4/51	W/O 4/51. Broke through ice; EX RCAF
Cessna Crane				
CF-FDR	2428	3/49	3/49	EX RCAF FJ227; parts used for VO-ACE
VO-ACE	----	3/49	1/50	W/O 1/50 Lascie; first EPA aircraft
Bell 47				
CF-IVE	1568	6/56	8/58	Sold; replaced by CF-IVF
CF-IVF	----	8/53	5/56	W/O 06/05/56 at Smallwood Farm
Sikorsky 55				
CF-HJS	55559	4/58	1/67	W/O 01/67 at St. Georges
CF-MEV	55103	4/58	3/67	ST CF-MEW Universal Helicopters

Maritime Central Airways

HEADQUARTERS:
Charlottetown, Prince Edward Island

MAIN BASES:
Charlottetown; Halifax

FINAL FLEET 1963:
1 - Dart Herald;
1 - DC4;
2 - Curtiss C-46s;
3 - DC3s

COLOURS:
The white upper fuselage was separated from the lower fuselage by a wide, light-blue cheat line (above and below the windows), with a narrow dark-blue cheat line above, both wrapping around the nose. The lower fuselage was silver on the Viscount and grey on the Heralds. Titles appeared in black. The tail was all white, except for a small Maritime Central logo.

ROUTES:
Charlottetown – Summerside – Moncton – St. John – Halifax – Sydney – Newfoundland;
DEW Line sites in Newfoundland and Labrador;
Magdelen Islands, St. Pierre;
Charters throughout the Maritimes and Newfoundland;
International Charters.

HISTORY:

Maritime Central Airways was formed on 30 September, 1941, at Charlottetown, PEI. Carl Burke, a native of P.E.I., and Josiah Anderson, were the two founders. Mr. Anderson was killed during WWII while flying with Ferry Command.

Carl Burke was awarded 'Member of the Order of the British Empire' (MBE) for a rescue, as described in this extract from the *Canada Gazette* of 21 August 1943:

> "When an Anson aircraft with a crew of four made a forced landing on an ice floe in the Gulf of St. Lawrence, Mr. Burke, a civilian pilot, made four landings in a Fleet aircraft on the ice floe, picking up one of the crew on each landing. He then returned to the ice floe and recovered certain valuable instruments. The whole operation incurred very considerable risk as he was by no means certain that the ice would hold his aircraft. By his outstanding skill and extremely courageous action this pilot undoubtedly saved the lives of the four crew members."

Service commenced on 8 December 1941, operating a Barclay-Grow seaplane, Fairchild 24 and Boeing 247D providing service between Charlottetown, P.E.I. and Moncton, N.B. In January 1942, service was started from Charlottetown to the Magdelen Islands.

The US government chartered the Barkley-Grow to search for a downed B-17 in December 1942. On 23 December 1942, while the Barkley-Grow was making a landing on the sea ice near Angmagssalik, Greenland, the plane broke through the ice. The pilots made their way to shore and were found six days later by a group of Inuit. After a few days recovering with the Inuit, the pilots were returned to a US Army base.

A DH-89A Rapide was added to the fleet in 1942. The first Lockheed 10 Electra was added in 1943, three more purchased in 1945, and another bought in 1946. A Lockheed 12A was operated for four months in 1945 and two ex-Royal Canadian Air Force Cessna T-50 Cranes were added to the fleet in 1945.

The arrival of the first DC-3 in February 1946 allowed MCA to operate the first P.E.I. to N.S. flight. Two more DC-3s were added later the same year, raising the MCA fleet to one Rapide, four Lockheed 10 Electras, two Cessna Cranes and three DC-3s. More than thirty-two thousand passengers were flown in 1946.

International service was begun by Maritime Central on 18 June 1948, with a flight from Sydney, Nova Scotia to the French Island of St. Pierre. The airline was kept busy with its other scheduled routes, plus charters for government officials, mail contracts, lobster hauling charters and ice patrols for the Federal Government in the late 1940s. A Canso was bought in 1948 only for its engines, but turned out to be in such good condition that it was refurbished and put into service. Two small Stinson aircraft were also purchased that year, but served only briefly.

A single Curtiss C-46 first saw service with Maritime Central in 1950, serving for only two years. An influx of six DC-3s in 1952 swelled the fleet size for this aircraft to eight, despite the loss of a DC-3 eighteen miles from Gaspe, Quebec on 22 March 1952.

In April 1953, the airline opened service to Frobisher Bay on Baffin Island. Fred Briggs and Carl Burke bought 50% of *Boreal Airways* that year and formed *Boreal Air Service. Boreal,* later renamed *Nordair,* was kept separate from the main operations of Maritime Central. *Boreal/Nordair* and MCA had a close working relationship and several aircraft were exchanged between the two companies.

The building of the Distant Early Warning Line (DEW Line) in 1955, allowed rapid expansion of Maritime Central. They received the contracts to supply air transport to seventeen of the forty-two DEW Line sites. Four Avro Yorks, four Curtiss C-46s, two DC-4s and another DC-3 were added to the fleet to carry out this service.

Maritime Central's lone Bristol Freighter, obtained in 1953 from *Associated Airways,* crashed on 13 February 1956. While taking off from Frobisher Bay on Baffin Island, a vehicle on board shifted to the rear of the cabin, causing the aircraft to stall and crash from about one thousand feet.

The company began operating international charters in 1956 and purchased three more DC-4s to service these flights. During the Hungarian airlift of 1956, the airline made numerous flights to Europe, returning to Canada with refugees.

One international charter ended in tragedy on 11 August 1957, when a DC-4, returning from the United Kingdom, crashed near Issoudun, Quebec and all seventy-nine on board were killed.

In 1958, MCA planned to purchase two DC-6As, but these aircraft were never delivered to the company. In June 1959 however, MCA became the second Canadian operator to fly the Vickers Viscount. The MCA aircraft was a series 800 Viscount, while the Viscounts flown by *Trans Canada Airlines* were Series 700 aircraft. The dif-

ference between these aircraft was that the series 800 had a 9'3" longer cabin, rectangular cabin doors (rather than the distinctive elliptical doors on the TCA aircraft) and increased engine power. The aircraft could cruise at 320 mph and carry up to seventy-one passengers. The MCA aircraft had removable bulkheads, permitting the passenger/freight ratio to be altered depending on the route being flown. This aircraft was flown throughout Newfoundland and the maritimes until sold in April 1962.

The DC-3 fleet was used extensively during the 1950s and right up until the merger in 1963. Three of these aircraft were written off in accidents during the period. The first, CF-BXZ, crashed ten miles northwest of Gaspe, Quebec on 22 March, 1955. The second accident occurred three years later, on 25 November 1955, at one of the DEW Line sites, (68.33N, 83.15W). The third accident occurred on 15 April 1961, when DC-3, CF-FKQ, crashed at Moncton, New Brunswick. In all, sixteen DC-3s served with Maritime Central Airways, more than with any of the other regional airlines.

To replace the Viscount, two Dart Heralds were ordered for delivery in 1962. One plane, CF-MCK, was painted in full Maritime Central colours and used by Handley Page for a 12,000 mile demonstration tour in 1962. The two ordered planes were not purchased by MCA, but the Company did buy one Herald from *Nordair,* CF-NAF, in November 1962. This thirty-six to forty-four passenger aircraft stayed with the company only for a short time, being sold to *Eastern Provincial* just prior to the merger of the two companies in 1963.

The Maritime Central Airways fleet in 1963 consisted of the Herald, one DC-4, four DC-3s, four C-46s and two Beech 18s. One C-46 was lost in a hangar fire in Moncton in January of that year and another was sold to *Nordair.* A DC-3 was also sold to *Nordair* and one of the Beech 18s was sold.

It was realized that the Maritimes and Newfoundland could only support one regional airline, thus after long negotiations, the smaller *Eastern Provincial Airways* took over Maritime Central Airways in September, 1963. One DC-4, three DC-3s, two C-46s and a Beech 18 went to the new company, called *Eastern Provincial Airways (1963) Ltd.* Thus ended the history of Maritime Central Airways.

FLEET LISTING
MARITIME CENTRAL AIRWAYS

REG'N	C/N	IS	WFU	NOTES	
Viscount					
CF-MCJ	258	6/59	4/62	ST EI-AMA Aer Lingus	
Dart Herald					
CF-NAF	160	11/62	5/63	ST CF-NAF Eastern Provincial; EX Nordair	
CF-MCK	161	NTU	NTU	Painted in MCA c/s for a tour in 1962 but NTU	
CF-MCM	162	NTU	NTU	Ordered in 1962 but NTU; ST HB-AAG Globe Air	
DC-6B					
CF-MCL	45506	NTU	NTU	Ordered but ST N4000S Overseas, 1958	
CF-MCK	45497	NTU	NTU	Ordered but NTU	
DC-4					
CF-MCA	10457	10/55	3/62	ST CF-NAA Nordair	
CF-MCB	10478	10/55	3/62	ST CF-NAB Nordair	
CF-MCD	10479	5/57	10/59	ST N8090 Aviation Business Sevice; EX CF-QBA	
CF-MCF	18374	5/57	8/57	W/O 11/08/57 Issoudun, Quebec; EX CF-HVL	
CF-MCI	27261	12/57	9/63	ST CF-MCI EPA in Merger; EX CF-CUJ	
DC-3					
CF-BXZ	4595	2/46	3/52	W/O 22/03/52 Gaspe, Quebec	
CF-BZH	6079	8/46	1/53	ST CF-BZH Spartan Air Service	
CF-BZI	13448	11/45	1/53	ST CF-BZI International Pipe Line Control	
CF-DJT	19039	1/50	8/53	ST CF-DJT A.V. Roe (Canada) Ltd.	
CF-FAJ	12099	2/52	9/63	ST CF-FAJ Eastern Provincial in merger	
CF-FBY	26888	6/52	4/56	ST N6067V G.H. Fuller, Miami	
CF-FCQ	620	7/52	7/55	ST N44F Beldex Corporation	
CF-FKQ	4301	12/52	4/61	W/O 15/04/61 Moncton, New Brunswick	
CF-GHQ	19122	3/52	9/59	ST CF-GHQ Northern Wings Ltd.	
CF-GKZ	9395	10/51	4/58	ST CF-GKZ Nordair	
CF-GOC	7362	4/51	9/63	ST CF-GOC Eastern Provincial in merger	
CF-HGD	13041	9/61	5/62	ST CF-HGD Nordair	
CF-HGL	12712	9/53	9/63	ST CF-HGL Eastern Provincial in merger	
CF-HTH	27000	2/55	8/58	ST CF-HTH Wheeler Aviation	
CF-HTP	19140	9/53	10/55	W/O 25/10/55 DEW Line Site 30 (68.33N, 83.15W)	
CF-MCC	13399	11/55	8/58	ST CF-MCC Wheeler Aviation	
Curtiss C-46					
CF-CZL	22494	1/60	3/63	ST CF-CZL Nordair; EX Canadian Pacific	
CF-GUU	2943	12/50	3/52	ST F-DAAR Air Maroc	
CF-HTI	2932	3/55	1/63	DBF 11/01/63 Moncton, N.B. in hangar fire	
CF-HTJ	22475	3/55	10/55	ACC 25/10/55; ST Mount Laurier 2/56	
CF-HTK	22530	2/55	9/63	ST CF-HTK Eastern Provincial in merger	
CF-HTL	22535	3/55	9/63	ST CF-HTL Eastern Provincial in merger	
Bristol 170					
CF-FZU	13136	3/53	2/56	W/O 13/02/56 Baffin Island	
DHC-2 Beaver					
CF-HGV	581	4/53	7/61	ST CF-HGV Abbott Industries Limited	
Beech C18S					
CF-MCE	35892	5/56	4/58	ST CF-MCE Nordair	
CF-MCG	35931	6/56	7/63	SOLD	
CF-MCH	35939	10/57	3/60	ST CF-MCH Curran & Briggs Limited	
CF-MCL	1347	7/61	9/63	ST CF-MCL Eastern Provincial in merger	
PBY-5A Canso					
CF-FKV	332	2/52	4/57	ST CF-FKV Mount Laurier Aviation	
CF-FVE	11052	7/48	3/59	ST CF-FVE Nordair	
CF-GBQ	456	3/52	4/57	SOLD	
CF-HTN	48275	9/55	3/57	ST CF-HTN Transair	
28-5ACF Canso					
CF-HTO	083	9/55	1/60	Sold	
Avro 685 York					
CF-HIP	MW287	4/55	12/56	ST CF-HIP Pacific Western Airlines	EX RAF MW287
CF-HMU	MW203	4/55	11/56	WFU	EX RAF MW203
CF-HMW	MW167	4/55	1/57	WFU	EX RAF MW167
CF-HTM	MW185	4/55	2/60	WFU	EX RAF MW185

FLEET LISTING
MARITIME CENTRAL AIRWAYS

REG'N	C/N	IS	WFU	NOTES	
Anson V					
CF-GMR	352C	3/51	8/56	WFU	
Cessna Crane					
CF-BTO	1397	11/45	12/48	WFU & scrapped	EX RCAF 7904
CF-BTQ	1543	11/45	4/51	ST CF-BTQ Nfld. Flying Club	EX RCAF 8050
Boeing 247D					
CF-BTB	1729	12/41	3/45	ST N13347 H.G. Chatterton, Dayton, Ohio	
Lockheed 12A					
CF-BXS	1240	3/45	7/45	ST N----- |H.G. Chatterton, Dayton, Ohio	
Lockheed 10B					
CF-BEH	1066	5/45	6/46	ST N---- H.G. Chatterton, Dayton, Ohio	
CF-BXQ	1040	3/45	5/56	ST CF-BXQ Matane Air Service	
CF-BYV	1059	8/45	11/56	ST CF-BYV Matane Air Service	
Lockheed 10A					
CF-BXE	1076	4/43	3/51	ST CF-BXE DOT; then to EPA	
CF-BYU	1013	1/46	11/56	ST CF-BYU Trans Gaspesian Airline	
DH-89A Rapide					
CF-BNJ	89232	6/42	4/52	ST CF-BNJ Spartan Air Service	
Fairchild 24					
CF-CCN	2801	10/41	11/43	ST N----- H.G. Chatterton, Dayton, Ohio	
Barkley Grow					
CF-BMV	5	10/41	12/42	W/O 23/12/42 near Angmagssalik, Greenland	

PART 3

Commuter Airlines

AIR BC

Air BC Dash-7, C-GJPI

ALLIANCE:
Air Canada Connector
(100% Owned by Air Canada)

HEADQUARTERS:
4680 Cowley Crescent, Richmond, B.C., V7B 1C1

MAJOR BASES:
Vancouver International Airport; Vancouver Harbour.

FLEET 1988:
4 - DASH-7s;
8 - DASH-8s;
8 - DHC-6 Twin Otters;
5 - Jetstream 3100s;
3 - BAe146s.

COLOURS:
Air Canada Connector colour scheme consisting of a white aircraft with a red cheat line which comes to a sharp point on the nose of the aircraft and runs below the windows, broadening downwards as it approaches the rear of the aircraft so that the rear lower fuselage is entirely red. A grey line starts at the same point on the forward fuselage and angles more sharply downwards ending at the lower portion of the rear door. The lines form two elongated darts meeting at the nose of the aircraft, with white fuselage between The tail is white at the top and red at the bottom with a large red maple

leaf on the white portion. The red colour on the tail follows the shape of the maple leaf above, and is separated from it by white. The registration appears above the title 'Air BC' on the rear upper fuselage, both in red, and the fleet number appears in red on the upper tail.

Air BC colours prior to adoption of the current scheme was an all white aircraft with a red cheat line (through the windows of the Dash-7 and below the windows on the other aircraft), which sweeps up to form an all red tail. A narrow blue and narrow red cheat line are below the broad red cheat, each separated by white. On the tail is a large White 'A.' The title 'Air BC' appears in blue on the forward upper fuselage of the Dash-7 and on the rear fuselage of the DHC-6 Otter and Islander. On the Dash-8, the title was in white on the broad red cheat line, forward of the engines. The wings were all white.

ROUTES:
Vancouver Harbour to Victoria Harbour.
Vancouver – Victoria – Seattle – Nanaimo – Port Hardy – Campbell River – Comox – Powell River – Quesnel – Williams Lake – Kamloops – Kelowna – Penticton – Castlegar – Cranbrook – Prince George – Fort St. John – Terrace – Prince Rupert – Dawson Creek – Whitehorse
Alberta:
Grande Prairie – Edmonton – Calgary – Lethbridge.

HISTORY:

In 1979, Jim Pattison Investments began to purchase regional commuter airlines in British Columbia. The key acquisition was *Air West Airlines Ltd.*, which had been founded in 1959 by Norman Gold under the name *Powell River Airways* and operated out of Powell River with a charter licence. In 1964, a Vancouver firm, *C and C Air Taxi*, was acquired by *Air West* thereby providing authority to operate a scheduled service between Vancouver, Texada Island and Powell River. In 1965, the acquisition *Nanaimo Airlines* was merged with *Powell River Airways* to form *Air West* with its main base located in Vancouver. More route authorities were obtained and in 1968 scheduled service between Vancouver Harbour, Nanaimo Harbour and Victoria Harbour were commenced as well as scheduled service to Duncan and Qualicum. In 1977 *Air West* further expanded, providing service between Victoria Harbour and Lake Union, Seattle.

West Coast Air Service Ltd. was founded by Lloyd and Al Michaud in 1956 as *Vancouver U-Fly,* providing flying training and charter service. The company was also a distributor for Cessna aircraft. As charter activities grew, the company changed its name to more appropriately reflect the services offered, becoming *West Coast Air Services* in 1956. Bases were established at Kamloops and Nelson, principally providing contract flying to the forest service. In 1963, the flying training section was sold to *Skyway Air Services* and the charter services were consolidated at Vancouver in 1970. In April 1974, *West Coast Air* acquired *Pacific Western's* Grumman Mallards and the routes they served on became the company's first scheduled service. *West Coast* then flew to Bella Coola, Namu and Bella Bella. Business grew and additional scheduled services were then provided to the Gulf Islands. Twin Otter float-equipped aircraft were acquired and *West Coast* went into direct competition with *Air West* on the lucrative Vancouver Harbour to Victoria Harbour route. Initially, *West Coast* aircraft had to make a 'technical stop' in the Gulf Islands. This varied from a touch and go in Lyle Harbour to a full stop in Bedwell Harbour with an immediate takeoff. This dangerous addition of a stop to meet a DOT rule was finally withdrawn but only after a large number of totally unnecessary landings and takeoffs had occurred. When *West Coast* was merged into Air BC, Al Michaud became Chairman of the Board of Air BC Ltd.

Gulf Air and *Island Air* operated charter and scheduled services out of Campbell River, mainly in support of the logging industry. Each operated one Twin Otter and several smaller aircraft. *Haida Airlines* flew from Vancouver Harbour in support of the logging industry.

Pacific Coastal Airlines was founded in 1960 by Don McGillvray and provided scheduled service between Nanaimo (Cassidy) Airport and Vancouver, as well as service to a number of Vancouver Island points including Victoria, Duncan, Port Alberni, Qualicum, Comox and Port Hardy. The airline was operating two DC-3s on the Vancouver – Nanaimo route when it was absorbed into *Air West* in February 1980.

Trans Provincial Airlines originally had its headquarters in Terrace, B.C. and operated scheduled and charter operations from bases at Prince Rupert, Prince George, Ocean Falls, Sandspit, and Smithers. It connected Prince Rupert to the Queen Charlotte Islands (Masset and Sandspit); to Stewart, Alice Arm, Hatley Bay, Bella Bella, and Ocean Falls; to Ketchikan, Alaska; and tried to make the Prince Rupert – Terrace – Smithers – Prince George route a viable operation. An F-27 flew this route as well as the two DC-3s later operated by *Pacific Coastal*. The bulk of its other operations were with amphibious aircraft such as Otters, Beavers, Cessnas and the renowned Grumman Goose.

By June 1980, Jim Pattison Industries had bought all of these airlines, and in December 1980, the first aircraft in the combined fleet, former *Gulf Air* Twin Otter C-FIOH, was rolled out in the new Air BC colour scheme. *Air West* aircraft had already adopted this colour scheme and its planes needed only a name change.

Air BC was at this time both a commuter and charter operation, serving coastal British Columbia from Victoria in the south to Stewart in the north. Air BC was divided into two operating companies: *Trans Provincial Airlines* and Air BC. *Trans Provincial Airlines* was based in Prince Rupert and served the Queen Charlotte Islands, northwestern BC and south to Ocean Falls. TPA aircraft adopted the white, red and blue colour scheme of Air BC but bore TPA titles and a TPA symbol on the tail. The other operating division, Air BC, had its headquarters at the Vancouver International Airport (south side) in the old *BC Airlines* hangar, and provided scheduled services throughout southern coastal BC and north to Campbell River, Port Hardy, Bella Coola and Ocean Falls. Its major route at this time was the Vancouver – Victoria service, both harbour to harbour and between the airports. It also had some services to the interior of British Columbia, with flights to Williams Lake and Quesnel from Vancouver.

Air West had started a service from Vancouver Harbour to Union Harbour in Seattle but this operation ceased in July 1980 and was never restarted. By September 1981, Air BC had sold many of its former Vancouver Island bases to *Air Nootka Ltd.* Charter work had suffered because of the slowdown in the forest industry and Air BC planned to concentrate on scheduled services. To this end, it started a Vancouver Airport (south terminal) – Victoria Airport service using Twin Otters and a Vancouver Airport – Comox Twin Otter service to complement its Vancouver – Nanaimo (Cassidy) flights.

In February 1982, Air BC's Campbell River operation was sold to *Coval Air*, although the company retained the Vancouver Harbour – Campbell River route. Because the only profitable route operated by the company had at that time was Vancouver Harbour – Victoria Harbour, it asked its union to accept a 10% pay cut but the union refused. This lead to the layoff of many mechanics, reservations staff and flight crews.

On April Fool's Day 1982, Air BC ran a promotion on their Vancouver Airport – Victoria Airport route, charging only 99 cents each way. More than a thousand passengers were carried but the company's licence for this route was cancelled by the DOT for one day (21 December 1982) because of the unauthorized fare! April also saw the Vancouver Harbour – Duncan route dropped. Air BC resumed flying from Vancouver Harbour to Gillies Bay and Powell River in September 1982 after dropping this route for nine months.

Two DC-3s were acquired by Air BC in 1983 for use on the Vancouver – Nanaimo and Port Hardy flights and also the Vancouver – Comox and Campbell River service. The company also used these aircraft for charters, but went back to using Twin Otters on these routes the following year.

Early in 1983, Air BC decided to obtain larger aircraft and attempted to purchase HS-748 aircraft without success. The F-27 was also considered, but Air BC finally settled on the Dash-7. Before gambling on these larger and comparatively expensive Canadian aircraft, the company requested a two-year, no-strike contract from its unions and this time the unions agreed. A former *Spantax* Dash-7 first flew Vancouver – Bella Bella and Bella Coola and Vancouver – Port Hardy on 29 July 1983. This flight was made possible by the upgrading of the Bella Bella airport, thus allowing the Grumman Mallards (which could land in the water) to be sold. The turbo Mallard and a piston Mallard were sold to *Air Witsunday* of Australia in January 1983.

CP Air's Boeing 737 service between Victoria and Vancouver was very expensive to operate and was in direct competition with the more frequently scheduled *Pacific Western Airlines* Boeing 737 service, so it entered into an agreement with Air BC for Air BC to operate the Vancouver to Victoria segment of these flights as a commuter service. The large, comfortable Dash-7 aircraft made this arrangement acceptable to the *CP Air* passengers. Air BC thus moved its operations from the south terminal at Vancouver International Airport to the main terminal, using *CP Air* docking bays and reservation services.

January 1984 saw two Cessna 185s, three Beavers and the Vancouver Harbour – Gulf Islands route sold to Vancouver-based *Harbour Air*, along with the Nanaimo Harbour charter licence. This was one step leading to Air BC getting out of the small aircraft charter business.

With Air BC's move from the Vancouver Airport south terminal, *Aztec Aviation* and *Burrard Air* applied to operate from the south terminal to Victoria Airport. To meet this competition, Air BC resumed service from the south terminal to Victoria Airport using the nine seat Britten Norman Islander, C-FDEB, and charged $25.00 each way (versus $47.00 each way from the main terminal with Dash-7 or Twin Otter aircraft).

Two former *Golden West* Dash-7s were acquired by Air BC early in 1984, the first registered as C-GJPI (JPI = Jim Pattison Industries) and the other as C-GXPO (XPO = EXPO 86). These Dash-7s replaced the DC-3s and Twin Otters on many of the land routes and would allow expansion into the BC Interior.

In May, Air BC took over *Powell Air*'s Vancouver – Powell River service, replacing *Powell Air*'s Convair 440 with a Twin Otter. The company had a minor accident involving two Twin Otters in Victoria Harbour. One aircraft moved forward rather than backing out of its moorings and sliced up the tail of the other. Both aircraft were repaired and returned to service.

Air BC transferred all its Port Hardy flight operations (Beavers, Otters, Islander) to its Trans Provincial affiliate during the summer of 1984. In October, all services to Bella Bella and Bella Coola were operated from Port Hardy by TPA. In October 1984, Air BC began operating two flights a day Vancouver – Port Hardy with Dash-7s, linking with the TPA flights.

In October, the Vancouver – Gillies Bay route was subcontracted to *Aquilla Air*. October also saw the operations between Vancouver and Williams Lake/Quesnel begun with Dash-7s, reminiscent of *BC Airlines*' expansion from a coastal operator to an interior operator with their Nord 262s.

Service using Twin Otters between Victoria and Seattle's SEA-TAC airport was begun in April 1986, with three flights daily. A former *Henson Airlines* Dash-7 was leased from deHavilland in June 1985, and operated in a hybrid colour scheme with a blue cheat line and blue titles, with the large white 'A' on a red tail. This aircraft allowed charter flights from Vancouver to Penticton to begin on behalf of *CP Air* holidays.

In the fall of 1985, Air BC announced the purchase of four Dash-8 aircraft for approximately $30 million. Five daily services Vancouver – Kamloops and Vancouver – Port Hardy were begun at this time and Vancouver – Kelowna service was started in December. At that time the company received permission to service Kamloops, Sandspit, Smithers, Kelowna, Cranbrook, Penticton, Castlegar and Calgary.

The first Dash-8 entered service in 1986. There were a number of problems with the first plane and future deliveries were postponed until the problems could be resolved. Charters between Vancouver and Tofino were operated for *Canadian Princess* and charters between Vancouver and Seattle or Portland were begun in May. September 1986 saw Vancouver – Castelgar (twice daily) and Vancouver – Penticton services begun.

In the fall of 1986, Vancouver – Nanaimo Harbour was permanently dropped, leaving only the Vancouver – Victoria Harbour float service on Air BC's schedule. Two Twin Otters were equipped with MLS receivers, the first aircraft in Canada to use Microwave Landing Systems. This allowed these aircraft to fly Vancouver – Nanaimo (Cassidy) Airport at night and in poor weather.

Trans Provincial Airlines was sold to an investor group led by former TPA chief pilot, Gene Story, in October 1986. The group acquired all TPA assets except the Port Hardy base which would now operate under the name *Pacific Coastal Airlines*. TPA adopted a colour scheme similar to the Air BC colours except that the blue cheat line ran above the red cheat line. Grumman Goose C-FAWH was the first aircraft to appear in this new colour scheme.

November 28, 1986 marked the end of the ownership of Air BC by Jim Pattison Group Ltd. when *Air Canada* purchased 100% of the company for between twenty and thirty million dollars. Air BC's three-year affiliation deal with *CP Air* would end in April 1987. Air BC and *Time Air* then changed their commuter affiliations, *Time Air* going with *CP Air (Canadian)* and Air BC with *Air Canada*. The year 1986 had shown a 28% growth in traffic for Air BC with more than 685,000 passengers carried during the year.

In March 1987, the *Air Canada* commuter colours began to appear when a second Dash-8 came into service. However, Air BC still needed only one Dash-8, so the other three were leased back to de Havilland, thus aiding de Havilland which was behind on delivery dates to several airlines following a lengthy strike. The three Air BC aircraft were leased out to several operators during 1987. April 26 saw the airline become a full *Air Canada* commuter, adopting the *Air Canada* four digit flight designators except on the Vancouver Harbour – Victoria Harbour route. New routes which commenced on this date included Vancouver – Seattle five times daily, Vancouver – Dawson Creek and on to Grande Prairie and Edmonton. Services between Kamloops, Kelowna, Castlegar and Calgary were also begun.

In May 1987, Air BC announced an order for sixteen Dash-8s to be delivered between the fall of 1987 and the fall of 1989. Four of these would be -100 models and twelve would be the stretched -300 aircraft. The total value of this order was in excess of $160 million. Two former *Air Wisconsin* Dash-7s were acquired at this time, bringing the Dash-7 fleet to six in number.

The additional aircraft made possible the inauguration of four daily flights between Vancouver and Prince George, with one of these continuing on the Dawson Creek and Grande Prairie. A Dash-7 was introduced on the Vancouver – Powell River service at this time.

The fall of 1987 saw Vancouver to Cranbrook, Castlegar and Calgary as well as Edmonton to Calgary, Castlegar and Penticton services begun. Flights between Edmonton Municipal and Kamloops were also begun.

Powell Air purchased 50% of Port Hardy based *Pacific Coastal Airlines* in January 1988.

Air BC entered the jet era in 1988 with the acquisition of three BAe 146-200 aircraft. These four engine jets allowed an expansion of routes and reduced times on the company's longer flights. On May 30, 1988, jet service five times daily began from Vancouver to Prince Rupert and Terrace; and on June 12, 1988, jet service began twice daily from Vancouver to Whitehorse. Service to Fort St. John also began in May 1988. Because of long delays in the delivery of the Dash-8-300s, Air BC cancelled its order for this aircraft early in 1989. Two BAe 146-200 jets were added to the fleet in January 1989 to operate a Super Shuttle service between the Calgary International Airport and the Edmonton Municipal Airport in direct competition with *Canadian*'s Chieftain service. All of the BAe 146s had their titles changed with the introduction of this service. The title 'Air BC' was moved to the rear of the aircraft and the new title 'Air Canada Connector' was added to the forward upper fuselage in two lines. This service began January 30, 1989, with eighteen flights a day. Four of the flights are operated using Dash-8 aircraft. The BAe 146s used on this service have five-abreast seating in an 83-seat configuration, providing more leg room than the Boeing 737s operated by *Canadian*. The aircraft is also much quieter than the 737.

To operate its shorter routes, Air BC purchased five BAe Jetstream-31s in March 1989. These were operated for a time with *Air Toronto*, until replaced in that company's fleet by Super Jetstreams. The BAe-31s will be used on flights to Comox, Port Hardy, Penticton, Seattle and Lethbridge. The Lethbridge flights are designed to further cut into the Alberta market by flying into *Time Air*'s original home base. April 1989 saw direct Vancouver to Whitehorse flights begun using the BAe-146 jets.

While Air BC is listed as a commuter airline, the move to jet aircraft continues the process of rebuilding the former regional airline concept with Air BC replacing *Pacific Western* as the BC/Alberta Regional, competing with *Time Air*.

FLEET LISTING
AIR BC

REG'N	C/N	F/N	IS	WFU	NOTES
BAE 146-200					
C-FBAB	E2090	041	5/88	C	EX G-5-090 British Aerospace
C-FBAE	E2092	042	6/88	C	EX G-5-092 British Aerospace
C-FBAF	E2096	043	6/88	C	EX G-5-096 British Aerospace
C-FBAO	E2111	044	1/89	C	EX G-5-111 British Aerospace
C-FBAV	E2121	045	2/89	C	EX G-5-121 British Aerospace
BAE 146-100A					
C-GNX	E1010	101	1/89	3/89	LF G-UKPC BAE; EX Air Nova
DASH-7					
C-GFEL	003	401	7/83	4/89	EX EC-DCB Spantax; EX C-GQIW
C-GHSL	080	404	6/85	3/88	ST DHC & RR N747BC Boeing
C-GJPI	036	403	3/84	C	EX N702GW Golden West
C-GXPO	021	402	5/84	C	EX N701GW Golden West
C-GYMC	059	405	5/87	C	EX N707ZW Air Wisconsin
C-GYXC	069	406	5/87	C	EX N709ZW Air Wisconsin
DASH-8-102					
C-FABA	080	085	2/88	C	
C-FABG	146	087	4/89	C	
C-FABN	044	083	8/86	C	LT DHC 3/87-4/87
C-FABT	049	084	10/86	C	
C-FABW	097	086	4/88	C	
C-FACD	150	088	4/89	C	
C-GABF	025	082	3/87	C	
C-GGOM	003	081	1/86	C	LT C-GGOM DHC 10/86-3/87
JETSTREAM 3100					
C-FBID	802	031	4/89	C	EX C-FBID Air Toronto
C-FBIE	815	032	4/89	C	EX C-FBIE Air Toronto
C-FB I I	816	033	3/89	C	EX C-FB I I Air Toronto
C-FB I J	817	034	4/89	C	EX C-FB I J Air Toronto
C-FBIP	820	035	4/89	C	EX C-FBIP Air Toronto
C-FCPF	827	036	4/89	C	NTU by Ontario Express
N331QV	806	---	2/89	4/89	LF BAE for pilot training
N331QV	811	---	2/89	4/89	LF BAE for pilot training
DHC-6 TWIN OTTER					
C-FAKM	078	604	1/77	C	EX C-FAKM Air West/Time Air
C-FAWC	108	061/607	5/72	3/89	EX CF-AWC North Cariboo; EX Air West
C-FGQE	040	069/601	8/73	C	EX C-FGQE Air West
C-FIOH	198	064/611	3/78	C	EX C-FIOH Gulf Air/ESSO
C-FJCL	151	062/608	5/78	C	EX C-FJCL West Coast
C-FOEQ	044	/602	9/79	4/88	ST C-FOEQ Borek/Harbour Air
C-FPAE	228	065/612	5/78	C	EX C-FPAE West Coast
C-GEAW	068	----	9/75	10/83	ST N44693 Royal Hawaiian
C-GFAW	163	----	7/76	10/83	ST N201RH Royal Hawaiian
C-GGAW	086	068/605	9/76	9/86	EX C-GGAW Air West, tt 20715
C-GIAW	060	/603	5/77	4/88	ST C-GIAW Borek/Harbour Air
C-GJAW	176	/609	8/78	9/86	EX C-GJAW Air West, tt 24661
C-GKBD	314	/067	11/87	11/87	LF C-GKBD Kenn Borek
C-GKNR	186	063/610	6/78	7/85	EX C-GKNR West Coast
C-GMKA	159	----	5/81	8/81	LF C-GMKA Kimba Air
C-GQKN	094	066/606	9/79	2/89	LT C-GQKN Echo Bay 1984
C-GEVL	762	----	NTU	NTU	NTU; ST C-GEVL Bannock Aero.
PA31-350					
C-GPCI	7652046	---	8/88	C	
DC-3					
C-GSCB	33441	----	6/83	5/84	LF C-GSCB Skycraft
C-GWUG	32963	----	4/83	6/85	ST C-GWUG Nahanni A/S 6/86
G-73 Mallard					
C-GHUB	J-22	----	4/74	4/83	ST VH-LAW Air Whitsunday; EX WCA
C-GIRL	J-53	----	4/74	7/83	Sold in USA 8/84; EX WCA
Turbo Mallard					
C-GHUM	J-26		5/75	7/83	ST VH-JAW Air Whitsunday; EX WCA

FLEET LISTING
AIR BC

REG'N	C/N	F/N	IS	WFU	NOTES
BN Islander					
C-FDEB	058		6/80	6/85	EX C-FDEB Gulf Air
C-GKAW	128		3/76	2/84	ST C-GKAW Viking Air
DHC-3 Otter					
C-FDJA	459		3/81	6/84	To C-FDJA TPA
C-FQEI	397		5/77	12/80	DMG by fire 12/80
C-FQRI	326		7/76	1/82	DBF 22/01/82
C-FXRI	258		9/68	6/84	EX C-FXRI Air West; to TPA
C-GUJM	159		2/77	6/84	EX C-FUJM West Coast/Gulf Air
C-GLCP	422		8/76	6/84	EX C-GLCP Gulf Air; to TPA

Time Air Dash-7, C-GTAD

TIME AIR

ALLIANCE:
Canadian Partner (46% owned by *Canadian*)

HEADQUARTERS:
Post Office Box 423,
Lethbridge, Alberta, T1J 3Z1

MAIN BASES:
Lethbridge, Edmonton Municipal,
Vancouver International

FLEET 1988:
3 - F28-1000s;
2 - SD-360s (1 on order 1989);
7 - DASH-7s;
5 - DASH-8-100s;
1 - DASH-8-300s (4 on order);
3 - CONVAIR 640s;
2 - CONVAIR 580s;
2 - BEECH 99s;
2 - F-27s.

COLOURS:
Canadian Partner colour scheme with titles 'TIME AIR'

ROUTES:
B.C.:
Vancouver – Victoria – Port Hardy – Campbell River – Comox – Nanaimo – Quesnel – Williams Lake – Dawson Creek – Kamloops – Kelowna – Penticton – Castlegar
Alberta:
Lethbridge – Medicine Hat – Calgary – Edmonton – Lloydminster – Cold Lake – Grande Prairie – Peace River – Rainbow Lake – Fort McMurray – Fort Chipewyan – High Level.
Saskatcewan:
Regina – Saskatoon – Prince Albert – La Ronge – Wollaston Lake – Stoney Rapid – Uranium City.
Manitoba:
Winnipeg
U.S.A.:
Minneapolis – Great Falls – Seattle.

HISTORY:

Founded as *Lethbridge Air Services*, the airline began operating in May 1966, connecting Lethbridge to Calgary and Medicine Hat with a Beech 18 and a Cessna 402. It's owner, W.R. 'Stubb' Ross, changed the name to Time Air in 1969 and expanded the company's routes throughout Alberta. A second Cessna 402, another Beech 18 and the airline's first Twin Otter were added in 1969. At that time the company's major routes were Lethbridge – Calgary – Red Deer – Edmonton Municipal Airport and a second route linking Calgary – Medicine Hat – Lethbridge.

The Twin Otter's eighteen-seat capacity was suited ideally to these routes and additional Twin Otter aircraft were purchased, one each in 1971, 1972 and 1973. One was sold in 1973, leaving the company with three Twin Otters. The Cessna 402s and Beech 18s were all withdrawn from service by 1974. A Beech 65 was operated, mainly on charter operations, from 1974 to 1977 .

Several services from Edmonton to Red Deer were inaugurated during this period but finally abandoned because the short driving distance between the two centres made air travel uneconomical. The success of the *Chieftain AirBus* operated between Edmonton and Calgary by *Pacific Western Airlines* led to the company's purchase of larger aircraft in an attempt to compete on this route. A forty-passenger F-27 was purchased in 1974 and a second obtained form *Trans Provincial Airlines* in 1975. These noisy turboprops operated in competition with Boeing 737 jets, but the route flourished because Time Air also flew on to Lethbridge.

The company's Cessna 402 and Beech 18 aircraft operated in standard factory colours. The first Twin Otter was flown as a white aircraft with a wide blue cheat line. A blue circle with a white 'T' in the centre appeared on the tail . Subsequent Twin Otters flew in colours which were to be the standard scheme of the airline for many years: a white aircraft with broad red cheat lines between narrower gold cheat lines. The tail displayed a red and gold panel containing a stylized white 'T.' One of the F-27s and all of the SD-330s bore this colour scheme. The ex-TPA F-27 retained an all yellow colour scheme while with the airline.

The success of the Edmonton – Calgary – Lethbridge route using F-27s prompted Stubb Ross to purchase new aircraft. The plane chosen was the thirty passenger Shorts SD-330 powered by twin Pratt & Whitney Aircraft (Canada) PT6A-45B turboprop engines, driving large-diameter, low-speed, five-blade propellers. The company initiated the first revenue service for this aircraft on 24 August 1976.

Three of the new aircraft were delivered in 1976 and the two F-27s along with one of the Twin Otters were sold the next year. At 7:15 a.m., 29 November 1977, a Time Air SD-330 was the first aircraft to arrive at the new Calgary International Terminal carrying revenue passengers.

The very roomy and quiet SD-330s were operated mainly on Edmonton – Calgary – Lethbridge flights while the Twin Otters were relegated to the role of back-up aircraft. In May 1978, service between Calgary and Pincher Creek was begun using Twin Otters, but ceased in October 1979 and service from Edmonton Municipal Airport to Grande Prairie was begun late in 1979.

Three Dash-7s were purchased in May 1980, and Time Air became the second Canadian airline (*Wardair* was the first) to fly these fifty-passenger, four engine Canadian built turbo aircraft. The Dash-7s appeared in an all-white colour scheme with a broad gold cheat line running through the windows and a narrow red cheat line below the gold. Both cheats swept up onto the tail where the gold cheat ended in the angled word 'SKY-DASH' in red.

In May 1980, Time Air acquired the *Northward Aviation* route from Edmonton Municipal Airport to Peace River and Rainbow Lake, Alberta. In October 1980, the airline purchased the assets of *Gateway Aviation* from bankrupt *Northward Aviation* for $1.8 million. A Convair 640 (ex PWA) was obtained in this purchase. The takeover of *Gateway* gave Time Air the Edmonton – Peace River – Rainbow Lake route on a permanent basis. The Convair 640, based in Edmonton, was used in the operation of this route.

Early in 1981 the Time Air fleet consisted of four different types of aircraft. The Twin Otters were sold that year and the decision was made to sell the SD-330s as well. These had been bought at a very good price with excellent financing terms and because of rapid inflation, were worth far more than when purchased. The sale of these planes helped finance the purchase of the three Dash-7s. One SD-330 was sold in each year, 1981, 1982 and 1983.

Time Air served Cold Lake briefly during 1980 but the route was abandoned when it proved uneconomical.

Pacific Western Airlines repeatedly applied for permission to fly Calgary – Lethbridge and Vancouver – Lethbridge only to be blocked by the CTC. PWA believed they had finally broken into the Lethbridge market when awarded a Vancouver – Kelowna – Lethbridge route in 1982. The federal cabinet, however, blocked this award, giving the route to Time Air instead. This service provided a more direct route linking *Japan Air Lines* Boeing 747 flights (Tokyo– Vancouver) with this southern Alberta city and its large Japanese population.

In February 1982, Time Air operated its first scheduled flight outside of Alberta when a Dash-7 flew from Lethbridge to Kelowna and on to Vancouver. This service has been a consistent money maker for the airline since that time.

In June 1982 Time Air's Dash-7s were sold to Westbank Lease (Bank of British Columbia) and taken back on long-term lease to improve the com-pany's finances. *Pacific Western* continued to covet access to Lethbridge and in October 1983, it purchased 40% of the stock and four of the nine seats on the Board of Directors of *Time Air* for $4.3 million . Stubb Ross remained as one of the directors.

In 1983, Time Air took over the *Pacific Western* routes Vancouver – Victoria and Vancouver – Comox – Campbell River, because the Boeing 737s of PWA were too large and uneconomical for these short routes. One Time Air Dash-7 was stationed in Vancouver, competing directly with the Dash-7 equipment of *Air BC* on these Vancouver – Vancouver Island routes.

In June 1984, Time Air began flying Calgary – Castlegar for PWA, but by September the route had become part of Time Air's licence. At that time, the company acquired a second Convair 640. This, like the company's first Convair 640, was a former PWA aircraft. In September 1984, Time Air acquired the Edmonton – Peace River – High Level and Edmonton – Fort Mc-Murray – Fort Chipewyan routes from PWA because *Pacific Western* once again found these routes uneconomical using a Boeing 737 and was not interested in maintaining the smaller turboprop aircraft needed to keep these routes viable.

When Time Air cancelled its order for four DHC-8 aircraft (cost $6.9 million each) in 1984, company President Richard Barton noted that the company would look at the aircraft again if better financing could be arranged.

In 1985 the company was in need of additional aircraft for its new routes and acquired *Inter City Air* and its Convair 580 in May, then leased two *Air Ontario* Convair 580s during the summer. The leased aircraft operated in the basic *Air Ontario* colour scheme with Time Air titles. The company also purchased its second Convair 580 in September 1985.

Time Air acquired all the shares of *Southern Frontier Airlines,* which operated out of Calgary, giving the company access again to Cold Lake and to Saskatoon and Lloydminster in Saskatchewan. The *Southern Frontier* Convair 440 was returned to *North Cariboo* and the charter division of *Southern Frontier* maintained intact.

The company had seen success operating the Shorts SD3-30 and returned to this aircraft when it purchased two SD-360s in October 1985. These aircraft are a stretched version of the SD3-30 with more than three feet added forward of the wings and a modified single-fin tail, resulting in an overall fuselage stretch of 12.5 feet. Powered by twin (Canadian PT6A-65R) turboprop engines, the SD-360 carries thirty-six passengers at a cruising speed of 243 mph. Both new aircraft are based in Vancouver and were initially operated on the *Connector* service between Vancouver and Victoria for PWA. Since July 1985 they have been completing thirteen flights a day for *Air Canada*. These aircraft or a Dash-7 also flew to Comox and Campbell River from Vancouver on behalf of PWA and *Air Canada*.

In June 1985, Time Air began flying the former *Southern Frontier* routes Calgary – Lloydminster and Cold Lake and back with a Convair 580 and flew Edmonton – Lloydminster and Saskatoon, and Edmonton – Cold Lake using Beech 99 aircraft. These were the company's first routes into Saskatchewan and northern Alberta.

The airline spent much of 1985 getting approval on its licence for all the former PWA services it had taken over, including Comox, Campbell River, Victoria and others. Late in the fall of 1985, services were begun Edmonton – Grande Prairie, Dawson Creek, Prince George and from Prince George, through the Okanagan, connecting Williams Lake, Kamloops, Kelowna and Penticton.

With EXPO 86 underway, additional capacity was required on all routes into Vancouver and the company used Convair 580 aircraft to augment its Dash-7 flights between Lethbridge and Vancouver. Time Air service to Saskatoon was halted early in 1986. In June, the company announced an order for four DASH-8-100s plus two optional as well as six DASH-8-300s, because it, like *Air BC*, would be standardizing on DASH-7 and DASH-8 aircraft. These orders gave the DASH-8-300 project a big boost.

In the summer of 1986, Time Air acquired some of *North Cariboo*'s charter operations out of Fort St. John and continued its takeover of shorter PWA routes. Vancouver – Port Hardy, Vancouver – Kamloops and Vancouver – Penticton and Castlegar services were all in operation.

In September 1986, Time Air joined PWA's *'Spirit Service,'* fully integrating its schedules with PWA. A modified PWA colour scheme displaying a double blue cheat line and the title 'PWA Spirit' was adopted, although only Dash-7 C-GTAJ was ever painted in this colour scheme. Several routes, including Prince George – Dawson Creek and Prince George – Kelowna, were dropped in the fall.

Time Air moved into the jet era on March 16, 1987 when it acquired 100% ownership of Saskatoon-based *Norcanair* and its two Fokker F28 jets from *North Canada Air Ltd.*, gaining CTC approval on 26 April 1987. Initially, Time Air and *Norcanair* continued to operate as separate *Canadian* Partner airlines but during the remainder of the year *Norcanair* was gradually absorbed and by January 1, 1988, only Time Air remained. *Pacific Western Airlines*, parent company of *Canadian*

Airlines International, owned 46% of Time Air. When the first Dash-8s were received by the airline, they appeared on the Lethbridge – Kelowna/Vancouver and Leth-bridge – Medicine Hat routes. The Vancouver – Naniamo route, however, was begun with a Beech 99 aircraft.

TIME AIR (via *Norcanair*) began a jet service linking Saskatoon to Regina and Winnipeg, thus becoming a presence in all four western provinces. In the fall of 1987 service was begun to Williams Lake/Quesnel from Vancouver and additional services between Vancouver and Vancouver Island were added (Comox and Campbell River). In 1987 when the Dash-8s were delivered, one Convair 580 was sold and an additional Dash-7 was acquired from *Air Atlantic*.

Prior to its affiliation with *Canadian Pacific*, the company's aircraft were all white with a broad gold cheat line through the windows and a narrow red cheat line below the gold. On the Dash-7s, both cheat lines swept up the tail to where the word SKYDASH appeared in red. The title 'Time Air' was displayed in red on the lower fuselage. The Convairs wore a variety of colours but the basic scheme was a white aircraft with a wide red cheat line, thin black cheat lines above and below the red and a lower fuselage of natural metal. The tail was white except for a red tip and the Time Air logo in red. The title 'TIME AIR' appeared in red on the upper fuselage and the nose was black. The Dash-7s were painted in this colour scheme in 1986, except one which bore the *PWA Spirit* colours and the *Air Atlantic* Dash-7 which arrived in the green CPA commuter colours to which the 'TIME AIR' title was added. The first Dash-8 arrived in the CPA green commuter colour scheme but all Time Air aircraft have since been converted to the *Canadian* colours.

TIME AIR Dash-7 C-GTAD was leased to *Wideroe's* from December 1987 until April 1988.

In May 1984, Walter Rodney (Stubb) Ross stepped down as Chairman of Time Air, after virtually running the airline as a one man show for eighteen years. Stubb Ross was awarded the Order of Canada in 1984. In September 1987, he died of a heart ailment, ending an important era in Canadian aviation. Richard H. Barton succeeded Ross as President and Chief Executive Officer of the airline.

Time Air's flights from Saskatoon to Edmonton also stopped in Lloydminster so the aircraft would qualify to land at the Municipal Airport in Edmonton. *NWT Air* successfully challenged the Airport's right to restrict the municipal airport's facilities to flights originating within Alberta. Time Air then dropped Lloydminster from the Saskatoon – Edmonton route as these flights could now land at the Edmonton Municipal Airport without landing elsewhere in Alberta first. Service between Calgary and Lloydminster was not affected.

In May 1988, *Canadian* dropped its Boeing 737 service to Castlegar, Dawson Creek, Penticton, Quesnel and Williams Lake and these cities are served by Time Air aircraft in the *Canadian* systems timetable. Service from Lethbridge to Great Falls, Montana was suspended at this time.

Time Air took over the Vancouver – Seattle route in October 1988, flying Dash-8 aircraft. Charter flights from Saskatoon and Victoria were started during the winter of 1988-89, flying F-28s. At that time, two Dash-

7s were added to the fleet, permitting the company to replace the aging F-27s on its Saskatchewan routes.

The first Dash-8, Series 300, was received by the company in February 1989, but was then used immediately for a demonstration tour by DHC. Time Air moved its maintenance base from Lethbridge to Calgary and downgraded its maintenance facilities at Victoria, Saskatoon, Edmonton and Lethbridge to perform only short-term maintenance.

FLEET LISTING
TIME AIR

REG'N	C/N	F/N	IS	WFU	NOTES
F28-1000					
C-GTAH	11082	130	3/88	C	EX VH-ATE Australian DOT
C-GTEO	11991	131	12/87	C	EX C-GTEO Norcanair
C-GTUU	11006	132	12/87	C	EX C-GTUU Norcanair
Shorts SD-360					
C-GTAU	3677	137	11/85	C	EX G-BLZU; Canadian c/s 6/87
C-GTAX	3679	136	11/85	C	Canadian c/s 6/87
C-			6/89	C	Canadian c/s 6/89
DASH-7					
C-FCOQ	044	177	10/88	C	EX OY-MBG Maersk Air
C-FDFK	045	175	12/88	C	EX OY-MBC Maersk Air
C-FDNR	024	176	1/89	C	EX N234SL Henson Aviation
C-GTAD	026	172	5/80	C	LT Wideroe 12/87-4/88; Canadian c/s
C-GTAJ	030	171	9/80	C	Skydash; PWA Spirit c/s; Canadian c/s
C-GTAZ	057	174	9/81	C	Skydash; Canadian c/s
C-GWTG	007	173	2/87	C	CPA c/s; EX Air Atlantic
DASH-8-100					
C-GEOA	072		3/87	C	Canadian c/s
C-GTAE	073	181	4/87	C	Canadian c/s
C-GTAF	083	183	7/87	C	Canadian c/s
C-GTAI	078	182	6/87	C	Canadian c/s
C-GWRR	070	180	4/87	C	Canadian c/s
DASH-8-300					
C-GKTA	124	184	3/89	C	First Series 300 production aircraft
C-					OO 1989
C-					OO 1989
C-					OO 1989
C-					OO 1989
CONVAIR 640					
C-FPWS	441	164	11/80	C	EX C-FPWS Gateway Aviation/PWA
C-FPWY	108	165	5/84	C	EX C-FPWY Worldways/PWA
C-GQCQ	451	161	12/87	8/88	ST C-GQCQ Canada West; EX Norcanair
C-GQCY	460	163	12/87	C	EX C-GQCY Norcanair/Highline
CONVAIR 580					
C-FICA	098		4/85	8/87	ST C-FICA Boeing/DHC; EX Intercity Air
C-GDTE	052		5/85	10/85	LF C-GDTE Air Ontario
C-GGWG	130		5/85	9/85	LF C-GGWG Air Ontario
C-GKFW	347	160	2/86	C	EX C-GKFW Kelowna Flightcraft
C-GTAO	116	134	9/85	12/87	ST C-GTAO DHC Canada/Air Ontario
C-GTAO	116	161	1/89	C	EX C-GTAO Air Ontario; Canadian c/s 1/89
Beech 99					
C-FAWX	U-64	192	6/88	C	EX N151CJ
C-FBRO	U-151		6/88	C	EX N300WP
C-GSFY	U-28	190	6/85	C	EX C-GSFY Southern Frontier
C-GSFP	U-43	191	6/85	C	EX C-GSFP Southern Frontier

FLEET LISTING
TIME AIR

REG'N	C/N	F/N	IS	WFU	NOTES
F-27					
C-FGZJ	53	160	3/87	C	EX C-FGZJ Norcanair
C-GCRA	52	161	3/87	11/88	ST C-GCRA Perimeter; EX C-GCRA Norcanair
F-27A					
CF-TPA	104		7/75	6/77	ST C-FTPA Norcanair; EX TPA
F-27J					
C-GWRR	013		10/74	11/77	ST N777DG Pacific Alaskan Airlines
Shorts SD-330					
C-GTAM	3006		10/76	2/84	ST G-BEEO Jersey European Airways
C-GTAS	3005		8/76	9/82	ST G-BKIE Genair
C-GTAV	3007		11/76	12/81	ST G-NICE Genair/Eastern Airways
DHC-6					
CF-AKM	078		12/69	1/77	ST C-FAKM Air West
C-FDKK*	177		10/72	6/81	ST C-FDKK Southern Frontier
CF-QHC	021		10/71	5/73	ST CF-QHC Northward Aviation
CF-QSC	174		2/73	1/81	ST C-FQSC Kenn Borek
Beech 65-B90					
C-GSFM	LJ422	905	6/88	C	
C-GWGT	LJ373		5/74	2/77	ST USA
Beech 18 (3NM)					
CF-WUW	CA250		5/66	7/74	EX CF-WUW Lethbridge Air
Beech D18S					
CF-YJG	A978		8/69	10/72	ST CF-YJG Comanche Aviation Ltd.
Cessna 402					
CF-WXQ	0217		5/66	11/71	EX CF-WXQ Lethbridge Air
Cessna 402A					
CF-YUT	0019		5/69	8/74	ST CF-YUT Atlantic Central

Calm Air International Ltd.

Calm Air DHC-6, C-FQBV

ALLIANCE:
Canadian Partner (45% owned by *Canadian*)

HEADQUARTERS:
60 Seal Road,
Thompson, Manitoba, R8N 1S4

MAIN BASES:
Thompson, Lynn Lake, Churchill

FLEET 1988:
4 - HS748s;
3 - DHC-6 Twin Otters;
5 - PA31-350 Navajo Chieftains;
1 - DC-3;
1 - Beech 200 Super King Air

COLOURS:
The upper fuselage and top of the tail are orange. A thin white cheat line starts at the nose and broadens until it covers the middle portion of the tail. A dark blue cheat line also broadens as it travels aft and covers the lower portion of the tail. Below the dark blue cheat line the lower fuselage is white. The title 'CALM AIR' appears in white on the dark blue cheat line covering the rear lower fuselage. The wings are orange. The registration appears in blue on the orange portion of the tail and the company logo, a script *CA,* is also displayed on the tail. In the logo, the bar in the *A* is replaced by a small maple leaf. The company adopted the *Canadian* colour scheme in 1988.

ROUTES:
Winnipeg – Thompson – Flin Flon – The Pas – Pik-witonei – Oxford House – God's Lake Narrows – Island Lake – St. Theresa – Kelsey – York Landing – Ilford – Gillam – Shamattawa – Pukatawagan – Leaf Rapids – Lynn Lake – South Indian Lake – Brochet – Lac Brochet – Tadoule Lake – Churchill – Eskimo Point (NWT) – Baker Lake – Repulse Bay – Coral Harbour – Chesterfield Inlet – Rankin Inlet – Whale Cove.

HISTORY:

Calm Air International was originally based in Lynn Lake and served many northern Manitoba commuties, connecting them with Churchill. It also had a base in the Keewatin District of the NWT, connecting Eskimo Point, Baker Lake, Repulse Bay, Coral Harbour, Chesterfield Inlet, Rankin Inlet and Whale Cove.

Calm Air operated small bush aircraft, including DHC-2 Beavers, and acquired its first Twin Otter in 1971 and two more during 1977-78. As its passenger and cargo routes grew, the company acquired an HS-748 from *Gateway Aviation* in 1979 and has operated two of these aircraft ever since.

One of the HS-748s had a serious accident in March 1982 and a replacement was leased from *Mount Cook Airlines* of New Zealand while it was completely rebuilt. To further expand the company's cargo capability, a DC-4 was acquired.

In September 1986, Calm Air began flights to Winnipeg. The routes flown were Lynn Lake to Thompson and Winnipeg; Thompson to Flin Flon and Winnipeg and Flin Flon to The Pas and Winnipeg. These routes were flown by the HS-748 aircraft. Calm Air also became a *PWA Spirit* partner at that time and HS-748 C-GSBF adopted the *PWA Spirit* colour scheme, adding the double blue cheat lines of *Pacific Western Airlines* to its own colourful paint scheme.

In June 1987, *PWA Corporation* bought 45% of Calm Air stock, thus taking a major interest in the airline and ensuring *Canadian Airlines International* a strong commuter network in northern Manitoba and the Keewatin District of the Northwest Territories. As the company's aircraft came due for painting in 1988, they were painted in the *Can-adian Partner* colour scheme.

In the spring of 1988, flights between Brandon and Winnipeg and between Lynn Lake and Winnipeg were begun using HS-748 aircraft. Two former *Eastern Provincial Airways* HS-748s were acquired for these routes.

Ontario Express took over the Winnipeg – Brandon route in 1989.

FLEET LISTING
CALM AIR

REG'N	C/N	IS	WFU	NOTES
HS-748				
C-FMAK	1668	12/79	C	ACC 19/03/82; rebuilt. EX C-FMAK Gateway Aviation
C-GDOP	1745	3/88	C	EX C-GDOP Eastern Provincial
C-GEPB	1686	9/87	C	LF C-GEPB Air Maritime/Canadian
C-GRCU	1697	6/82	8/83	LF ZX-MCF Mount Cook Airlines
C-GSBF	1662	9/84	C	EX G-11-3 British Aerospace; PWA Spirit c/s.
DC-4				
C-GPFG	42917	1/82	10/87	W/O 16/06/87 at Hidden Bay, Saskatchewan
C-GPSH	7458	4/82	7/85	ST C-GPSH Soundair
DHC-6				
C-FCIJ	71	6/78	C	EX C-FCIJ St. Andrews Airways
C-FQBV	103	3/77	C	EX C-FQBV Transair/Quebecair
C-FQXW	121	9/71	C	EX N1372T Trans East Airlines
Skyvan				
C-GHBQ	1859	3/79	1/80	ST N101WA Lodi Airport Corp.
C-GWCY	1862	4/71	1/80	EX CF-YQY Selkirk Air; ST USA
DHC-2				
C-GEXX	699	3/76	7/87	
BEECH 200				
C-GMMK	88-214	5/85	C	EX N441PS
Beech B90				
C-GPPN	L J389	2/84	12/84	W/O 22/12/84 Sanikiluaq
DC-3				
C-GCKE	27203	2/87	C	EX C-GCKE
PA-31-350				
C-FAKZ	7852147	10/87	C	EX N27754
C-GALP	7405441	10/87	C	EX N54317
C-GITW	7652114	9/87	C	EX N59891
C-GURM	7752184	9/87	C	EX N273RH
C-GVOX	7552067	10/87	C	EX N59976

AIR ONTARIO
GREAT LAKES AIRLINES

Air Ontario Dash-8, C-GJMI

ALLIANCE:
Air Canada Connector
(75% owned by *Air Canada*)

HEADQUARTERS:
380 Wellington Street, Suite 1100,
London, Ontario, N6A 5B5

MAIN BASES:
London, Sarnia, hub at
Toronto International Airport

FLEET 1989:
2 - F28-1000s;
5 - Convair 580s;
13 - DASH-8-100s;
3 - HS748s;
9 - DASH-8-300s on order;
7 - Catpas 200s.

COLOURS:
Air Canada Connector colour scheme as described for
Air BC aircraft but with *Air Ontario* titles.

ROUTES:
Toronto – London – Sarnia – Windsor – Ottawa –
Montreal – Trenton – Kingston – North Bay – Sudbury
– Sault Ste Marie – Thunder Bay – Dryden – Winnipeg
USA:
Hartford/Springfield – Cleveland – Minneapolis

AUSTIN Routes:
Toronto – Elliot Lake – Timmins – Kapuskasing –
Cochrane – Moosonee – Rupert House – East Main –
Weminkji – Paint Mills – Chasasibi/La Grande 2 – Great
Whale – Fort Albany – Kashechewan – Attawapiskat –
Winisk/Peawaniuck – Fort Severn – Big Trout Lake –
Kasabonika – Bearskin Lake – Sachigo – Round Lake
– Muskrat Dam – Cat Lake – Pickle Lake – Webequie
– Lansdowne – Fort Hope – Geralton – Manitouwadge
– Hornepayne – Mara-thon – Sioux Lookout – Kenora/
Minaki – Red Lake – Pakangikum – Deer Lake – Sandy
Lake

HISTORY:

Great Lakes Airlines was formed in January 1961 to provide executive transport for the Homes-Blunt Company of Sarnia. Most of the traffic was to Toronto and back utilizing light twin engine aircraft.

Two DC-3s were purchased in 1967 to supplement the company's Cessna 310 and tri-gear Beech 18 as it began a scheduled service between Sarnia and Toronto.

Two Convair 440 aircraft were bought in 1969 from *Swissair.* Called the *Metropolitan,* the piston twin engine Convair 440 carried forty-four passengers and bore a colour scheme with a broad red cheat line running through the windows of the white aircraft. The upper three quarters of the tail was red and displayed a white map of the Great Lakes within a white circle. Once the Convairs arrived, the Beech 18 was sold to *Air Windsor* and the two DC-3s sold to *Pem Air* of Pembroke.

When London, Ontario, was added to the Sarnia to Toronto route in 1973, four more Convair 440s were purchased from *Linjeflyg* of Sweden. These white aircraft had a broad blue cheat line above a thin white cheat line and a thin dark blue cheat line below both and had an all-white tail. One of a variety of symbols was found on the tail, including a map of the Great Lakes in blue but with no circle, a stylized 'GLA' or no symbol at all.

With the additional aircraft, Peterborough, Ottawa and Kitchener were added to flights from Toronto. This rapid expansion of routes using old, unreliable equipment proved to be uneconomical and the three cities were quickly dropped. For a short period in 1975, all operations were halted except the Sarnia to Toronto route. An analysis of the problems faced by the airline showed that many flights had to be unexpectedly cancelled due to aircraft unserviceability; the new routes had not been properly publicized; and no feasibility studies had been made before opening new routes.

A group of Toronto businessmen bought the airline in 1975 and started to rejuvenate it. They moved the Toronto operations from Terminal One to Terminal Two and turned over the flight handling to *Air Canada* in Toronto and London. *Air Canada* also handled all Great Lakes' ticket sales and reservations on its computerized system. The Toronto to Ottawa via Peterborough route was resumed in April 1976 but Kitchener was never reintroduced to the schedule.

When *Air Canada* retired its Viscounts, there was a hockey charter market for a forty to fifty passenger aircraft in Southern Ontario. Professional hockey teams, however, refused to fly in old piston equipment and the decision was made to purchase Convair 580 aircraft from *Allegheny Airlines.* The Convair 580 was a Convair 340 piston aircraft re-engined with twin Allison jet props. The interior of this aircraft was the same size as the Convair 440 except that the galley and lavatory had

been moved to the front of the plane permitting two additional rows of seats to be added, thus increasing the capacity to fifty-two passengers.

These aircraft were all white with a brown cheat line through the windows. Below this an orange cheat line broadened downwards as it swept aft. Below this was another brown cheat. The new company logo was displayed on the white tail and the airline's name appeared in brown on the upper fuselage. The Convair 440s were kept for a short time as backup aircraft before being sold or broken up.

The Convair 580 entered service with the company in March 1976 using experienced *Allegheny* pilots as co-pilots. Four aircraft were purchased within a year and the company was once again on solid financial footing. In October 1976, Great Lakes took over all but one flight per day between London and Toronto from *Air Canada.*

In January 1977, the company moved its headquarters from Sarnia to London, Ontario, and later that year purchased *Flightexec Ltd.* of London, which operated executive aircraft charters in southwestern Ontario using a Piper Aztec. The company continued to operate *Flightexec Ltd.* as a separate airline.

Great Lakes applied for the Toronto – Sault Ste Marie – Thunder Bay – Dryden – Winnipeg route relinquished by *Transair* when it merged with PWA, but the route was awarded to *Nordair.* In need of expanding its routes, Great Lakes also hoped that *Air Canada* would phase out its short DC-9 routes in Ontario (such as Toronto to North Bay and Sudbury), but it would be another decade before these routes would come available to the airline. Thus the company continued to operate with only Sarnia, London, Toronto, Peterborough to Ottawa route, with the London to Toronto segment being the most profitable.

During the summer of 1979, Great Lakes began flying small package charters from Toronto to Western Canada. The aircraft involved were stripped of their normal passenger seats and soon Great Lakes Convair 580s were seen frequently in Vancouver, Calgary, Edmonton and Winnipeg. In October of that year, *Flightexec* added Cessna Citation C-GJTX raising the fleet of this subsidiary to seven aircraft based in London and Windsor.

A fifth Convair 580, added in December 1979, carried the registration C-GJRP, JRP being the initials of the company President, James Robertson Plaxton. Regular scheduled flights and charter flights kept the airline so busy during February 1980 that it was necessary to drop the flights to Western Canada for *Purolator Courier* until April 1980.

In January 1981, the company again dropped its Toronto to Peterborough and Ottawa service which was picked up by *Air Atonabee.* In February, *Great Lakes* introduced its direct Toronto to Ottawa service operating Monday to Friday only. *Great Lakes* also formed an off-shore helicopter support division which included five Sikorsky S76As. The S76s were delivered in 1985.

The company changed its name to AIR ONTARIO on 27 April 1981. Convair 580 C-GDTC was the first aircraft flown in the company's new colour scheme: a white aircraft with no cheat line, the title 'AIR ONTARIO' displayed in dark purple on the upper fuselage. The purple tail was broken by a horizontal green stripe with a narrow white strip above it.

Purolator Courier services were reduced in March 1981 and discontinued altogether in April 1981 being taken over by *Kelowna Flightcraft* Convair 580s. In December 1981, 50% of the stock of the parent holding company was purchased by the Deluce family of Timmins who were the owners of *Austin Airways* and *White River Air Service*.

In April 1982, an interline agreement was arranged with *Wardair* permitting passengers in Ottawa or London to connect on *Wardair* flights at Toronto.

By 1982, the Toronto to Ottawa route was proving to be very successful as the flights were scheduled between *Air Canada* flights, thus creating very good load factors. The rights for an Ottawa to Montreal service (with no local traffic) were obtained early in 1982 but never used because the company had also received the rights to fly London – Ottawa and London – Montreal direct. Aircraft on the London to Montreal route arrived in Montreal from London early in the morning and would sit unused all day before returning to London at night. When *Eastern Provincial Airways* was on strike in January 1983, Air Ontario Convair 580s operated Montreal to Charlo and Chatham daily services.

The company became an international airline in 1983 when it was awarded flights from London to Cleveland. London, Ontario, was now the hub of operations for Air Ontario, with flights to Sarnia, Cleveland, Toronto, Ottawa and Montreal direct from that city.

Early in 1984, Delplax Holdings Limited, the holding company for Air Ontario, tried to buy *Nordair* but was unsuccessful. A major expansion of the company's fleet occurred that year when a Convair 580 was purchased from South Africa and five Convair 580s from *Freedom Airlines* in the United States bringing the airline's total to 11 Convair 580s. These aircraft were required for the new routes being opened by the company. Toronto – Hartford and Toronto – North Bay routes began in September, and Toronto – Sudbury was started in November.

The company changed its colour scheme in 1984, adding three cheat lines to the white aircraft. A narrow green cheat line running through the middle of the windows was separated from a broader dark purple line below by a white cheat line. The dark purple tail is split horizontally by a white band with a broader green band below, which cross the tail approximately one-third from the top. The title 'AIR ONTARIO' appears in dark purple on the upper fuselage and the company's logo (linked spheres) is displayed forward of the title, in green. The white registration is on the purple cheat line at the rear of the fuselage and the last three letters of the registration are on the purple cheat line near the nose. The wing tips have dark purple, white, green and dark purple stripes.

A considerable expansion in routes within Ontario and its two neighbouring provinces occurred in 1985 with the addition of routes between Windsor, London, Ottawa and Montreal. Thunder Bay was also linked to Sudbury, Ottawa and Montreal and in mid-year this flight was extended to Winnipeg. Toronto to Atlantic City service was begun in the fall.

In October 1985, forty-nine percent of Air Ontario shares were sold to *Air Canada* and *Pacific Western Airlines* (each receiving half of the shares), while Delplax Holdings Limited, (owned by the Deluce Family), retained fifty-one percent of the airline. Air Ontario was now established as a commuter airline serving the large national airline (*Air Canada*) and the rapidly expanding regional airline (*Pacific Western*).

In May 1986, Sault Ste. Marie was added to the Ontario cities served by the company as it continued to take over many of the shorter *Air Canada* routes which could be better served by the smaller Convair 580s. The company announced plans to build a $3 million hangar and new head office at the London Ontario airport by 1990. In October, the future aircraft plans of the company were announced with an order for 15 Dash-8-100s (plus four optional) and five Dash-8-300 aircraft. As the two national airlines lined up commuter airlines, *Air Canada* purchased Air Ontario shares from the Deluce Family and *Pacific Western,* resulting in *Air Canada* holding seventy-five percent of the company's stock.

The beginning of 1987 saw the first Convair 580s dressed in the *Air Canada Commuter* red and white colour scheme. One Convair, however, flew in an interim scheme displaying the Air Ontario logo on the tail rather than the red maple leaf. The first Dash-8 aircraft arrived in full commuter colour scheme in April and were used on the Sarnia – Toronto – North Bay and Toronto – Cleveland routes. The *Air Canada* designator replaced Air Ontario's designator (GX) for all flights shown in the schedule of either airline.

Air Canada, through the purchase of Air Ontario, also acquired 75% of *Austin Airways* which serviced more than thirty-five centres in Ontario (mostly in the north), and five centres in northern Quebec as well as Minneapolis and Toronto. *Austin* also switched to four digit AC flight designators in April 1987 and in June 1987, amalgamated with Air Ontario. At that time, *Austin Airways* was the longest-operating airline in Canada having started operations on 1 March 1934. A complete history of this airline can be found in Canav Books' *Austin Airways* by Larry Milberry.

Although principally a northern Ontario operator, *Austin Airways* was able to fly routes from Toronto International Airport beginning in 1984, first linking Toronto to Timmins and Kapuskasing and later to Marathon and Manitouwadge. HS748 and Beech 99 aircraft were used on these flights, operating in a colourful scheme of yellow aircraft with a broad expanding cheat line of orange, red, black, red, orange that swept up the tail.

Geraldton and Elliot Lake were added to routes from Toronto in 1985. In June 1986, *Austin Airways* took over *Torontair*'s flights between Toronto, Trenton and Kingston using HS748 aircraft. All of these routes will be merged into the Air Ontario schedule and the fleet of HS748s, Beech 99s, Twin Otters, Cessna Citation (operated as an air ambulance for the Ontario Ministry of Health), DC-3s and smaller aircraft assimilated over the next few years.

Austin Airways ordered eight Dash-8s at the time Air Ontario announced its order of twenty-two Dash-8s, so these *Austin* aircraft will join the Air Ontario fleet when delivered. *Austin Airways* began flying in *Air Canada*'s red, white and grey colour scheme in mid-1987.

In 1988, a strike by Air Ontario pilots in early March grounded the airline until May 4. The new contract with the pilots, expiring in November 1990, provided for a newly-hired co-pilot on the new CATPASS 200 aircraft to make $20,000 a year while a four year captain flying a Fokker F-28 would receive $71,400 per year.

Flights to Trenton and Kingston and those to Kapuskasing were delayed in restarting following the strike.

Scheduled flights to Kasabonika, Round Lake, Sachigo, Bearskin Lake, Geraldton and Hornepayne were suspended indefinetly; and London – Cleveland was never restarted.

Air Ontario joined the other regional airlines in going to small jet aircraft early in 1988 when they acquired two Fokker F-28-1000 jets. These entered service in May on the Toronto – Sault Ste. Marie – Thunder Bay – Winnipeg route, with three flights a day. Some flights on this route would also stop at Dryden and/or Kenora. The airline also began operating the Toronto – Syracuse and Albany route at that time.

In addition to the new jets, Air Ontario purchased ten *Commuter Air Transport* Catpas 200 (CATPASS 200) aircraft. These modified Beech King Air 200s will replace the Beech 99s and Cessna 402s acquired in the takeover of *Austin Airlines*. Nine of the Cessna 402s were sold by the time the Cat 200s began arriving in June 1988. Eventually all the Beech 99s, Cessna 402s and Twin Otters will be replaced with these aircraft.

During the latter part of 1988, Air Ontario began selling off the Northern Ontario routes it had acquired from *Austin Airways*. Timmins-based aircraft and routes were sold to *Air Creebec*, including most of the company's HS748 aircraft. The Twin Otters and Beech 99s were sold and the newly-arriving CATPUS 200s would also be sold. Aircraft and routes based in Thunder Bay went to *Bearskin Lake Air Service*, and the company's Thunder Bay – Minneapolis route was dropped.

Air Ontario suffered a tragic accident on 10 March 1989 when its new F-28 jet crashed on takeoff from Dryden. Twenty-four passengers and crew were killed in the accident which was likely caused by ice on the wings. Convairs had to be brought back into service to replace the lost aircraft.

FLEET LISTING
AIR ONTARIO

REG'N	C/N	F/N	IS	WFU	NOTES
F28-1000					
C-FONF	11060	281	5/88	3/89	W/O 10/03/89 on takeoff from Dryden, Ont.; 24 killed.
C-FONG	11070	282	4/88	C	
DASH-8-102					
C-FABN	044	---	9/86	3/87	LF C-FABN Air BC
C-GION	127	805	12/88	C	
C-GJIG	068	801	4/87	C	AC Commuter c/s
C-GJMI	077	802	7/87	C	AC Commuter c/s; LT Air Alliance 1988
C-GJMO	079	803	7/87	C	AC Commuter c/s; LT Air Alliance 1988
C-GJMK	081	804	7/87	C	AC Commuter c/s
C-GJSV	085	805	7/87	C	AC Commuter c/s; LT Air Alliance 1988
C-GJSX	088	806	11/87	C	AC Commuter c/s
C-GKON	130	815	1/89	C	
C-GLON	133	816	3/89	C	LT Air Nova 3/89-4/89
C-GOND	090	807	1/88	C	AC Commuter c/s
C-GONH	093	808	2/88	C	AC Commuter c/s
C-GONJ	095	809	3/88	C	AC Commuter c/s
C-GONN	101	810	6/88	C	AC Commuter c/s
C-GONO	102	887	5/88	6/88	LF Air Nova (Air Nova c/s)
C-GONR	109	811	7/88	C	LT DHC 9/88-10/88
C-GONW	112	812	9/88	C	
C-GONX	118	803	10/88	C	
C-GONY	115	802	9/88	C	
DASH-8-301					
C-----		---	----	OO	OO 1989
C-----		---	----	OO	OO 1989
C-----		---	----	OO	OO 1989
C-----		---	----	OO	OO 1989
C-----		---	----	OO	OO 1989
C-----		---	----	OO	OO 1989
C-----		---	----	OO	OO 1989
C-----		---	----	OO	OO 1989
C-----		---	----	OO	OO 1989
CONVAIR 580					
C-GDTC	089	546	4/81	C	EX N5846 Allegheny; full c/s 2/81
C-GDTD	028	540	4/81	7/87	ST OO-VGH European Air Transport
C-GDTE	052	545	4/81	12/87	ST OO-EAT; full c/s 5/81
C-GGWF	459	511	1/85	8/87	ST OO-DHL EAT; LT Time 5 - 9/85
C-GGWG	130	513	12/84	9/87	ST OO-HUB EAT; LT Time 5 - 7/85
C-GGWH	456	535	3/85	C	LT C-GGWH Soundair 5/88-8/88
C-GGWI	169	536	3/85	C	EX N5836 Freedom.
C-GGWJ	127	537	11/84	8/88	EX N5837 Freedom; LT C-GGWJ Gelco Express
C-GJRP	466	551	4/81	C	EX N21466 Time; full c/s 7/84
C-GQHA	147	538	4/81	5/88	ST OO-EAT; full c/s 4/82
C-GQHB	376	531	10/84	C	EX ZS-KRX Air Cape.
C-GTAO	116	560	12/87	8/88	LF C-GTAO DHC Canada; EX Time Air
HS748					
C-GFFU	1579		8/87	2/89	EX TR-0203 Venezuelan Navy; ST C-GFFU Air Creebec
C-GGNZ	1690	721	8/87	2/89	ST C-GGNZ Air Creebec; Air Canada Connector c/s 6/88
C-GGOO	1692	722	8/87	2/89	EX ZS-SBV South African Airways; ST C-GGOO Air Creebec
C-GLTC	1656	788	8/87	3/89	RT C-GLTC (Lessor)
C-GOUT	1621	724	8/87	2/89	ST C-GOUT Air Creebec
C-GMAA	1576		8/87	C	EX TR-LQY; Trans Gabon
C-GQSV	1618		8/87	2/89	LT OY-MBY Maersk 8/80-7/81; ST C-GQSV Air Creebec
C-GQTG	1619		8/87	C	EX CC-CEH Lan Chile
C-GQTH	1617		8/87	C	LT OY-MBY Maersk Air 4/80-4/81
C-GSXS	1674		8/87	2/89	EX XA-SAC SAESA; ST C-GSXS Air Creebec
C-GQWO	1597	723	8/87	2/89	EX T-03 Fuerza Aera Argentina; ST C-GQWO Air Creebec
DHC-6 TWIN OTTER					
C-GDAA	475		8/87	12/88	WFU
C-GNPS	558		8/87	2/89	ST C-GNPS Latham Island Airways
Beech 99					
C-FJEZ	U--15	917	8/87	10/88	EX N199Gl
C-GDFX	U-123		8/87	3/89	EX C-GDFX Torontair; ST C-GDFX Bearskin Lake Airways

FLEET LISTING
AIR ONTARIO

REG'N	C/N	F/N	IS	WFU	NOTES
Beech 99 (Continued)					
C-GEOI	U-152	988	8/87	2/89	EX C-GEOI Torontair; ST C-GEOI Bearskin Lake Airways
C-GFKB	U--55		8/87	4/89	EX C-GFKB Torontair
C-GFQC	U-120		8/87	2/89	EX HS-SKF; ST C-GFQC Bearskin Lake Airways
C-GGLE	U-207		8/87	4/89	WFU
C-GGPP	U-216		8/87	4/89	WFU
C-GQAH	U--58	914	8/87	2/89	EX C-GQAH Quebec Aviation; ST C-GQAH Bearskin Lake Airways
DC-3					
CF-AAM	9862		8/87	12/88	EX 10910 RCAF; ST CF-AAM Central Mountain Airways
CF-BJE	13453		8/87	11/88	EX CF-BJE Ontario Central; W/O 01/11/88 Pikangikum Lake, Ont., 2 killed
C-FQBC	27026		8/87	12/88	WFU; EX C-FQBC Quebecair
C-GNNA	12483		8/87	12/88	WFU; EX CF 12964
Citation 501					
C-GFEE	0169		8/87	11/88	EX C-GFEE Austin Airways; ST C-GFEE Voyageur Airways
C-GRQA	0374		8/87	11/88	EX C-GRQZ Austin Airways; ST C-GRQA Voyageur Airways
Beech KingAir					
C-GQXF	BB285	201	8/87	2/89	ST C-GQXF Central Mountain Airways
CATPAS 200					
C-FBWX	BB341	202	8/88	C	AC Connector c/s
C-FCGB	BB246	203	9/88	C	EX N183MC
C-FCGC	BB236	204	9/88	C	EX N46KA
C-FCGL	BB190	207	10/88	12/88	EX N190MD
C-FCGM	BB236	205	8/88	C	EX N200CD
C-FCGT	BB159	206	10/88	C	EX N47FH
C-FCGU	BB301	208	11/88	C	
C-FCGX	BB250	209	2/89	C	EX N1008J
C-F	BB342				
C-F	BB343				
C-F	BB344				
C-F	BB345				

GREAT LAKES AIRLINES

REG'N	C/N	F/N	IS	WFU	NOTES
CONVAIR 580					
C-GDTC	089	DTC	2/76	4/81	EX N5846 Allegheny
C-GDTD	028	DTD	4/76	4/81	EX N5840 Allegheny
C-GJRP	466	JRP	12/79	4/81	EX N21466 Time Aviation Services
C-GQHA	147	QHA	1/77	4/81	EX N5838 Allegheny
N5826	385		11/77	12/77	LF N5826 Allegheny
N5831	376		10/78	12/78	LF N5831 Allegheny
N580GN	376		12/79	3/80	LF N580GN Great Northern; CONVAIR 440
CF-GLC	360		12/69	9/75	BU 1976
CF-GLD	364		12/69	9/75	ST N30KA Sun Valley Key Airlines
CF-GLK	325		12/73	5/77	ST N21DR 324 Inc.; EX CF-GHQ
CF-GLM	393		2/74	5/77	ST N24DR 393 Inc.; EX Linjeflyg
CF-GLR	350		6/74	6/76	ST N25DR Onyx Aviation Inc.
CF-GLT	351		1/74	7/77	ST N26DR San Jaun International Airway
DC-3					
CF-GLA	2140		6/67	11/72	ST CF-GLA Pem Air
CF-GLB	1547		11/67	5/71	ST CF-GLB Pem Air
CF-YED	4433		1/71	5/71	LF CF-YED Greyhound Leasing
PA-31-350					
C-GQNC	52176		7/78	9/79	ST C-GQNC Flightexec Ltd.
BEECH D-18S					
CF-LLF	A352		4/60	1/72	ST CF-LLF Air Windsor
CESSNA 310					
CF-KAY	35624		4/60	5/68	ST CF-KAY Hughes Marine Sales Ltd.

AUSTIN
AIRWAYS

Austin Airways HS-748, C-GSXS

ALLIANCE:
Air Canada Connector

HEADQUARTERS:
RR2, Timmins Airport,
Timmins, Ontario, P4N 7C3

MAIN BASES:
Timmins Airport; Toronto International

FLEET 1988:
9 - HS748s;
2- Twin Otters;
7 - Beech 99s;
4 - DC-3s;
2 - Cessna Citations;
12 - Cessna 402s.

COLOURS:
A yellow aircraft with a broad black cheat line running through the windows and a thin red cheat line above and below the black. The cheat lines sweep up the yellow tail ending in a point at the rear of the tail, just below the top. Austin titles appear in black on the upper fuselage and the black registration is displayed near the rear of the fuselage.

ROUTES:
Toronto – Elliot Lake – Timmins – Kapuskasing – Cochrane – Moosonee – Rupert House – East Main – Weminkji – Paint Mills – Chasasibi/La Grande 2 – Great Whale – Fort Albany – Kashechewan – Attawapiskat – Winisk/Peawaniuck – Fort Severn – Big Trout Lake – Kasabonika – Bearskin Lake – Sachigo – Round Lake – Muskrat Dam – Cat Lake – Pickle Lake – Webequie – Lansdowne – Fort Hope – Geralton – Manitouwadge – Hornepayne – Marathon – Sioux Lookout – Kenora/Minaki – Red Lake – Pikangikum – Deer Lake – Sandy Lake

HISTORY:

In 1934, Jack and Chuck Austin began flying a Tiger Moth and a pair of Wacos out of Toronto Island Airport. However, it was not for flights out of Toronto that Austin Airways would build its name, but for service to northern Ontario based out of Timmins.

The company operated a multitude of small aircraft and as with other Canadian airlines, the DEW Line and Mid-Canada Line made it possible for Austin Airways to acquire larger aircraft, like the DC-3 and Canso for its fleet.

The Austin's finally gave up operating their airline in 1974 when they sold out to Stan Deluce. Deluce had been operating *White River Airways,* out of White River, since 1951, using a fleet of Otters, Beavers, and smaller aircraft. *White River Airways* was awarded one of the contracts to operate the Twin Otters when *NorOntair* began operations..

Under the Deluce family, Austin expanded its fleet in 1976 by adding HS748s. The Cansos were phased out in 1977. The DC-3 fleet was greatly reduced at this time and additional Twin Otters purchased. The Cessna 402 aircraft was added to the fleet in 1979 and would eventually reach twelve in number.

Austin Airways bought *Ontario Central Airlines* of Gimli, Manitoba, in 1979, acquiring its fleet of DC-3s but, more importantly, acquired further scheduled services. In 1980, Austin leased three HS-748s to *Maersk* of Denmark and provided maintenance and crew training with these aircraft.

Austin Airways had a contract to operate *NorOntair* Twin Otters on the Timmins to Sudbury, Kapuskasing and Cochrane route and also operated a Twin Otter out of Pickle Lake for Bell Canada. An Air Ambulance service for the Ontario Government called 'Bandage 4' was begun in July 1981 using a Cessna Citation based at Timmins. In 1981, Austin Airways took over another large DC-3 operator, *Superior Airways* of Thunder Bay, providing Austin Airways access to Thunder Bay and enabling the company to begin a scheduled Thunder Bay – Minneapolis service.

The Deluce family purchased 50% of *Air Ontario* in 1981, setting up the inevitable merger of the large northern Ontario operator with the large southern Ontario operator. The new holding company for Austin Airways and *Air Ontario* was called Delplex Holdings. The company also acquired a 49% ownership of *Air Creebec* which was based at Val d'Or.

Austin Airways took over the *Torontair* routes between Kingston and Toronto when that company folded in 1984. When *Air Canada* purchased further shares from Delplex Holdings giving it 75% of *Air Ontario* and Austin Airways, plans were begun to merge the two companies into one under the *Air Ontario* name. Thus in 1987, the name Austin disappeared from the Canadian Airline register and the aircraft and routes began to operate as *Air Ontario*.

FLEET LISTING
AUSTIN AIRWAYS

REG'N	C/N	IS	WFU	NOTES
HS748				
C-GDOP	1745	12/80	4/82	ST C-GDOP Eastern Provincial; LF EPA 7 - 9/88
C-GFFU	1579	9/81	8/87	EX TR-0203 Venezuelan Navy
C-GGNZ	1690	11/83	8/87	EX ZS-SBU South African Airways
C-GGOB	1691	12/83	2/88	EX ZS-SBW South African Airways
C-GGOO	1692	11/83	8/87	EX ZS-SBV South African Airways
C-GMAA	1576	5/76	8/87	EX TR-LQY Trans Gabon
C-GOUT	1621	5/79	4/84	ST C-GOUT Air Inuit; LT Maersk 6/80 - 4/81
C-GPAA	1675	12/76	7/79	W/O 17/07/79 at Moosonee
C-GQSV	1618	6/79	8/87	LT OY-MBY Maersk 8/80 - 7/81
C-GQTG	1619	5/79	8/87	EX CC-CEH Lan Chile
C-GQTH	1617	5/79	8/87	LT OY-MBY Maersk Air 4/80 - 4/81
C-GQWO	1597	10/78	8/87	EX T-03 Fuerza Aera Argentina
C-GSXS	1674	11/77	8/87	EX XA-SAC SAESA
DHC-6				
C-FGON	369	6/81	6/83	OF Norontair; Air Dale took over 1983
C-FZKP	290	7/75	10/82	ST C-FZKP Air Crebec; LT Air Inuit 10/78 - 6/80
C-GBOX	672	2/80	6/84	LT Air Inuit and sold 10/87
C-GCVZ	726	11/80	6/82	ST Air Creebec
C-GDAA	475	2/76	8/87	
C-GFJC	768	5/81	2/85	ST AP-BCH Pakistan International Airline
C-GGAA	477	4/76	4/84	LT C-GGAA Air Inuit
C-GNPS	558	3/78	8/87	
C-GOVG	592	5/78	6/85	OF Norontair; AirDale took over
C-GTJA	630	6/79	11/79	W/O 01/11/79 Big Trout Lake, Ontario
C-GTLA	632	6/79	11/84	W/O 23/11/84 Lansdowne House
Beech 99				
C-FJEZ	U--15	10/86	8/87	EX N199Gl
C-GDFX	U-123	4/86	8/87	EX C-GDFX Torontair
C-GEOI	U-152	6/86	8/87	EX C-GEOI Torontair
C-GFKB	U--55	1/86	8/87	EX C-GFKB Torontair
C-GGLE	U-207	8/84	8/87	
C-GGPP	U-216	1/84	8/87	
C-GQAH	U--58	9/85	8/87	EX C-GQAH Quebec Aviation
DC-3				
CF-AAB	12289	1/65	7/78	ST N2290L Federal Land Corp.; EX RCAF 961
CF-AAC	25369	4/65	6/70	W/O 19/06/70 Val d'Or, Quebec
CF-AAH	12528	4/72	4/78	ST N45860 Southern Flyer Inc.
CF-AAL	26828	2/64	11/69	W/O 09/11/69 2 miles west of Timmins
CF-AAL	10202	2/70	8/77	ST CF-TKX Alberta Northern A/L
CF-AAM	9862	9/70	8/87	EX 10910 RCAF
CF-BJE	13453	8/79	8/87	EX CF-BJE Ontario Central
C-FIAX	19499	9/74	12/76	W/O 10/12/76 Ft. George, Quebec
CF-ILQ	12377	1/56	1/64	W/O 09/01/64 near Rupert River, PQ
CF-JMX	25615	1/57	4/59	ST CF-DTT DOT
C-FQBC	27026	2/87	C	EX C-FQBC Quebecair
C-GNNA	12483	3/75	C	EX CF 12964
Citation				
C-GJOE	0049	5/81	6/86	Sold
C-GFEE	0169	12/81	8/87	To C-GFEE Air Ontario; ST Voyageur 11/88
C-GRQA	0374	6/86	8/87	To C-GRQA Air Ontario; ST Voyageur 11/88
Beech 200				
C-GQXF	BB285	10/85	6/88	Repainted in Air Ontario AC Connector c/s 6/88

Aircraft shown as 8/87 were transferred to Air Ontario.

ONTARIO EXPRESS

Ontario Express ATR-42, C-FLCP

ALLIANCE:
Canadian Partner (45% owned by *Canadian*)

HEADQUARTERS:
Box 69, Toronto AMF, Ontario, L5P 1A5

MAIN BASE:
Toronto (Pearson) International Airport
(Terminal 1)

FLEET 1989:
14 - BAe 3101 Jetstream 31s;
3 - Aerospatiale ATR-42s with 6 on order.

COLOURS:
The *Canadian* colour scheme with large titles on the upper fuselage: 'CANADIAN PARTNER' ("Canadian" in Blue, "Partner" in Red) and smaller titles on the rear fuselage: 'Operated by Ontario Express.' The grey cheat line above the red line running along the fuselage has been dropped because the grey paint has not stood up well on the *Canadian* jets.

ROUTES:
Toronto – London – Sarnia – Windsor – Hamilton – Kingston – Ottawa – North Bay – Sudbury – Sault Ste. Marie - Thunder Bay – Dryden – Winnipeg – Brandon – Montreal – Timmins – Pittsburgh.

HISTORY:

When *Air Canada* purchased *Air Ontario, Canadian Airlines International* did not have a commuter airline partner in Ontario. Rather than purchase an existing airline, it decided to set up a new company, Ontario Express. The aircraft chosen for this new commuter airline was the British nineteen-passenger Aerospace Jet-stream 31. The new company was owned 45% by *PWA Corporation*, parent company of *Canadian Airlines International,* with 10% of the stock being reserved for employees. The remaining 45% of the shares was offered on the Toronto Stock Exchange.

Ronald L. Patmore, former Vice-President (Ontario) for *Canadian,* became the company's first president and Anthony Man Son Hing was the director of flight operations.

The airline began operations on July 15, 1987 with service to five cities: Toronto, Ottawa, London, Sarnia and Windsor. As the new Jetstream aircraft were received, routes were added to service Kingston, Sudbury, Sault Ste. Marie and Thunder Bay.

Service from Toronto to Pittsburgh was started on April 3, replacing the Boeing 737 service then operated by *Canadian.* On the same date, flights began between Toronto and North Bay.

Six ATR aircraft were ordered in February 1988, with an option for six more. The first two ATR 42s were flown on Toronto – Pittsburgh, Toronto – Sault Ste. Marie, and Toronto – Windsor routes. Service to Dryden and Winnipeg from Thunder Bay was added in June 1988.

Later in 1988, Ontario Express took over the Winnipeg – Brandon route from *Calm Air.* Hamilton – Ottawa and flights to Timmins were begun early in 1989.

FLEET LISTING
ONTARIO EXPRESS

REG'N	C/N	F/N	IS	WFU	NOTES
BAe 3100 Jetstream					
C-FAMJ	772	107	12/87	C	EX G-31-772
C-FAMK	773	108	12/87	C	EX G-31-773
C-FASJ	781	107	12/87	C	
C-FCOE	783	110	2/88	C	
C-FCPD	822	115	11/88	C	
C-FCPE	825	116	2/89	C	
C-FCPF	827	117	NTU	NTU	To C-FCPF Air BC
C-FCPG	829	118	NTU	NTU	NTU
C-FHOE	785	114	3/88	C	
C-FIOE	786	112	3/88	C	
C-GJPC	733	101	5/87	C	
C-GJPH	738	102	5/87	C	
C-GJPO	740	103	5/87	C	
C-GJPQ	745	104	6/87	C	
C-GJPU	749	105	6/87	C	
C-GJPX	756	106	8/87	C	
N331QX	811	---	8/88		Used for crew training.
AEROSPATIALE ATR 42					
C-FLCP	085	201	6/88	C	EX F-WWEK
C-FNCP	088	202	6/88	C	EX F-WWEN
C-FPCP	124	205	/88	C	EX F-WWEU
C-FQCP	116	203	12/88	C	EX F-WWEM
C-GCXP	139	206	/89	C	EX F-WWEL
C-GHCP	123	204	2/89	C	EX F-WWET
C-	143	207	/89	C	

AIR TORONTO
(COMMUTER EXPRESS)
SOUNDAIR EXPRESS
EXECUTIVE JET

Commuter Express (Soundair) Metroliner, C-GJWS

ALLIANCE:
Air Canada Connector

HEADQUARTERS:
6303 Airport Road, Ste 502,
Mississauga, Ontario, L4V 1R8.

MAIN BASES:
Toronto International Airport;
Montreal (Mirabel).

FLEET 1989:
Air Toronto
7 - Super Jetstream 3201s;
1 - SA226TC Metro.

Soundair Express
5 - SA226TC Metro IIs;
4 - SA226AT Merlin IVs;
5 - Convair 580s;

4 - DC-3s;
1 - F27F;

Executive Jet
2 - Falcon 20Ds;
2 - Learjets.

COLOURS:
Air Toronto aircraft fly in the red, white and grey *Air Canada Commuter* colours.

ROUTES:
Toronto – Saginaw – Grand Rapids (Michigan);
Toronto – Indianapolis;
Toronto – Kalamazoo;
Toronto – Columbus – Dayton (Ohio);
Toronto – Louisville, Kentucky;
Toronto – Harrisburg – Allentown (Pennsylvania);
Cargo and passenger charters

151

HISTORY:

Soundair was formed in 1980 in Wiarton, Ontario, and began as a charter service with a fleet of several single- and double-engine Cessnas, Swearingen Metro IIs and Merlin aircraft. The headquarters of the company was later moved from Wiarton to Toronto.

Soundair is the parent company for three operations: Soundair Express, Air Toronto (Commuter Express) and Odyssey International Charter Operations. Commuter Express flew Fairchild Metro II and Merlin IV aircraft out of Terminal 2 at Toronto International Airport. The company began December 17, 1984, with service to Columbus, Ohio. Dayton, Ohio was added and a third Ohio city, Toledo, was serviced in January 1986. In November, 1986, two daily flights to Fort Wayne, Indiana were inaugurated. In April 1987, service from Toronto to Saginaw and Grand Rapids, Michigan were begun but Fort Wayne and Toledo flights were discontinued. August 1987 saw service between Toronto and Harrisburg and Allentown started.

In November 1987, Commuter Express became an *Air Canada* Commuter airline and switched to AC designator codes in the timetables. The company's aircraft (which had operated in an all white colour scheme with a brown 'COMMUTER EXPRESS' title and a brown cheat line), began to be re-painted in *Air Canada* Commuter colours in 1987. The name of the company was changed to Air Toronto in March 1988.

Soundair operated a Lear Jet Freighter service from Vancouver to Calgary, Winnipeg into Columbus, Ohio in February 1984. The company started a passenger service Winnipeg – Prince Albert – Yorkton in the summer of 1984, flying Metro II aircraft. At the beginning of 1985, a Montreal – Burlington – Hartford cargo service was begun for *Emery Express*. As its Commuter Express operation expanded, the company required additional equipment and Winnipeg – Yorkton – Prince Albert passenger service was halted to free up aircraft.

A DC-4 aircraft, C-GPSH, was purchased in July 1985 from *Calm Air* and flown Quebec City – Montreal – Ottawa – Dayton and Toronto/Hamilton – Dayton for *Emery Express*. A second Learjet was also acquired at this time for cargo services.

In November 1986, Soundair established a jet charter operation, *Executive Jet Canada,* which flew Lear Jets from bases in Vancouver, Winnipeg, Wiarton, Toronto, and Montreal.

The company acquired a Fairchild F-27F (C-FIOG) in April 1987 for cargo work and in July acquired a former *Kelowna* Convair 580 (C-GKFP). The company had also operated another Convair 580 (C-FJEE), since 1986 to replace the DC-4 and late in 1987 purchased three more Convair 580s.

In March 1988, Commuter Express was renamed Air Toronto. With the name change, the company announced that it would begin flying from Toronto to Indianapolis using recently acquried Convair 580 aircraft. Service to Louisville, Kentucky would commence as soon as the American paperwork was complete.

Air Toronto decided on the Super Jetstream 3201 for its fleet replacement program. Six regular Jetstream 3100s were leased from BAE late in 1988. These were returned to BAE as the Super Jetstreams became available in March 1989. One Metroliner was retained as a backup aircraft with the remaining going to *Soundair Express* after being converted back to cargo aircraft. The six leased Jetstream 3100s were sent to *Air BC* by BAE. Also in March 1989, Saginaw was dropped and the flight to Grande Rapids rerouted to include Kalamazoo. Toronto to Green Bay and Madison was also begun at that time.

Soundair began *Odyssey International* using two Boeing 757s in the fall of 1988 to operate a charter service out of the Toronto International Airport and details are provided under Odyssey's own listing. Mr. Brian Walker, a former vice-president of Wardair, heads up this new service.

Thus Soundair operates Air Toronto (Commuter Express) as an *Air Canada* Connector, Executive Jet Canada operates Lear Jets throughout Canada, Falcon jets for *Purolator Courier*, a freight operation for *Emery Express* with Convair 580, DC-4 and F-27 Aircraft and Odyssey International using Boeing 767s.

FLEET LISTING

AIR TORONTO (COMMUTER EXPRESS)

REG'N	C/N	F/N	IS	WFU	NOTES
JETSTREAM 3201					
C-FBDR	830	610	2/89	C	EX G-31-830
C-FDBR	831	611	2/89	C	EX G-31-831
C-FTAR	832	612	3/89	C	EX G-31-832
C-FTDB	833	613	4/89	C	EX G-31-833
C-GZRT	835	614	3/89	C	EX G-31-835
C-FFPA	837	615	3/89	C	EX G-31-837
C-GQRO	843	616	4/89	C	EX G-31-843 (C-GKXW NTU)
C-		617	6/89	C	
C-		618	7/89	C	
JETSTREAM 3100					
C-FBID	802	601	8/88	3/89	LF BAE; To C-FBID Air BC
C-FBIE	815	602	8/88	4/89	LF BAE; To C-FBIE Air BC
C-FBI I	816	603	8/88	3/89	LF BAE; To C-FBI I Air BC
C-FBI J	817	604	8/88	4/89	LF BAE; To C-FBI J Air BC
C-FBIP	820	605	8/88	4/89	LF BAE; To C-FBIP Air BC
N331QV	806		7/88	1/89	LF BAE for crew training
SA226TC METRO II					
C-GBDF	TC-258	104	4/80	3/89	Cvt cargo Soundair Express
C-GDAU	TC-213	102	5/85	3/89	Cvt cargo Soundair Express
C-GFAP	TC-220	103	12/87	C	EX N443JA (backup aircraft)
C-GFBF	TC-317		10/81	11/82	
C-GGRX	TC-212	101	6/86	3/89	Cvt cargo Soundair Express
C-GGSW	TC-290	105	4/84	3/89	Cvt cargo Soundair Express
C-GJWS	TC-211	100	4/87	3/89	Cvt cargo Soundair Express
SA226AT MERLIN IV					
C-GJWW	AT-013	107	8/81	3/88	EX N720R; Cargo a/c
C-GPCL	AT-017	109	2/80	3/89	EX N511M; Cargo a/c
C-GSDR	AT-014	108	8/81	7/87	LT Tempus Air; Cargo a/c
C-GSWF	AT-011	106	4/85	3/89	EX N400PL
C-GVEJ	AT-039	111	7/87	3/89	EX C-GVEJ Eastern Flying
C-GWSL	AT-028	110	5/85	3/89	EX C-GWSL Provincial Aviation

SOUNDAIR EXPRESS

REG'N	C/N	F/N	IS	WFU	NOTES
F-27F					
C-FIOG	109		5/87	C	EX C-FIOG
CONVAIR 580					
C-FAUF	24	302	3/88	C	EX N585PL
C-FBHW	29		3/88	C	EX N581P Plymouth Lsg
C-FICA	98	333	3/88	C	EX C-FICA Time Air
C-GGWH	465		5/88	8/88	LF C-GGWH Air Ontario
C-GJEE	65		10/86	C	EX N5821
C-GKFP	168		7/87	C	EX C-GKFP Kelowna Flightcraft
DC-4					
C-FGNI	10389		3/84	9/86	WFU; ST C-FGNI Air North 11/88
C-GCXG	10644		3/84	9/86	WFU; EX C-GCXG Aero Trades
C-GPSH	7458		7/85	9/86	WFU; EX C-GPSH Calm Air
DC-3					
C-FFBS	6070		8/83	C	EX C-FFBS Questor
C-FIAR	20877		11/81	4/83	ST C-FIAR Ontario Central
C-FIMA	13070		8/83	10/88	EX C-FIMA Questor; ST Air North
C-FKAZ	19345		7/82	6/85	ST N5831B
C-FQBI	6179		2/83	5/83	ST C-FQBI Northwest Leasing
C-FTVL	32855		/82	10/83	LF C-FTVL Bradley Air Service
C-GCXD	25612		/84	C	EX 12948 CAF
C-GSCA	27190		11/81	6/84	W/O 10/06/84 at St. Louis
C-GCCB	33441		6/84	C	EX C-GSCB Skycraft
C-GYBA	20215		6/84	C	EX C-GYBA Yellowbird Air

FLEET LISTING
EXECUTIVE JET CANADA

REG'N	C/N	IS	WFU	NOTES
LEAR JET 35				
C-GBWL	35-049	11/84	C	
C-GFRK	35A-093	1/84	10/84	ST N5474G Templair Air
LEAR JET 25				
C-GHMH	25-011	7/85	8/86	EX C-GHMH Provincial
Falcon 20D				
C-FONX	225	4/87	C	OF Purolator Courier
C-GTAK	197	11/85	C	OF Purolator Courier

City Express ST-27, C-FJFH

CITY EXPRESS

AFFILIATION:
None

HEADQUARTERS:
545 Lakeshore Blvd W.,
Toronto, Ontario, M5V 1A3

MAIN BASE:
Toronto Island Airport

FLEET 1989:
4 - DASH-7s;
4 - DASH-8s;

COLOURS:
From the nose to aft of the rear door the aircraft is white, followed by a series of inclined vertical stripes which wrap around the fuselage and alternate broad orange, narrow white, broad red and narrow white. Everything aft of the final white stripe is dark blue. The engines are painted with the same series of coloured stripes. A large stylized 'C' covers most of the dark blue tail. The titles: 'CITY EXPRESS' (port) and 'CITÉ EXPRESS' (starboard) appear on the forward fuselage below the cockpit. The stylized 'City/Cité' is displayed in white on a dark blue pattern in the shape of the word, while the red 'EXPRESS' is rendered in smal-ler italicized block letters beneath. The registration appears on the dark blue lower rear fuselage in white block letters.

ROUTES:
Toronto Island Airport – London – Ottawa – Montreal (Dorval) – Quebec City – Sept-Iles – Wabush.
Toronto Island – Detroit – Newark.

HISTORY:

The airline known now as City Express was established in 1971 as *Otonabee Airways Ltd*. The company was formed in Peterborough and began operating a scheduled service on variations of the St. Lawrence route between Toronto Island Airport, Peterborough, Kingston and Montreal.

When the Saunders company went bankrupt, *Otonabee* purchased its available ST-27 aircraft, including all the jigs and tooling. Although the company never proceeded with production of the ST-27 and ST-28 as planned, these aircraft became the mainstay of the fleet for *Otanabee Airways/Air Atonabee*.

Service to Kingston was ended in the late 1970s and Ottawa was substituted. After the name was changed to *Air Atonabee* in 1979, the company established two routes: Toronto Island – Peterborough and Ottawa; and Toronto Island – Montreal (Dorval), with some of these latter flights also going through Peterborough.

The airline's name was changed to City Express in 1984 when a former *Arkia Israeli* Dash-7 was acquired and its headquarters was moved from Peterborough to Toronto. A regular commuter service was established, flying Dash-7 and ST-27 aircraft on its major Toronto Island – Ottawa route. One flight a day went from Ottawa to the Toronto International Airport, while two trips a day were flown between Toronto Island, Peterborough and Montreal (Dorval), using ST-27 aircraft .

By March 1985, City Express had acquired a second Dash-7 and the Dash-7s were used mainly on the Ottawa flights. At Toronto Island Airport, passengers were picked up in a City Express bus and taken to the Royal York Hotel, thus placing business and government officials in the heart of Toronto. The Toronto Island – Montreal schedule was reduced to weekend flights only for the winter of 1985, using Dash-7s and ST-27s.

June 1985 saw the takeover of the former *Nordair* Hamilton – Pittsburgh route using ST-27 aircraft. In August, two flights a day on the Ottawa – Toronto route were extended to include Hamilton. When the Dash-8 was acquired in September 1985, the Montreal – Toronto route was also extended to Hamilton. A Hamilton – Ottawa – Montreal route was added at this time using a leased Grumman Gulfstream G-159.

The Hamilton – Pittsburgh route turned out to be a money loser and was dropped in January 1986, as were flights between Toronto Island and Peterborough, but the Peterborough – Ottawa – Montreal flights continued. In April 1986, charter flights from Ottawa/Montreal/ Hamilton to Atlantic City were started under the title 'Atlantic City Express Flights.' In May the company began service between Toronto Island and Quebec City on a charter basis. A Toronto Island – London (Ontario) service was begun in September 1986, flying nine ST-27 flights daily.

Twice weekly ski charters between Toronto Island and Quebec City were begun in February 1987. The following month, all flights to Peterborough were cancelled and all flights to Hamilton were discontinued in May. Routes from Toronto Island to Newark and Detroit were inaugurated in May.

Hunting charters were operated in the fall of 1987 between Montreal and Schefferville using a Dash-7, with a ST-27 as backup. The Toronto – Montreal service was extended to Quebec City and Sept Iles in December 1987 and later to Wabush.

At the beginning of 1988, the airline was operating eight weekday Dash-7 flights between Toronto and Ottawa; nine weekday Dash-8 flights between Toronto and Montreal, one of them extending to Quebec City and Sept-Iles; eight daily Toronto to London flights using ST-27 aircraft; five daily Toronto to Newark flights with Dash-8s; and, one flight per day between Toronto and Detroit City Airport. Courtesy shuttle buses connect the flights to check in locations in the centre of each city. The sites are: Toronto – the Royal York; Ottawa – Westin Hotel; Montreal – Dominion Square on Metcalfe Street; London – City Centre on King Street.

On August 15, 1988, all ST-27 aircraft were retired and all flights from Toronto Island Airport to London, Ontario and Rochester, NY were cancelled.

In February 1989, all flights from Montreal to Quebec City, Wabush and Sept Iles were cancelled because of poor load factors. A Dash-7 was leased to Sudan to operate as a cargo aircraft on relief flights.

FLEET LISTING

CITY EXPRESS

REG'N	C/N	IS	WFU	NOTES
DASH-7				
C-GGXS	064	6/84	C	LT Brymon Airways 10/87; Air BC 11/87-12/87
C-GHRV	074	3/85	C	EX N903HA Henson Aviation
C-GJVY	011	8/87	C	EX N210AW Southern Jersey Airways
C-GJKS	072	5/87	3/89	EX P2-ANO Air Niugini; LT Sudan
DASH-8				
C-FCTE	027	3/86	C	
C-GCTC	065	1/87	C	
C-GCTX	014	9/85	C	
C-GGTO	005	9/85	C	
C-GIQQ	010	1/86	2/86	LF C-GIQQ DHC
C-GGOM	003	2/87	4/87	LF C-GGOM DHC
ST-27				
C-FCNX	08	8/87	8/88	EX C-FCNX Air Atonabee; WFU
C-FFZP	10	6/84	8/88	EX C-FFZP Air Atonabee; WFU
C-FHMQ	12	6/84	8/88	EX C-FHMQ Air Atonabee; WFU
C-FJFH	11	6/84	8/88	EX C-FJFH Air Atonabee; WFU
C-FXOK	02	6/84	8/88	EX C-FXOK Air Atonabee; WFU
C-GYCR	04	6/84	8/88	EX C-GYCR Air Atonabee; WFU
G-159				
C-FMUR	54	5/86	5/87	LF C-FMUR Air Inuit

FIRST AIR
(BRADLEY AIR SERVICE)

First Air HS-748, C-GDUN

ALLIANCE:
Air Canada Aero Plan Partner;
uses *Air Canada* reservac

HEADQUARTERS:
Carp Airport, Carp, Ontario, K0A 1L0

MAIN BASES:
Ottawa International; Carp Airport

FLEET 1989:
4 - Boeing 727-100s;
10 - HS748;
7 - DHC-6s;

COLOURS:
All white aircraft with a rainbow cheat line: yellow above the window; orange through the top of the windows; red through the bottom of the window and dark blue below the window. The cheat line starts as a point near the nose of the aircraft and expands to equal lines through the main part of the body, then sweeps up onto the rear portion of the tail. On the 727s the cheat line ends at a point at the top of the tail, but on some of the HS748s it ends part way up the solid blue top to the tail. There is a Canadian flag on the lower forward fuselage and the registration appears in black on the lower rear fuselage. Angled on the leading edge of the tail in black is the word 'FIRST' and the second part of the title 'AIR' appears on the top engine on the 727s. The HS748s display the full title 'FIRST AIR' in black on the upper forward fuselage, preceded by the company symbol.

ROUTES:
Ottawa – Montreal (Mirabel); Ottawa – Boston;
Ottawa – Iqaluit (Frobisher Bay) – Nuuk (Greenland) – Broughton Island – Clyde River – Pond Inlet – Nanisivik – Igloolik – Hall Beach – Cape Dorset – Coral Harbour – Lake Harbour – Pelly Bay – Spence Bay – Gjoa Haven – Cambridge Bay – Yellowknife.

HISTORY:

Bradley Air Service was formed in 1946 by R. Bradley, connecting many small communities in the eastern Northwest Territories. It was also a flying school and Piper dealer.

Nordair dropped its *Nordair Arctic* operations from Frobisher Bay in 1976, which were taken over by *Survair*. In October 1978, Bradley Air Service acquired these routes and the former *Nordair* Twin Otters from *Survair*. Once Bradley Air Service had developed into a more scheduled airline the name was changed to First Air.

The airline's first services outside of the north began with the opening of Montreal's Mirabel Airport, operating several DC-3 flights per day between Ottawa and Mirabel. To handle increasing passenger loads, the DC-3s were later replaced by HS748 aircraft. The first international flight by the airline was between Frobisher Bay and Nuuk, Greenland. First Air also began an Ottawa – Val d'Or and Rouyn service in November, 1984 using *Voyageur Airways* ST-27s. Later the company flew its own aircraft on this route.

In November 1984, Ottawa to Boston flights were begun using HS748 aircraft. The company also won a $9 million contract to maintain the DOT's DASH-7 ice reconnaissance aircraft based in Ottawa. At the end of 1985, First Air was finally able to link their northern and southern routes when permission for an Ottawa to Frobisher Bay route was granted.

To operate this long haul route, a Boeing 727 combi aircraft was acquired early in 1986 and the first Ottawa to Frobisher Bay flight took place on 31 March 1986. These 727 flights were scheduled for three times a week, and the aircraft was also used to fly weekend charters from Toronto to St. Petersburgh for *Nordair*. To accomplish this, the aircraft was converted from combi to full passenger configuration and back every weekend. The 727 was also leased during the week by *Air Canada* for flying nightly cargo service between Ottawa, Toronto, Winnipeg, Toronto and back to Ottawa to supplement DC-8 cargo flights.

In July 1986, the 727 was used on a charter between Frobisher Bay, Yellowknife and Kotzebue for the Inuit Circumpolar Conference. In the same month the Ottawa – Val d'Or – Rouyn service was discontinued. During the winter of 1986, the 727 flew charters from Toronto, Windsor and Ottawa to Caracas, Montego Bay and Puerto Vallarta.

A second Boeing 727 was acquired in 1987 and used occasionally on the Ottawa to Montreal route. In October of that year, service was extended from the eastern Arctic into the central and western Arctic using a HS748 to connect Iqaluit, Igloolik, Pelly Bay, Spence Bay, Gjoa Haven, Cambridge Bay and Yellowknife.

During the winter of 1987-88, First Air used its Boeing 727s on twice-weekly Montreal – Detroit service on behalf of *Sabena Belgian World Airlines*, replacing *Nordair* as the operator of this service.

A third Boeing 727 was purchased in June 1988, enabling the airline to establish a jet service between Ottawa – Iqaluit (Frobisher Bay) – Yellowknife. This was the first jet service linking eastern Canada with the western Arctic.

First Air is a member of *Air Canada*'s Aero Plan Program and uses the *Air Canada* reservac system but is not part of *Air Canada*'s connector service.

First Air suffered two serious accidents involving its HS-748 aircraft while on night express service flights within a four month period. On 15 September 1988, one HS-748 crashed near Cheney while on route from Montreal to Ottawa with the loss of the crew. The second aircraft crashed on takeoff from Dayton, Ohio, again with all crew members killed.

During the winter of 1988-89, First Air provided Boeing 727 aircraft to *Mirabelle Tours* of Montreal for use on charters from Montreal and Ottawa to sun spots such as Orlando, Acapulco, Freeport, Curacao, Cuba and Santo Domingo. Late in December 1988, a Boeing 727 carried Canadian medical supplies from Ottawa to Moscow for victims of the earthquake in Armenia.

Ottawa – Newark and Ottawa – Goose Bay routes were begun early in 1989. First Air and *NWT Air* agreed to co-operate on trans-Canada flights north of the 60th parallel. Previously, both airlines flew Yellowknife – Rankin Inlet and Iqaluit on Mondays, but beginning in May 1989 the agreement permits one airline to fly this route on Mondays and the other on Fridays. By coordinating their schedules the two airlines will now be able to provide daily air service to the Keewatin and Kitikmeot regions. Through-service flights between the two airlines are also now offered.

FLEET LISTING
BRADLEY AIR/FIRST AIR

REG'N	C/N	IS	WFU	NOTES	MODEL	AIRCRAFT NAME
727-100						
C-FRST	19169	12/85	C	EX N797AS Alaska;	-90QC	SPIRIT OF IQALUIT
C-FFRB	19120	2/87	C	EX 5N-AWH Kabo Air	-27C	
C-GOFA	18815	6/88	C	EX N154N Pride Air	-35	
C-GVFA	20475	8/88	C	EX N26879 IASCO/Federal Express	-44C	
HS748						
C-FBNW	1759	9/87	C	EX 9Y-TGD BWIA International		
C-GBFA	1781	5/88	C	EX N117CA Cascade		
C-GDOV	1582	4/84	1/89	EX C-GDOV Quebecair/Regionair; W/O 12/01/89 on takeoff, Dayton, Ohio		
C-GDUN	1581	4/84	C	EX C-GDUN Quebecair/Regionair		
C-GDUI	1577	12/87	C	EX C-GDUI Regionair/Quebecair		
C-GDUL	1578	12/87	C	EX C-GDUL Regionair/Quebecair		
C-GFFA	1789	5/88	9/88	EX N118CA Cascade; W/O 15/09/88 Cheney, between YUL-XOW Montreal-Ottawa		
C-GFNW	1758	9/87	C	EX 9Y-TFX BWIA International		
C-GJVN	1640	2/80	C	EX RP-C1016 Philippine Airlines		
C-GLTC	1656	5/87	C	EX D-ASFD BFS		
C-GRXE	1783	5/85	2/86	LF C-GRXE Air Martin		
C-GTLD	1722	12/78	C	EX PK-IHR Bouraq		
C-GYMX	1665	11/80	C	EX DQ-FBK Air Pacific		
Cessna 550						
C-GJAP	0051	5/79	5/80	ST C-GBCB Province of British Columbia		
Cessna 650						
C-GJOE	0049	6/87	C	Citation III		
Cessna 501						
C-GPTC	0377	1/84	6/87	ST C-GPTC Central Airways. Citation I		
DHC-6						
C-FASG	373	11/73	C			
C-FASS	362	4/82	C	Operated 7/73 - 1/80 also		
C-FDHT	130	5/71	3/81	W/O 12/03/81		
C-FNAN	242	10/78	C	EX CF-NAN Nordair Arctic/Survair		
C-FQDG	246	5/72	8/78	W/O 28/08/78 Frobisher Bay		
C-FTVO	334	4/84	6/85	OF NorOntair; back to Air Dale		
C-GNDN	427	10/78	C	EX Nordair/Survair		
C-GNDO	430	10/78	C	EX Nordair/Survair		
C-GNHB	462	4/84	9/84	OF NorOntair; back to Bearskin Lake A/S		
C-GOES	247	5/74	C	EX N384EX Executive Airlines		
C-GPJB	507	6/82	C	EX C-GPJB Air Gava/Kimba Air		
C-GQKZ	441	4/84	9/84	OF NorOnatair; back to Bearskin Lake A/S		
DASH-7						
C-GCFR	102	11/85	C	OF Canadian Coast Guard; based in Ottawa		
Bandeirante						
C-GYQT	3313	1/87	10/87	ST C-GYQT Skycraft		
Beech 99						
C-GDSL	U-92	4/84	9/87			
C-GPEM	U-98	2/82	9/87	EX C-GPEM Pem Air		
DC-3						
CF-FAX	33518	3/74	9/74	ST CF-FAX Golfe Air Quebec Ltee.		
C-FFST	9041	5/79	9/82	WFU at Carp, Ontario		
CF-GKZ	9395	4/78	4/81	WFU at Carp, Ontario		
C-FIQR	11876	2/76	10/76	ST C-FIQR Kenting Aviation		
CF-ITH	20228	5/77	3/78	ST C-FITH Terra Surveys Ltd.		
C-FKBU	4683	7/85	10/86	EX C-FKBU Bearskin Lake Air Svces Ltd.		
CF-LFR	13155	11/78	8/88	EX CF-LFR Survair; EX RCAF U.N. a/c; WFU		
CF-MOC	12741	9/74	8/88	EX CF-MOC Mobil Oil; WFU		
CF-QNF	26643	5/75	6/87	EX 12959 CF "Pinocchio"; ST Central Mountain		
CF-TVK	27004	4/72	1/74	W/O 28/01/74 in hangar fire, Carp, Ontario		
C-FTVL	32855	6/72	8/88	LT C-FTVL Soundair 10/82 - 8/83; WFU		
C-GUBT	12424	10/75	8/79	ST C-GUBT Soundair		
C-GWUG	32963	5/78	6/80	ST C-GWUG Trans Provincial Airlines		
C-GWMY	25368	6/77	9/78	ST C-GWMY Modern Air Spray; EX CAF 12956		
C-GWUH	33046	2/78	11/78	ST C-GWUH Alberta Northern Airline		

AIR ALLIANCE

Air Alliance Dash-8, C-GJMO

ALLIANCE:
Air Canada Connector
(75% owned by *Air Canada*)

HEADQUARTERS:
6th Avenue, Aeroport de Quebec,
Ste. Foy, Quebec, G2E 3L9

MAIN BASES:
Quebec City; Montreal

FLEET 1989:
5 - Dash-8s

COLOURS:
Full red and white *Air Canada* Connector colour scheme
as described for Air Ontario but with 'AIR ALLIANCE' titles on the rear.

ROUTES:
Quebec City – Montreal (Dorval) – Ottawa – Saguenay/
Bagotville – Sept-Iles – Mont Joli – Baie Comeau –
Wabush – Montreal (Mirabel) – Val d'Or – Rouyn/
Noranda – Gaspe – Iles de la Madeleine

HISTORY:

Air Alliance was formed in 1988 as a commuter
airline to feed *Air Canada* routes in Quebec.
Canadian Airlines International was already in
possession of a strong commuter service with *Inter-
Canadian,* the merged *Nordair Metro Express/Quebec-
air* operation, while *Air Canada* had only its DC-9
aircraft flying into the smaller Quebec communities
before the formation of Air Alliance.

Air Alliance is a joint venture between *Air Canada*
(75%) and the Deluce family who own the other 25%
— the same arrangement as the ownership of *Air Ontario.* The company commenced operations on March
27, 1988 using *Air Ontario* Dash-8 aircraft and will acquire their own aircraft as positions become available.

Service began on the Quebec City – Dorval, Quebec
City, Ottawa, Dorval – Ottawa and Dorval – Saguenay/
Bagotville routes. Baie Comeau and Mont Joli were
added in June 1988. Rouyn, Sept Iles and Val d'Or were
added as aircraft became available.

Flights from Montreal's Mirabel Airport to Quebec
City were added in January 1989 to assist international
passengers. Wabush was also added at this time.

FLEET LISTING
AIR ALLIANCE

REG'N	C/N	F/N	IS	WFU	NOTES
DASH-8-102					
C-FOOJ	128		1/89	C	New Aircraft
C-GJMI	077	802	3/88	C	LF C-GJMI Air Ontario
C-GJMO	079	803	3/88	C	LF C-GJMO Air Ontario
C-GJSV	085	805	3/88	C	LF C-GJSV Air Ontario
C-GONH	093	808	1/89	C	LF C-GONH Air Ontario

INTER-CANADIAN

Inter-Canadian Boeing 737, N322XV

ALLIANCE:
Canadian Partner (35% owned by *Canadian*)

HEADQUARTERS:
Quebecair:
CP 490, Montreal International Airport,
Dorval, Quebec, H4Y 1B5
Inter-Quebec:
Hangar No. 2, Aeroport de Quebec,
Ste Foy, Quebec G2E 3M3

MAJOR BASES:
Montreal (Dorval); Quebec City

FLEET 1989:
2 - Fokker F28;
7 - Convair 580s;
12 - F-28-0100s (F100) on order;
3 - Convair 580s (of SEBJ);
5 - Swearingen Metroliners;
3 - Boeing 737s (leased);
2 - ATR42s.

COLOURS:
Initially the aircraft wore 'INTER-CANADIAN' titles over their former red, white and blue (*Quebecair*) or yellow and blue (*Nordair Metro*) colours. Later the aircraft were repainted in the full *Canadian Airlines* colour scheme with 'INTER-CANADIAN' appearing on the upper fuselage in dark blue.

ROUTES:
Montreal (Dorval) – Quebec City – Gatineau/Hull – Montreal (Mirabel) – Ottawa – Rouyn/Noranda – Val d'Or – Chibougamau – Saguenay/Bagotville – Baie Comeau/Hauterive – Sept-Iles – Wabush/Labrador City – Schefferville – Rimouski/Mont Joli – Iles-de-la-Madeleine – Bonaventure – Port Menier – Gaspe – Havre St. Pierre – Baie Johan-Beetz – Natashquan – Kegaska – Gethsemaine (La Romaine) – Harbour Chevery – Harrington – Tete a la Baleine La Tabatiere – St. Augustine – Blanc Sablon – Charlo – Chatham – Moncton – Saint John – Charlottetown – Iles-de-la-Madeleine. (Boston)

HISTORY:

Inter-Canadian was formed on January 17, 1988 by the merger of *Quebecair, Nordair Metro Express* and *Quebecair Inter*. Although the public will deal with only one airline, two companies in fact control Inter-Canadian. The first, *Quebecair,* is the holding company for the jet aircraft of the Inter-Canadian fleet. The second, *Les Lignes Aeriennes Inter-Quebec,* a combination of *Les Lignes Aeriennes A+* (Nordair Metro Express) and *Quebec Aviation* (Quebecair Inter), operates the turboprop section of the Inter-Canadian fleet.

Both companies are owned by *Canadian Airlines* (35%), Michel Leblanc (35%), Marc Racicot (20%) and Marcel Dutil (10%). All flights are listed under one timetable which is fully coordinated with the *Canadian* schedule. The company uses the flight designator 'ND.'

Quebecair had operated a fleet of two F28-1000 jets and five Convair 580s, one of which was a cargo aircraft until its merger with *Nordair Metro Express* and *Quebecair Inter*. In July 1986, *Nordair Metro* bought *Quebecair* for $21 million and assumed *Quebecair*'s long term debt of $64 million. The takeover cost was to be offset by the sale of the four Boeing 737s to *Canadian Pacific,* but in fact only two 737s went to CPA. A third was sold in Norway and the fourth remained with the re-vamped *Quebecair* for another year.

Many of *Quebecair'* s other assets were sold off or redistributed among *Nordair Metro* companies. *Nationair* bought the two DC-8-63s for $10 million; *Quebecair*'s consulting division went to Lavalin Inc (Montreal), owned by *Nordair Metro*; the maintenance of the Quebec government's CL215 fleet went to *Conifair* in St. Jean.

Quebecair would continue as a separate entity for a time, retaining its three Convair 580s and operating three additional Convairs 580s on behalf of *Société d'-Energy de la Baie James* (SEBJ), but would immediately drop the Toronto – Montreal route. *Quebecair* was now in friendly hands, including the 22% of *Nordair* stock owned by the Quebec government.

Inter-Canadian began flying the Montreal to Toronto corridor in February 1988. Most of the company's aircraft were repainted to display the CPA designator by the end of March, 1988. Flights between Montreal and Dolbeau and Alma using Metro II aircraft also commenced in March. A Montreal – Moncton route was initiated during the Spring of 1988 with one flight carrying on to Charlottetown, and in June the company took over the *Canadian* flights from Montreal to Charlottetown and Chatham, New Brunswick. The Fokker F-28 jets were used on this route, with one flight in the morning from Charlottetown to Montreal and an evening flight from Chatham to Montreal.

Early in 1988, Inter-Canadian ordered four F28-0100 (F100) jets to begin the modernization of its fleet. A further three were ordered mid-1988 and by the end of the year a total of 12 were on order. When these new aircraft began arriving early in 1989, they were used on the Toronto – Montreal and Toronto – Quebec City routes. Because the F100s had sixteen Business Class seats, *Air Canada* put Business Class sections on its aircraft flying these routes.

One Convair 580 remained in SEBJ colours while two were painted in Hydro Quebec colours. The balance of the Convairs and the Metroliners were painted in full *Canadian* colours.

In addition, to replace the aging Convair 580s, five ATR-42s (plus four options) were ordered at the same time. A Montreal – Boston jet service will begin once the company's new jet aircraft arrive.

In its first year, the new management turned the company around from a loser to a winner with a bright future.

FLEET LISTING
INTER-CANADIAN

REG'N	C/N	F/N	IS	WFU	NOTES	AIRCRAFT NAME
F-28-1000						
C-GQBR	11012	511	9/87	C	EX LN-SUN Braathens	
C-GQBS	11013	512	9/87	C	EX LN-SUO Braathens	
F-28-0100 (F100)						
C-FICB	11248	500	1/89	C		
C-FICO	11249	501	1/89	C		
C-FICP	11259	502	2/89	C		
C-FICQ	11260	503	3/89	C		
C-FICW	11247	505	5/89	C		
C-FICY	11246	504	4/89	C		
C-FIC	11263	506	6/89	C		
C-F						
C-F						
C-F						
C-F						
C-F						
737-219						
N303XV	20255	563	8/88	4/89		
N321XV	19929	561	5/88	2/89	LF N321XV Aviation Sales; EX ZK-NAC Air New Zealand	
N322XV	19930	562	5/88	11/89	LF N322XV Aviation Sales; EX ZK-NAP Air New Zealand	
CONVAIR 580						
C-GKFR	454		9/87	3/88	ST C-GKFR Jetall Corp. (Cargo aircraft)	
C-GQBM	49	539	9/87	C	EX N26KA Key Airlines	
C-GQBN	50	538	9/87	C	EX N90855 Republic	
C-GQBO	30	532	9/87	C	EX N4801C Republic/Gulf Air Transport; Canadian c/s 4/89	
C-GQBP	137	536	9/87	C	EX N7528U Republic/Gulf Air Transport	
C-GNMO	15	531	9/87	C	EX YV-64C Avens	
C-GNMQ	161	537	9/87	C	EX YV-78C Avensa	
C-GNMR	485		9/87	C	EX YV-61C Avensa	
C-GFHB	38		10/76	C	OF S.E.B.J.; Repainted Hydro Quebec, 1988	SAKAMI
C-GFHF	176		4/77	C	OF S.E.B.J.; Repainted Hydro Quebec, 1988	OPINACA
C-GFHH	109		7/78	C	OF S.E.B.J	RUPERT
SA226TC						
C-GKFS	TC215E		9/87	C	EX C-GKFS Kelowna Flightcraft	
C-GQAJ	TC295	524	10/87	C	EX N104UR	
C-GQAK	TC321		11/87	C	EX N105UR	
C-GQAL	TC233		11/87	C	EX N101UR	
C-GQAP	TC263	523	11/87	C	EX N103UR	
ATR-42-300						
C-FIQB	112	514	12/88	C	EX F-WWEI test registration	
C-FIQN	118	515	12/88	C	EX F-WWEO test registration	
C-			/89	OO		
C-			/89	OO		
C-			/89	OO		

NORDAIR METRO

REG'N	C/N	F/N	IS	WFU	NOTES	AIRCRAFT NAME
CONVAIR 580						
C-GNMO	15		3/86	9/87	EX YV-64C Avensa	
C-GNMQ	161		3/86	9/87	EX YV-78C Avensa	
C-GNMR	485		3/86	9/87	EX YV-61C Avensa	

AIR ATLANTIC

Air Atlantic Dash-7, C-GILF

ALLIANCE:
Canadian Partner
(20% owned by *Canadian*)

HEADQUARTERS:
PO Box 9040,
St. John's, Newfoundland, A1A 2X3

MAJOR BASES:
Halifax;
St. John's is the servicing base

FLEET 1989:
10 - Dash-8-101s

COLOURS:
Air Atlantic aircraft are painted in full *Canadian* Partner colour scheme without the grey cheat line.

ROUTES:
Halifax – Sydney – Yarmouth – Saint John – Moncton – Fredericton – Charlottetown – Illes de la Madelaine – Stephenville – Deer Lake – Deer Lake – Gander – St. John's – Quebec City – Ottawa – Montreal.
USA:
Boston – Portland – Bangor.

HISTORY:

When CPA acquired *Air Maritime* with the purchase of *Eastern Provincial Airways,* it was decided to phase out *Air Maritime* and replace it with a new airline. Air Atlantic was formed with *Sealand Helicopters* of St. John's, Newfoundland with *Sealand* as the principal owner and *Canadian Pacific* owning only 20%. The company's main operating base was Halifax, but its service base would be at *Sealand*'s facilities at St. John's Airport. Craig L. Dobbin was the first Chairman and Chief Executive Officer of the new company.

Air Atlantic began operations in February 1986 using two Dash-7 aircraft — one leased and the other a former Canadian Forces aircraft. These planes were the first to appear in the new *Canadian Pacific* Partner colour scheme which was identical to the *Canadian Pacific Airlines* standard colour scheme except that the aircraft was painted a sea green colour rather than dark blue. The CPA symbol appeared on the tail.

When *Pacific Western* took over CPA, changing its name to *Canadian Airlines International,* the standard *Canadian Airlines* colour scheme was displayed on all subsequent Dash-8s as they were delivered, although the first Dash-8s retained the green CPA commuter colour for a time.

On 28 February 1986, Air Atlantic's initial services were to Moncton, Fredericton, Saint John and Charlottetown from Halifax and Gander; and to Deer Lake and Stephenville from St. John's. Service from Halifax to Sydney and Charlottetown were added in May with Moncton and Iles de Madeleine added in July. *Air Maritime* was kept in operation during this period (flying HS748 aircraft) and was gradually phased out as Air Atlantic was able to take over the routes.

When the new Dash-8 aircraft began arriving in the fall of 1986, they were placed on routes in Newfoundland, while the Dash-7s continued to operate out of Halifax. Although CPA had not operated a Halifax – Yarmouth route, Air Atlantic introduced this service in October following deregulation and also linked Moncton to Charlottetown at this time.

With the arrival of three Dash-8s in February 1987, one of the Dash-7s was sold to *Time Air* of Lethbridge. The company's first international route (Saint John to Boston) was started in August 1987. The final Dash-7 was sold in January 1988 when the company standardized on the Dash-8 aircraft.

In February 1989, Quebec City – Halifax and Saint John began with routes from Halifax to Bangor and Portland starting a month later. With Boston, Air Atlantic now has regularly scheduled routes to three cities in the USA.

FLEET LISTING

AIR ATLANTIC

REG'N	C/N	F/N	IS	WFU	NOTES
DASH-8-102					
C-FATA	091	806	3/88	C	EX OE-LLO Tyrolean
C-FCIZ	138		3/89	C	
C-FDAO	123		11/88	C	
C-FDNE	141		3/89	C	
C-GAAC	047	801	9/86	C	originally in CPA green c/s
C-GAAN	051		12/86	C	
C-GAAM	059		1/87	C	
C-GABF	025		8/86	10/86	LF C-GABF DHC; Air BC aircraft
C-GDND	129		1/89	C	
C-GGOM	003		12/86	2/87	LF C-GGOM City Express
C-GTBP	066	804	2/87	C	originally in CPA green c/s
C-GTBU	086		/88	C	
C-GTBZ	010		12/87	4/88	LF OE-HLR Tyrolean
C-GTCO	119		10/88	C	
C-GGPJ	004		6/88	10/88	LF C-GGPJ DHC
DASH-8-300					
C-G					
C-G					
DASH-7-103					
C-GILE	012		1/86	9/87	ST N678MA Markair: EX 13202 CF
C-GWTG	007		5/86	2/87	ST C-GWTG Time; EX N27AP ERA Jet Alaska
C-GSEV	006		2/86	1/88	ST N926RM Rocky Mountain (Continental Express); EX N37RM Rocky Mountain/Ransome

AIR NOVA

Air Nova BAe 146-100, C-GNVY

ALLIANCE:
Air Canada Connector
(49% owned by *Air Canada*)

HEADQUARTERS:
PO Box 158 Elmsdale,
Nova Scotia, B0N 1M0

MAIN BASE:
Halifax

FLEET 1989:
6 - Dash-8s;
4 - BAe 146-200s;
1 - Beech 99.

COLOURS:
Air Nova was the first airline to appear in the *Air Canada* Connector colour scheme, which differs slightly from that appearing on *Air BC* and *Air Ontario* aircraft. The aircraft is all white but rather than a single red cheat line, the aircraft have two red cheat lines separated by a white stripe. The two cheats begin on the nose of the aircraft as very thin lines which gradually thicken to broad cheat lines with the lower line angling slightly downward. The tail is white at the top and red at the bottom with a large red maple leaf. This maple leaf is comprised of alternating light and dark red portions, producing a three-dimensional appearance. The title 'AIR NOVA' appears on the rear fuselage in large red letters and is repeated in smaller size just forward of the door with 'Air Canada Connector' immediately beneath in very small lettering. The registration is on the top rear fuselage in red and the fleet number appears in red at the top of the tail.

ROUTES:
Halifax – Sydney – Charlottetown – Moncton – Fredericton – Saint John – Yarmouth – Boston – St. John's – Gander – Deer Lake – St. Anthony – Stephenville – Blanc Sablon – Goose Bay – Ottawa – Montreal.

HISTORY:

CPA, and later *Canadian*, held Newfoundland and the Maritimes in a firm grip after acquiring *Eastern Provincial Airways* and establishing *Air Atlantic*.Air Nova was created in 1986 to provide *Air Canada* with a smaller airline to operate propjet equipment in the Maritimes and act as a feeder airline for its longer range flights.

Air Nova's principal owners are *Labrador Airways* (Atlantis Investments Ltd.) with 34%, *Air Nova* Board Chairman Roger Pike with (17%) and *Air Canada* with 49%.

The company began operations on 14 July 1986 with flights from Halifax to Sydney and from Halifax to Deer Lake, St. John's, and Goose Bay, operating Dash-8-100 aircraft. When the Halifax – Yarmouth route was dropped by *Air Canada* in October it was picked up by Air Nova. Halifax – Charlottetown was also added at this time, both routes being flown by a leased Dash-8 aircraft. *Labrador Airways* scheduled their flights to feed Air Nova and thus Newfoundland and Labrador were tied into both the Air Nova and *Air Canada* network.

January 1987 saw Gander added to the Halifax – St. John's route. In August, Yarmouth – Boston, Halifax – Moncton and Halifax – Saint John were also added.

In June 1988, Halifax – Moncton and Quebec City and Halifax – Bathurst and Montreal were added, linking the Maritimes to the province of Quebec. Jets may soon be introduced into the Air Nova fleet with the BAe-146 being a strong possibility.

In March 1988 Atlantis Investments Ltd. (controlled by Atlantis Corp. of St. John's, Newfoundland), purchased the 17% held by Air Nova Board Chairman Roger Pike. This gave Atlantis 51% of the total shares while *Air Canada* continued with 49%.

Air Nova now flies to all maritime provinces as well as Newfoundland and Labrador and has begun spreading into Quebec providing links similar to those previously provided by *Eastern Provincial Airways*. The company's red and white Dash-8s provide a feeder network to *Air Canada* at principal cities, with the operational hub at Halifax, NS.

Air Nova followed the lead of *Air BC* and ordered BAe 146 jet aircraft. Two Series 100 (with 69 economy seats) were leased in September 1988 for use until the larger Series 200 jets (with 85 economy seats) are received in 1989. Flights to Montreal and Ottawa were added to the company's routes and the BAe jets were used by *Air Canada*'s Touram for Halifax – Orlando charters during the winter of 1988-89.

A Beech 99 was acquired for use between St. Anthony, Newfoundland, and Blanc Sablon. The company also ordered Dash-8-300 aircraft for delivery during the summer of 1989.

FLEET LISTING
AIR NOVA

REG'N	C/N	F/N	IS	WFU	NOTES
BAE-146-200					
C-GRNY	E2115	201	12/88	C	EX G-11-115
C-GRNZ	E2106	202	1/89	C	EX G-05-106
C-G	E21	203	6/89	C	
C-G	E21	204	6/89	C	
C-G	E21	205	/89	OO	
BAE-146-100					
C-GNVX	E1010	101	9/88	12/88	LF G-UKPC BAe; To C-GNVX Air BC
C-GNVY	E1011	102	9/88	6/89	LF G-UKJF BAe (Air UK)
DASH-8-101					
C-FCTA	039	801	7/86	C	
C-GABF	025	---	10/86	2/87	LF C-GABF DHC; to Air BC
C-GANF	042	802	7/86	C	
C-GANI	064	804	2/87	C	
C-GANK	087	806	/88	C	
C-GANQ	096	805	3/88	C	
C-GANS	057	803	3/87	C	
C-GLON	133	816	2/89	3/89	LF C-GLON Air Ontario
C-GONO	102	807	5/88	6/88	LF C-GONO Air Ontario
BEECH 99					
C-		6/86	C		

NORTHWEST TERRITORIAL AIRWAYS

Northwest Territorial Air Lockheed Electra, C-FIJV

ALLIANCE:
Air Canada Connector
(90% owned by *Air Canada*)

HEADQUARTERS:
Yellowknife Airport,
Postal Service 9000,
Yellowknife, N.W.T. X1A 2R3

MAJOR BASES:
Yellowknife, Winnipeg, Edmonton

FLEET 1989:
4 - Lockheed Electras;
1 - Lockheed 382G Hercules (for sale);
2 - Boeing 737s;
2 - DC-3s

COLOURS:
The aircraft has a white upper fuselage and natural metal below the wings. A broad three-colour cheat line runs from nose to tail extending above and below the windows. The top and bottom of the cheat consists of a nar- row black stripe with narrow strips of white separating the black lines from the broad red band forming the mid- dle of the cheat. The tail is red with a large Red maple leaf inside a stylized 'N.' The titles apear in black letters on the upper fuselage and read either 'NORTHWEST TERRI-TORIAL' or 'NORTHWEST TERRITORIAL CARGO.' The nose, which was formerly black, is now white on most Electras. When new aircraft are added, they will probably appear in the *Air Canada* Commuter colours which have many similarities to the current scheme, in- cluding the large maple leaf on the tail.

ROUTES:
Edmonton Municipal – Yellowknife – Fort Simpson – Holman Island – Coppermine – Cambridge Bay – Gjoa Haven – Spence Bay – Pelly Bay – Rankin Inlet – Iqaluit (Frobisher Bay) – Winnipeg.
Inuvik – Yellowknife – Edmonton Municipal – Calgary.
Cargo:
Winnipeg – Regina – Saskatoon – Edmonton

HISTORY:

Bob Engle, a Yale graduate in business administration, is President of NWT Air. He became a bush pilot in Yellowknife in 1958 and formed NWT Air in 1962. The company flew small aircraft out of Yellowknife, including an Otter, Piper Aztec, and Beechcraft 18, but the DC-3 was tobecome the backbone of its passenger and charter service in the mid-sixties.

As Yellowknife grew in size and importance, it became obvious that the possibility existed for a sixth regional airline in Canada, this one operating in the north. NWT Air decided to become that sixth regional airline. When *Wardair* phased out all but one of its Bristol Freighters in 1970, the need for equipment larger than the DC-3 became obvious to NWT Air, and early in 1971 a former *Canadian Pacific* DC-6 was purchased and based in Yellowknife. A second DC-6 was added the following year. The DC-3 and DC-6 aircraft displayed a variety of colour schemes at that time but were basically white aircraft with a red cheat line and a red tail. Either 'NORTHWEST' or 'NWT AIR' titles appeared in white on the red tail and the title 'NORTHWEST' was displayed in black on either the upper or lower fuselage of the DC-6s.

NWT Air purchased its first Lockheed Electra (from *International Jet Air* of Calgary) in 1976, which flew out of the company's Calgary base. Bob Engle had been awarded a licence to operate a Hercules aircraft in 1973 but it carried the restriction that the company must keep the aircraft for a minimum of four years. At the time, *Pacific Western Airlines* possessed a fleet of four Hercules operating in the north and around the world, and Engle did not feel he could purchase a Hercules and honour the restriction in the licence. In 1978, NWT acquired its first Hercules with a second due to arrive the following year. The first Hercules was based in London, England and operated on a variety of services including gold bullion flights.

The old piston engine DC-6s were retired upon arrival of the Hercules aircraft, which were the first of the fleet to appear in the current NWT colour scheme. The Electras and DC-3s were repainted during the next few years.

NWT Air was awarded a scheduled Yellowknife to Cambridge Bay and Coppermine service in November 1978. Initially a DC-6 (and later an Electra or DC-3) was used on this route. When *Wardair* closed down its Yellowknife operations in 1979, NWT Air picked up much of the work. The airline also picked up the plum northern transcontinental route, Yellowknife – Rankin Inlet – Frobisher Bay, in December 1979. This route linked the capital of the NWT to the administrative centres of the central and eastern Arctic, and operated twice a week using the Electra in a passenger (59 seat) and cargo (3 pallets) configuration. NWT Air flights connected with those of PWA, *Nordair* and *Calm Air* at locations in the north served by these airlines, thus providing its customers access to the south.

In October 1980, Spence Bay, Pelly Bay and Gjoa Haven were added to the company's scheduled routes from Yellowknife. The second Hercules was replaced in 1981 by a former PWA Hercules, and the two Hercules operated trans-Canada flights for Purolator Courier until replaced by Electras in mid-1981, when the second Electra was added to the fleet.

In June 1981, *Pacific Western Airlines* dropped its route from Winnipeg to Yellowknife. NWT acquired the route, the company's first scheduled route to the south, and operated it using an Electra aircraft. In mid-August 1981, the Electra aircraft were required for scheduled services and *Austin Airways* took over the Purolator flights. In mid-December of the same year, the airline began flying Winnipeg to Rankin Inlet and Yellowknife twice a week and Winnipeg to Yellowknife direct three times a week. NWT Air also began flying Yellowknife to Fort Simpson to Fort Liard and Fort Nelson with DC-3 aircraft at this time.

In mid-April 1982, the former PWA Hercules was destroyed by fire in a ground accident. *Swiftair Cargo* folded in mid-1982 and NWT Air picked up its trans-Canada cargo route in October and operated the route out of Vancouver International Airport instead of Abbottsford Airport. Two more Electras were acquired to fly this nightly service between Toronto, Winnipeg, Edmonton, and Vancouver, with one Electra flying in each direction.

The first Hercules was returned to *Safeair* in 1983 and replaced by the last PWA Hercules, C-GHPW, on a lease/purchase arrangement. DC-3 aircraft, mostly former *Canadian Forces* aircraft, provide the short haul service for NWT Air and the Electras operate the long haul passenger and cargo scheduled and charter services.

In May 1984, the company acquired its fifth Electra which flew on the trans-Canada cargo service, initially wearing 'NORTHWEST TERRITORIAL' titles while retaining the green *Transamerica* cheat line. The two former *Transamerica* Electras were leased until 1985 when they were purchased and repainted in full NWT colours with 'NORTHWEST TERRITORIAL CARGO' titles. Early in 1984, NWT Air began operating *Air Canada*'s high-priority freighter service between Vancouver and Edmonton, replacing the *North Cariboo* Convair 440s. This service was incorporated into their nightly trans-Canda scheduled cargo route. Hall Beach and Norman Wells were new communities added to NWT Air's routes in 1984. Fort Liard was dropped in 1984.

In June 1984, Cambridge Bay – Holman Island non-stop and Pelly Bay – Hall Beach weekly were begun using DC-3 aircraft. Winnipeg to Frobisher Bay direct was discontinued but a DC-3 flight from Yellowknife to Wrigley, Fort Simpson and Norman Wells was added.

In April 1985, the trans-Canada cargo route was adjusted so the Electras flew Toronto to Winnipeg, Calgary and Vancouver westbound and eastbound from Vancouver to Calgary to Toronto with a DC-3 cargo flight from Edmonton connecting at Calgary. In October, a *City Express* ST-27 was wet-leased to connect Montreal and Ottawa to the Toronto cargo flights.

A significant new passenger route was won late in 1985 when NWT began operating passenger service between Yellowknife and the Edmonton International Airport, with the route also continuing on to the Edmonton Municipal Airport. This route provided direct competition to PWA's Boeing 737 aircraft. Hall Beach to Pelly Bay service was discontinued in October but Pelly Bay to Gjoa Haven was added.

Air Canada and NWT signed a formal agreement in March 1986, co-ordinating schedules. The Edmonton to Calgary DC-3 cargo route was then used to link up with *Air Canada*'s nightly DC-8 cargo flight. Regina replaced Winnipeg on the trans-Canada route and a DC-3 was used to link Saskatoon, Winnipeg and Regina. Later in the year, under a new cargo arrangement with *Air Canada*, Vancouver was removed from the trans-Canada cargo route and Electras were flown Toronto – Regina or Winnipeg – Calgary, turning around at Calgary. Cargo DC-3s were flown Edmonton – Calgary, Saskatoon – Regina, and Montreal, Ottawa – Toronto to link with the Electras, the City Express ST-27 service having ceased.

Late in 1986, two Electras were sold to *Falcon Cargo* in Sweden and a former *Reeve Aleutian* cargo Electra acquired. Another Electra was leased early in 1987.

Northwest Territorial became an *Air Canada* Connector service on selected routes in April 1987. Specifically, the Edmonton – Yellowknife as well as Cambridge Bay – Coppermine and Holman Island were connector routes.

Air Canada purchased 90% of the shares in Northwest Territorial in November, 1987, providing *Air Canada* with a north-south link to its major routes. The aircraft colours already matched the *Air Canada* Commuter colour scheme closely, but any new aircraft will be painted in the full commuter colours. Toronto was dropped from the Electra cargo flights when *Air Canada*'s 7th and 8th DC-8 cargo jets went into service at the beginning of 1988 and flew Winnipeg – Regina – Saskatoon – Edmonton. The last Hercules remaining with NWT was put up for sale in early 1988.

Inuvik – Yellowknife (and on to the Edmonton Municipal Airport) commenced in 1988 using Lockheed Electra aircraft. During the summer, flights from Inuvik to Yellowknife, Rankin Inlet and Iqaluit (Frobisher Bay) in the eastern arctic were flown three times a week, eliminating the passenger overnight stay in Yellowknife. A Boeing 737 was added to the fleet in 1988 to compete directly with the *Canadian* jet flights. This aircraft was painted in the full *Air Canada* connector colour scheme, as was the second Boeing 737 acquired early in 1989.

The company dropped its nightly Winnipeg – Regina – Saskatoon – Edmonton cargo flights to concentrate on north-south flights to the arctic and trans-Canada flights within the arctic. The direct Winnipeg – Yellowknife route was dropped in March 1989, but Winnipeg – Rankin Inlet was continued.

In 1989 NWT began co-operating with *First Air* on trans-Canada flights north of the 60th parallel by interlining with *First Air* and scheduling flights at complimentary times. With the addition of the company's second Boeing 737 in 1989 the flights to Edmonton were extended to Calgary.

FLEET LISTING
NWT AIRWAYS

REG'N	C/N	F/N	IS	WFU	NOTES
Boeing 737-210C					
N4951W	21066	661	2/89	C	EX N4951W Wien Airlines
N4952W	21067	662	11/88	C	EX N4952W Wien Airlines
L-188 Electra					
C-F I JR	1138		6/83	C	EX C-F I JR Imperial Oil
C-F I JV	1129		9/76	C	EX CF-I JV International Jet Air
C-FNWY	1036		7/81	C	EX N83MR Cardinal Corporation
C-GNWC (1)	2015		5/84	10/86	ST SE-IVT Falcon Cargo
C-GNWC (2)	2010		11/86	11/88	LF N178RV Reeve Aleutian/bought 4/87
C-GNWD	2003		5/84	9/86	ST SE-IVS Falcon Cargo
N864U	1135		2/87	10/87	LF N864U
N1968R	2007		11/88	C	LF N1968R
L-382G Hercules					
C-FNWF	4562		9/78	12/83	LF ZS-RSF Safeair
C-FNWY	4600		5/79	5/81	LF ZS-RSI Safeair
C-GHPW	4799		12/83	C	EX C-GHPW Pacific Western Airlines
L-382B Hercules					
C-FPWK	4170		6/81	4/82	DBF mid-April 1982; EX PWA
DC-6AB					
C-FCZZ*	45498		6/72	1/79	EX CF-CZZ Canadian Pacific/PWA
DC-6B					
C-FNWY*	45500		3/71	7/78	ST ET-AGY Ethiopia; EX CF-CPC CPA
DC-3					
CF-BZI	13448		12/65	5/71	W/O 13/05/71 Somerset Island, NWT.
C-FNTF*	12344		1/72	11/88	EX 12914 Canadian Armed Forces; ST C-FNTF Air North
C-FNWS*	12419		4/68	11/88	EX KG389 Royal Canadian Air Force; ST C-FNWS Buffalo Airways
C-FNWU*	6095		7/71	C	EX N51F General Mills Inc.
C-FQHF	13392		9/75	7/76	ST C-FQHF Kenting Avn.; EX 12934 CAF
C-FQHY	26005		9/75	9/77	LF C-FQHY Merlyn Carter; EX 12958 CAF
C-GWIR	9271		4/82	C	EX C-GWIR Alberta Northern; EX F-WSGY
C-GWMX	12357		7/77	10/78	ST C-GWMX Kenn Borek; EX 12915 CAF
C-GWMY	25368		9/75	12/75	LF C-GWMY R. Carruthers; EX 12956 CAF
C-GWZS	12327		4/80	10/88	EX 12913 Canadian Armed Forces; ST C-GWZS Buffalo Airways
Beech 18C (C45)					
CF-PCK	AF479		7/70	10/74	ST CF-PCK Parsons Airways
PA-23 Aztec					
CF-NWT	27-2980		4/67	3/74	ST CF-NWT La Ronge Aviation
DHC-3 Otter					
CF-NTR	054		4/63	1/70	ST N3904 Western Rotocraft Ltd.

PART 4

JET
CHARTER
AIRLINES

Worldways
Canada Ltd.

Worldways Canada L-1011, C-GIES

HEADQUARTERS:
6299 Airport Road,
Mississauga, Ontario, L4V 1N3

MAIN BASE:
Toronto International (Pearson) Airport

FLEET 1989:
2 - L1011-193Ls;
4 - DC-8-63s;
2 - L1011-1s (on lease).

COLOURS:
All of the aircraft above the wings is white; the wings and lower fuselage are silver. A dark blue cheat line, covering the cockpit and passenger windows, sweeps upward over the fuselage immediately forward of the tail. A narrower light blue line runs immediately below the dark blue, with a portion of the white fuselage appearing below the light blue. The company logo, a dark blue 'W' inside a light blue globe, is displayed in the centre of the white tail. The title 'WORLDWAYS' appears in dark blue block letters on the white upper fuselage, followed by 'CANADA' in smaller block letters (in either light or dark blue). The Convairs did not display the word 'CANADA' following the 'WORLDWAYS' title.

ROUTES:
Charters worldwide, mostly out of Toronto with some from Vancouver and Calgary.
Summer Charters:
Amsterdam – Athens – Belfast – Dublin – Brussels – Copenhagen – Frankfurt – Malaga – Munich – Leeds/Bradford – Lisbon – London – Oporto – Paris – Rome – Shannon – Venice – Vienna.
Winter Charters:
Acapulco – Aruba – Barbados – Cartagena – Curacao – Holguin – La Paz – Las Vegas – Lisbon – Marguarita Island – Montego Bay – Oporto – Puerto Plata – Puerto Vallarta – Santiago de Cuba – Santo Domingo.

175

HISTORY:

Worldways Airlines was formed in Toronto in April 1975, and flew a DC-4 (formerly flown on ice patrols by *Kenting Aviation*) painted in a pale blue colour scheme with a large 'W' on the tail. This aircraft was used for cargo work only. The withdrawal of the *Air Canada* Viscount fleet in 1974 left a void for short haul sports charters in the Southern Ontario region. *Great Lakes Airlines* had been filling this void when Worldways purchased a Convair 640 from *Pacific Western Airlines* in May 1976. In addition to the Convair and the DC-4, Worldways also had a fleet of business jets at that time. One of its Learjets was based in Vancouver and operated by *Canada Learjet*.

A second Convair 640 was purchased from *Pacific Western* in 1978. These aircraft began flying across Canada for *Loomis Couriers* in December 1980. The Learjets were also used on cross-Canada cargo flights for *Loomis*.

When *Ontario Worldair* folded in December 1980, there was still a market for long haul charters out of Toronto and Worldways Canada Ltd. (the name under which Worldways Airlines operates its long-haul charter operations), was formed. The first aircraft acquired by Worldways Canada was a former *Ontario Worldair* Boeing 707 and the first charter was flown 21 June 1981 from Toronto to Terciera in the Azores. In December 1981, Toronto – Venezuela became a regular charter flight for the company and two more 707s were purchased from *British Caledonian*.

Only two 707s were operated for the first part of 1982, with the third remaining as a spare until the summer. By March 1982, charters were being flown from Toronto to Prestwick, Shannon, Dublin and Belfast. Oslo, Helsinki, Zagreb and Skopje were added in the months to follow. Charters were also flown from Montreal to Paris and Athens and from Vancouver to Amsterdam.

One of the Convair 640s was leased to *Petrocan* in St. John's Newfoundland in the summer of 1982 to fly crews to Goose Bay and Sagluk. In the winter of 1982, the two Convair 640s were sold to *Wright Airlines* of Detroit. During the summer of that year the company's administration and flight operations were moved into the former *Wardair* building opposite the *CP Air* hangars at Toronto International Airport. The 186-seat Boeing 707s were given a brighter decor and wide-body overhead bins, as well as being converted to 195 seat aircraft with the addition of slim-line seats at that time.

The 707s were still too small despite the increase in seat capacity and alternate aircraft were sought. The best available planes were four *CP Air* DC-8-63s with seating capacity of 250 passengers. The first DC-8-63 arrived in March 1983 and the other three soon after. Two of the 707s were sold to the *Royal Australian Air Force* and the third used as a backup aircraft to the DC-8s.

In April 1983, Worldways took over operation of the *Echo Bay Mines* Hercules, based in Calgary. The former *Aero Trades* Convair 640 appeared in full Worldways colour scheme in May of that year. It was actually leased from *Air Niagara* and used by Worldways in support of the Petrocan contract out of St. John's. For the winter of 1983-84, two DC-8-63s were based in Montreal and two were based in Toronto.

During the summer of 1984, Worldways flew Toronto to Edinburgh, Scotland twice weekly. The company also flew Vancouver to Copenhagen as well as to London and Amsterdam from Vancouver and Calgary. The DC-8-63s were overhauled by Aviation Traders of Stanstead, England in 1984. The company leased C-FCPP to *Icelandair* who in turn leased it to *Air Algeria* for use on the Hadj pilgrimage in August 1984. Worldways could not meet FAR noise standards in 1984 and had to give up flights into the USA. Its Boeing 707 continued as a backup aircraft that year but also operated weekly from Vancouver to Calgary to Copenhagen during the summer. The Convair 640 that had been leased from *Air Niagara* was returned to them and immediately sold to *Time Air*.

The Hercules operated by Worldways on behalf of *Echo Bay Mines* was sold to *TransAmerica Airlines* for $6.5 million (US) in December 1984. This Hercules had set a world record, in 1980, by carrying 47 million pounds of supplies to the Lupin gold mine. The Hercules often flew up to nine trips a day between Yellowknife and Lupin, a distance of 400 kilometers. An ice road during the winter allowed ground transportation to replace air transportation.

Early in 1985, Worldways signed a contract with Aviation Accoustics Technology Inc. for two of their DC-8s to have "hush kits" installed. This would enable them to fly into the United States again, particularly to the Ft. Lauderdale and Las Vagas markets. Flights from Vancouver to London and Vancouver to Prestwick and Manchester commenced again in spring 1985.

The *Canadian Forces* require complete overhaul of their 707s every five years, with usually one plane overhauled each year. In 1985, *Pacific Western Airlines* had the contract to overhaul all five *Canadian Forces* 707s in one year and the Forces chartered the Worldways aircraft as a replacement for the year. The Worldways 707 could carry twenty-five passengers more than the Forces aircraft. Worldways flights crews, many of them former pilots with 437 Squadron, and Worldways cabin crews flew the aircraft from Shearwater to Comox via Ottawa, Trenton, Winnipeg, Namao and Vancouver.

Worldways acquired two former PSA Lockheed L-

1011s in 1985. These aircraft had a lower-deck lounge and retractable stairways from their commuter days with PSA. They began in service, as delivered, on August 29, 1985 from Toronto to London but were modified in November.

Extensive charter operations were carried out during the winter of 1985 with flights from Toronto to Santo Domingo, Puerto Vallarta, Barcelona (Venezuala), Cartagena (Colombia), Bridgetown (Barbados), and Banjul (Gambia) using DC-8 aircraft as well as Toronto to London, Acapulco, Montego Bay and Puerto Plata using L-1011s.

The company received temporary exemption from FAR 36 noise regulations and was permitted to continue its Toronto to Ft. Lauderdale, Orlando, St. Petersburgh and Las Vagas flights throughout the winter.

The Boeing 707 was finally sold in January 1986. The Canadian Forces, however, continued to charter aircraft from Worldways; with a DC-8-63 flying nine overseas flights as well as performing domestically for the Forces during February and March 1986. Charters from Vancouver via Calgary to Copenhagen were begun during the summer of 1986. The L-1011s were upgraded to L1011-50 standards enabling the aircraft to operate non-stop from Toronto to London. All DC-8s were hush-kitted in the fall of 1986 so they could to continue to fly into the United States.

The summer charter flights in 1987 included Toronto to Shannon, Dublin, Belfast, Amsterdam, Brussels, Paris (Orly), Frankfurt, Munich, Vienna, Venice, Rome, Athens, Leeds/Bradford, Prestwick, London, Lisbon, Oporto, Copenhagen and Malaga. Extensive charters during the winter of 1987 were flown from Toronto to southern sun spots including Acapulco, Aruba, Barbados, Cartagena, Curacao, Holguin, La Paz, Las Vegas, Lisbon, Margarita Island, Montego Bay, Oporto, Puerto Plata, Puerto Vallarta, Santiago de Cuba and Santo Domingo.

For the winter of 1988-89, Worldways supplied aircraft for *Regent Holidays*. Two L-1011-1 aircraft were leased from *British Caledonian* and operated in *British Caledonian* colour schemes with Worldways Canada titles.

One of the company's DC-8s will have twelve "Big Seats" added for the trans-Atlantic flights during the summer of 1989. Another of the DC-8s will be leased to *Air Jamaica* for fifteen months. This aircraft will be based in Toronto and fly to Jamaica five days a week.

FLEET LISTING
WORLDWAYS CANADA LTD.

REG'N	C/N	F/N	IS	WFU	NOTES
L1011-385 (193L)					
C-GIES	1064	101	8/85	C	EX N10112 PSA; CVT -50 1/87
C-GIFE	1079	102	9/85	C	EX N10114 PSA; CVT -50 1/87
C-FCXB	1083	199	11/88	4/89	LF G-BBAE British Caledonian
C-FCXJ	1102	198	12/88	5/89	LF G-BBAI British Caledonian
DC-8-63					
C-FCPO	45926	801	5/83	C	EX C-FCPO CP Air
C-FCPP	45927	802	3/83	C	EX C-FCPP CP Air
C-FCPQ	45928	803	5/83	C	EX C-FCPQ CP Air
C-FCPS	45929	804	6/83	C	EX C-FCPS CP Air; LT Air Algeria for Hadj 1984 & 1985
707-365C					
C-GFLG	19416	32	11/81	2/86	ST PT-TCP Transbrasil
707-338C					
C-GGAB	19629	33	1/82	5/83	ST A20-629 Royal Australian Air Force
C-GRYN	19623	31	6/81	5/83	ST A20-623 Royal Australian Air Force
L382E Hercules					
C-FDSX	4303		3/83	12/84	ST TransAmerica; OF Echo Bay Mines
CONVAIR 640					
C-FPWT	009		5/76	12/82	ST N2691W Wright Air Line; EX PWA
C-FPWU	010		5/78	12/82	ST N2569D Wright Air Line; EX PWA
C-FPWY	108		4/83	5/84	ST C-FPWY Time Air; EX PWA/Aero Trade
DC-4					
CF-KAD	18356		4/75	2/78	EX CF-KAD Kenting; EX CF-PWA & CF-TAM
DC-3					
C-FWBN	25888		9/79	1/81	EX CF-WBN Millardair; ST USA
Learjet 25					
C-FTXT	25-057		7/78	4/79	ST C-FTXT Business Flights
Learjet 25B					
C-GBFP	25-167		6/80	3/82	LF C-GBFP Burmac Corporation
Learjet 35A					
C-GBLF	35-091		12/79	2/81	ST C-GBLF Loram
Learjet 35					
C-GGYV	35-040		4/76	8/77	ST C-GGYV Business Flights
C-GPUN	35-058		4/76	4/82	ST C-GPUN Canada Jet Charters
HS 125-3A					
C-FQNS	25152		4/76	7/77	EX CF-QNS Ontario Paper Company
HS 125-1A					
C-GFCL	25107		6/85	7/87	EX C-GFCL Fiberglas Canada Limited; Sold

Nationair
Canada Inc.

Nationair DC8-63, C-GQBF

HEADQUARTERS:
Mirabel International Airport
Administration Building,
P.O. Box 300, Montreal, P.Q., J7N 1A3

MAIN BASE:
Mirabel Airport

FLEET 1989:
2 - DC-8-62s;
5 - DC-8-61s;
2 - DC-8-63s.

COLOURS:
The white upper fuselage displays a small Canadian flag just aft of the front door. A grey cheat line extending above and below the windows runs the full length of the fuselage and sweeps upward to form an 'N' outlined in white on the red tail. The red lower fuselage is separated from the grey cheat line by a thin white cheat line. The title 'NATIONAIR CANADA' appears in white on the lower forward fuselage. The registration is in black on the rear upper fuselage.

A new colour scheme was introduced when the former *Quebecair* aircraft were repainted. This con-sisted of a white aircraft with only a small Canadian flag on the upper fuselage, just forward of the front door. 'NATIONAIR' appears in large red letters on the lower forward fuselage (below the windows), with 'CANADA' in smaller red letters below. There is a thin red cheat line at the bottom of the fuselage running the length of the aircraft but interrupted by the lower wing root. The registration is shown in black on the rear fuselage at window level. The tail is all white except for a large green 'N' with a red box below it, which fits into the lower part of the 'N.'

ROUTES:
Scheduled:
Montreal (Mirabel) to Brussels;
Toronto to Reclife (Brazil)
Domestic Charter:
Montreal (Mirabel), Toronto, Vancouver, Calgary, Edmonton, Hamilton, Windsor.
Charters:
Acapulco, Barbados, Cancun, Cartagen, Curacao, Las Vagas, London, Manchester, Montego Bay, Nassau, New Delhi, Puerto Vallarta, Rio de Janeiro, Prestwick, San Jose (Costa Rica), Tenerife, Venezuela.

179

HISTORY:

Nationair Canada Inc. is the operating name for Nolisair International which commenced charter service in December 1984 from Mirabel using two former *Capitol* DC-8-61s. Charter routes in 1985 included Mirabel to Rio de Janeiro, Barbados, Acapulco, Nassau and Montego Bay. One of the DC-8-61s was leased to *Air Jamaica* from 1 July to 9 September, 1985 for use on *Air Jamaica*'s scheduled route from Toronto to Montego Bay and Kingston five days a week.

Two DC-8-62s were purchased in 1985, the first aircraft of this type in Canada. The DC-8-62 is designed for long haul work such as charters from Toronto/Montreal to Rio de Janeiro and Recife, Brazil. It is a stretched version of the DC-8-50 series with a seven foot plug added, giving the aircraft an overall length of 157.5 feet.

The winter of 1985 saw charters operated from Montreal, Ottawa, Quebec City and Toronto to Recife, Maragita Island and Venezuela. One DC-8 was based in Quebec City for the winter. An *Eagle Air* DC-8-61 was acquired on a 90 day lease in December but was in such bad shape that a Certificate of Airworthiness was not granted.

Weekly services from Toronto to Vancouver, followed by Vancouver to Manchester and Prestwick, were inaugurated in May 1986. During the summer, Nationair also began flying Toronto – New Delhi charters. Flights from Hamilton to London (Gatwick) were also inaugurated and an extensive winter charter season followed.

A Montreal – Brussels service, three times a week, was initiated on March 5, 1987 as the company's first scheduled service. This was followed shortly by scheduled service between Toronto and Reclife, Brazil. Vancouver and Winnipeg to London flights were begun in May 1987. Toronto to Montreal flights were operated on behalf of *El Al Israel Airlines* in the summer of 1987.

Service from Toronto to New Delhi was begun in June 1987 and then almost immediately cancelled as the Indian Government cancelled every second flight to protest the lack of a bilateral agreement with Canada. Weekly flights Montreal – Vancouver; Toronto – Vancouver; Toronto – Calgary; and Toronto – Edmonton were undertaken in the summer of 1987.

Numerous Toronto to Acapulco, Cartagena, Curacao, Puerto Vallarta, San Jose (Costa Rica) and Tenerife flights took place during the winter charter season in 1987.

Scheduled flights, perhaps daily, from Hamilton to London began during the summer of 1988. Domestic charters during the summer of 1988 included Toronto to Edmonton and Toronto to Vancouver.

Construction on Nationair's $13.5 million maintenance hangar at Montreal's Mirabel Airport was started during the summer of 1988.

Because it could not obtain early morning departure times from Toronto International Airport, the company operated all of its southern sun spot charters from the Hamilton airport during the 1988-89 winter, with some of the flights originating in Windsor but routing through Hamilton.

The summer of 1989 will see a resumption of flights from Montreal to Los Angeles and from Montreal to Vancouver.

Nationair will acquire two used Boeing 747-200s early in 1990.

FLEET LISTING
NATIONAIR CANADA INC.

REG'N	C/N	F/N	IS	WFU	NOTES
DC - 8 - 61					
C-GMXB	45943	801	12/84	C	EX N4578C/JA8059 Capitol/JAL; LT Sudan 3/88-6/88; LT Hispania 6/88-8/88
C-GMXD	45912	805	5/86	C	EX N914CL Capitol International
C-GMXL	45981	802	3/88	C	EX N911CL Capitol International
C-GMXQ	45982		12/84	C	EX N4582N/JA8057 Capitol/JAL; LT Hispania 6/88-7/88
N22UA	45892		1/88	C	LF United; EX C-FTJV Air Canada; LF 1/88-4/88, then again 12/88-
N23UA	45893		1/88	5/88	LF Aviation; EX C-FTJW Air Canada; (all white c/s & titles)
DC - 8 - 62					
C-GMXR	45925	803	7/85	C	EX HB-IDG/N922CL Swissair
C-GMXY	45920	804	8/85	C	EX HB-IDF Swissai
DC - 8 - 63					
C-GQBA	46155	806	9/86	C	EX C-GQBA Quebecair
C-GQBF	46116	807	9/86	C	EX C-GQBF Quebecair
DC - 8 - 55F					
C-GMXP	45804		5/86	11/86	ST CX-BLN Aero Uruguay-EX N855BC
747-200					
C-			1/90	OO	
C-			2/90	OO	

Air Transat

Air Transat L-1011, C-FTNC (with Air Canada L-1011 in background)

HEADQUARTERS:
Aeroport International de Mirabel,
Edifice D, Local 242,
Mirabel, Quebec, J7N 1C2

MAIN BASE:
Montreal (Mirabel)

FLEET 1989:
2 - L1011-1s

COLOURS:
The white upper fuselage is separated from the silver lower fuselage by a broad, dark blue cheat line. The tail is all blue with a White 'at' near the top. The blue title 'air transat' appears in lower case on the upper fuselage, with the second 'a' of 'transat' in red.

ROUTES:
International Charters:
Toronto – London – Prestwick – Manchester;
Vancouver – London;
Montreal – Paris;
Toronto – southern sun spots.

HISTORY:
This International Charter operator, based in Montreal, became operational during the *Air Canada* strike when it leased two *Air Canada* L1011s (C-FTNG and C-FTNH) and operated several of that airline's charters during the strike period. The company's first president was Jean-Marc Eustache.

Air Transat's first L-1011 was former *Air Canada* C-FTNC, which was painted in full colour scheme in December 1987. A second L-1011 joined the fleet during the summer of 1988. Up to four Toronto – London flights operated weekly during the spring and weekly Vancouver – London (Stan-sted) flights commenced in May 1988. The London charters from Toronto were increased to three times per week in May. Other Toronto Atlantic charters included flights to Dublin and Shannon. Flights to Paris from Montreal, Quebec City and Toronto began in May/June 1988.

Late in 1988, *Treasure Tours* cut back on several Transat charters from Toronto. For the summer of 1989, Toronto – London will be flown three times a week, while Toronto – Manchester and Toronto – Prestwick will operate weekly. An additional L-1011 will be leased to fly charters Montreal – Paris for two French wholesalers during the summer of 1989.

181

FLEET LISTING
AIR TRANSAT

REG'N	C/N	IS	WFU	NOTES
L-1011-1				
C-FTNA	1014	5/88	C	EX C-FTNA Air Canada
C-FTNC	1023	11/87	C	EX C-FTNC Air Canada
C-FTNG	1048	11/87	12/88	LF C-FTNG Air Canada; operated charters during strike; full Air Canada c/s
C-FTNH	1049	11/87	12/87	LF C-FTNH Air Canada; operated charters during strike; full Air Canada c/s
L-1011-150				
C-	1010	6/89	C	EX N309EA Eastern

Swiftair Cargo DC8, C-GSWX

Swiftair Cargo

HEADQUARTERS:
P.O. Box 156, Abbottsford, B.C. V2S 4N9

MAIN BASE:
Abbottsford Airport, B.C.

FINAL FLEET 1982:
2 - DC-8-33Fs

COLOURS:
The aircraft had a silver lower fuselage and wings while the nose and upper fuselage were white. Broad dark brown, tan and gold cheat lines curved up from the lower fuselage near the nose then ran horizontally the length of the aircraft from aft of the forward door. The three cheat lines were separated, permitting a narrow strip of the white upper fuselage to be seen between each pair of colours. The tail was all dark brown with the company logo in gold. The title 'SWIFTAIR CARGO' appeared in dark brown on the upper fuselage with a Canadian flag immediately aft of the cockpit.

ROUTE:
Abbottsford – Calgary – Winnipeg – Toronto – Montreal (Mirabel) and back.

HISTORY:

In 1953, *Canadian Pacific Airlines* attempted a trans-Canada cargo service using DC-6A aircraft, but was stymied by *Trans-Canada Airlines* which purchased three Bristol Freighters to compete in the air cargo market. The air cargo business during 1953-55 was not very good and soon all three aircraft were sold. Since that time, various Canadian airlines have proposed operating trans-Canada cargo services.

During the summer of 1979, *Conair Aviation* of Abbottsford, B.C., applied for a licence to operate a cargo service using jet aircraft. *Conair* flies a large fleet of DC-6, A-26 and Tracker water bombers and operates an aerial spray service out of Abbottsford.

Finally in September 1980, *Conair Aviation* and *Frontier Helicopters,* as joint owners, successfully initiated an all-jet cargo service under the name 'SWIFTAIR CARGO'. Two DC-8-33F all-cargo jets were purchased from *Rosenbalm Aviation* and painted in the colours of the new company. These aircraft operated from Abbottsford Airport, sixty kilometers east of Vancouver. Each evening, one plane would leave Abbottsford and fly to Calgary, Winnipeg, Toronto and finish its flight at Mirabel Airport in Montreal. The second plane would fly the reverse route simultaneously, providing overnight jet cargo between these five major Canadian cities.

Unfortunately, the airline faced heavy competition from the major air carriers in Canada which operated into more cities than Swiftair and could carry large cargos on their regularly scheduled services. *Air Canada* had been operating all-cargo DC-8-55Fs and DC-8-63AFs for several years. As well, *Purolator Courier* had started a trans-Canada service out of Vancouver with Convair 580 aircraft and *Northwest Territorial Airways* was operating an Electra or Hercules on a trans-Canada flight out of Vancouver.

In March 1982, *Pacific Western Airlines* proposed buying 40% of Swiftair's stock. Approval from the Canadian Transportation Commission for this purchase would take a few months to obtain, however, and the airline was deeply in debt. The proposed bailout by *Pacific Western* did not occur and on 11 May 1982, the Canadian Imperial Bank of Commerce put the airline into receivership. One DC-8 was soon sold but the other remained at the Abbottsford Airport. This aircraft was sold in May 1983, but continued to remain at Abbottsford Airport.

Avionics Components acquired the DC-8 in March 1986, and on April 3 began to dismantle the aircraft. A spark from one of the saws ignited more than 22,000 litres of fuel which remained in the fuel tanks and the aircraft exploded and burned out.

FLEET LISTING

SWIFTAIR

REG'N	C/N	F/N	IS	WFU	NOTES
DC-8-33F					
C-GSWQ	45387		9/80	5/82	ST HI-413 5/83
C-GSWX	45388		9/80	5/82	ST C-GSWX Dunwoody Ltd. 5/82; Destroyed by fire 03/04/86.

Ontario Worldair

HEADQUARTERS:
Suite 206A, 6205 Airport Road,
Building B,
Mississauga, Ontario, L4V 1E3

MAIN BASE:
Toronto International Airport

FINAL FLEET 1980:
2 - Boeing 707s

COLOURS:
The aircraft has a white upper fuselage and the lower fuselage and wings are silver in colour. A broad dark-blue cheat line covering from above to below the windows runs the length of the aircraft, wrapping around the cockpit windows and broadening upwards at the rear of the fuselage to form a dark blue tail. Butting the blue cheat from below is a narrower orange line, below which a narrow strip of the white upper fuselage can be seen. In the middle of the tail is the company logo, a stylized trilium within a white circle, and three horizontal orange lines appear near the top of the tail. The title 'ONTARIO WORLDAIR' appears in dark blue on the upper fuselage.

ROUTES:
Mostly international charters out of Toronto to Europe, South America and the Caribbean.

HISTORY:

A group headed by Jim Mclean had planned to form a jet charter operation, flying DC-8-63 aircraft out of Toronto, as early as January 1976. It was not until November 1978, however, that a Boeing 707 was purchased and ONTARIO WORLDAIR flew its first revenue charter from Toronto to Montego Bay, Jamaica on December 1, 1978.

During the summer of 1979, the 707 was used by *Sunflight Tours* for charters to Europe, South America and the Caribbean, and that fall, charters were operated for the federal government bringing Viet Nam refugees to Canada. The 707 flew from Kuala Lumpur in Malaysia or Bangkok in Thailand to Montreal and Toronto. The aircraft was also used during the Hadj pilgrimage, flying from Manilla to Jeddah. In the first year of operations, this aircraft logged 3,939 hours, flying out of sixty-eight cities in thirty-one countries.

A second 707 was purchased from *Abelag* of Belgium in January 1980. This aircraft had been operated from 1973 to 1979 by *Pacific Western Airlines*. A third Boeing 707, planned to be added to the fleet, was never delivered.

Ontario Worldair continued to operate through-out the world during 1980. In October, the aircraft flew from Kano, Nigeria to Jeddah for the Hadj pilgrimage until *Nigerian Airways* protested that this Canadian airline was operating out of Nigeria and the contract was cancelled. The cancellation was enough of a financial blow to put the airline into receivership by 6 November 1980. Ontario Worldair continued to operate its contracted flights and a proposal to buy the airline was received from *Sunquest Holidays* and a realty company. The purchase never took place and the second Boeing 707 was returned to Belgium in December. The original 707 continued to operate until 13 January 1981 when Ontario Worldair ceased all operations.

FLEET LISTING
ONTARIO WORLDAIR

REG'N	C/N	F/N	IS	WFU	NOTES
707-338C					
C-GRYN	19623	701	11/78	1/81	ST C-GRYN Worldways Canada
707-351C					
C-GRYO	18746	702	1/80	12/80	ST OO-ABA Air Belgium; EX C-FPWJ PWA

Kelowna Flightcraft
Air Charter

INTER CITY – PUROLATOR COURIER

HEADQUARTERS:
RR2, Kelowna Airport,
Kelowna, B.C. V1Y 7R1

MAIN BASES:
Kelowna
Purolator:
Edmonton Municipal, Hamilton,
Halifax and Vancouver.

FLEET 1989:
2 - Boeing 727-100s;
3 - Convair 580s;
1 - Grumman G-1;
1 - Aero Commander;
1 - Cessna 402;
1 - Beech A60.

COLOURS:
Kelowna Flightcraft aircraft have cheat lines of red, white, orange, white and dark blue. The company's logo is a modified 'F' with the outside red and the small bar orange. The *Purolator* Convairs are all white cargo aircraft with two vertical dark blue stripes on the tail extending to the bottom of the fuselage. The lines bend where the body and tail meet. The title 'PUROLATOR COURIER' in red was added on the upper fuselage late in 1987. The 727s are painted in the same colour scheme as the Convairs with red *Purolator Courier* titles and a Canadian flag on the third engine.

ROUTES:
Charter flights, mostly in B.C. and Alberta;
Purolator cargo flights with bases at Toronto (Hamilton), Halifax, Edmonton & Vancouver.

HISTORY:

Kelowna Flightcraft, operating from the Kelowna Airport in the Okanagan Valley of British Columbia, is comprised of three main divisions: a charter operation; an overhaul operation for Convair 580s and Lockheed Electras, and a division which provides aircraft for *Purolator Courier* cargo flights.

In 1980, Kelowna Flightcraft operated a Convair 440 (C-GKFC) on charter operations through-out B.C. This aircraft had full titles and displayed large wrap-around stripes of orange, red and dark blue on the rear of the aircraft, with 'KF' on the tail. It was sold to *Powell Air* in April 1981.

In 1981, Kelowna purchased a Convair 580 to operate trans-Canada cargo flights for *Purolator Courier* and added a second Convair 580 in March 1982. Originally both aircraft carried *Purolator Courier* titles. Additional Convair 580s purchased between 1982 and present fly in an all white colour scheme with no titles and display two vertical blue stripes on the tail (*Purolator Courier* colours). During the summer of 1987, two Boeing 727-100 cargo jets were purchased for operation on the *Purolator Courier* routes.

Kelowna Flightcraft started its own scheduled service in 1984 with a single Convair 580. The aircraft was painted white with a black cheat line (between two narrow red lines) running through the windows and a modified 'F' displayed on the tail. The title 'INTER CITY' appeared on the upper fuselage in black. The first scheduled route was between Kelowna, Kamloops and Vancouver twice a day. Kelowna direct to Vancouver began in October 1984. Penticton was added but dropped in the winter of 1984-85 and Spokane not added until spring 1985. However, the Convair 580 and the routes were sold to *Time Air* in April 1985. *CP Air* had begun direct Boeing 737 charters to Kelowna and *Pacific Western* had countered with excellent air fares, thus making the Convair 580 unattractive. Futhermore, the airline was operating out of the south terminal at Vancouver while its competitors operated out of the main terminal.

The company's overhaul work included *Lincoln Air*'s Convairs in 1984. Former *Department of Transport* DC-3, C-FGXW, was overhauled in 1985 in preparation for its around the world flight to promote EXPO 86 carrying the title 'ODYSSEY 86.' The company overhauled *Prinair*'s Convair 580s in 1986, and when *Northwest Territorial* sold its Electra to *Falcon Cargo* of

Sweden that same year, Kelowna Flightcraft did the overhaul and painting of the aircraft.

The company continued to operate its charter service in 1986, employing an Aero Commander and a Gulfstream 1.

Two Boeing 727s were added in 1987 to be used on the cross Canada *Purolator Courier* flights. These have an all white colour scheme with the *Purolator* twin blue stripes on the tail and display a maple leaf and the registration number on the third engine. Kelowna Flightcraft's main hub is the Hamilton Airport. Each weekday, turboprop aircraft arrive from Halifax, Montreal and Ottawa and transport trucks from various centres arrive at

the airport between 10:00 pm and midnight. The packages carried by these aircraft and trucks are loaded onto a 727 which flies to Winnipeg, Calgary and Vancouver. The other jet leaves Vancouver and stops in Calgary and Winnipeg before arriving at Hamilton at about 4:00 am.

Purolator Courier bought *Gelco Express* from *Air Canada* for $31 million in January 1989, leaving the fate of the Kelowna Flightcraft/*Purolator* contract in question. The immediate effect was the moving of the 727s from Hamilton to Montreal and the linking of Toronto and Hamilton to Montreal using Convair 580 aircraft. The *Purolator* titles were removed from the 727 aircraft at that time.

FLEET LISTING
KELOWNA FLIGHTCRAFT

REG'N	C/N	F/N	IS	WFU	NOTES	MODEL	
727-100							
C-GKFC	18897	171	9/87	C	EX OB-R-1115 Faucett	-51C	OF Purolator
C-GKFT	19807	172	8/87	C	EX N722JE WSE Inc./Flying Tigers	-172C	OF Purolator
CONVAIR 580							
C-FARO	382		11/87	3/88	ST C-FARO Air Niagara		
C-GKFF	160		1/89	C	EX N9067R Gulf Air/Republic		OF Purolator
C-GKFL	372		3/87	C	EX SE-IBY Kungsair/Scabee;		OF Purolator
C-GKFP	168		11/83	7/87	ST C-GKFP Soundair;		OF Purolator
C-GKFQ	62		1/88	11/88	EX N5820 Sea Airmotive; ST N580EH Evergreen Equity		OF Purolator
C-GKFR	454		12/85	11/86	ST C-GKFR Quebecair;		OF Purolator
C-GKFT	115		11/86	6/87	ST N584PL Air Traffic Service;		OF Purolator
C-GKFT	56		5/86	NTU	ST LN-PAA Partinair Norway; rebuilt only		
C-GKFW	347		3/82	2/86	ST C-GKFW Time Air;		OF Purolator
C-GKFY	91		6/81	C	EX N2042 Jay-Dee Aircraft;		OF Purolator
C-GKFZ	79		7/87	C	EX N2261N Jay-Dee Aircraft;		OF Purolator
N110AS	154		11/86	1/87	LF N110AS All Star Leasing;		OF Purolator
C-FICA	98		6/84	4/85	ST C-FICA Time Air;	**OB INTER CITY**	
CONVAIR 440							
C-GKFC	504		1/80	4/81	ST C-GKFC Powell Air:	**OB KELOWNA FLIGHTCRAFT**	
DC-6							
C-GKFF	44645		7/85	1/88	LT C-GKFF Conair summer 1986/1987		
DC-3							
C-FGXW	25313		7/85	C	EX C-FGXW DOT; Odyssey 86 a/c based YVR		
Gulfstream 1							
C-GKFG	22		6/86	C	EX N88G		OF Purolator
METRO II							
C-GKFS	TC215E		5/86	7/87	ST C-GKFS Quebecair Inter		
DHC-4 Caribou							
C-GVYX	292		5/80	6/84	EX C-GVYX La Sarre Aviation		
C-GYYZ	97		5/83	6/84	ST C-GYYZ Air North		
Jet Commander							
C-GKFS	62		8/78	5/84	EX N1777T		
C-GKFT	5		1/78	5/84	EX N18CA		
Aero Commander							
C-GKFR	6044		11/78	10/79	ST C-GKFR Futura Airlines		
C-GKFV	1704-80		5/85	C	EX N2KS		OF Purolator
Cessna 402B							
C-GKFK	0213		5/87	C	EX N2261N		OF Purolator
Beech A60							
C-GKFX	P335		9/85	3/87	EX N60GF		

Points Of Call
Airlines Limited

Points of Call DC-8, C-FNZE

HEADQUARTERS:
200 Royal Lepage Bldg., 10130-103,
Edmonton, Alberta, T5J 3N9

MAIN BASES:
Vancouver International; Edmonton International

FLEET 1989:
1 - DC-8-52

COLOURS:
A white aircraft with a blue cheat line which wraps around the nose and runs through the windows, changing to black for the aft third of the aircraft. Below the blue cheat line is a broad band of the white fuselage with a thin red cheat line running through its middle. The lower fuselage is silver. The tail is blue with a black on white symbol near the top. One half of the Canadian flag appears on the tip of the tail. The title 'POINTS OF CALL CANADA' is displayed in black on the upper fuselage. The registration, in white, is near the rear of the fuselage on the black cheat line. The nose is white.

ROUTES:
Charters from Edmonton, Calgary and Vancouver to sun spots such as Honolulu.
Flights to Amsterdam.

HISTORY:
Points Of Call filed an application with the CTC in January 1985, to operate international and domestic charter flights. Permission was received in July 1985 and a share offering was finally realised on the Alberta Stock Exchange in June 1987. The stock is listed under PSA on the Alberta Stock Exchange. With the money raised from this offering, President Jan Backe was able to negotiate a lease-to-purchase agreement for a DC-8-52 aircraft in September 1987.

This aircraft once belonged to *Air New Zealand* and has a long range capability. The DC-8 is intended to carry 159 passengers with some seats set at 34" and others at 38" and its four Pratt & Whitney JTD-3B engines were each fitted with "Hush Kits" to meet US noise standards. The aircraft has a range of 5200 statute miles at 550 mph and carries a flight crew of three and a cabin crew of five.

The aircraft arrived at the Edmonton International Airport on 9 April 1988 but because most of its flights now originate in Vancouver, the aircraft base was moved to Vancouver late in 1988. Points Of Call received its operating certificate in May 1988 and negotiated a contract that same month with *Fiesta Holidays* to provide flights to Amsterdam from Vancouver, Edmonton and Calgary. On 28 June 1988 the company's first revenue flight was made from Edmonton to Amsterdam.

Points Of Call received permission from the DOT in the US to operate charters from Canada to any US destination and also received third freedom rights to operate from or to the US from other than Canada. This allowed the company to finalize an agreement with *General Tours* to operate charters to Honolulu, the first such flight to take place in September 1989.

Points Of Call also contracted with *Fiesta Tours* to fly from Vancouver to San Jose and Jaco Beach in Costa Rica during the winter of 1988-89. Flights from Vancouver, Edmonton and Calgary to Varadero, Cuba; Puerto Plata, Sosua and Boca Chica in the Dominican Republic; and to Cancun, Cozumel, Ixtapa and Zihuatanejo, Mexico were also contracted with *Fiesta Tours*.

To encourage repeat use of the airline, the company offers to its shareholders the opportunity to become members of its 'Partner In Travel' plan, which offers special discounts on inclusive tour packages and discounts on hotels and car rentals.

The author and his family travelled on Points Of Call from Vancouver to Honolulu in March 1989 and were very impressed with the service. Flights to Amsterdam will again be made during the summer of 1989, as will flights to Manchester from Vancouver, Calgary and Edmonton.

FLEET LISTING
POINTS OF CALL

REG'N	C/N	IS	WFU	NOTES
DC-8-52				
C-FNZE	45985	1/88	C	EX N4292P/N60X/ZK-NZE Air New Zealand

Minerve Canada

HEADQUARTERS:
980 St. Antoine West, Suite 201,
Montreal, Quebec, H3C 1A8

MAIN BASE:
Mirabel International Airport

FLEET 1989:
2 - DC-8-61

ROUTES:
International Charters

HISTORY:

Minerve Canada was granted a temporary three month licence on December 16, 1987 and scheduled to receive a permanent licence once it demonstrates that 75% of its shares are controlled by citizens or residents of Canada. The company is based in Montreal and its first president is Mr. Alfred Hamel.

The company's first charter flight departed Montreal for Varadero Beach, December 19, 1987 after a delay of 24 hours — not an auspicious beginning for the airline.

FLEET LISTING
MINERVE CANADA

REG'N	C/N	IS	WFU	NOTES
DC-8-61				
C-FCMV	46038	12/87	C	EX F-GETM Minerve/N8762 Eastern A/L
C-GEMV	46032	2/89	C	EX N51UA / JA8039 Japan Air Lines (all white c/s)

ACS Charter
AIR CHARTER SYSTEMS

HEADQUARTERS:
780 , Magenta Blve, Farnham, Quebec, J2N 1B8

MAIN BASE;
Montreal (Mirabel Airport)

FLEET 1989;
2 - DC-8-55Fs

COLOURS:
The ACS Charter colour scheme is an all-white aircraft with a narrow brown cheat line which starts at the nose and is broken near the front door by the title 'ACS' in large brown letters. Aft of the title, the cheat line broadens steadily until a small portion of the rear fuselage is all brown. One-third of a maple leaf appears in brown on the white tail and the registration is on the upper rear fuselage in brown.

ROUTES:
The airline operates cargo charters from Canadian cities to points around the world.

HISTORY:
In July 1986 the company acquired its first DC-8-55F and began an ad hoc cargo service. The aircraft was registered to *Worldwide Air Cargo* of Montreal, and flew out of Montreal Mirabel Airport with the ACS (Air Charter Systems) title displayed on the tail. A second DC-8-55F was obtained in February 1987and both aircraft have done work for *Air Canada Cargo* operations. ACS operated many charters for Iberia and Saudia during the winter of 1988-89.

FLEET LISTING
A C S

REG'N	C/N	IS	WFU	NOTES	AIRCRAFT NAME
DC-8-55F					
C-FCWW	45762	9/86	C	EX N4809E Arrow Air/PH-DCW KLM	
C-FDWW	45856	2/87	C	EX EC-DEM Spantax/PH-MAU Martinair	GILLES RONDEAU

Odyssey International Boeing 757, C-FNBC

Odyssey International

HEADQUARTERS:
6303 Airport Road, Ste. 502,
Mississauga, Ontario, L4V 1R8

MAIN BASE:
Toronto International

FLEET 1989:
3 - Boeing 767-28As

COLOURS:
The company's colour scheme consists of a white aircraft with a purple lower fuselage. Four narrow blue cheat lines separated by white lines run the length of the fuselage well below the windows. A broad stylized 'V' is displayed on the white tail. The 'V' consists of six narrow parallel blue lines which begin on the lower half of the leading edge of the tail and give the illusion of folding under at the lowest part of the 'V.' The trailing arm of the 'V' finishes much higher at the rear of the tail and consists of three maroon and three blue lines. The title "ODYSSEY international" appears on the forward upper fuselage in dark blue. A red Canadian flag followed by the registration in dark blue appear on the upper rear fuselage.

ROUTES:
The company operates charters including Toronto – Las Vegas – Rome (Italy) – Catania (Italy) – Palomo (Sicily)

HISTORY:
Odyssey International began operating from Toronto to Mexico, Florida and the Caribbean Islands in November 1988, using a Boeing 757 leased from *Air Holland*. Odyssey's principal tour operator is *Thomson Vacations*, but the company will also sell seats to *Sunquest, Paramount Holidays, Toram, Alba Tours* and *Skican*. The airline's initial flight was from Toronto to Las Vegas. It had been planned to make several flights from London, Ontario to the southern sun spots during the 1988-89 winter, but poor loads led to the cancellation of these flights.

Odyssey International began flying to Italy twice weekly for *Alba Tours*, one flight to Rome and the other to Catania and Palermo in Sicily. The company intends to build a new hangar near the *Worldways* hangar at the Toronto International Airport to service its aircraft.

The *Air Holland* 757 was operated with Odyssey International titles but retained the Air Holland colour scheme. This aircraft had 231 economy seats. When the company's new aircraft arrived they were equipped with only 218 seats for better passenger comfort.

FLEET LISTING
ODYSSEY INTERNATIONAL

REG'N	C/N		IS	WFU	NOTES	
BOEING 757						
C-FNBC	24260	501	12/88	C		-28A
C-GAWB	24367	502	2/89	C		-28A
C-		503	/89	C		-28A
PH-AHF	24136		11/88	3/89	LF PH-AHF Air Holland (Air Holland c/s)	-27B

Air 3000
(AIR 2000)

HEADQUARTERS:
27 Fasken Drive, Toronto, Ontario
M9W 1K6

MAIN BASE:
Toronto

FLEET 1989:
3 - 757-28As.

COLOURS:
Air 2000 (now Air 3000) flies a white aircraft with two narrow cheat lines (the upper is gold and the lower is red), separated by a narrow strip of white fuselage. The cheat lines begin under the second forward window, leaving the forward portion of the aircraft white, run aft below the windows until they sweep upwards through the rear four windows onto the lower portion of the tail. The lines broaden as they run across the tail. The title 'AIR 2000'appears in two lines on the middle portion of the tail in red italicized block letters, with the letters outlined in gold. The title 'AIR 2000' is displayed again on the upper fuselage, ending above the forward end of the cheat lines. This title appears in one line with a maple leaf immediately aft of the title. Both the maple leaf and the title are in red, outlined in gold.The registration is in red immediately aft of the rear door. The top and bottom of the engines are red leaving a broad white band between the two red portions. Two narrow lines, separated by white, run through the middle of this white area; the upper line is gold and the lower is red.

ROUTES:
Charters from Toronto – St. Petersburg – Fort Lauderdale – St. Kitts – St. Lucia – Puerto Rico – Montego Bay – Acapulco – Cancun – Mananillo – Grenada – Puerto Vallarta.

HISTORY:
Air 2000, based in Toronto, was delayed in beginning its charter service during the latter part of 1988 because *Air 2000*, based in Manchester, England, held too large a share of the Canadian company. *Air 2000* of Manchester sold its 25% holdings to Deluce Investments of Toronto (the holding company for *Air Ontario*), clearing the way for the airline to begin operations in December, 1988. In order to meet its commitments for November, the company sub-chartered its bookings through *Air Transat, First Air, Canadian, Minerve, Nationair* and *Wardair*.

The airline was forced to change its name by May, 1989, to disassociate itself from the Manchester-based Air 2000. When its first non-leased aircraft was delivered in May it bore the title 'AIR 3000' which will be the company's interim name until a permanent name is selected.

Robert Deluce is the first President of the airline which will fly charters to the southern sun spots in the winter and to Europe in the summer. The company started with a staff of one hundred and sixty-five personnel.

The airline's first Boeing 757, leased from *Air 2000* in Manchester, arrived early in November, 1988, but did not go into service until the following month. Air 3000 flew the first Boeing 757s operated in Canada (Odyssey International also began flying Boeing 757s in December 1988). The company pre-sold all 60,000 charter seats it had available for the 1988-89 winter.

FLEET LISTING

AIR 3000

REG'N	C/N	IS	WFU	NOTES	MODEL
BOEING 757-28A					
C-FOOB	23822	12/88	5/89	LF G-OOOB Air 2000 (UK)	
C-FOOE	24369	5/89	C	Titles 'AIR 3000'	
C-FXOD	24235	12/88	5/89	LF G-OOOD Air 2000 (arrived 11/88)	

Air 2000 (Now Air 3000) Boeing 757, C-FXOD

Vacationair Boeing 737, C-GVRD

Vacationair

HEADQUARTERS;
220 Atwell Drive, Rexdale, Ontario, M9W 5B2

MAIN BASE:
Toronto

FLEET 1989:
2 - Boeing 737-200s.

COLOURS:
The Vacationair colour scheme consists of a white aircraft with a broad, multicoloured line running below the windows from just forward of the front door, then sweeping upward at the rear of the windows (broadening as it sweeps up to a point near the top at the rear of the tail). The multicoloured line is actually composed of four butting cheat lines: red on top, then red-orange, orange and finally orange-yellow at the bottom. Forward of the multicoloured cheat line, a single narrow orange-yellow cheat line runs around the front of the aircraft, and is separated from the multicoloured line by a large stylized 'V' in dark blue. Beginning above the front window, the title 'VACATIONAIR' appears in dark blue, followed by a Canadian flag in red. A large 'VACATIONAIR' title runs upward on the forward half of the tail. The registration appears in small blue letters on the rear lower fuselage and the final three letters are on the front wheel well.

ROUTES:
Charters from Toronto – Provinciales (Turks & Caicos) – Camaguey (Cuba) – Tobago – Santo Domingo – Cancun – Puerto Plata.
U.S.A.
Fort Lauderdale – Orlando – St. Petersburg – West Palm Beach – Sarasota – Harlingen (Texas).

HISTORY:
This Toronto based charter operator began flying in December 1988, with two Boeing 737-200 aircraft. The company is owned by *International Travel Group*, a joint venture of *Conquest Tours, Regent Holidays* and *Gray Coach Lines Ltd.* The company's aircraft are based at the *Skycharter* hangar at the general aviation area of Pearson (Toronto) International Airport. On of its Boeing 737 aircraft was formerly operated by PWA.

FLEET LISTING
VACATIONAIR

REG'N	C/N	IS	WFU	NOTES	MODEL
BOEING 737					
C-GVRD	20956	01/89	5/89	LT YU-ANZ Aviogenex; EX N131AW GPA/C-FTAQ Transair/PWA	-2Q8A
C-GVRE	22396	12/88	C	EX G-BHVH Air Europe/Orion Airways	-2T5A
C-GVRD	21735	NTU	NTU	C/N 20956 was leased rather than C/N 21735	-2Q8A

Crownair
(Canadian Aviation Express Airlines Inc.)

HEADQUARTERS:
Toronto

MAIN BASE:
Edmonton International

FLEET:
1 - DC-8-52

COLOURS:
Crownair flies a white aircraft with a dark lower fuselage. The title 'CROWNAIR' appears on the forward upper fuselage and a large crown is displayed on the tail. A narrow cheat line runs the length of the fuselage, below the windows.

ROUTES:
Worldwide charters from Toronto – Puerto Plata – Montego Bay – Puerto Vallarta – Acapulco – Orlando.
Summer: Toronto – Stansted – Prestwick – Manchester.

HISTORY:
The airlines first flight was made on 17 February 1989 from Calgary to MBJ with a hush-kitted DC-8-52. The Airline's full name is Canadian Aviation Express Airlines Inc. and it uses the callsign 'Regal.'

FLEET LISTING
CROWNAIR

REG'N	C/N	IS	WFU	NOTES
DC-8-52				
C-FCRN	45752	2/89	C	EX N42920 / ZK-NZC Air New Zealand

Holidair

HEADQUARTERS:
Rexdale, Ontario
(Travel 'N' Save Holding Company)

MAIN BASE:
Edmonton, Alberta

FLEET 1989:
1 - DC-8-52

COLOURS:
The dark blue upper fuselage of the aircraft is separated from the grey lower fuselage by narrow cheat lines running the length of the fuselage below the windows. These cheat lines alternate with gold at the top, followed by dark blue, gold, and finally dark blue. The title 'HOLIDAIR' appears in white on the forward upper fuselage and a large gold maple leaf is displayed on the tail. The registration, followed by a maple leaf appears in black on the rear lower fuselage.

ROUTES:
Charters Edmonton/Calgary – Las Vegas – Cancun – Honolulu.

HISTORY:
This new charter operator bases its single DC-8-52 in Alberta. The company is a wholly-owned subsidiary of Travel 'N' Save Holding Company of Toronto, which is owned by Harry Borenstein. The airline's first President is Joe Garrihy.

Holidair was forced to bring in subcontracted aircraft and American crews to operate its charters during mid-December because of a delay in delivery of the DC-8. A Boeing 727 and an L-1011 were chartered from the US, the L-1011 charters costing as much as $200,000. The company finally flew its DC-8 from Calgary to Las Vegas late in December. Direct flights Calgary or Edmonton – Cancun and Honolulu were also flown. Charter flights from Vancouver will commence during 1989.

Summer flights during 1989 will include Vancouver via Edmonton to Prestwick, London, Amsterdam or Frankfurt.

FLEET LISTING
HOLIDAIR

REG'N	C/N	IS	WFU	NOTES
DC-8-52				
C-FHAB	45658	12/88	C	EX T.15-2 Spanish Air Force/EC-ATP Iberia/N42920

PART 5

Small Carriers
Past and Present
by
Province

with
Representative
Aircraft Listings

BRITISH COLUMBIA

BURRARD AIR

A Vancouver-based charter operator, Burrard Air began in 1981. The company flies the scheduled routes formerly operated by *Pacific Coastal Airlines* between Vancouver (south terminal) and Nanaimo (Cassidy), using Britten Norman Islanders. The company acquired *Yellowbird Air* in March 1984 and in June of that year became the fifth carrier operating from the Vancouver south terminal to Victoria Airport. In April 1985, it expanded with service to Gillies Bay, Sechelt, Powell River, and Campbell River from Vancouver and later added flights to the interior of B.C., using Piper PA31 aircraft in addition to the Britten Norman Islanders. To better serve its customers, the company moved its operations to the main terminal at Vancouver International Airport.

The company briefly became a *Canadian* Partner in 1987 for flights to Campbell River and Nanaimo and planned to paint their aircraft in full *Canadian* colour scheme. The arrangement was ended abruptly, however, on October 24, 1987, probably because the company was in direct competition with another *Canadian* Partner (*Time Air*), on these routes.

On December 4, 1987, the airline voluntarily shut down operations after an audit by the *Department of Transport* revealed numerous discrepancies in its aircraft maintenance records. This was a major blow to the company, occurring during an *Air Canada* strike which, combined with the anticipated heavy Christmas traffic, had been expected to help the company's bottom line. The company had just acquired a Metro II aircraft at that time, which was leased to *Air BC* from November 30 to December 4 to fly one return Vancouver to Penticton flight and the aircraft was sold to *Skylink*. The company started up again on February 1, 1988 from their new base in Victoria with flights between Vancouver and Nanaimo, Powell River, Victoria , Campbell River and Port Hardy.

CANADA WEST AIR LTD.

This is a Vancouver based airline which began as a charter operation in 1986 with a fleet of two Convair 440 aircraft . One of the Convair 440s was former *North Cariboo* Convair 440, C-GRWW, which had been purchased in May 1986.

Canada West's colour scheme consists of a white aircraft with a blue cheat line through the windows. Narrow lines of white, yellow and white run immediately below the blue and the airline's name appears in black on the upper fuselage. The company logo, the italicised initialst '*CW*' in red, appears on the tail with a red maple leaf plus a vertical blue bar broken in three parts at the top. A Canadian flag is displayed immediately aft of the cockpit.

In June 1988, *Air Niagara* Convair 580, C-FARO, was leased in full *Air Niagara* colours and titles, and the following month Convair 640, C-GQCQ, was acquired from *Time Air*.

CONAIR AVIATION LIMITED

Based at Abbottsford, 60 km from Vancouver, the company operates a large fleet of fire control and spraying aircraft. Twin-engined Douglas A-26C Invaders were used as water bombers until sold in 1988. Two major aircraft types make up the bulk of the fleet: four-engine piston DC-6s and former *Canadian Forces* Grumman CS2F-1 Trackers, which the company calls Firecats. The first European built Fokker F-27 was acquired in 1986 and converted to a water bomber. The company plans are to convert several more of these aircraft as they are received. Conair took over the former PWA hangar in Edmonton in 1985 and opened a water tanker base there.

Conair was a major shareholder in *Swiftair Cargo*. A Firecat crashed in central British Columbia on 27 August 1988.

THE FLYING FIREMAN LIMITED

The company operates from the Victoria Airport using a large fleet of PBY Cansos water bombers for fire control. The aircraft winter in Victoria and are based at strategic points in the province during the forest fire season.

FOREST INDUSTRIES FLYING TANKER LIMITED

Formed by six B.C. companies in the forest industry to protect the forests from fire, the company operates two giant Martin Mars water bombers, a VIP Grumman Goose and some helicopters. The aircraft are based at Sproat Lake near Port Alberni.

HARBOUR AIR

Formerly, as Windoak Air Services, the company operated service between Vancouver Harbour and Duncan, B.C. This company took over the *Air BC* float base and hangar at the Vancouver International Airport (south side), and operates a large fleet of Cessnas (185s, 206, 210, 402, 414, and 421), Beech and Piper aircraft. It also has several float Beavers and Otters. The company operates a fleet of up to five Twin Otters each summer, usually leasing the aircraft from *Kenn Borek Air*. All the Twin Otters operate on floats and usually retain the *Kenn Borek* colour scheme with Harbour Air titles and/or symbols.

BRITISH COLUMBIA

HYACK AIR

Based on the Fraser River in New Westminster, this small charter company operates a fleet of Beavers and at one time flew a former RCMP Otter.

NORTH CARIBOO FLYING SERVICES LIMITED

Based in Fort St. John, the company operates a general charter air service and has flown some regularly scheduled flights. It has linked Fort St. John to Hudson Hope, Chetwynd, Dawson Creek, Fort Nelson and Grande Prairie (Alberta) with a Twin Otter and DC-3. Service is also provided to the townsite of Tumbler Ridge.

From its Edmonton base, the company flew several large aircraft on charters, especially for Edmonton baseball and hockey teams. A former *Echo Bay Mines*/PWA Convair 640 and two Convair 440s have been operated at various times. North Cariboo also operated a small parcel air cargo service on behalf of *Air Canada* for a while.

The company still has two DC-3s, one being C-FJUV, painted all green and used to shuttle BC firefighters during the summer.

NORTH COAST AIR SERVICE

Based at Prince Rupert, this airline was formed in 1961 to provide service to the Queen Charlotte Islands and the north coast of British Columbia. A fleet comprised mostly of amphibious aircraft includes a Grumman Mallard and Beavers as its mainstays. The company has operated a DC-3 and a C-46.

NORTHERN THUNDERBIRD AIR LTD.

The merger of *Northern Mountain Airlines* and *Thunderbird Air* created this airline in 1973. The companyird has attempted on several occasions to make the Prince George – Prince Rupert and the Prince George – Quesnel – Williams Lake – Kamloops – Penticton – Kelowna routes profitable. Four Twin Otters and one DC-3 were used on these routes but one Twin Otter crashed into a mountain on the approach to Terrace on 14 January 1977. The company continues to provide charter operations in northern British Columbia flying a variety of Cessnas, Pipers and deHavilland aircraft.

POWELL AIR

Powell Air operated an extensive seaplane operation from Powell River with a large fleet of Beavers and an Otter plus smaller aircraft. The company purchased the *Kelowna Flightcraft* Convair 440 in 1981. This aircraft maintained the *Kelowna* paint scheme with added Powell Air titles and operated between Powell River and Vancouver until the route was purchased by *Air BC* in 1984.

TRANS PROVINCIAL AIRLINES

Trans Provincial originally had its headquarters in Terrace, B.C. and operated scheduled and charter services from bases at Prince Rupert, Prince George, Ocean Falls, Sandspit and Smithers. The airline connected Prince Rupert to the Queen Charlotte Islands (Masset and Sandspit) and provided service from Prince Rupert to Stewart, Alice Arm, Hartley Bay, Bella Bella, Ocean Falls, and Ketchi-kan, Alaska.

The company attempted to make the Prince Rupert – Terrace – Smithers – Prince George route a viable operation. An F-27 in an all yellow colour scheme flew this route between 1973-75 and an all yellow DC-3 also flew the route, but the low volume of passengers could not sustain the operation.

Trans Provincial was purchased by Jim Pattison Industries in 1979 and, although retaining a separate identity from *Air BC*, it operated in the full *Air BC* colour scheme of red and blue, with its own symbol (rather than the 'A') displayed on the tail. Port Hardy became a major base with TPA operating smaller aircraft and connecting with *Air BC* flights from Vancouver.

In October 1986, Gene Story, former chief pilot for TPA, headed a group of investors who purchased Trans Provincial Airlines from the Jim Pattison Group. Story had managed the airline since 1968 from its base at Prince Rupert. The Port Hardy operation was retained by the Jim Pattison Group and operated under one of the names *Air West* had acquired in 1980: *Pacific Coastal Airlines*. TPA again became a northern BC charter and scheduled service operator.

In 1987 the company acquired the only Bristol Freighter in operation in Canada, adding a second in 1988.

Conair DC-6B, C-GIOY

AIRCRAFT LISTING
BRITISH COLUMBIA

REG'N	C/N	F/N	IS	WFU	NOTES	TITLE
BURRARD AIR						
BN Islander						
C-GIHF	475		81	C		
DHC-3 Otter						
C-FBCG	408		83	86	EX Province of B.C.	
C-FMPP	42		83	87	EX RCMP	
Piper Navajo						
C-GSUY	52143		86	C	EX C-GSUY Skylink	
CANADA WEST						
Convair 440						
C-GCWF	196		86	C	EX N96CF Combs Airways	
C-GRWW	156		86	C	EX C-GRWW North Cariboo	
Convair 580						
C-FARO	382		88	88	LF C-FARO Air Niagara	
Convair 640						
C-GQCQ	451		88	C	EX C-GQCQ Time Air	
CONAIR AVIATION						
DC-6AB						
C-FCZZ	45498		88	C	EX C-FCZZ CPA/PWA/NWT Air	
C-GJKT	45179	49	82	C		
DC-6						
CF-PWA	4469	41	72	74	W/O 02/08/74 near Kamloops	
CF-PWF	43537	42	76	82	WFU/BU; EX PWA	
C-GBYS	44658		86	C	EX Conifair	
C-GHCA	45197	44	73	C		
C-GHCB	44893	43	74	C		
C-GHLY	45501	46	75	C		
C-GHLZ	45478	45	75	C		
C-GICD	45496	47	76	C		
C-GIOY	45506	48	76	C		
C-GKUG	45177	50	82	C		
DC-6A/C						
C-GIBS	45531	51	82	C		
CS2F Tracker						
C-FODU	38		80	82	EX CF 3680; EX Ontario Gov't	
C-GWUO	39	63	80	82	EX CF 12140	
C-GWUP	19	68	80	82	EX CF 1520	
Fokker F-27						
C-GSFS	10473	27	86	C		
FLYING FIREMAN						
PBY-5A Canso						
C-FFFW	46596	4	67	C		
C-FFFZ	46602	3	66	86	ST N4NC	
C-GFFD	414	6	75	84	W/O 14/05/84 YQT	
FOREST INDUSTRIES						
Martin JRM-3 Mars						
C-FLYK	76820		62	C	.	PHILLIPINE MARS
Gumman G-21 Goose						
C-FVFU	B-101		75	C		
Martin JRM-3 Mars						
C-FLYL	76823		59	C	Flying Tankers	HAWAII MARS
Bell 206L						
C-GWPW	45248		79	C		

AIRCRAFT LISTING
BRITISH COLUMBIA

REG'N	C/N	IS	WFU	NOTES
HARBOUR AIR				
DHC-6 Twin Otter				
C-FKBI	25	86	C	LF C-FKBI Kenn Borek
C-FOEQ	44	88	C	EX C-FOEQ Kenn Borek
C-FPAT	2	86	87	LF C-FPAT Kenn Borek
C-FQHC	21	86	C	LF C-FQHC Kenn Borek
C-GIAW	60	88	C	LF C-GIAW Kenn Borek
C-GKBD	314	88	C	LF C-GKBD Kenn Borek
C-GNTA	146	87	C	LF C-GNTA Kenn Borek
DHC-3 Otter				
C-FSUB	8	85	87	EX C-FSUB Tyee
C-FQRI	326	84	C	Rebuilt after fire, Air BC
DHC-2 Beaver				
C-FAXI	1514	84	C	EX C-FAXI West Coast Air
C-FOCN	44	84	C	EX C-FOCN Hyack Air
C-FOSP	1501	84	C	EX C-FOSP West Coast Air
HYACK AIR				
DHC-3 Otter				
CF-MPX	280	82	83	EX RCMP
DHC-2 Beaver				
C-FOCN	44	75	84	EX Ontario Government
C-GFDD	273	75	84	
Cessna 185				
C-GHPI	03806	80	86	
Cessna 206				
C-GSAI	04745	80	87	
NORTH CARIBOO FLYING SERVICES				
DC-3				
C-FBXY	25980	80	C	EX C-FBXY Knight Air
C-FJUV	19394	80	88	LF C-FJUV Knight Air
DHC-6				
C-FDKK	177	82	84	ST C-FDKK Inuvik Coastal
Convair 440				
C-GRNB	497	79	86	ST Renown Aviation, USA
C-GRWW	156	80	86	ST C-GRWW Canada West
Convair 640				
C-FPWO	463	84	86	ST N587CA Corporate Air
Viscount 806				
C-GWPY	311	83	85	ST G-BNAA Euroair
NORTHCOAST				
C-46				
C-GIXZ	22453	78	80	ST C-GIXZ Lambair
DC-3				
CF-CQT	9813	70	75	ST C-FCQT Ilford-Riverton
Grumman Mallard				
C-GHDD	J-23	78	87	ST C-FHDD Waglisla Air
C-FMHG	J-21	78	87	EX C-FMHG West Coast Air
DHC-3 Otter				
C-FSUB	8	86	87	EX C-FSUB Harbour Air
DHC-2 Beaver				
C-FJAA	961	75	87	
NORTHERN THUNDERBIRD				
DC-3				
CF-JUV	19394	76	78	ST C-FJUV Knight Air

AIRCRAFT LISTING
BRITISH COLUMBIA

REG'N	C/N	IS	WFU	NOTES
NORTHERN THUNDERBIRD (Continued)				
DHC-6 Twin Otter				
C-FMHU	142	72	75	W/O 30/09/75 365 miles NW of Prince George
C-GDHC	494	77	85	Sold
C-GNTA	146	75	78	ST West Coast Air
C-GNTB	463	75	77	W/O 14/01/77 near Terrace
C-GNTD	533	77	82	ST HK-2821 Aeroejecutives
POWELL AIR				
Convair 440				
C-GKFC	504	81	85	EX Kelowna Flightcraft
TRANS PROVINCIAL				
DHC-6 Twin Otter				
C-FCSL	64	87	C	EX C-FCSL Cdn Superior Oil
C-GGNI	32	87	C	EX N332MA Alaska Aeronaut.
F-27				
C-FTPA	104	73	74	ST C-FTPA Time Air
DC-3				
C-FKAZ	19345	70	78	ST C-FKAZ Pacific Coastal
C-FPWI	4880	72	78	ST C-FPWI Pacific Coastal
C-GWUG	32963	80	83	ST C-GWUG Air BC
Grumman Goose				
C-FBXR	1059	74	C	
C-FEFN	1157	76	C	EX C-FEFN Gulf Air
Grumman Goose				
C-FNIF	B-129	68	87	EX CF-NIF Pacific Western
C-FUAZ	1077	69	87	EX CF-UAZ BC Air
C-FUMG	B-145	68	C	EX CF-UMG Pacific Western
C-FUVJ	B-6	68	78	W/O 30/08/79
BN Islander				
C-GTPB	223	80	87	EX N41JA
DHC-3 Otter				
C-FKLC	255	70	C	
C-FRHW	445	64	81	W/O 12/06/81 near Smithers
C-FRNO	21	69	C	EX CF-RNO Pacific Western
CF-ROW	449	64	67	W/O 18/04/67 at Stewart BC
C-FXUY	142	70	C	OB C-FXUY Gulf Air 76-78
Bristol Freighter				
C-GYQS	13060	87	C	EX ZK-EPD
C-GYQY	13134	88	C	EX ZK-EPF
SKYLINK				
Cessna 402				
C-GULD	0004	86	C	EX N5404M
Piper Navajo				
C-GJTE	----	85	C	
C-GSUY	----	85	C	
TYEE				
DHC-2 Beaver				
C-FMAW	1201	80	87	EX CF-MAW Manitoba Air Service
C-FHGX	604	75	87	
CF-HRT	1203	75	C	
DHC-3 Otter				
C-FSUB	8	78	80	ST C-FSUB Trans North

AIRCRAFT LISTING
BRITISH COLUMBIA

REG'N	C/N	IS	WFU	NOTES

AIR CALEDONIA

Convair 440

C-GTVU	173	NTU	X	reg'n applied 10/85 - 2/86 at Miami

Cessna 421B

C-GTVU	0238	86	87	
C-GTWU	0098	85	87	

PBY-5A Canso

C-FJCV	CV357	82	C	EX C-FJCB Aero Trades

AIR WEST

DHC-6 Twin Otter

C-FAKM*	78	77	80	ST Air BC; EX Time Air
C-FAWC*	108	72	80	ST Air BC; EX N204E
C-FAWF*	67	73	76	W/O 22/09/76 Bella Coola
C-FAIV	215	74	78	W/O 02/09/78 Vancouver
C-FGQE	40	73	80	ST C-FGQE Air BC
C-GEAW	68	75	80	ST C-GEAW Air BC
C-GFAW	163	76	80	ST C-GFAW Air BC
C-GGAW	86	76	80	ST C-GGAW Air BC
C-GIAW	60	77	80	EX JDF-T1 Jamaica Air Def.
C-GJAW	176	78	80	ST C-GJAW Air BC
C-GPBO	100	76	77	W/O 01/12/77 Saturna Isle.
C-GQKN	94	80	90	EX PZ-TAV Surinam

BN-2A Islander

C-GKAW	128			

DHC-2 TurboBeaver

C-FOEX	TB-52			
C-FOEY	TB-54			

BC AIRLINES

Nord 262

CF-BCR	16	69	72	ST CF-BCR PWA
CF-BCS	23	69	72	ST CF-BCS PWA
CF-BCT	24	69	72	ST CF-BCT PWA
CF-BCU	9	69	72	ST CF-BCU PWA

DHC-6 Twin Otter

CF-WZH	132	68	69	ST CF-WZH Falconbridge

Grumman Mallard

CF-HPA	J--7	61	70	ST CF-HPA Abitibi Paper
CF-HPU	J--9	60	70	ST CF-HPU West Coast
CF-MHG	J-21	60	70	ST CF-MHG West Coast

Grumman Goose

CF-RQI	1145	65	68	ST CF-RQI Northland
CF-UAZ	1077	66	69	ST CF-UAZ Trans Provincial

HARRISON AIRWAYS

DC-3

CF-CPX	6085	69	79	EX CPAL
CF-CRX	19276	74	77	EX CPAL
CF-CRZ	20180	69	77	EX CPAL

Viscount 757

CF-THG	224	77	79	ST Pacific Vocational Ins.
CF-TIC	383	77	78	ST 318975 Ontario Ltd.

Convair 440

CF-HAF	432	73	78	ST N27KA Key Airlines
C-GBHA	447	75	78	ST N440AD Aero Dyne; NIS

AIRCRAFT LISTING
BRITISH COLUMBIA

REG'N	C/N	IS	WFU	NOTES
PACIFIC COASTAL				
DC-3				
C-FKAZ	19345	78	80	ST C-FKAZ Air West
C-FPWI	4880	77	80	ST C-FPWI Air West
BN Islander				
C-GPCF	----	75	83	
VANCOUVER CANUCKS				
727-22				
C-GVCH	18853	84	85	ST YV-87C Avenza
WEST COAST AIR				
DHC-2 Beaver				
C-FAXI	1514			
CF-JOM	1204			
CF-OSP	1501			
C-FVFS	1616			
C-FYYU	1573			
DHC-6 Twin Otter				
C-FJCL	151	78	80	ST Air BC; EX Gateway
C-FPAE	228	78	80	OF PWA; EX Survair
C-FWAF	122	79	80	W/O
C-GKNR	186	78	80	ST C-GKNR Air West/Air BC
C-GQKN	94	79	80	ST C-GQKN Air West/Air BC
Grumman T-Mallard				
C-GHUM	J-26	73	80	ST C-GHUM Air BC
Cessna 185				
CF-YNO	----	70	80	Sold

Echo Bay Mines Convair 640, C-FPWO

ALBERTA

ECHO BAY MINES –
JASPER HINTON AIR
AURIC AIR

This airline first operated from the Edmonton Municipal Airport as part of *Eldorado Aviation,* using *Eldorado* DC-3s. However, the company set up its own flight operations in 1975 acquiring an *Eldorado* DC-3 (CF-CUG) and DC-3 (C-GWMX). In June 1976, a Convair 640 (C-FPWO) was acquired from PWA and based at the Edmonton Municipal Airport. This aircraft was sold to *North Cariboo Air Services* in 1984 when the company bought a former PWA Boeing 727. A Hercules aircraft was purchased from SEBJ in 1981 and used to carry oversize equipment into the north until it was sold in 1984.

The Echo Bay Mines 727 continues in operation in 1988 from the Edmonton International Airport, and the company also operates a Twin Otter. Echo Bay Mines changed the name of its aircraft operations to Jasper-Hinton Air and again, more recently, to Auric Air.

ESSO RESOURCES

Esso operated a Lockheed Electra from the Edmonton International Airport in support of its northern operations from 1972. This aircraft was sold in 1983 when the company acquired the former *Eldorado* Boeing 737. The 737 was sold in 1987 to *Aloha Airlines.*

KENN BOREK AIR LTD

Kenn Borek Air has its main base at the Calgary International Airport with satelite bases at Inuvik, Resolute Bay and Dawson Creek. The company owns thirteen de Havillland Twin Otters and one Caribou as well as several Beechcraft and Cessna aircraft. It currently has one DC-4 and operates several Bell JetRangers. The company leases its Twin Otters to many operators such as *Harbour Air* in British Columbia and *Empire Airways* in the United States. The company also provides scheduled service out of Inuvik and Resolute Bay.

SOUTHERN FRONTIER AIRLINES

Formed in 1978, this Calgary based airline was a charter operation until it acquired the Calgary licence of *Gateway Aviation,* and began operating daily flights from Calgary to Lloydminster and Cold Lake. The company operated from its own hangar at the old site of the Calgary Airport until 1984 when it moved to the new terminal. Operating DC-3s, Twin Otters, Beech King Airs and a Beech 99, the airline expanded to Edmonton, flying from the Municipal Airport to Lloydminster and Saskatoon. The company also leased a Convair 440 from *North Cariboo Air* for a short period in 1984.

Time Air took over the airline in January 1985 and operated the scheduled services of Southern Frontier but left the charter operations intact. A citation jet and Piper Navajo are included in their 1988 fleet.

SHELL OIL – MOBIL OIL –
INEXCO – AMOCO

These oil companies operated a number of large aircraft out of the Calgary International Airport. Shell operated an F-27 (CF-SHA) as did Mobil Oil (CF-IOG). Inexco and Amoco operated HS-748s from Calgary through the Edmonton Municipal Airport to their northern operations.

Former Airlines of Alberta

AIR ALBERTA

Air Alberta commenced operations in 1985 with two EMB 110 Banderiante to operate between the Edmonton Municipal Airport, Red Deer and Calgary. However, after only 5 months of service, the company folded on 3 February 1986.

DOME PETROLEUM

The Canadian energy policy of the 1970s encouraged this Calgary based company to expand its northern operations. To connect these operations with their Calgary base, a large fleet of aircraft were operated including two Cessna Citations, a Grumman Gulfstream II (executive transport only), a Beech King Air and a Boeing 737. The operation of the Boeing 737 was taken over by *Pacific Western Airlines* in 1984, with *Pacific Western* operating charters for the company after this date.

ELDORADO AVIATION

This company was formed in 1944 and operated until 1984, providing air support for its parent company *Eldorado Mining and Refining Limited.* Two Norseman aircraft provided service to Port Radium (now Echo Bay) in 1944. When the aviation division was formally set up in 1952 as Eldorado Aviation, a DC-3 (CF-DGJ) was acquired. A second DC-3 (CF-GEI), a Curtiss C-46 and the two Norseman aircraft made up the fleet at that time. In 1957, the company acquired DC-4 (CF-JRW) and accumulated more than 65,000 flying hours before being sold in 1980. This aircraft was based at the Edmonton Municipal Airport and each day flew crews north to the high Arctic. The aircraft carried fifty-six passengers plus cargo. A second DC-4 (CF-GNI), was acquired by Eldorado from the defunct *Great Northern*

ALBERTA

Airways of Calgary in 1973 with the intention of using this aircraft as a spare, but it was in such good condition it was placed into regular service. The DC-4s and DC-3s carried passengers and cargo between Edmonton and Uranium City. The DC-3s also flew on behalf of Eldorado's sister company, *Northern Transportation Company Limited,* hauling passengers and freight to Inuvik, Tuktoyaktuk, Hay River, Norman Wells, Bear River and other northern locations. The DC-3s and DC-4s originally operated with a white upper fuselage which was separated from the silver lower fuselage by a dark blue cheat line. The tail was dark blue and the title 'ELDORADO' appeared in large blue letters on the upper fuselage. When the DC-3s were repainted, they flew with an orange cheat line, orange tail and the title changed to 'ELDORADO - N.T.C.L.' The DC-4s also received the orange cheat line and tail but continued to carry the title 'ELDORADO.'

In 1980, Eldorado bought a Boeing 737 to use on its northern flights. The aircraft was white, with an orange and blue cheat line sweeping up the tail. About that time, the company moved its headquarters from Edmonton to Saskatoon to shorten the travel time between its headquarters and Uran-ium City. When Uranium City was shut down in 1983, the 737 was sold to *Esso Resources.* The company's remaining aircraft were sold in 1984.

GATEWAY AVIATION LTD.
Formed in 1952, this operator was based at the Edmonton Municipal Airport and flew passenger and cargo charters between Edmonton, the Yukon and the Northwest Territories. The company operated a large fleet of DC-3s and Twin Otters as well as many smaller aircraft. In April 1972, Gateway Aviation acquired an HS-748 from *Transair,* which flew for the company for more than seven years. The HS-748 was replaced by a former PWA Convair 640 in June 1978.

Gateway flew some scheduled services on behalf of PWA from then until the company was taken over by *Northward* in December 1979.

GREAT NORTHERN AIRWAYS
This airline operated three F-27s, a DC-4, a former *Wardair* DHC-6 and several DC-3 aircraft from the Calgary Airport during the early 1960s. However, the crash of F-27, CF-GND at Resolute Bay in June 1968 coupled with the crash of F-27, CF-GNG at Inuvik in December 1969 led to the airline going out of business early in 1970.

INTERNATIONAL JET AIR
From 1969 to 1976, this company operated a fleet of former *Northwest Airlines* Electras out of the Calgary International Airport. Jet Commander and Aero Commander aircraft were also operated on a charter basis, as was an F-27.

KIER AIR
AIR COMMONWEALTH
McKENZIE AIR
From the mid-1960s until 1975, the Edmonton Municipal Airport saw the same fleet flown by a succession of airlines, each acquiring the aircraft of a predecessor. *Kier Air* was a company which operated DC-3s and Aztecs on charters. When it folded, its aircraft were acquired by *Air Commonwealth,* which added a DC-4 (CF-QIX) to the DC-3s but this company also folded within a couple of years. *McKenzie Air* emerged as the owner of the DC-3s and operated a large fleet of aircraft which included Twin Otters, an F-27 (CF-BNX) and an F-227 (C-GMAL). The company also operated a Lear Jet. However, in April 1975, it also folded operations.

NORTHWARD AIRLINES LTD.
Formed in 1965, this company had its headquarters in Edmonton but most of its operations were in the Yukon and Northwest Territories. Northward Airlines operated a large fleet of Twin Otters, DC-3s and an F-27. It acquired several ST-27s to operate scheduled services out of Edmonton and acquired *Gateway Aviation* in 1979, but as with many operators who tried to expand too rapidly, the company could not properly fund the expansion and folded in 1980.

PAN ARCTIC
This oil company operated a fleet of Electras and Twin Otters from its base at the Calgary International Airport, later moving to the Edmonton International Airport. Pan Arctic flew the former PWA Electra from 1972 until it was burned out at the Edmonton International Airport after its gear collapsed in January 1976. The aircraft was rebuilt and later sold. The other Electra crashed through the ice at Rea Point, NWT, on 29 October 1974. PWA operated charters for Pan Arctic after the Electras were no longer available but the Twin Otters continued in operation with Pan Arctic.

WESTBORNE INDUSTRIAL ENTERPRISES
From its base at the Calgary International Airport, Westbourne operated the former *Quebecair* Boeing 727 on charters from 1980 until 1987 when the aircraft was sold.

AIRCRAFT LISTING
ALBERTA

REG'N	C/N	IS	WFU	NOTES

AMOCO

HS-748

| C-FAMO* | 1669 | 69 | C | |

DHC-6 Twin Otter

| C-FQBT | 95 | 71 | C | |

ECHO BAY MINES

Boeing 727-171C

| C-FPXD | 19859 | 84 | C | EX C-FPXD PWA |

Convair 640

| C-FPWO | 463 | 76 | 84 | ST C-FPWO North Cariboo |

DC-3

| CF-CUG | 9891 | 74 | 76 | LF CF-CUG Eldorado |
| C-GWMX | 12357 | 78 | 79 | ST C-GWMX Kenn Borek |

L-382E Hercules

| C-FDSX | 4303 | 80 | 84 | OB Worldways |

DHC-6

| C-GFLS | 341 | 85 | C | JASPER HINTON AIR; EX C-GFLS Labrador Airways |

ESSO RESOURCES

Boeing 737-255C

| C-GENL | 22148 | 83 | 87 | ST N802AL Aloha Airlines |

DHC-4A

| CF-LAN | 2 | 61 | 61 | LF CF-LAN de Havilland |

DC-3

| CF-IOC | 13456 | 51 | 69 | ST CF-IOC Hudson Bay Air |

F-27

| CF-IOG | 109 | NTU | X | ST CF-IOG Mobile Oil |

DHC-6

CF-IOH	198	69	78	ST C-FIOH Gulf Air
CF-IOJ	261	69	C	
CF-IOK	273	70	82	ST C-FIOK Armamco

Gulfstream I

| CF-IOM | 60 | 72 | 88 | |

Gulfstream II

| CF-IOT | 078 | 72 | 80 | |

L-188 Electra

| C-FIJR | 1138 | 72 | 83 | ST C-FIJR NWT Air |

Convair 240

| CF-IOK | 126 | 64 | 66 | ESSO/Imperial Oil; ST N400M Fluor Corp. |

KENN BOREK

Beech 99

| C-GXFC | U--18 | 79 | C | DHC-6 Twin Otter; EX Wardair |

DHC-6 Twin Otter

C-GBDR	417	74	C	
C-GKBD	314	76	C	
C-GKBE	693	80	C	LT Emirates A/S 1982-84

DC-3

| C-FQHF | 13392 | 76 | 82 | W/O 07/05/82 Calgary |
| C-GWMX | 12357 | 79 | 80 | ST C-GWMX Southern Front. |

DHC-4A Caribou

| C-GVYX | 292 | 82 | C | W/O 10/11/87 near XRR |

MOBILE OIL

F-27

| CF-IOG | 109 | 65 | 87 | ST C-FIOG Soundair |

AIRCRAFT LISTING
ALBERTA

REG'N	C/N	IS	WFU	NOTES
MOBILE OIL (Continued)				
DC-3				
CF-MOC	12741	67	74	ST C-FMOC Bradley A/S
DHC-6 Twin Otter				
CF-MOL	147	72	C	EX XA-BOR SAESA
DASH-8				
C-GMOK	024	86	C	
SHELL OIL				
F-27				
CF-SHA	89	69	83	ST N4425B Pacific Alaska
DHC-6 Twin Otter				
CF-SCA	17	66	78	ST Athabaska Airways
CF-SCF	82	71	C	EX 392 Fuerza Aerea Peru
DC-3				
CF-HXS	4854	55	58	ST CF-HXS Quebec Cartier
CF-IAE	4563	55	69	ST CF-IAE Alberta Gov't
CF-JRY	4585	57	69	ST CF-JRY Arctic 7
Convair 440				
CF-KQI	390	58	65	ST N7743U North Central AL
SOUTHERN FRONTIER				
Convair 440				
C-GRNB	497	84	86	LF C-GRNB North Cariboo
DHC-6 Twin Otter				
C-FWAG	343	79	85	ST C-FWAG Pace Aviation
DC-3				
C-FCUC	19366	78	85	EX CF-CUC GNA/Gateway
Beech 99				
C-GPFF	U-12	83	84	ST C-GPFF Quebec Aviation
C-GSFP	U-43	84	87	ST C-GSFP Time Air
AIR ALBERTA				
Banderiante				
C-GPNW	1100413	85	86	ST N199PB Mountain Pacific
C-GPRV	1100424	85	86	ST USA
AIR COMMONWEALTH				
DC-4				
CF-QIX	7476	69	71	ST CF-QIX Can Arctic Co-op
CARNEGIE HOLDINGS				
DC-6				
C-GPEG	43576	78	80	ST C-GPEG GO Enterprises
DOME PETROLEUM				
Boeing 737-2T2C				
C-GDPA	22056	80	84	ST C-GDPA Pacific Western
Gulfstream II				
C-GDPB	232	79	84	
Beech 65 -B90				
C-GDPC	LJ671	85	86	
Cessna Citation				
C-GDPD	0071	80	86	
C-GDPF	0112	79	85	ST C-GDPF Esso Canada
DHC-6 Twin Otter				
C-GDMP	489	76	83	ST C-GDMP Air Bras d'OR

AIRCRAFT LISTING
ALBERTA

REG'N	C/N	IS	WFU	NOTES

ELDORADO AVIATION

Curtiss C-46

CF-FCI	22393	51	57	W/O 31/05/57 near Edmonton

Norseman V

CF-BSB	N29-15	46	64	W/O 05/64 near Sawmill Bay

Norseman VI

CB-BZW	825	48	48	W/O 20/11/48 Leith Point

DC-3

CF-CUG	9891	58	79	ST Air North Training
CF-DGJ	25454	46	57	W/O 04/10/57 at Fort Murry
CF-GEI	12377	47	52	W/O 12/09/52 Goldfield
CF-OVW	12267	63	80	ST C-FOVW Air North Train.

DC-4

CF-GNI	10389	73	80	ST C-FGNI Aero Trades
CF-JRW	42983	56	80	ST C-FJRW Aero Trades

Boeing 737-255C

C-GENL	22148	80	83	ST C-GENL Esso Resources

GATEWAY

Convair 640

C-FPWS	441	78	79	ST C-FPWS Northward

HS-748

CF-MAK	1668	72	79	CF-MAK Calm Air

DHC-6 Twin Otter

CF-JCL	151	74	78	ST C-FJCL West Coast Air

DC-3

CF-CUC	19366	75	78	ST C-FCUC Southern Frontier
CF-PWG	20439	69	73	WFU; EX Pacific Western

GREAT NORTHERN

F-27

CF-BNX	94	69	72	ST CF-BNX McKenzie Air
CF-GND	113	65	68	W/O 13/06/68 Resolute Bay
CF-GNG	114	68	69	W/O 20/09/69 Inuvik
CF-GNJ	118	68	70	LF N2707J Allegheny

DHC-3 Otter

CF-SUB	8	67	71	ST CF-SUB International Jet

DHC-6 Twin Otter

CF-WAF	122	68	70	ST CF-WAF Northward Air

DC-3

CF-CPY	4665	66	71	On display CPA Whitehorse
CF-CUC	19366	66	71	ST CF-CUC Northward
CF-JWP	9089	67	71	ST CF-JWP Northward

DC-4

CF-GNI	10389	69	71	ST CF-GNI Eldorado in 1973

INTERNATIONAL JETAIR

F-27

CF-IJI	120	73	75	ST C-FIJI Northward

L-188 Electra

CF-IJJ	1145	NTU	X	NTU; remained Western c/s
CF-IJM	1108	69	73	ST California Airmotive BU
CF-IJR	1138	71	72	ST C-FIJR Esso Resources
CF-IJV	1129	71	76	ST C-FIJV NWT Air
CF-IJW	1131	73	76	ST N133AJ American Jet
CF-IJY	1094	71	76	ST N7139C Great Northern

AIRCRAFT LISTING
ALBERTA

REG'N	C/N	IS	WFU	NOTES
INEXCO				
HS-748				
CF-INE	1611	68	75	ST C-FINE EPA
KIER AIR				
DC-3				
CF-KAH	27184	68	69	ST CF-KAH Air Commonwealth
CF-KAZ	19345	67	69	ST CF-KAZ Air Commonwealth
CF-PIK	27202	68	69	ST CF-PIK Air Commonwealth
MCKENZIE AIR				
DHC-6 Twin Otter				
C-FCCE	8	77	78	ST C-FCCE La Ronge
C-GMAS	438	76	78	ST C-GMAS La Ronge
F-27				
CF-BNX	94	72	77	ST N88973 National Aero.
CF-LWN	72	72	76	ST N225 Flying Fireman Inc.
F-227				
C-GMAL	514	75	78	ST N4216 Air New England
NORTHWARD				
F-27				
C-FIJI	120	75	79	ST N2709J Indust. Fabrics
Beech 99				
C-GXFC	U-18	77	79	ST C-GXFC Kenn Borek
DC-3				
CF-JWP	9089	71	75	St C-FJWP Gateway Aviation
DHC-6 Twin Otter				
CF-QHC	21	73	80	ST C-FQHC Kenn Borek
CF-WAF	122	70	79	ST C-FWAF West Coast Air
CF-WZH	132	72	73	ST CF-WZH Trans North Tu
ST-27				
C-FCNT	008	79	80	RT C-FCNT Air Atonabee
CF-LOL	006	79	80	RT C-FLOL Air Atonabee
C-GHMQ	012	79	80	RT C-GHMQ Air Atonabee
C-GCML	009	79	80	RT C-GCML Air Atonabee
PAN ARCTIC				
L-188 Electra				
CF-PAB	1141	70	74	W/O 29/10/74 Rae Point NWT
CF-PAK	1127	73	76	DMG 30/01/76 Edmonton.
DHC-6 Twin Otter				
CF-PAE	228	69	75	St C-FPAE Survair
CF-PAT	2	69	75	ST C-FPAT Ptarmigan
C-GPAO	447	75	84	ST Rigel Airways
C-GPAZ	729	80	84	ST Rigel Airways
TEXACO CANADA				
Convair 340				
CF-TCL	013	62	65	ST N7517U North Central Airlines
WESTBURNE INDUSTRIAL				
Boeing 727-25				
C-GQBE	18970	80	87	ST N682FM Freeport McMoran

SASKATCHEWAN

ATHABASKA AIRWAYS LIMITED

This company operates from Prince Albert with main bases at Buffalo Narrows, Lac-la-Ronge, and Isle à la Crosse. Since 1955 it has operated helicopters and fixed wing aircraft on charters throughout Saskatchewan. The 1988 fleet includes Twin Otters, Otters, Beavers and turbo Beavers plus several Cessnas. Five Sikorsky 55BTs and four Jet Ranger IIs are also in operation.

LA RONGE AVIATION SERVICE LTD

Since 1960, La Ronge Aviation has been providing charter service from La Ronge, Saskatchewan and Lynn Lake, Manitoba to northern Saskatchewan, northern Manitoba and the Arctic. The company operates a large fleet of Twin Otters (five at present), Beavers, Otters, Cessna 185s and two Beech Barons.

Former Airlines of Saskatchewan

HIGHLINE AIRWAYS INC.

The company was formed in 1978 by several Saskatchewan resource companies to provide charter work to their northern bases. The initial fleet consisted of three Beech King Airs and a Convair 640 (C-GMUM). The Convair 640 was flown for two years, then sold and replaced by two Convair 640s in 1982. The company also leased a Convair 580 from a US operator which was flown under US registration with Highline titles on the Saskatoon – Edmonton route following the company's merger with *Norcanair* in November 1984 .

Highline Airways' Convairs were finally repainted with *Norcanair* titles and, in 1987, following the takeover by *Time Air,* the Convair 640s became a part of the larger *Time Air* fleet of Convair 580s and 640s.

NORCANAIR – NORTH CANADA AIR LTD.

Formed in 1947 by the Saskatchewan Government as Saskair, the name of this Prince Albert based company was changed in 1955 to Norcanair. The company's main scheduled service was Prince Albert to Saskatoon and Regina. It also served La Ronge, Cluff Lake, Sony Rapids, Uranium City and Willaston Lake using DC-3s, F-27s and leased YS-11 aircraft. In 1984, the company

merged with High-Line Airways Inc. of Saskatoon but the Norcanair titles remained.

In the summer of 1984, a Bandeirante aircraft was put into service when the North Battleford to Lloydminster and Edmonton route was opened. During the winter of 1984, ski charters to Cran-brook were operated from Saskatoon, Lloydminster and North Battleford using *Highline*'s Convair 640s.

May 1985 saw the startup of service between Saskatoon, Regina and Minneapolis using F-27s and Convair 640s. Norcanair entered the jet era in January 1986 with the purchase of two F-28 jets which were used on the services to Minneapolis and Edmonton.

In 1986, *Canadian Pacific Airlines* acquired a 25% equity in the company and Norcanair adopted the green CPA partner colour scheme. That fall, Saskatoon and Regina to Calgary were commenced using the F-28s and linking into the full *Canadian Pacific* network at Calgary. Canadian Pacific flight designators were used.

On 16 March, 1987, *Time Air* of Lethbridge took over 100% ownership of Norcanair and on 26 April 1987, with CTC approval, *Time Air* officially took over operation of all Norcanair flights.

AIRCRAFT LISTING
SASKATCHEWAN

REG'N	C/N	IS	WFU	NOTES
ATHABASKA AIRWAYS				
DHC-6 Twin Otter				
C-FCHE	162	73	87	
C-FSCA	17	78	C	EX Shell Oil
C-FWGE	58	68	87	W/O 13/06/87 Maudsley Lake
LA RONGE AVIATION				
DHC-6 Twin Otter				
C-FCCE	8	78	C	EX McKenzie
C-FVOG	35	68	C	EX Wardair

AIRCRAFT LISTING
SASKATCHEWAN

REG'N	C/N	IS	WFU	NOTES
HIGHLINE				
Convair 640				
C-GQCQ	451	82	87	ST C-GQCQ Time Air
C-GQCY	460	82	87	ST C-GQCY Time Air
C-GMUM	203	81	82	ST N865TA Atlas Aircraft
NORCANAIR				
F-27				
C-FGVL*	51	73	81	ST SE-IGZ Swedair
C-FGZJ*	53	73	87	EX N2775R Hughes Air West
C-FTPA	104	77	85	EX Trans Provincial/Time Air
C-GCRA	52	74	87	EX N2774R Hughes Air West
C-GEGH	48	75	82	ST N274PH Horizon Air
YS-11				
N273P	2122	82	82	LF N273P Piedmont Airline
DHC-6 Twin Otter				
CF-AIV	215	74	74	ST Air West
C-GQOQ	155	79	83	ST Nipawin Air Service
Bristol Freighter				
CF-WAE	13219	70	78	On display Western Aviation Museum
DC-3				
CF-KBU	4683	57	78	ST Aero Trades
C-FCTA	32843	72	85	WFU; EX 10196 RCAF
EMB-110P1				
C-GPDI	110207	84	87	ST C-GPDI Time Air

Selkirk Air Short Skyvan, CF-YQY

MANITOBA

NORTHLAND AIR MANITOBA
ILFORD RIVERTON AIRWAYS LTD.

The company has its main base at the Winnipeg International Airport and operates charter and passenger service to Manitoba and the Arctic. A large fleet of DC-3s and, in the late 1980s, Curtiss C-46s are the backbone of the fleet. A Canso was used for flying fishermen into northern Manitoba lakes during the 1970s and 1980s.

Ilford Riverton tried to change its name to Air Manitoba in 1987 but the provincial government would not permit it and the name Northland Air Manitoba was chosen instead. When the airline acquired HS-748 aircraft in 1987, the title 'NORTH-LAND' was painted in small letters but the rejected title 'AIR MANITOBA' was displayed in large letters on these aircraft.

Former Airlines of Manitoba

AERO TRADES WESTERN LIMITED

Aero Trades Western was a large passenger and cargo charter operator out of the Winnipeg International Airport until it folded in 1984. The company operated a large fleet of DC-3s, most of them former *Canadian Forces* C-47 Dakotas. A Convair 640 was acquired from PWA in May 1978 for both passenger and cargo charter operations and was sold to *Worldways* in 1984. Two DC-4s were acquired for cargo operations, one being the former *Eldorado* C-FGNI. A Saunders ST-27 was acquired by the company just before it ceased operations.

LAMBAIR

Thomas Lamb started an air service in 1938 to support his fishing and lumber industries. The name Lambair was adopted in 1969 when the company operated charters and scheduled routes to The Pas, Thompson, Churchill and Rankin Inlet. Lambair's large fleet included DC-3s, Twin Otters, an F-27, a C-46, and a Bristol Freighter.

After Thomas Lamb's death, his sons tried to keep the company operating but in February 1981, Lambair ceased all operations.

ONTARIO CENTRAL AIRLINES LIMITED

Formed in 1947, this airline's headquarters was at Gimli, with bases at Red Lake, Ball Lake and Kenora, all in Ontario. It operated a large fleet of DC-3s, Beavers and Otters and at one time flew a former *Quebecair* Curtiss C-46. The company was purchased by *Austin Airways* in 1979.

SAUNDERS AIRCRAFT COMPANY

Saunders Aircraft company moved to the former RCAF Station at Gimli in the early 1970s with plans to produce the ST-27 and the ST-28 aircraft. However, the company was never fully financed and after losing out on further sales to *ACES Col-ombia,* the company was sold to *Otanabee Airways* of Peterborough, Ontario.

SELKIRK AIR SERVICES

In the early 1970s, Selkirk Air Services operated a Short Skyvan from its base in Winnipeg.

AIRCRAFT LISTING
MANITOBA

REG'N	C/N	IS	WFU	NOTES
AIR MANITOBA				
Curtiss C-46				
C-GAVO	33242	88	C	EX N9891Z
C-GIXZ	22495	87	C	EX N7923C (2nd Reg'n)
C-GTPO	22556	86	C	EX N1258N
C-GTXW	30386	87	C	EX N4803J
HS-748				
C-FAGI	1699	88	C	EX C-FAGI Quebecair
C-FTTW	1681	86	C	EX G-AYIR
C-GQTH	1617	86	C	EX C-GQTH Austin Airways

AIRCRAFT LISTING
MANITOBA

REG'N	C/N	IS	WFU	NOTES
ILFORD-RIVERTON				
DC-3				
C-FCQT	9813	75	C	NN Air Manitoba
C-GSCC	33352	82	C	EX CF 12965
Curtiss C-46				
C-FFNC	22388	82	C	NN Air Manitoba
CF-ZQX	22595	72	73	ST CF-ZQX Nordair
C-GIXZ	22453	81	82	W/O 31/10/82 Shama Hawa
C-GRLQ	22469	82	87	NN Air Manitoba
C-GRXL	22405	84	85	LF N5076N Casair
AERO TRADES WESTERN				
Convair 640				
C-FPWY	108	78	83	ST C-FPWY Worldways
DHC-6 Twin Otter				
CF-MHR	51	74	78	ST C-FMHR Miksoo Aviation
DC-4				
C-FGNI	10389	80	84	ST C-FGNI Soundair
C-FJRW	42983	80	81	W/O 02/12/81 near YHH
C-FQIX	7476	78	79	W/O 01/06/79 Thompson
C-GCXG	10644	79	84	ST C-GCXG Soundair
DC-3				
C-FKBU	4683	76	78	ST C-FKBU Slate Fall A/W
LAMBAIR				
F-27				
C-GJON	31	74	78	ST N54506 Pacific Alaska
Bristol Freighter				
CF-YDO	12827	69	81	WFU
CF-YDP	13250	69	81	WFU
Curtiss C-46				
C-GYHT	22375	78	79	W/O 13/11/79 Churchill
BN Islander				
CF-XYK	23	68	81	ST C-FXYK Simpson Air
DHC-6 Twin Otter				
C-FAUS	34	69	71	ST C-FAUS Air Inuit
C-FOOL	159	71	81	ST C-GMKA Kimba Air
C-GRDD	54	76	81	ST C-GRDD Nahanni Air
C-GGDZ	201	75	77	ST N851T Fel Air Inc.
DC-3				
CF-BKX	32813	76	80	ST C-FBKX Ontario Central
CF-DBJ	6135	72	82	ST C-FDBJ Perimeter A/L
C-FBFV	7340	74	81	ST C-FBFV Perimeter A/L
C-GWIR	9371	77	78	ST C-GWIR NWT Air
ONTARIO CENTRAL				
DC-3				
C-FBKX	32813	81	83	EX RCAF KN392
C-FGHL	12475	79	86	EX RCAF KG440
C-FYQG	4654	69	80	EX N99U Bolder Corp. WFU
C-GCKE	27203	76	86	ST C-GCKE Perimeter
SELKIRK AIR				
Short Skyvan				
CF-YQY	1862	69	71	ST C-GWCY Calm Air

ONTARIO

AIR DALE LTD.

Based in Sault Ste Marie, the company operates a charter service with Beavers, Cessnas, Beech 18s and formerly DC-3s. It also operates several Twin Otters for *NorOntair* between Sault Ste Marie, Wawa, Hornpayne, Geraldton, Terrace Bay, Thunder Bay, Elliot Lake, Timmins, Sudbury, Chapleau, North Bay, Earlton, and Kirkland Lake. Airdale operates the Dash-8 for *NorOntair* and an air ambulance service on behalf of the Ontario government.

AIR NIAGARA EXPRESS

This airline operates cargo and charter services from the Toronto International Airport and St Catharines. The bulk of the company's fleet consists of seven Citation jets, a Challenger, two Swearingen Merlin/Metros plus a Convair 580. The company was established in 1978.

JETALL

Based at the Toronto International Airport, this cargo operator was formed in 1987. Four Swearingen Merlins, a Cessna 402 and a Convair 580 make up the 1988 fleet.

KENTING EARTH SCIENCE LTD.

Formerly called Atlas Aviation and Kenting Atlas Aviation, the company operated DC-4s CF-KAD and CF-KAE on ice patrols until *Nordair* resumed these services with their Electras. Cansos and DC-3 were used during the early 1980s but the company now operates Piper Navajos, a Cessna 404 Titan and two Belsl 412s. The airline is based in Ottawa.

MILLARDAIR

A large charter operator based at the Toronto International Airport, Millardair operates the largest fleet of DC-3s and DC-4s in Canada. Two former *US Navy* C-117s (a variant of the DC-3) are operated as well as several Beech 18s. The company also operates a Cessna Citation and smaller fixed wing aircraft.

NORONTAIR

This airline was created by the Ontario Government as a subsidiary of *Northland Transportation Commission,* a crown corporation. The airline was established in 1971 to suppy scheduled service to the northern Ontario communities of Sudbury, Timmins, Kirkland Lake, Earlton, Kapuskasing, North Bay, Elliot Lake, Sault Ste Marie, Chapleau, Wawa, Thunder Bay, Pickle Lake, Atikokan, Fort Frances, Kenora and Dryden. The company initially flew only Twin Otters but in 1985 became the first operator of the Dash-8 aircraft. The Twin Otters were originally orange in colour with a large purple and white goose on the side. The company's colours were changed to white, orange, dark blue, light blue with the name On-tario Northland Transportation Commission added to the NorOntair titles. Several private operators have flown the Twin Otters on behalf of NorOntair. The original companies were *Austin Airways, White River Air Service, Bradley Air Service, On Air* and *Air Dale.* The current operators are *Air Dale,* (5 Twin Otters), *Bearskin Air* (3 Twin Otters), and *Austin Airways* (one Twin Otter). The company's headquarters is at North Bay.

Air Dale operated the Dash-8 for NorOntair. In January 1985, the Dash-8 began service on the Sault Ste Marie to Elliot Lake, Sudbury, Timmins and Kapuskasing route. After a year of service, the aircraft landed short of the runway at Sault Ste Marie on February 2, 1986 and was seriously damaged. However, the Dash-8 was repaired and returned to service in 1987.

The original mandate of the airline was to serve remote northern Ontario communities that were not receiving regular air service from other commercial carriers. Therefore, in 1988, the two Dash-8s were to be sold to *Air Ontario* and the Twin Otters were also to be sold. A fleet of smaller aircraft will be acquired and those communities serviced by the regular airlines will be dropped from the schedules while other smaller centres will be added.

PEM AIR

Pem Air operates between Pembroke and Toronto International Airport. Service began in 1970 with a Beech 18 aircraft. Two former *Great Lakes* DC-3s were used for much of the 1970s and a Beech 99 in the early 1980s. The airline now uses Piper Chieftains and Aztecs.

SKYCRAFT AIR TRANSPORT INC.

Based at the Oshawa Airport, the company was formed in 1972 to provide cargo and charter services to the car industry. The original fleet included several Cessnas and DC-3s. In January 1985, the company began scheduled service between Montreal, Ottawa, Oshawa and Windsor using two Embraer Bandeirante aircraft. By mid-1985, the airline offered flights twice daily Oshawa – Montreal and Oshawa – Ottawa with *CP Air* handling the aircraft at Ottawa and Montreal. Daily Oshawa – Windsor flights were also operated.

In April 1986, flights between Oshawa and Detroit City airport began. Skycraft switched affiliations in mid-1986, moving from *CP Air* to *Air Canada.* In June 1987, a former *Time Air* SD3-30 was purchased for use on the passenger runs and flights from Oshawa to both Windsor and Detroit City airport were operated. An SD-360 was added in the summer of 1988 for use on the Oshawa to Windsor route.

ONTARIO

VOYAGEUR AIRWAYS LTD.
Based at North Bay, this company was initially granted permission to fly between Toronto Island Airport and North Bay/Sudbury in 1984. However, because of problems at Toronto Island Airport, the flights were permitted to begin from the Toronto International Airport during July 1984 and have operated from there ever since. ST-27s were the main aircraft used with Beech King Airs also in operation. Flights between Toronto and Windsor were begun and stopped in 1984.

In January, 1985, the Toronto to Sudbury route was extended to Marathon and Manitouwadge. Later the same year, the company signed a cooperative scheduling agreement with *NorOntair* to connect Voyageur's passengers on the Ottawa – Sudbury route with the *Nor-Ontair* flights to Timmins and Kapuskasing.

Extensive expansion took place during 1986. In April direct Ottawa to Sudbury flights (not via North Bay) were begun using a Beech 100 and in July the Ottawa – Rouyn and Val d'Or route was initiated. A route linking Marathon to Sudbury, North Bay and Montreal was started in December.

The company took over the *City Express* Toronto – Peterborough and Peterborough – Ottawa and Montreal routes in 1987. Beech King Airs and Super King Airs form the bulk of the fleet, with PA31 Cheyennes and three ST-27s also in use.

Former Airlines of Ontario

GREAT LAKE PAPER COMPANY
This company operated an executive Convair 580 from 1960 to 1963. The aircraft returned to Canada several years later with *Energy Mines and Resources* as C-GRSC.

INTER CITY
Inter City began flying between Oshawa and Windsor in March 1986, using two HS748 aircraft. Oshawa – Montreal and Oshawa – Ottawa routes began in June 1986 but the service to Ottawa was dropped in September 1987. The company planned to become a *Canadian* Partner in 1987 but before the aircraft could be painted in partner colours, the company was dropped from the *Canadian* computer reservation system. On October 3, 1987, the company ceased all operations. There were discussions about Inter City operating a commuter service for *Wardair* in Ontario and British Columbia using HS748s but this never came about and the aircraft were sold.

LAURENTIAN AIR SERVICE
Based at Ottawa, this company operated a large charter fleet of DC-3s, Twin Otters, Otters, Beavers and Grumman Goose aircraft. The company is now called Air Schefferville and is based in Schefferville, Quebec.

MID AIR
A little known company based at London, Ontario, Mid Air operated a single DC-7 aircraft in *Delta Airlines* colour scheme on aerial sprays during 1972-73 but the aircraft spent most of the time sitting at the airport.

ON AIR (1979) LIMITED
Based at Thunder Bay, this company provided service to Atikokan, Fort Francis, Dryden, Kenora, Red Lake and Pickle Lake. For a period of time, it operated ST-27, C-GCAT between Thunder Bay, Red Lake, Kenora and Winnipeg but the ST-27 has been in open storage at Toronto International Airport for several years. On Air also operated Twin Otters for *NorOntair*.

SURVAIR
Survair took over the *Nordair Arctic* services out of Frobisher Bay before selling out to *Bradley Air Service*. Twin Otters and DC-3s were the main aircraft in the company fleet.

TORONTAIR
Owned by *Toronto Airways* and originally based at the Toronto-Buttonville Airport, this company flew charter and scheduled services throughout southern Ontario. Using Beech 99 and later a Twin Otter, the company began flying Toronto International Airport to Trenton/Ottawa and Trenton/Kingston in October 1984. By April 1985, the Toronto to Kingston route was flown five times daily and Toronto to CFB Trenton, Brockville and Ottawa was flown daily. A Beech 90 was acquired in December 1985 and used when passenger traffic was light.

Torontair planned a new operation with *Nordair* and leased a *Nordair* FH-227 prior to the startup. The company also moved its operations from Buttonville airport to the Field Aviation site at Toronto International in February 1986 and moved from Terminal 2 to Terminal 1 at Toronto in May 1986. The arrangement with *Nordair* fell through, however, and the company ceased operations in June 1986, with *Austin Airways* taking over the Toronto to Kingston routes. The FH-227 was returned to *Nordair*.

AIRCRAFT LISTING
ONTARIO

REG'N	C/N	IS	WFU	NOTES	TITLE
AIR DALE					
DC-3					
C-FLED	43375	82	C	EX ESN C117 Bu 17182	
C-FOOW	13342	76	C	LT 8P-OOW Tropical 79-80	
C-FWGO	4932	75	C	EX Millardair	
AIR NIAGARA					
Convair 580					
C-FARO	382	88	C	EX C-FARO Kelowna Flight.	
C-GKFZ	079	88	89	ST C-GKFZ Tempus Air	ELGIN
JETALL					
SA226AT					
C-FJTA	AT492	87	C	EX N30HE	
C-FJTC	AT009	87	C		
SA226TC					
C-FJTD	TC377	87	C	EX N5052H Tempus Air	
Convair 580					
C-GKFR	454	88	C	EX C-GKFR Quebecair	
KENTING AVIATION					
DC-4					
CF-KAD	18356	66	75	ST C-FKAD Worldways	
CF-KAE	36029	66	74	ST 9Q-COF SOMA	
DHC-6 Twin Otter					
CF-KAS	339	72	78	ST N983FL Frontier A/L	
DC-3					
C-GOZA	26111	75	77	ST C-GOZA Kenn Borek	
PBY Canso					
C-FJJG	48423	75	86	ST N423RS	
MILLARDAIR					
DC-3					
C-FDTV	12192	75	C	EX DOT	THE CARGOLINER
C-FITQ*	9108	72	80	ST 6Y-IT	EXECUTIVE II
C-FWBN*	25888	69	79	ST Worldways	EXECUTIVE III
C-FWCO*	43082	67	79	ST N37490	THE COURIER
C-FWGN*	33368	67	C	EX 1000 RCAF	CARGOLINER
C-FWTU*	25802	73	78	ST N3146Z	THE EXECUTIVE
C-FWTV*	12300	68	C	EX RCAF	MERCHANTMAN
CF-WIC	11625	70	73	ST C-FWIC	THE TRAVELLER
CF-WGM	10168	72	73	ST CF-WGM	THE PRESIDENT
CF-WGN	33368	67	C	EX KN665 RCAF	
CF-WGO	4932	67	68	ST C-FWGO	
C-GGCS	32529	75	83	ST C-GGCS B. Andrews	
C-GNOA	19627	78	85	EX USAF #3-15160	
DC-3 - C117					
C-GDIK	43369	83	C	EX US Navy C117	
C-GDOG	43374	85	C	EX US Navy C117	
C-GGKE	43366	83	C	EX US Navy C117	
C-GGKG	43354	83	C	EX US Navy C117	
C-GJGN	43312	87	C	EX US Navy C117	
DC-4					
C-GDWZ	10636	82	C	Stored Tucson until 1987	
C-GFFQ	27298	82	C	Stored Tucson until 1987	
C-GFMQ	27265	82	C	Stored Tucson	
C-GQIA	10464	77	87	WFU Tucson	CARGOLINER I
C-GQIB	27370	77	C	EX US Navy	
C-GQIC	27302	77	86	EX USAF - WFU	
C-GRYZ	10811	79	NTU	EX Royal Danish A.F.; WFU	
C-GRYY	22192	79	NTU	EX Royal Danish A.F.; WFU	

AIRCRAFT LISTING
ONTARIO

REG'N	C/N	IS	WFU	NOTES	TITLE
MILLARDAIR (Continued)					
Citation 500					
C-GOCM	0154	74	C		
Hansa Jet					
CF-WDU	1039	73	73	RT Manufacturer	
Beech 18					
C-FSIJ	35552	65	C		
NORONTAIR					
DASH-8					
C-GJCB	6	84	88	ST Air Ont.	JIM C. BELL
C-GPYD	12	85	88	ACC 02/02/86	PY DAVOUD
DHC-6 Twin Otter					
C-FGON*	369	73	85	ST Lab Air/OB Air Dale	
C-FTVO*	334	71	87	ST C-FTVO OPP/OB Air Dale	
C-FTVP*	335	71	77	W/O 31/12/77 Kenora, Ont.	
C-GGUX	462	75	C	OB Bearskin A/S	
C-GHRB	673	80	C	OB Air Dale	
C-GNHB	441	74	87	OB Bearskin A/S	
C-GNQY	450	75	87	OB Air Dale	
C-GOVG	592	78	C	OB Austin Airlines	
C-GQKZ	532	77	C	OB Bearskin A/S	
C-GRBY	741	81	C	OB Air Dale	
PEM AIR					
DC-3					
C-FGLA*	2140	72	78	EX Great Lakes Airlilnes	
C-FGLB*	1547	71	79	EX Great Lakes Airlines	
C-FTKX	10202	76	79	ST N211Q S.S. Airways 1981	
Beech 99					
C-GPEM	U-98	78	82	ST C-GPEM Bearskin Lake AS	
Beech A100					
C-GJVK	B-127	86	C	EX N128F	
QUESTOR					
Shorts Skyvan					
C-FQSL	1883	70	C		
C-GDRG	1847	80	C		
B.N. Islander					
C-GSZI	360	74	87	EX JS-JJC	
SKYCRAFT					
SD3-30					
C-GSKW	3007	87	C	EX C-GTAV Time Air	
SD-360					
C-G	88		C		
Banderiante					
C-GHOV	377	85	C	EX G-RVIP Genair	
C-GHOY	277	85	C	EX G-BHYT Genair	
DC-3					
C-GSCA	27190	76	81	ST C-GSCA Soundair EX	
C-GSCB	33441	77	C	EX C-GSCB Wildwood A/L	
C-GSCC	33352	79	85	ST C-GSCC Ilford Riverton	
C-GUBT	12424	85	83	W/O 22/06/83 \EX 1000 RCAF	
C-GYBA	20215	85	C	ST C-GYBA Soundair	
Cessna Citation					
C-GMAT	0231		C		

AIRCRAFT LISTING
ONTARIO

REG'N	C/N	IS	WFU	NOTES
VOYAGEUR AIRWAYS				
Saunders ST-27				
C-FCNX	008	83	C	EX Air Atonabee
C-FLOL	006	86	C	EX Labrador Airways
C-GCML	009	83	C	EX Northward
Beech A100				
C-GILM	B-124	86	C	
GREAT LAKES PAPER CO.				
Convair 580				
CF-BGY	72	70	73	Now C-GRSC Dept. E.M.R.
INTER CITY				
HS-748				
C-GEGJ	1711	86	86	ST C-GEFJ Air Inuit
C-GLTC	1656	86	86	
LAURENTIAN A/S				
DC-3				
C-FIAR	20877	75	78	ST C-FIAR Slate Falls A/S
C-FPOX*	20875	72	75	ACC 03/05/75 Schefferville
AIR SCHEFFERVILLE				
DHC-6 Twin Otter				
C-GPJQ	505	81	83	ST J6-SLH Winlink
MID AIR				
DC-7				
CF-GEQ	45352	72	73	WFU EX N4888C Delta
SURVAIR				
DHC-6 Twin Otter				
C-FYPP	223	72	76	ST C-FYPP Air Inuit
C-FPAE	228	75	77	ST C-FPAE West Coast Air
C-FNAN	242	76	78	ST C-FNAN Bradley A/S
DC-3				
CF-FBS	6070	67	77	ST C-FFBS Northway Survey
TORONTAIR				
Beech 99				
C-GDFX	U-123	80	86	ST C-GDFX Austin Airways
C-GEOI	U-152	81	86	ST C-GEOI Austin Airways
C-GFKB	U--55	81	86	ST C-GFKB Austin Airways
DHC-6 Twin Otter				
C-FQSC	174	82	85	ST N9762E Jack Wall Sales
F-227				
C-GNDI	564	86	86	LF C-GNDI Nordair

QUEBEC

AIR CREEBEC

Air Creebec is a Native Airline begun with the assistance of *Austin Airways* in 1982. The airline links the Quebec communities of Val d'Or, Matagami, Rupert House, Eastmain, Paint Hills, Fort George and Great Whale Lake. Air Creebec underwent a major expansion late in 1988 when it purchased many former *Austin Airways* routes and aircraft from *Air Ontario*. Seven HS748s and most of the routes to the smaller communities in Northern Ontario were obtained.

AIR INUIT

Air Inuit is based at Fort Chimo and operates a large fleet of Twin Otters and two HS748. The aircraft are blue in colour with a broad, bright yellow cheat line. The company operates scheduled service from Fort Chimo (Kuujjuaq) to the villages of Port Nouveau, Leaf Bay, Payne Bay, Koartak, Sugluk, Wakeban Bay, Nain Labrador and Aupaluk. Air Inuit scheduled services interline with *Canadian Airlines* Boeing 737 flights from the south. *Chaperal Charters Ltd.* of Montreal merged its fleet of Twin Otters and DC-3s with Air Inuit in 1984.

CANADAIR

Many of Canadair's aircraft, such as its initial Convair 540s, have appeared in civilian registration representing the company on sales tours. For many years, Canadair operated an all white Convair 240 as a corporate aircraft.

CONIFAIR AVIATION

The company formed in 1979 to perform aerial spraying and operates from St. Jean, just outside of Montreal. At one time, the airline operated two Lockheed 749A Constellations, four DC-4s and three DC-6s but the L749s have been removed from service and some of the DC-6s have been sold. The company has operated a Mont Joli – Port Menier (Anticosti Island) route for wildlife hunters every fall, using DC-4s. The fleet is based at the Quebec City airport and uses a hangar beside the *Quebec Government Air Fleet* hangar built in 1988.

PROPAIR

Based at Rouyn, this is the name used following the merger of *La Sarre Air Service* and *Air Fecteau*. A large fleet of Cessna Skywagons, Beavers (13), Otters (13), and Caribou (2) aircraft was operated under the name Propair in 1986. Charter services were flown from bases at La Sarre, Rouyn, Senneterre, Chibougamau and Matagami. Propair, then 50% owned by *Quebecair,* purchased *Quebec Aviation Ltee* in December 1985 and merged the two operations. The new operation flew Montreal – Chibougamau, Bagotville – Chibougamau and Ottawa, Rouyn/ Noranda – Montreal and Val d'Or, and Quebec City – Sherbrooke and Montreal. The Quebec City – Murray Bay route was subcontracted to *Les Ailes de Charloevoix*. In June 1986, Propair became *Quebecair Inter* and adopted QB flight designators. The Propair name is retained by a small company which operates charter flights with Cessna 185 Skywagons from Rouyn.

QUEBEC NORTH SHORE & LABRADOR RAILWAYS QUEBEC CARTIER MINING

These two companies each operate an F-27 aircraft within the Province of Quebec.

TRANSFAIR INC.

Called *Transports Aeriens Sept-Iles Inc.* in 1971, the company adopted the name Transfair Inc. in 1985, and currently operates a fleet of DC-3s and a single DC-4 on passenger and cargo charters out of Sept-Iles.

UNITED TECHNOLOGIES PRATT & WHITNEY AIRCRAFT OF CANADA LTD.

The manufacturer of the PT series of turboprop engines, the company is based at Longueuil, Quebec. Its engines power the deHavilland Buffalo, Twin Otter, Dash-7 and Dash-8 as well as many other aircraft such as the Embraer EMB-110 Bandeirante. The company has operated several large aircraft to test its engines, including a five-engine Viscount, and currently operate the only Boeing 720 ever registered in Canada. The Boeing 720 flew for the first time in May 1988, after extensive modifications.

Former Airlines of Quebec

AIR CARAVANE
AIR CARDINAL

This Montreal based operator flew a fleet of DC-3s and two former *Air Canada* Viscounts in the 1970s and early 1980s.

AIR GASPÉ

Formed in 1952 as *Trans-Gaspian Airlines,* the company operated a HS-748 and Beech 99 in the Gaspé and Quebec North Shore areas of Quebec until merged with *Regionair* in 1982.

CANAIRELIEF

The company was formed in Quebec by a church group in 1968 to operate a food lift into war torn Biafra. Four Super Constellations were obtained from *Nordair* and a

QUEBEC

fifth purchased in the United States. The aircraft flew from the Portuguese island of Sao Tome to Uli, Biafra. Air and ground crews from *Nordair* ran the operation, which carried up to sixteen tons each trip. Three trips were made by each plane every night possible. All of the flights had to be made at night to avoid being shot down. One plane was destroyed in the air and another was destroyed on the ground in Uli. When the operation was ended on January 17, 1970, over 10,000 tons of food and supplies had been delivered by the airlift.

CANHELLLANAS
When the RCAF phased out the Yukon aircraft, the company acquired one plane, planning to fly it from Dorval in Montreal. However, the company operated only briefly before the Yukon (CL-44) was sold.

CURTISS REID FLYING SERVICE
Dorval based Curtiss Reid flew charters to Europe from Montreal between 1950 and 1953 using two DC-4s. One DC-4, carrying the name "Canadian Pilgrim" crashed in the Alps in November 1950.

DORVAL AIR TRANSPORT
Operating from Dorval with a fleet of five Curtiss C-46s, this airline provided contract and charter operations into northern Quebec during the DEW Line constructioin work in the 1950s.

EASTERN CANADA STEVEDORING
This company operated a fleet of large aircraft in Eastern Canada between 1957 and 1965. A Convair 440 and DC-4 were among the aircraft used in support of the Dew Line Construction.

QUEBEC AVIATION LTÉE
Based at the Quebec City Airport, Quebec Aviation Ltée was known as *Air Brazeau* until 1978. The airline operated scheduled passenger service between Quebec City, Hull, Boston, Bagotville and Chibougamau, as well as Edmunston and Fredericton in New Brunswick. The company operated Beech 99, Piper Navajos and a Metro II aircraft. In December 1985, *Propair* bought out Quebec Aviation and merged the two companies, standardizing izingizingizingizingizingizingit its fleet on Fairchild Metro aircraft.

WABUSH RAILWAY
KRUGER PULP AND PAPER
Both of these companies operated large aircraft in the province of Quebec: Wabush flew former *Air Canada* Viscounts and a DC-3; Kruger operated using an F-227.

WHEELER AIRLINES LTD.
The history of this airline dates back to 1921. At the height of the DEW Line construction in the mid-1950s, it operated a large fleet of Curtiss C-46s and DC-4s. The heavy section of the company was sold to *Nordair* in April 1960 and the smaller aircraft component continued in operation for several more years.

WORLD WIDE AIRWAYS INC
MONTREAL AIR SERVICE
World Wide Airways was formed in 1945. The company obtained several DEW Line contracts in the 1950s and bought many larger aircraft to meet the requirements of these contracts. One unusual aircraft was a Lancaster which was used to carry fuel. This plane crashed on landing at a DEW Line site in July 1953, with the crew just able to escape.

The fleet of DC-3 and Curtiss C-46s were mixed with those registered to *Montreal Air Service*. World Wide Airways also controlled *Canadian Aircraft Renters* to whom several of the DC-4s and DC-3s were registered. When *Trans-Canada Airlines* disposed of their fleet of North Stars, World Wide Airways purchased and flew two of them for just under eleven months. During the mid-1960s, the company also acquired Super Constellations for charter work .

Great Lakes Convair 580, C-GDTC

Canhellas Yukon, CF-CHC

AIRCRAFT LISTING
QUEBEC

REG'N	C/N	F/N	IS	WFU	NOTES
AIR CREEBEC					
HS-748					
C-GQSV	1618		87	C	EX C-GQSV Austin A/W
C-GQTG	1619		87	C	EX C-GQTG Austin A/W
DHC-6					
C-FZKP	290		82	C	EX C-FZKP Austin/Air Inuit
AIR INUIT					
HS-748					
C-GCUK	1762		85	C	EX V2-LAZ LIAT
C-GEFJ	1711		87	C	EX C-GEGJ Inter City
C-GOUT	1621		84	C	EX C-GOUT Austin Airways
DHC-6 Twin Otter					
C-GGAA	477		84	C	EX C-GGAA Austin Airways
C-GBOX	672		84	87	LF C-GBOX Austin Airways
C-GMDC	763		81	C	
DC-3					
C-FIRW	9834		80	82	ST C-FIRW Tpt Aer. Sept Il
C-FTAS	4666		85	87	WFU
DHC-4 Caribou					
C-GVYX	292		79	81	ST C-GVYX Max Ward
Grumman G-1					
C-GMJS	81		81	86	LT C-GMJS City Express
CANADAIR					
Convair 240					
CF-UOJ	160		67	C	
CONIFAIR					
L-749A					
C-GXKO	2601	01	79	85	ST N494TW Star
C-GXKR	2604	02	79	85	WFU
DC-6					
C-GBYA	43717	07	83	C	
C-GBYS	44658	08	83	C	
C-GBZC	45458	09	83	87	EX C-FCZZ NWT Air
DC-4 C54					
C-GBNV	35988	18	81	C	EX N3303F
C-GBPA	10673	16	81	84	ST N87591
C-GBSK	36049	15	82	C	
C-GDCH	10614		85	C	EX N21VC
C-GXKN	36090	17	81	C	EX N4958P
PROPAIR					
DHC-4A Caribou					
C-GVGW	107		79	85	EX Kuwait A/F
C-GVGX	23		77	86	EX 805 Sultan of Oman
QUEBEC CARTIER MINING					
F-27					
C-GQCM	110		74	C	
QUEBEC NORTH SHORE					
F-27					
CF-QYP	95		72	79	W/O 10/12/79 Sept Iles
TRANSFAIR					
DC-4 C54					
C-GCTF	27281		82	C	

AIRCRAFT LISTING
QUEBEC

REG'N	C/N	IS	WFU	NOTES
TRANSFAIR (Continued)				
DC-3				
C-FBZN	25290	82	C	EX KG746 RCAF
C-FDTT	25615	78	C	EX Dept of Transport
C-FPOY	10028	78	C	
CONVAIR 240				
C-GTFC	279	79	C	EX USAF T29
UNITED AIRCRAFT				
Viscount				
C-FTID	384	75	85	WFU; 5 engine test-bed a/c
720				
C-FETB	18024	88	C	Pratt & Whitney; EX OD-AFQ; engine test bed
AIR CARDINAL				
Viscount				
CF-TGZ	144	79	80	WFU Montreal
CF-THZ	308	79	80	WFU Montreal
AIR CARAVANE				
DC-3				
CF-TAS	4666	74	80	ST Chaperal Charters
CF-WIC	11625	77	81	ST N115NA North American
CANAIRELIEF				
L-1049G				
CF-AEN	4821	68	72	WFU at St. Hubert, PQ
CF-NAJ	4828	68	69	W/O 03/08/69 Uli, Biafra
CF-NAK	4829	68	69	W/O 17/12/69 Uli, Biafra
CF-NAL	4831	68	72	WFU
CF-NAM	4832	68	72	WFU
CANHELLANAS				
CL-44 (Yukon)				
CF-CHC	3	71	73	EX RCAF 15923/ CF 106923
CURTISS REID F/S				
DC-4				
CF-EDM	3110	50	53	ST EC-APQ Iberia
CF-EDN	10518	50	50	W/O 13/11/50 in the Alps
DORVAL AIR TRANSPORT				
Curtiss C-46F				
CF-HEI	22419	59	61	ST CF-HEI Wheeler A/L
CF-IHU	22476	56	62	ST CF-IHU Nordair
CF-IHV	22551	56	59	ST CF-IHV Wheeler A/L
Curtiss C-46F				
CF-JIK	22519	57	60	ST N420TT Tanis Co. Inc.
Curtiss C-46E				
CF-FBJ	2941	52	58	ST CF-FBJ East. Cdn Stev.
EASTERN CANADA STEVEDORING CO.				
Convair 440				
CF-ECS	135	62	66	ST N7600 Union Oil Corp.
DC-4				
CF-JIR	10362	57	58	ST CF-JIR Notre Dame A/T
DC-3				
CF-ILW	4352	56	62	ST CF-ILW EPA

AIRCRAFT LISTING
QUEBEC

REG'N	C/N	IS	WFU	NOTES

EASTERN CANADA STEVEDORING CO. (Continued)

Curtiss C-46E

REG'N	C/N	IS	WFU	NOTES
CF-FBJ	2941	58	60	ST CF-FBJ Wheeler Airlines

KRUGER PULP & PAPER

F-227

REG'N	C/N	IS	WFU	NOTES
C-GGHK	560	72	78	ST EP-AMT Air Service Co.

QUEBEC AVIATION LTEE

Beech 99

REG'N	C/N	IS	WFU	NOTES
C-GPFF	U-12	80	85	ST C-GPFF Propair
C-GQAG	U-74	80	85	ST C-GQAG Propair
C-GQAH	U-58	81	85	ST C-GQAH Propair

WABUSH LAKE RAILWAY

Viscount

REG'N	C/N	IS	WFU	NOTES
CF-THA	218	68	78	WFU; EX TCA
C-FTHQ	227	78	88	ST 9Q-CTU Zaire Aero Service

WHEELER AIRLINE

DC-4

REG'N	C/N	IS	WFU	NOTES
CF-ILI	10360	56	59	W/O 04/11/59 St. Cleophas
CF-IQM	36088	56	60	ST CF-IQM Nordair
CF-JIR	10362	58	60	ST CF-JIR Nordair

WORLD WIDE AIRWAYS

DC-4 C54D

REG'N	C/N	IS	WFU	NOTES
CF-NNN	10826	61	64	ACC 10/03/64 Montreal; Sold

North Star

REG'N	C/N	IS	WFU	NOTES
CF-TFP	140	61	62	WFU
CF-TFR	142	61	61	ST CF-TFR International Leases

L1049G

REG'N	C/N	IS	WFU	NOTES
CF-PXX	4580	65	66	EX VH-EAA Qantas
CF-RNR	4544	65	65	EX CF-TGE, WFU
CF-WWH	4820	65	66	LT CF-WWH Nordair

Lancaster

REG'N	C/N	IS	WFU	NOTES
CF-GBA	----	52	53	W/O 28/06/5;3 Menihek

DC-3

REG'N	C/N	IS	WFU	NOTES
CF-DME	20432	56	57	OB Montreal Air Service
CF-IQK	25944	56	61	ST CF-IQK Mont Laurier
CF-IQR	11876	56	58	ST CF-IQR Cdn A/C Renters
CF-JIZ	26700	56	63	ST CF-JIZ GR Macleod
CF-JNN	20058	57	57	ACC 05/05/57 Fox; ST N4207

Curtiss C-46A

REG'N	C/N	IS	WFU	NOTES
CF-IHQ	448	55	60	W/O 25/03/60 DEW Line 28
CF-IHR	32866	55	56	W/O 23/09/56 DEW Line 28
CF-IQQ	369	56	62	ST N4631S B.D. Agardy
CF-HVJ	30222	55	55	W/O 18/06/55 North PQ

Curtiss C-46D

REG'N	C/N	IS	WFU	NOTES
CF-IQJ	33595	56	65	ST CF-IQJ Associated Aviation

Curtiss C-46F

REG'N	C/N	IS	WFU	NOTES
CF-IQX	22369	56	56	ACC 25/03/56; Fixed CF-HVJ
CF-JIL	32699	56	59	OB Montreal Air Service
CF-MKV	22369	60	65	ST N323V Atlantic A/C

ATLANTIC PROVINCES

LABRADOR AIRWAYS LTD. – LAB AIR

Eastern Provincial Airways sold its bush operations in 1969 to a group of its employees. The company was based in Goose Bay and began with two Twin Otters, Beavers, Otters and smaller aircraft. Charter and schedules services were flown from bases at Goose Bay, Deer Lake and St. Anthony. Two ST-27 aircraft were leased in 1985.

Labrador Airways is a major owner of *Air Nova* and feeds that airline in Newfoundland.

NEWFOUNDLAND LABRADOR AIR TRANSPORT LTD.

Based at Corner Brook, Newfoundland, the company was formed in 1961 to fly charter services. A fleet of small aircraft is operated, the largest being a Beech 99.

Former Airlines in the Atlantic Provinces

AIR BRAS d'OR

On September 22, 1986, the company began operations using two Twin Otters to provide scheduled service in the Atlantic provinces. The company was affiliated with *Air Dale* and flew Sydney to Digby, Port Hawkesbury, Halifax, Fredericton, St. Leonard, Charlo and Charlottetown. Port Hawkesbury was dropped in February 1987. The company did not last for even a year and all services were suspended and the company disbanded on 17 July 1987.

DOWNAIR

In 1972, a former USAF Super Constellation was flown out of St. John's, Newfoundland, carrying fresh fish to the eastern United States and returning with fresh vegetables. The company purchased a second Constellation but went bankrupt before it was registered in Canada and the company went out of existence in 1975.

GOOSE BAY AIR SERVICE

In 1983, the Labrador division of Newfoundland *Labrador Air Transport Ltd.* was transferred to Goose Bay Air Service, based at Goose Bay. The fleet included four Otters, two Beavers, one turbo Beaver, a BN Islander and some smaller aircraft which operated charters in Labrador. The company was taken over by *Labrador Airways* in 1987.

AIRCRAFT LISTING

ATLANTIC PROVINCES

REG'N	C/N	IS	WFU	NOTES

LABRADOR AIRWAYS

DHC-6 Twin Otter

REG'N	C/N	IS	WFU	NOTES
C-FGON	369	85	C	EX C-FGON Norontair
C-GDQY	77	78	C	

Saunders ST-27

REG'N	C/N	IS	WFU	NOTES
C-FCNT	007	84	84	W/O 25/08/84 at YYT

NEWFOUNDLAND LABRADOR

Beech 99

REG'N	C/N	IS	WFU	NOTES
C-GJKO	U-128	87	C	

AIR BRAS D'OR

DHC-6 Twin Otter

REG'N	C/N	IS	WFU	NOTES
C-GDMP	489	87	87	ST N707PV; EX C-GDMP Dome
C-GJAT	400	87	87	ST N708PV Princeville 3/88

DOWNAIR

L-1049H

REG'N	C/N	IS	WFU	NOTES
CF-BFN	4825	73	75	WFU & BU Stephenville

NORTHWEST TERRITORIES

AKLAK AIR LTD.
This Inuvik based company has been in operation since 1977. A fleet of Twin Otters, Beech 99s, Piper Navajo Chieftains and Cessna Skywagons is used to operate charters from this base. The company is associated with the Inuvialuit Development Corporation.

BUFFALO AIRWAYS LTD.
Based in Fort Smith, Buffalo Airways operates fixed wing and helicopter services from Fort Smith and Fort Simpson. Its fleet of DC-3s include three former *Canadian Forces* Dakotas. The aircraft are white with a green cheat line and display a Buffalo on the tail. The title 'BUFFALO' appears in black on the upper fuselage.

CARTER AIR SERVICES LTD.
This company operates an Otter and Twin Otter from its base at Hay River.

NAHANNI AIR SERVICES LTD.
From its base at Norman Wells, Nahhanni provides charter services in the western Arctic using Twin Otters, DC-3s, Otters, Islanders and other small aircraft.

PTARMIGAN AIRWAYS LTD.
Based at Yellowknife, the company took over the *Wardair* scheduled services from Yellowknife to Snowdrift, Fort Resolution and Hay River when *Wardair*'s northern operations were discontinued. A fleet of Twin Otters, turbo Beavers and Piper aircraft is operated in bright yellow colour scheme with black titles.

RIGEL AIRWAYS LTD.
A division of *Panarctic Oils,* Rigel operates Twin Otters from its bases at Resolute Bay and Roe Point on behalf of the parent company.

SIMPSON AIR (1981) LTD.
From its major base at Fort Simpson, a Twin Otter and Islander as well as several smaller aircraft are used to provide charter services in the western Arctic.

Large Four Engine Piston Operators

Several large piston-engine aircraft have been operated in the Northwest Territories by Co-ops. From 1971 to 1972, a DC-4 (CF-PBC) was operated by the *Koonuit Co-operative* until the aircraft had an accident at Pelly Bay on November 21, 1972.

The *Pelly Bay Co-operative* flew the former *Nordair* DC-4, C-FIQM, out of Yellowknife from 1975 to 1979. *Aero Trades Western* of Winnipeg operated a DC-4 (C-FQIX) on behalf of *Can Arctic Co-op Federation* from June 1978 to June 1979. This aircraft operated with the title 'CO-OP FEDERATION N.W.T.' plus Inuit script. The DC-4 burned at Thompson, Manitoba, on June 1, 1979. *Go Enterprises* of Yellowknife operated the former *Pelly Bay Co-Op* DC-4 (C-FIQM) and later flew the former *Carnegie* DC-6. The DC-6 had a colourful western scene painted on one side of the aircraft.

AIRCRAFT LISTING
NORTHWEST TERRITORIES

REG'N	C/N	IS	WFU	NOTES
AKLAK AIR				
DHC-6 Twin Otter				
C-FIOJ	261		C	EX C-FIOJ Esso Resources
C-FIOK	273		C	EX C-GIOK Esso/Aramco
C-GDHC	494		C	EX C-GDHC Northnern Thund.
C-GZFP	72		C	EX C-GZFP Nahanni Air Svc.
BUFFALO AIRWAYS				
DC-3				
C-GJKM	13580	80	C	EX CF 12946
C-GPNR	13333	81	C	EX CF 12932
C-GPNW	13028	80	87	EX CF 12927
C-GPOA	12307	80	83	EX CF 12912
CARTER AIR SERVICE				
DHC-6 Twin Otter				
C-FMHR	51	79	C	
NAHANNI AIR SERVICE				
DHC-6 Twin Otter				
C-GRDD	54	81	C	ST C-GRDD La Ronge
C-GZFP	72	85	87	EX PH-DDC Travelair Cargo
RIGEL AIRWAYS LTD.				
DHC-6 Twin Otter				
C-GPAO	447	84	C	EX C-GPAO Pan Arctic
C-GPAZ	729	84	86	ST C-GPAZ Ptarmigan
SIMPSON AIR (1981)				
DHC-6 Twin Otter				
C-GJLZ	220	85	C	
PTARMIGAN AIRWAYS				
DHC-6 Twin Otter				
C-FTFX	340	79	C	EX Wardair
C-FWAB	349	80	C	EX Wardair
C-GARW	367	76	C	
C-GKAZ	3	80	87	
CAN ARCTIC CO-OP FED.				
DC-4				
C-FQIX	7476	78	79	W/O 01/06/79 Thompson
GO ENTERPRISES				
DC-4				
CF-IQM	36088	78	80	EX CF-IQM Pelly Bay Co-op
DC-6				
C-GPEG	43576	80	87	EX C-GPEG Carnegie
KOONUIT CO-OPERATIVE				
DC-4				
CF-PBC	10296	71	72	W/O 21/11/72 Pelly Bay
PELLY BAY CO-OPERATIVE				
DC-4				
C-FIQM	36088	75	78	EX CF-IQM Nordair

YUKON

ALKAN AIR LTD.

Alkan Air Ltd. began in 1977 as a charter operator out of Whitehorse. The company operates a Twin Otter, Beaver and Otter, plus several smaller air-craft, in the Yukon.

B C YUKON AIR SERVICE LTD.

Originally called *Northern British Columbia Air Service,* the present name was adopted in 1953. Based at Watson Lake, Yukon and Dease Lake, B.C., the company operates a small fleet of Otters and Beavers on charter services.

TRANS NORTH AIR
TRANS NORTH TURBO AIR LTD.

A large operator of helicopters as well as fixed wing aircraft, Trans North Air is based at Whitehorse and provides both charter and scheduled service. Twin Otter and DC-3 aircraft were flown originally to provide service from Whitehorse to Watson Lake, Yellowknife, and Dawson Creek. In May 1984, the company began service between Whitehorse and Juneau, Alaska. The company has replaced the Twin Otters and DC-3s with an Embraer Bandeirante and Cessna Titans.

The Bell 206 Jet Ranger is the helicopter preferred by the company with more than ten of these in operation at one time.

AIRCRAFT LISTING
YUKON

REG'N	C/N	IS	WFU	NOTES
ALKAN AIR LTD				
DHC-6 Twin Otter				
C-FKBI	259	81	82	ST C-FKBI Kenn Borek
DHC-3 Otter				
C-FAYR	436	86	C	
TRANS NORTH AIR				
DHC-6 Twin Otter				
C-FWZH	132	73	83	ST N/Baker Aviation

PART 6

Provincial

Government

Operations

BRITISH COLUMBIA

The Department of Highways, Department of Public Works and Department of Lands and Forests all operated aircraft for the BC government in the 1940s and 1950s. The fleet at that time consisting of Ansons, a Grumman Widgeon and a Beaver. In the 1960s, four Beech 18s, an Otter, a Grummand Goose and the famous Lear Jet of Highways Minister Gaglardi were operated. Beech 18, CF-BCF, was modified to a trigear, turboprop aircraft and used throughout the 1970s. The Grumman Goose was also converted to a turbo-prop. In the early 1970s, the BC government modernized the fleet by adding three Cessna Citation jets for air ambulance and executive transport services. Two Citation IIs were added later for executive transport. The Beech 18s were replaced by two Beech 200 aircraft. A Challenger jet joined the fleet in the summer of 1988.

The BC government did not join the CL-215 program preferring to use *Conair* and the *Flying Firemen* for forest fire control.

Two older Cessna Citation 500s were sold late in 1988 and two newer and larger Cessna Citation 550s were purchased.

FLEET LISTINGS
BRITISH COLUMBIA

REG'N	C/N	IS	WFU	NOTES
Challenger 600S				
C-GBCC	1005	88	C	
Citation 500				
C-FBCL*	0042	73	89	ST C-FBCL Voyageur Airways
C-FBCM*	0071	73	88	ST C-FBCM South West Air Lines
C-GBCK	0204	74	C	
Citation 550				
C-GBCA	0590	88	C	
C-GBCB	0051	80	C	
C-GBCD	0591	88	C	
C-GHYD	0063	85	C	
Lear Jet 24A				
CF-BCJ	100	67	68	
Anson V				
CF-EZI	MDF118	46	65	
CF-EZN	12537	46	64	
CF-BCA	MDF305	47	62	W/O 24/05/62 Victoria
Beech 18				
CF-BCB	4335634	61	75	WFU; EX 1404 RCAF
CF-BCC	CA003	62	75	WFU; EX 1428 RCAF
CF-BCD	CA011	63	75	
CF-BCE	CA038	61	75	ST C-FBCE NT Air
Tri/Turbo Beech 18				
CF-BCF	CA176	66	80	
DHC-3 Otter				
CF-BCG	408	65	85	ST Burrard Air
Turbo Goose				
CF-BCI	1203	68	72	ST Air West
Grumman G44				
CF-GPJ	1230	65	70	WFU
DHC-2 Beaver				
C-FFHF*	19	48	87	
Beech 200				
C-FBCN*	BB-7	74	C	
C-FBCO*	BB-8	74	C	

ALBERTA

The Forest Service of the Province of Alberta operated Helio Couriers, a Dornier DO28, a Bell 47 and a DC-3 for many years. In the 1980s the government added executive transport, consisting of three Beech 200 Super King Airs and a Navajo. An executive DASH-8 aircraft and two CL-215s were added in 1986. and two more CL-215s in 1987 under the federal government's scheme to provide aircraft for fighting forest fires and to assist Canadair. Five Bell Jetranger IIIs and a Bell 222 are also used for fire fighting operations by the province.

FLEET LISTINGS
ALBERTA

REG'N	C/N	IS	WFU	NOTES
DC-3				
C-FIAE*	4563	69	86	ST Reynolds Museum
Cessna 337G				
C-FFSC	01793	78	85	Sold
Helio Courier				
CF-IYZ	04F	57	66	ST CF-IYZ Estabrook
CF-AFA	1004	60	76	ST CF-AFA Richard Reid
Dornier DO28B1				
CF-AFB	3063	64	78	Sold
CF-AFC	3069	65	78	ST C-FAFC Ilford River.
Beech 100				
CF-AFD	B-42	72	82	ST CF-AFD Kenn Borek
Bell 206B				
CF-AFH	979	73	80	Sold
Bell 47J				
CF-AFI	2630	66	80	ST C-FAFI Shirley Heli.
CF-AFJ	1421	63	80	ST C-FAFJ Shirley Heli.
CF-AFK	1805	60	80	ST C-FAFK Echo Bay
Bell 47G				
CF-KEY	1735	57	78	Sold
Bell 206B				
CF-AFL	1256	74	80	ST C-FAFL Shirley Heli.
CF-AFM	1260	74	80	ST C-FAFM Shirley Heli.
C-GFSA	1317	74	C	
C-GFSD	2658	79	C	
C-GFSE	2659	79	C	
Piper PA31				
C-GFSF	112043	81	C	
Beech 200				
C-GFSB	BB084	75	C	
C-GFSG	BB671	80	C	
C-GFSH	BB912	78	C	
Beech 58				
C-GXJW	TH815	77	87	
Beech 70				
C-FCKM	LB24	70	83	ST C-FCKM Krause Enter.
CL-215 -1A10				
C-GFSK	1085	86	C	EX C-GKDN Canadair
C-GFSL	1086	86	C	EX C-GKDP
C-GFSM	1098	88	C	
C-GFSN	1099	88	C	
DASH-8				
C-GFSJ	017	85	C	
Challenger				
C-GRVC	---	87	C	

SASKATCHEWAN

The Saskatchewan Government has long operated air services, introducing the Cessna 195 in the late 1940s for use by the *Air Ambulance Service* of the *Department of Public Health*. Other Cessnas and the Beech 18 were operated as well. The province formed SASKAIR to operate a scheduled service between Prince Alberta, Saskatoon and Regina and renamed it *Norcanair* when it was privatized. Several former *Canadian*

Forces Tracker aircraft, converted by *Conair* to Firecats, and two Cansos are currently in operation.

Four CL-215s were purchased under the federal government's fire fighting initiative to increase sales of Canadair CL-215s while upgrading fire fighting services in Canada. Presently, two Piper PA31s, three turbo PA31s and a small fleet of Beech 95 King Airs provide executive transport for the provincial government.

Alberta Beech 100, CF-AFD

Saskatchewan CS2F2, C-GEHR

FLEET LISTINGS
SASKATCHEWAN

REG'N	C/N	F/N	IS	WFU	NOTES
CL-215					
C-FAFN	1093		87	C	
C-FAFO	1094		87	C	
C-FAFP	1100		8	C	
C-FAFQ	1101		88	C	
CS2F2 Tracker					
C-GEHP	97	1	77	C	
C-GEHQ	59	2	77	C	
C-GEHR	51	3	77	C	
C-GEQC	53	4	77	C	
C-GEQD	98	5	76	C	
C-GEQE	92	6	76	C	
C-GWHK	37		84	C	
PBY-5A Canso					
C-FNJB	CV549		81	C	EX CF-NJB Norcanair
C-FNJF	CV283	7	81	C	EX CF-NJF Norcanair
C-FUAW	CV201		81	C	EX CF-UAW Norcanair
Beech 95 B55 Baron					
C-FSPG	TC-940		65	C	
C-FSPM	TC1008		66	C	
C-GNBA	TC1787		75	C	
C-GPVD	TC1966		76	C	
Piper PA31 Navajo					
C-FSPX	3134268		68	87	
C-GPJT	1200877		77	C	
Piper PA31T Cheyenne					
C-GGPS	20023		77	C	
C-GJPT	20039		75	C	
C-GNKP	20008		75	C	

MANITOBA

Over the years, Manitoba's "Government Air Division" has used Norseman, Fairchild F-11 Husky, Beaver, Turbo Beaver and Otter aircraft. Piper Aztec, Cessna 337 and MU2 aircraft were used in the 1970s. Manitoba purchased three CL-215 Water Bombers and added two more in 1986 under the federal deal. A Cessna Citation I (C-GBNE) was added for air ambulance service in 1978. It was replaced as an air ambulance by a Citation II (C-FEMA) in 1985 and the original Citation used for executive transport. Three Turbo Beavers and a Navajo Chieftain are part of the current fleet.

FLEET LISTINGS

REG'N	C/N	IS	WFU	NOTES
Cessna Citation 550				
C-FEMA	0040	85	C	
Cessna Citation 500				
C-GBNE	0378	78	C	
DHC-2 Beaver				
CF-MAA	1500	58	86	ST W.C.A.Museum
DHC-2 Turbo Beaver				
CF-MAB	TB-21	72	C	
Cessna 180H				
CF-MAC	51819	67	C	
Piper PA23				
CF-MAD	4737	71	86	
Cessna 337F				
CF-MAE	01397	71	86	ST C-FMAE Ontario Cent.
Norseman V				
CF-MAM	N2910	46	56	ST CF-MAM Lambair
Fairchild Husky				
CF-MAN	9	47	59	ST CF-MAN Northl'd Fish
CF-MAO	10	47	59	ST CF-MAO Northl'd Fish
DHC-2 Beaver				
CF-MAP	10	48	59	ST C-FMAP Austin A/W
CF-MAQ	14	48	70	ST CF-MAQ Ilford-River.
CF-MAS	38	49	69	ST CF-MAS Intern'l Jet
CF-MAT	659	54	80	ST C-FMAT Stewart Lake
C-FMAV*	1056	57	77	ST C-FMAV R & N Logging
C-FMAW*	1201	57	80	ST C-FMAW Gulf Air
C-FMAY*	1254	57	77	ST C-FMAY Arnold Bros.
C-FMAZ*	1413	57	78	ST C-FMAZ Ellair Ltd.
DHC-2 Turbo Beaver				
C-FOEA	TB-03	72	C	EX Ontario Government
C-FOEB	TB-05	72	C	EX Ontario Government
C-FOED	TB-09	72	C	EX Ontario Government
C-FOEE	TB-10	72	C	EX Ontario Government
DHC-3 Otter				
C-FMAU*	74	56	C	
C-FMAX*	267	58	C	
MU-2				
CF-ROM	601	78	83	Sold
PA 31 Navajo Chief.				
C-GRNE	2224	79	C	
CL-215				
C-GMAF	1044	74	C	
C-GMAK	1107	87	C	
C-GUMW	1065	80	C	
C-GYJB	1068	80	C	
CL-215-1A10				
C-GBOW	1087	86	C	EX C-GKDY Canadair

ONTARIO

The Ontario Provincial Air Service (OPAS) began in May 1924 operating Curtiss HS-2L, G-CAOA. In 1927, DH60 Moth, G-CAOU, was added with a total of eighteen of these aircraft seeing service with OPAS. A DH61 Giant Moth, G-CAPG, was purchased in August 1928 and with its partner, CF-OAK (purchased in 1933), operated mainly as a freighter aircraft. CF-OAK crashed in 1933 but Giant Moth G-CAPG continued in service until 1941. In the 1940s, OPAS operated Hamilton H-47s, Vickers Vedette flying boats, Fairchile 71s, Wacos and Noorduyn Norsemen.

The Ontario Provincial Air Service operated a huge fleet of aircraft in the 1940s and 1950s. Norseman made up much of the fleet until the de Havilland Beaver was introduced in 1948. Forty-four standard Beavers were used on general transport and fire support duties. Turbo Beavers also saw service with the fleet with three (CF-OEM, OEX & OEY) going to *Air West*. Eleven Otters were purchased new from de Havilland. One *US Army* Otter and seven former *Canadian Forces* Otters were added during 1978-1979. The first was former CA aircraft C-GOFA from 418 Squadron (3677), which was acquired in March 1978. These aircraft operate as fire bombers and are based at Sault Ste. Marie.

The name of the service was changed later to *Province of Ontario, Ministry of Natural Resources Aviation and Fire Management Division.* Grumman Trackers were operated for a short time before being sold to *Conair.* Four Canadair CL-215 Water Bombers are currently with the fleet, two from the federal government scheme. Grumman Trackers operated for a short time but all were sold to *Conair.* Four Twin Otters, a Beech Baron, a Beech King Air and two Beech 200s are the current aircraft used for transport duties. The water bombing fleet is painted bright yellow with large black lettering, while the transport fleet is white with a light blue cheat line and no titles. The government had planned to buy a Challenger jet in the mid-1980s but it became politically inopportune to do so during a restraint period.

Manitoba Canadair CL-215, C-GUMN

Ontario DHC-2 Beaver, CF-OBS

FLEET LISTINGS
ONTARIO

REG'N	C/N	F/N	IS	WFU	NOTES
CL-215					
C-GUKM	1049	260	83	C	EX C-GUKM Canadair
C-GBXQ	1076	261	83	C	EX C-GBXQ Canadair
C-GDRS	1081	262	86	C	EX C-GKDN Canadair
C-GENU	1082	263	86	C	EX C-GKDP Canadair
C-GQFM	1090	264	86	C	EX C-GQFM Canadair
C-GOFN	1097	265	87	C	EX C-GQFN Canadair
C-GOFO	1102	266	87	C	EX C-GOFO Canadair
C-GOFP	1103	267	87	C	EX C-GOFP Canadair
C-GOFR	1104	268	87	C	EX C-GOFR Canadair

FLEET LISTINGS
ONTARIO

REG'N	C/N	F/N	IS	WFU	NOTES
DHC-6 Twin Otter					
C-FOEG	4		67	69	ST N508NA NASA
CF-OEQ	44		67	72	ST C-FOEQ Calm Air
C-FOPG*	232		69	C	ON Wheels
C-FOPI*	243	48	69	C	ON Floats
C-FOPJ	344	47	72	C	ON Floats
C-FTVO	334		87	C	OF Ont. Prov. Police
C-GOGA	739		81	C	On Floats
C-GOGB	761		81	C	On Floats
C-GOGC	750		81	C	On Floats
Beech 200					
C-GOGT	BB535		79	C	
C-GQNJ	BB275		77	C	
Piper Navajo Chief.					
C-GCJX	7552064		75	C	
CS2F1 Tracker					
C-FOPU	38		74	77	ST C-FOPU Conair
C-FOPV	34		74	77	ST C-FOPV Convair
DHC-2 Beaver					
CF-OBS	2		48	86	
CF-OCN	44		48	75	ST Hyack Air
CF-ODS	984		55	69	Sold; Last of 41 Beavers
DHC-2 Turbo Beaver					
C-FOEC*	TB-08		65	C	
C-FOEH*	TB-24		66	C	
C-FOEJ*	TB-27		66	C	
C-FOEK*	TB-28		66	C	
C-FOER*	TB-41		67	C	
C-FOES*	TB-43		67	C	
C-FOET*	TB-44		67	C	
C-FOEU*	TB-46		67	C	
C-FOEV*	TB-48		67	C	
C-FOEW*	TB-50		67	C	
C-FOEX*	TB-52		67	78	ST Air West; now RCMP
C-FOEY*	TB-54		67	78	ST Air West
C-FOPA*	TB-56		68	C	
C-FOPD*	TB-58		68	C	
C-FOPE*	TB-59		68	C	Last of 19 Turbo DHC-2s
DHC-3 Otter					
C-FODJ*	14		53	87	
C-FODK*	13		53	87	
C-FODU*	369		60	C	On Floats/Skis
C-FODW*	403		61	C	On Floats/Skis
C-FODX*	427		62	C	On Floats/Skis
C-FODY*	429		62	C	Last of initial 11 Otters
C-GOFA	35		78	86	EX CF 3677 RCAF (418)
C-GOFG	188		79	81	W/O 19/08/81 Linklater Lake
C-GOPP	355		76	86	EX US Army
Bell 206L-1					
C-GEOM	45625		81	C	
C-GGHA	45525		80	C	
C-GOGH	45359		80	C	
C-GOFI	45342		79	C	
MBB BK117A-3					
C-GOFJ	S7085		86	C	
Bell 212					
C-GONT	30824		77	80	Bandage 1 Toronto Heli.

QUEBEC

Like Ontario, Quebec operates a large fleet of water bombing and transport aircraft. Beaver, Otter, Beech 18s, Grumman Mallard and Grumman Goose aircraft made up the fleet during the 1950s and 1960s.

The Department of Transportation and Communication is currently responsible for air transportation for the province. The fleet of fire suppression aircraft includes seventeen CL-215s augmented by five Cansos. A DC-3 and two Fairchild F-27s provide large executive trans-

port. Two DH-125 jets are used for air ambulance and executive transport service. A DH125 (C-FHLL) was purchased after it crashed so that its wings could be used on C-FPQG. A Challenger jet has been purchased for executive transport and one of the DH-125s used for air ambulance service. An accident near Chibougamau in July 1987 involving Canso C-FPQP was the first fatality in more than 26 years of water bombing operations. Eight Jet Ranger helicopters make up the remainder of the current fleet.

Quebec Challenger, C-FURG

FLEET LISTINGS

QUEBEC

REG'N	C/N	F/N	IS	WFU	NOTES	AIRCRAFT NAME
Challenger 601						
C-FURP			88	C	Ambulance A/C	
DH-125 Jet						
C-FSEN	25027		79	C		
C-FPQG *	25036		65	C		VALENTINE LUPIEN
DHC-3 Otter						
CF-PQH	417		61	63	W/O 1963 in a fire	
F-27						
C-FPQH *	84		71	C		
C-FPQI *	66		73	C		
DC-3						
C-FPQE *	6319		62	C	EX CF-CBL/CF-RBC/CF-ICK	
Beech 18						
CF-PQA	A765		59	73	ST S. Desjardins	
DHC-2 Beaver						
C-FPQB *	166		58	80	RR from CF-GCS 1958	
C-FPQC *	873		58	80	RR from CF-ILQ 1958	
PBY-5A Canso						
C-FPQF *	CV333	11	62	C		
C-FPQK *	9830	12	62	C		
C-FPQL *	CV417	13	63	C		
C-FPQM *	CV425	14	63	C		
C-FPQO *	CV427	15	63	C		
C-FPQP *	11079	64	87	16	W/O 10/07/87 La Cache	

FLEET LISTINGS
QUEBEC

REG'N	C/N	F/N	IS	WFU	NOTES
CL-215					
C-FTUU*	1011	221	69	C	
C-FTUV*	1020	222	71	C	
C-FTUW*	1030	223	71	C	
C-FTXA*	1006	224	70	C	
C-FTXB*	1007	225	70	C	
C-FTXC*	1008	226	70	C	
C-FTXE*	1012	227	70	C	
C-FTXG*	1014	228	70	C	
C-FTXI*	1016	229	70	C	
C-FTXJ*	1017	230	70	C	
C-FTXK*	1018	231	70	C	
C-FYWO*	1003	232	69	C	
C-FYWP*	1002	233	69	C	
C-FYWQ*	1004	234	70	C	
C-FYXG*	1009	235	69	C	
C-GFQA	1091	236	86	C	
C-GFQB	1092	237	86	C	
Bell 206B					
C-FPQR*	1263		74	C	
C-FPQT	733		71	C	
C-FPQU	1000		73	C	
C-FPQV	1056		73	C	
C-FPQX	1330		74	C	
C-GBPQ	2897		79	C	
C-GPQS	2382		78	C	
C-GPQY	1638		75	C	
Hughes 369H					
CF-PQS	1190212		70	85	Sold
Bell 47					
CF-PQZ	1827		62	69	Sold
G-73 Mallard					
CF-PQE	J-55		55	72	RR from CF-HAV 1960
G-21 Goose					
CF-EXA	B-50		49	57	ST CF-EXA O'Connell
G-44 Widgeon					
CF-BVN	1240		51	58	ST Trans Gaspesian A/L
Piaggio P-136-4					
CF-PQD	207		57	61	RR from CF-IZG 1960
Cessna T-50					
CF-DAC	1230		58	62	ST CF-DAC J. Lachance

Yukon Grumman Gulfstream, CF-COL

ATLANTIC PROVINCES

Like four of the other Canadian provinces, New Brunswick operated a Beech 200, C-GPNB, for executive transport until the new Liberal government (elected in 1987) decided to sell this aircraft. It was sold to *Air Vende,* a regional French airline, in June 1988 for $731,000.

Nova Scotia also operates a Beech 200 and a DHC-2 Beaver (C-FUCU). The remainder of the current fleet consists of a Cessna 185 Skywagon, as well as Bell 212

and Hughes 369D helicopters.

Eastern Provincial Airways operated several aircraft including Cansos and Twin Otters for the Newfoundland government. In 1967, the government took over operation of the Cansos and in the mid-1980s operated a fleet of five Cansos. Two CL-215s and a Cessna 337 are also currently in use. A Beech A100 is used for executive transport.

FLEET LISTINGS
NEW BRUNSWICK

REG'N	C/N	F/N	IS	WFU	NOTES
Hughes 369HS					
C-FFGI	520380S		87	C	
Beech B60 Duke					
C-FLJL	P531		80	C	
Aero Commander 680W					
C-GFAB	160143		87	C	
Beech 200					
C-GPNB	BB102		75	88	
Cessna 185F					
C-GYAZ	03668		87	C	

NEWFOUNDLAND

REG'N	C/N	F/N	IS	WFU	NOTES
Beech A100 King Air					
C-FGNL *	B-184		73	C	
Cessna 337G					
C-GLFY	01700		82	C	
PBY-5A Canso					
C-FCRP	9837		67	C	EX CF-CRP CPA/RCAF 9837
C-FDFB *	605		78	C	EX CF-DFB Austin A/W
C-FIGI	48429		65	87	
C-FIGJ	48429		66	80	
C-FIZU *	46655		67	C	
C-FNJC *	CV430	5	67	C	
C-FNJE *	CV437		67	C	EX RCAF 11094
C-FOFI *	CV343	3	67	85	SANK 30/06/85 20 KmNorth of YYR
285ACF Canso					
C-GGDW	98837		68	C	
CL-215					
C-GDKW	1095	281	87	C	
C-GDXY	1096	282	87	C	
C-FAYN	1105	283	88	C	
Piper PA18					
C-FNVM	187749		65	C	EX CF-NVM EPA
C-FNVN	187761		65	C	EX CF-NVN EPA
DHC-2 Turbo Beaver					
CF-UKK	TB-18		67	73	ST CF-UKK Gander Avn.
CF-VPV	TB-37		67	73	
DHC-6 Twin Otter					
CF-DMR	36		67	72	OB EPA for Gov't.

FLEET LISTINGS
NOVA SCOTIA

REG'N	C/N	IS	WFU	NOTES
Hughes 369HS				
C-FDUA	530479S	82	87	One of 3 Hughes
DHC-2 Beaver				
C-FODS	984	69	77	EX CF-ODS Ontario Govt
C-FUCU	1611	65	C	
Beech 200				
C-GEVN	BB898	81	C	
Bell 206B				
C-GLCD	1284	80	87	
C-GLET	1643	80	87	
Bell 212				
C-GPNS	31148	80	C	

YUKON – NORTHWEST TERRITORIES

Prince Edward Island does not operate any aircraft. A Grumman Gulfstream 1 was operated for the Yukon Government by *Wardair* in the 1970s. In the Federal CL-215 costsharing, the Yukon acquired one CL-215 to be operated by *Conair*.

The Northwest Territories acquired two CL-215s during the federal forest fire control deal, to be operated by *Conair*.

FLEET LISTINGS
YUKON

REG'N	C/N	F/N	IS	WFU	NOTES
CL-215					
C-GCSX	1088		86	C	EX C-GKEA Canadair
Grumman Gulfstream					
CF-COL	64		77	78	OB Wardair for Gov't.

NWT

REG'N	C/N	F/N	IS	WFU	NOTES
CL-215 -1A10					
C-GBYU	1083	290	86	C	OB Conair
C-GBPM	1084	291	86	C	OB Conair

PART 7

Federal
Government
Agencies

CANADIAN ARMED FORCES

The air branch of the Canadian Armed Forces was called the Royal Canadian Air Force until integration in 1968. After 1970, aircraft carried the titles 'Canadian Armed Forces' on one side of the aircraft and the French equivalent on the other. In the mid-1970s, these titles were replaced by the word 'Canada.'

The Canadian Armed Forces had many transport aircraft before and during WWII. This history will deal only with post-war transport aircraft. The C-47 Dakota (DC-3) served with the RCAF during WWII and continues to serve into 1989 with the Air Reserve Unit in Winnipeg. The other WWII aircraft which continued in service until 1970 was the Beechcraft C-45 Expeditor which was used for short haul transport and as a trainer, ending its career with the Air Reserve Units.

The Canadair North Star marked the entry of the RCAF into the field of large four-engine aircraft. The North Star was basically a DC-4, unpressurized and extremely noisy, and was powered by four Rolls-Royce Merlin 620s instead of the DC-4's Pratt & Whitney engines. The first four aircraft destined for the RCAF were leased to *Trans-Canada Airlines*. One of these was destroyed while with TCA and three were returned. The first RCAF North Star began service in 1947 with 426 Transport Squadron, based at Dorval. This squadron received the bulk of the North Stars, operating them as part of the United Nations airlift during the Korean conflict. One North Star (17513) underwent special modifications for use in testing icing conditions for aircraft and became known as the 'Rockcliffe Ice Wagon.' The first North Star returned from TCA went to 412 Squadron for VIP transport duties. Because North Star CF-TEL was written-off with TCA, Canadair produced one extra aircraft, the C-5, for the RCAF. This was the only C-5 built and was designated as a VIP transport. The C-5 was pressurized, used four Pratt & Whitney R-2800 engines rather than the noisy Merlins and had an elongated DC-4 fuselage with a DC-6 undercarriage. It was set-up to carry twenty-four passengers. The C-5 was originally registered as number 17524, but was quickly changed to 1000. One North Star, 17514, after being retired by the RCAF, flew for several years with the National Aeronautical Establishment.

The RCAF became the first air force in the world to operate jet transports when it purchased two de Havilland DH-106 Comet 1As. While the Comet 1As did not have a distinguished record in civilian operation, these two aircraft served very well with the RCAF for a decade. Operated by 412 Squadron out of Ottawa's Uplands Airport, they bridged the Atlantic and were also used to exercise Canada's air defences. During RCAF operations,

these aircraft carried thirty-six passengers, a crew of seven and up to 5,000 pounds of freight.

The turboprop era for passenger transport began in 1960 with the introduction of the CC-109 Cosmopolitan. Canadair used Napier Eland turboprop engines to convert ten Convair 440 airframes to Convair 540 status. These ten aircraft were then converted to Convair 580 status in 1966 with Allison engines replacing the Napier Eland engines. One of the ten was destroyed in a fire and two were scrapped, but seven are still serving with the Canadian Armed Forces in 1989. Three Convair 440 aircraft (as opposed to the above airframes) were acquired by Canadair and converted to Convair 540 status using Napier Eland engines. These were used as demonstrators by Canadair, two of them serving with *Quebecair* before being acquired by the RCAF in 1962. These aircraft were sold in 1966-67 having been converted to Convair 580 status following service with the RCAF.

The North Star replacement showed up in 1961 with the introduction of the CC-106 Yukon aircraft. A derivative of the Bristol Britannia aircraft which served in Canada with *Canadian Pacific Airlines,* this pressurized four-engine turboprop carried one hundred and thirty-four passengers and a crew of ten and was the largest aircraft in Canada at the time. Twelve Yukons served for just over a decade with none of these aircraft being written-off.

The Yukons were replaced in 1970 by five Boeing 707s destined for *Western Airlines*. These aircraft are used on trans-Canada runs three times per week for the Canadian Forces and on the trans-Atlantic flights linking Trenton/Ottawa with Lahr, Germany as well as serving as VIP transport aircraft. The 707s also serve as inflight tanker refueling aircraft for the CF-18 Hornets and CF-5s. From a fleet of twenty-four North Stars (including the C-5), to 12 Yukons, these 5 Boeing 707s have served the Canadian Forces extremely well.

Short haul passenger and cargo fights in Europe were handled by Bristol 170s from 1953 to 1967. Two of the six aircraft operated briefly in Canada during the winter of 1951-1952, while undergoing cold weather testing in Edmonton. In Canada, the C-119 Flying Boxcar (Fairchild Packet) served with 435 and 436 Squadron as short haul passenger and cargo aircraft. Twelve of these also served with the *United Nations Emergency Force* (UNEF) in the Middle East during 1956. The twelve C-119s were replaced in 1957 by four Otters, two C-47s and four C-119s as part of 115 Communication Flight. The aircraft were based at El Arish. The Flying Boxcar served until 28 July 1965 when the main wing

CANADIAN ARMED FORCES

spars on several of the aircraft were found to be damaged and the aircraft were considered uneconomical to repair. The effect of this decision was to leave the RCAF very short of aircraft during the summer of 1965, thus eliminating many flights. As a result, the author's summer posting to France was replaced by a posting to Gimli, Manitoba and he travelled there not by air but by train and 'The Red River Grey Goose Bus Line'!

The first of the Lockheed Hercules aircraft entered service with the RCAF on 28 October 1960 when four C-130B aircraft were delivered to 435 Squadron. Subsequent aircraft were the larger C-130E aircraft which continue to form the bulk of the Canadian Forces cargo transport and troop carriers operating throughout the world. Several C-130Es have operated out of Winnipeg with the Air Navigation School, but will be returned to cargo duties once the Dash-8 Air Navigation aircraft are received. With the loss of several aircraft through accidents, replacement Hercules aircraft have been purchased, these being the larger C-130H models. Two of the C-130Hs were lost in an unfortunate accident at an airshow at CFB Namao when they collided while turning in for landing.

De Havilland Canada aircraft have served with the RCAF and Canadian Armed Forces as short range transport and as search and rescue aircraft, although surprisingly, the de Havilland Beaver has never seen military service in Canada. The DHC-3 Otter entered service in 1953 and in addition to serving in the Middle East, served with the United Nations in West Guinea. The DHC-4 Caribou entered service in 1960, three of them immediately flying with 115 Air Transport Unit at El Arish, Egypt. The Caribou had a short service with the RCAF, being replaced by the DHC-5 Buffalo in 1966.

One Buffalo was shot down in the desert while serving with the United Nations in the Middle East. These aircraft continue to serve as troop carriers and as search and rescue aircraft in 1989.

Two Dash-7 aircraft were purchased in 1979 to replace the Cosmopolitans in Europe. However, the Canadian Forces decided to operate Dash-8 aircraft for the Air Navigation School in Winnipeg and realized that by also using Dash-8 aircraft in Europe, the number of types of aircraft in the fleet could be reduced. Thus the Dash-7s were sold in 1986 and Cosmopolitans used until two Dash-8s were sent to Europe in 1987.

Short haul jet service has been operated by 412 Squadron in Ottawa using seven Dassault Fan-Jet Falcons. These VIP aircraft carry only ten passengers, and several were transferred to 414 Squadron for use as electronic jamming aircraft being replaced in passenger service by Canadair Challenger aircraft. One Falcon was purchased for use as an electronic recording aircraft but was later transferred to the Department of Energy, Mines and Resources and operated by *Innotech Aviation*.

In 1985, the Conservative government under Brian Mulroney decided to transfer all Department of Transport VIP flight operations to the Canadian Forces. The Jetstars then still in service with the DOT remained until retired but the Challenger jets were transferred to the Canadian Forces, except for two which are used for calibration. Thus, in 1989, the Canadian Forces operate a large VIP jet service for the Government of Canada using Challenger jets based with 412 Squadron. All the remaining Falcons were transferred to 414 Squadron and the older of these phased out.

CAF Dakota, 957

CF Falcon, 117501

FLEET LISTING
CANADIAN ARMED FORCES

REG'N	C/N	IS	WFU	NOTES	MODEL	AGENCY
Boeing 707-347CH						
13701	20315	70	C			Canadian Forces
13702	20316	70	C			Canadian Forces
13703	20317	70	C			Canadian Forces
13704	20318	70	C			Canadian Forces
13705	20319	70	C			Canadian Forces
CC-109 Cosmopolitan						
109151	001	60	C	EX 11151 RCAF		RCAF/CAF
109152	002	60	C	EX 11152 RCAF		RCAF/CAF
109154	004	60	C	EX 11154 RCAF		RCAF/CAF
109155	005	60	72	EX 11155 RCAF; Scrapped		RCAF/CAF
109156	006	60	C	EX 11156 RCAF		RCAF/CAF
109157	007	60	C	EX 11157 RCAF		RCAF/CAF
109158	008	60	72	EX 11158 RCAF; Scrapped		RCAF/CAF
109159	009	60	C	EX 11159 RCAF		RCAF/CAF
109160	010	61	C	EX 11160 RCAF		RCAF/CAF
11153	003	60	67	DBF 11/04/67		RCAF
CC-109 (Convair 540)						
11161	475	62	66	ST N969N General Motors		RCAF
11162	454	62	67	EX CF-LMA Quebecair		RCAF
11163	462	62	66	EX CF-MKP Quebecair		RCAF
CC-132 Dash-7						
132001	8	79	86	ST 4X-AHI Arkia		Canadian Forces
132002	12	79	86	ST C-GILE Air Atlantic		Canadian Forces
CC-142 Dash-8						
142801	38	87	C	OB 412 ATS CFB Lahr		Canadian Forces
142802	46	87	C	OB 412 ATS CFB Lahr		Canadian Forces
142803	071	88	C	EX C-GESR DHC		
142804	080	88	C	EX C-GFRP DHC		
142805	103	89	C			
142806	107	89	C			
CC-138 Twin Otter						
13801	303	71	C			Canadian Forces
13802	304	71	C			Canadian Forces
13803	305	71	C			Canadian Forces
13804	306	71	C			Canadian Forces
13805	307	71	C			Canadian Forces
13806	308	71	C			Canadian Forces
13807	309	71	86	W/O 14/06/86 Alberta		Canadian Forces
13808	310	71	71	W/O 05/12/71 Kashmir-UN		Canadian Forces
13809	382	73	C			Canadian Forces
CC-144 Challenger						
144601	1040	83	C		CL600	Canadian Forces
144602	1065	84	C		CL600	Canadian Forces
144604	1007	86	C	EX C-GBKC DOT;	CL600	Canadian Forces
144605	1008	86	C	EX C-GBEY DOT;	CL600	Canadian Forces
144606	1009	86	C	EX C-GCVQ	CL600	Canadian Forces
144608	1015	86	C	EX C-GBLN	CL600	Canadian Forces
144609	1017	86	C	EX	CL600	Canadian Forces
144610	1022	86	C	EX	CL600	Canadian Forces
144613	3035	84	C		CL601	Canadian Forces
144614	3036	84	C		CL601	Canadian Forces
144615	3037	84	C		CL601	Canadian Forces
144616	3038	84	C		CL601	Canadian Forces
CC-117 Falcon 20C						
117501	82	67	C	EX 20501 RCAF; 414 Sqd		RCAF/CAF
117502	87	67	C	EX 20502 RCAF; 414 Sqd		RCAF/CAF
117503	92	67	C	EX 20503 RCAF; 414 Sqd		RCAF/CAF
117504	97	67	C	EX 20504 RCAF; 414 Sqd		RCAF/CAF
117505	103	67	87	EX 20505 RCAF		RCAF/CAF
117506	109	67	87	EX 20506 RCAF		RCAF/CAF
117507	114	67	87	EX 20507 RCAF		RCAF/CAF
117508	157	71	75	ST C-GRSD-X E.M.R.		Canadian Forces

FLEET LISTING
CANADIAN ARMED FORCES

REG'N	C/N	IS	WFU	NOTES	AGENCY
CC-130 Hercules-B					
10301	3572	60	66	ST N4652 Gelac; 435 Sqd	RCAF
10302	3575	60	66	ST N4653 Gelac; 435 Sqd	RCAF
10303	3587	60	66	ST N4654 Gelac; 435 Sqd	RCAF
10304	3590	60	66	W/O 04/66 nr. Saskatoon	RCAF
CC-130 Hercules-E					
130305	4020	64	C	EX 10305 RCAF	RCAF/CAF
130306	4026	64	C	EX 10306 RCAF	RCAF/CAF
130307	4041	64	C	EX 10307 RCAF	RCAF/CAF
130308	4042	64	C	EX 10308 RCAF	RCAF/CAF
130309	4050	64	67	W/O 28/04/67 Trenton	RCAF
130310	4051	64	C	EX 10310 RCAF	RCAF/CAF
130311	4060	64	C	EX 10311 RCAF	RCAF/CAF
130312	4061	64	80	W/O 15/10/80 Quebec	RCAF/CAF
130313	4066	64	C	EX 10313 RCAF	RCAF/CAF
130314	4067	64	C	EX 10314 RCAF	RCAF/CAF
130315	4070	64	C	EX 10315 RCAF	RCAF/CAF
130316	4075	64	C	EX 10316 RCAF	RCAF/CAF
130317	4095	64	C	EX 10317 RCAF	RCAF/CAF
130318	4096	64	89	EX 10318 RCAF; W/O 27/01/89 Fort Wainwright, Alaska	RCAF/CAF
130319	4122	64	C	EX 10319 RCAF	RCAF/CAF
130320	4124	64	C	EX 10320 RCAF	RCAF/CAF
130321	4191	65	C	EX 10321 RCAF	RCAF/CAF
130322	4192	65	C	EX 10322 RCAF	RCAF/CAF
130323	4193	65	C	EX 10323 RCAF	RCAF/CAF
130324	4194	65	C	EX 10324 RCAF	RCAF/CAF
130325	4285	68	C	EX 10325 RCAF	RCAF/CAF
130326	4286	68	C	EX 10326 RCAF	RCAF/CAF
130327	4288	68	C	EX 10328 RCAF	RCAF/CAF
130328	4289	68	C	EX 10328 RCAF	RCAF/CAF
CC-130 Hercules-H					
130329	4553	74	C	EX 73-1589	Canadian Forces
130330	4555	74	85	W/O 29/03/85 CFB Namao	Canadian Forces
130331	4559	74	85	W/O 29/03/85 CFB Namao	Canadian Forces
130332	4568	75	C	EX 73-1596	Canadian Forces
130333	4574	75	C	EX 73-1599	Canadian Forces
130334	4994	86	C		Canadian Forces
130335	4995	86	C		Canadian Forces
130336	4580	86	C	EX 1211 Abu Dhabi	Canadian Forces
130337	4584	86	C	EX 1212 Abu Dhabi	Canadian Forces
CC-115 Buffalo					
115451	05	67	C	EX 9451 RCAF	Canadian Forces
115452	06	67	C	EX 9452 RCAF	Canadian Forces
115453	07	67	C	EX 9453 RCAF	Canadian Forces
115454	08	67	C	EX 9454 RCAF 442 Sqd.	Canadian Forces
115455	09	67	C	EX 9455 RCAF	Canadian Forces
115456	10	67	C	EX 9456 RCAF	Canadian Forces
115457	11	68	C	EX 9457 RCAF	Canadian Forces
115458	12	68	C	EX 9458 RCAF 442 Sqd.	Canadian Forces
115459	13	68	C	EX 9459 RCAF	Canadian Forces
115460	14	68	C	EX 9460 RCAF; UNEF II	Canadian Forces
115461	16	68	74	W/O 09/08/74 Syria - UN	Canadian Forces
115462	19	68	C	EX 9462 RCAF; EX C-FNUZ	Canadian Forces
115463	21	68	C	EX 9463 RCAF; EX CF-DJU	Canadian Forces
115464	23	68	C	EX 9464 RCAF	Canadian Forces
115465	25	68	C	EX 9465 RCAF	Canadian Forces
CC-106 Yukon					
15921/106921	001	62	71	ST YS-04C TACA	RCAF/CAF
15922/106922	002	62	71	ST 9X-CWN SGA	RCAF/CAF
15923/106923	003	60	71	ST CF-CHC Canhellanas	RCAF/CAF
15924/106924	004	60	71	ST LV-LBS AER	RCAF/CAF
15925/106925	005	61	70	ST LV-PQL AER	RCAF/CAF
15926/106926	006	61	70	ST LV-JSR AER	RCAF/CAF
15927/106927	007	61	71	ST LV-JYR AER	RCAF/CAF

FLEET LISTING
CANADIAN ARMED FORCES

REG'N	C/N	IS	WFU	NOTES	AGENCY
CC-106 Yukon (Continued)					
15928/106928	008	61	70	ST LV-PRX TARP	RCAF/CAF
15929/106929	009	61	70	EX 15555/CF-MKP-X	RCAF/CAF
15930/106930	010	61	70	ST 9Q-CWK SGA	RCAF/CAF
15931/106931	011	61	70	ST C-GACH Beaver Enter	RCAF/CAF.
15932/106932	012	62	70	ST CF-JSN Beaver Enter.	RCAF/CAF
North Star C-54GM					
17501	108	47	53	W/O 23/07/53	RCAF
17502	109	47	65	ST CF-UXA Air Caicos	RCAF
17503	110	47	53	W/O 30/12/53 Vancouver	RCAF
17504	111	47	65	Sold & Scrapped	RCAF
17505	112	47	53	W/O 27/12/53 Shemya	RCAF
17506	113	47	65	Sold & Scrapped Florida	RCAF
17507	114	47	65	ST CF-UOY, YS-27C	RCAF
17508	115	47	65	Sold & Scrapped Florida	RCAF
17509	116	47	60	DBF 24/03/60 Trenton	RCAF
17510	117	48	65	ST CF-UXB Air Caicos	RCAF
17511	118	48	64	Sold & Scrapped Florida	RCAF
17512	119	48	64	Sold & Scrapped Florida	RCAF
17513	120	48	56	DBF 19/03/56 Dorval RIW	RCAF
17514	121	48	65	ST CF-SVP-X NAE	RCAF
17515	122	48	65	On Display Ottawa	RCAF
17516	123	48	65	Sold & Scrapped Florida	RCAF
17517	124	48	65	Sold & Scrapped Florida	RCAF
North Star DC-4M1					
17518	102	49	62	WFU 9/62 & Scrapped	RCAF
17519	103	NTU	NTU	W/O while LT CF-TEL TCA	RCAF
17520	104	49	62	W/O 26/04/62 Hall Lake	RCAF
17521	105	49	65	WFU 3/65 & Scrapped	RCAF
17522	106	49	54	W/O 08/05/54 U.K.	RCAF
17523	107	49	51	W/O 15/03/51 Resolute	RCAF
17525	101	52	59	DBF 21/06/59 Athens	RCAF
C - 5					
17524	171	50	66	RR 10000; ST N17599	RCAF
DH-106 Comet 1A					
5301	06017	53	65	WFU & Scrapped	RCAF
5302	06018	53	65	WFU & Scrapped	RCAF
Bristol 170					
9696	12829	51	65	W/O 03/12/65 France	RCAF
9697	12830	51	63	W/O 31/12/63 Marville	RCAF
9698	13079	53	67	ST CF-WAC Wardair	RCAF
9699	13219	55	67	ST CF-WAE Wardair	RCAF
9700	13249	55	67	ST CF-WAG Wardair	RCAF
9850	13253	57	67	ST CF-WAD Wardair	RCAF
CC-108 Caribou					
5303	001	60	71	ST JW9011 Tanzanian AF	RCAF
5320	009	60	71	ST JW9012 Tanzanian AF	RCAF/UNEF Svc.
5321	010	60	71	ST JW9013 Tanzanian AF	RCAF/UNEF Svc.
5322	011	60	71	ST JW9014 Tanzanian AF	RCAF/UNEF Svc.
5323	012	60	71	ST JW9015 Tanzanian AF	RCAF
5324	113	64	65	W/O 08/09/65 India	RCAF /UNMOGIP
5325	115	64	71	ST JW9016 Tanzanian AF	RCAF /UNMOGIP
5326	166	64	71	ST JW9017 Tanzanian AF	RCAF
5327	206	64	71	ST JW9005 Tanzanian AF	RCAF /UNMOGIP
C-119 Boxcar					
22101	10676	52	67	OB 435/436 Squadrons	RCAF
22102	10677	52	67	OB 435/436 Squadrons	RCAF
22103	10678	52	67	OB 435/436 Squadrons	RCAF
22104	10735	52	66	OB 435/436 Squadrons	RCAF
22105	10736	52	67	OB 435/436 Squadrons	RCAF
22106	10737	52	67	OB 435 Squadron	RCAF
22107	10738	53	67	OB 408/436 Squadrons	RCAF
22108	10773	53	67	OB 436 Squadron	RCAF

FLEET LISTING
CANADIAN ARMED FORCES

REG'N	C/N	IS	WFU	NOTES	AGENCY
C-119 Boxcar (Continued)					
22109	10774	53	66	OB 435/436 Squadrons	RCAF
22110	10775	53	67	OB 435 & 4 OTU	RCAF
22111	10776	53	67	OB 104 Comm. Flight	RCAF
22112	10823	53	67		RCAF
22113	10824	53	67		RCAF
22114	10825	53	67		RCAF
22115	10859	53	67		RCAF
22116	10860	53	67	OB 436 Squadron	RCAF
22117	10861	53	67		RCAF
22118	10870	53	67		RCAF
22119	10871	53	67		RCAF
22120	10872	53	67		RCAF
22121	10905	53	67	OB 436 Squadron	RCAF
22122	10906	53	67		RCAF
22123	10907	53	67	OB 435 Squadron	RCAF
22124	10908	53	56	W/O 27/04/56	RCAF
22125	10942	53	68	W/O 20/01/68 RCAF Namao	RCAF
22126	10943	53	67	OB 436 Squadron	RCAF
22127	10944	53	60	W/O 21/09/60	RCAF
22128	10945	53	59	W/O 04/03/59	RCAF
22129	10954	53	67		RCAF
22130	10955	53	67		RCAF
22131	10956	53	67	OB 436 Squadron	RCAF
22132	10957	53	67		RCAF
22133	10992	53	67		RCAF
22134	10993	53	67		RCAF
22135	10994	53	67	OB 435/436 Squadrons	RCAF
DHC-3 Otter					
3661	007	53	63	ST BM-1004 Indian AF	RCAF
3662	008	53	65	ST CF-SUB	RCAF
3663	009	53	82	OB 408, 102 CU, 400, 438 Sqds.	RCAF/CAF
3664	010	53	63	ST CF-GTL Lambair; OB 408 Sqd.	RCAF
3665	011	53	63	ST BM-1003 Indian AF	RCAF
3666	012	53	56	W/O 10/04/56 Goose Bay	RCAF
3667	001	52	52	LT CF-DYK DHC indefinite	RCAF
3668	022	53	64	ST CF-OVN Gateway Aviation	RCAF
3669	023	53	82	OB 105 SAR, 102 CU, 400 Sqd.	RCAF/CAF
3670	025	53	54	DBF 04/05/54 Vancouver	RCAF
3671	026	53	82	OB 408, 411, 424, 400 Sqds.	RCAF/CAF
3672	027	54	54	W/O 26/04/54 Churchill	RCAF
3673	028	54	82	OB 103, 111, 4 OTU, 411 Sqd.	RCAF/CAF
3674	032	54	68	W/O 16/02/68 Montreal, 438 Sqd.	RCAF
3675	033	54	57	W/O 15/04/57 Egypt	RCAF/UNEF
3676	034	54	54	DBF 04/05/54 Vancouver	RCAF
3677	035	54	67	ST C-GOFA OPAS, 418 Sqd.	RCAF/UNEF
3678	036	54	66	W/O 25/04/66 Egypt	RCAF/UNEF
3679	037	54	63	ST BM-1001 Indian AF	RCAF
3780	038	54	64	ST CF-MPK/CF-EBX RCMP	RCAF
3781	039	54	67	ST C-GOFB OPAS; 401 Sqd.	RCAF
3782	040	54	67	WFU & Scapped 03/67	RCAF
3783	044	54	78	ST C-GOFC OPAS; LT CF-MPU	RCAF/CAF
3784	045	54	56	W/O 15/12/56 Goose Bay	RCAF
3785	046	54	71	ST CF-QOQ Gander Aviation	RCAF/CAF
3786	052	54	64	ST CF-MPO RCMP	RCAF
3787	053	54	56	W/O 18/03/56 Knob Lake	RCAF
3788	055	54	63	ST BM-1000 Indian AF	RCAF
3789	056	54	71	W/O 15/05/71 Montreal; 438 Sqd.	RCAF/CAF
3790	057	54	63	ST BM-1002 Indian AF	RCAF
3791	058	54	78	ST C-GOFD OPAS; 400 Sqd.	RCAF/CAF
3792	059	54	82	OB 102 SAF, 103 SAR, 438 Sqd.	RCAF/CAF
3793	060	54	55	ST 144259 US Navy	RCAF
3794	061	55	78	ST C-GOFE OPAS; 438 Sqd.	RCAF/CAF
3795	062	55	55	ST 144260 US Navy	RCAF
3796	063	55	69	W/O 12/06/69 Montreal, 438 Sqd.	RCAF/UNEF

FLEET LISTING
CANADIAN ARMED FORCES

REG'N	C/N	IS	WFU	NOTES	AGENCY
DHC-3 Otter (Continued)					
3797	064	55	65	ST CF-SME Sask. Government	RCAF
3798	065	55	78	ST C-GOFF OPAS; 438 Sqd.	RCAF/CAF
3799	066	55	55	ST 144261 US Navy	RCAF
3743	183	56	65	ST CF-WJB Gander Aviation	RCAF/UNEF
3744	185	56	58	W/O 19/09/58 Egypt	RCAF/UNEF
3745	188	56	79	ST C-GOFG OPAS; 402 Sqd.	RCAF/CAF/UNEF
9401	356	60	61	W/O 30/05/61 Toronto; 400 Sqd.	RCAF/CAF
9402	357	60	82	OB 438 & 431 Sqds., Montreal	RCAF/CAF
9403	359	60	82	OB 402 Sqd Winnipeg/1ARW	RCAF/CAF
9404	361	60	82	OB 400 & 418 Sqd.	RCAF/CAF/UNMOGIP
9405	363	60	82	OB 402 Sqd & 2 ARW	RCAF/CAF
9406	365	60	82	OB 438, 424, 401, 402 Sqds.	RCAF/CAF/UNMOGIP
9407	367	60	82	OB 418, 403, 1 ARW	RCAF/CAF
9408	370	60	82	OB 418; Nat'l Aero Coll	RCAF/CAF
9409	375	60	71	ST CF-QOR Gander Aviation	RCAF/CAF
9410	380	60	71	W/O 15/06/71 Toronto; 400 Sqd.	RCAF/CAF
9411	384	60	74	W/O 19/05/74 Winnipeg	RCAF/CAF
9412	387	60	82	OB 400, 411 & 401 Sqds.	RCAF/CAF
9413	389	60	75	W/O 16/07/75 NWT	RCAF/CAF
9414	391	60	61	W/O 13/10/61 St. Hyacinthe	RCAF
9415	393	60	82	OB 402, 406, 411 Sqds.	RCAF/CAF/UNMOGIP
9416	394	60	82	OB 402, 406, 2 ARW	RCAF/CAF
9417	396	60	82	OB 418 Sqd. & 1 ARW	RCAF/CAF
9418	398	60	68	ACC 1968 CFB Namao & WFU	RCAF
9419	399	60	70	W/O 07/05/70 Montreal; 401 Sqd.	RCAF/CAF
9420	401	60	82	OB 442 & 411 Sqds.	RCAF/CAF
9421	402	60	82	OB 424 & 400 Sqds.	RCAF/CAF
9422	404	60	82	OB 424 & 411 Sqds.	RCAF/CAF/UNMOGIP
9423	405	60	82	OB 438, 116 ATU, 400 Sqds.	RCAF/CAF/UNTEA
9424	407	60	82	OB 418, 400, 116ATU, 401 Sqds.	RCAF/CAF/UNTEA
9425	408	60	63	ST CF-BCG B.C. Govt.	RCAF/CAF
9426	409	60	82	OB 400, 443, 401 Sqds.	RCAF/CAF/UNMOGIP
9427	410	60	65	ST CF-VVY Northward; 438 Sqd.	RCAF/CAF
C-47 Dakota					
650/ A508	9015	43	46	TO A508 Instucttional Airframe	RCAF
651/12936	9290	43	75	WFU 1975	RCAF
652/ A509	9108	43	46	TO A509 Instuctional Airframe	RCAF
653/12937	9415	43	82	FOR Display in Calgary	RCAF
654/-----	9595	43	52	WFU; OB 165 Sqd.	RCAF
655/-----	9831	43	70	ST CF-QJZ Gateway Aviation	RCAF
656/12938	9832	53	89	NASARR-"Dolly's Folly"	RCAF/UN Congo
657/12939	9834	43	73	ST CF-IRW Ste Felicien	RCAF
658/-----	9830	43	70	ST N8563 Bush Aviation	RCAF
659/12940	9833	43	74	ST N300ZZ Zoom Zoom Aviation	RCAF
660/12941	10199	43	75	ST N64767 Sharvas Investments	RCAF
661/-----	10200	43	69	ST KG661 RAF/RAE	RCAF
662/-----	10201	43	69	ST 502 Muscat & Oman AF	RCAF Europe
663/-----	10202	43	70	ST CF-AAL Austin Airways	RCAF
664/-----	10203	43	50	WFU; OB 146 Sqd.	RCAF
960/ A628	12267	44	51	TO A628 Instructional Airframe	RCAF
961/-----	12289	44	64	ST CF-AAB Austin Airways	RCAF
962/-----	12544	44	46	W/O 16/09/46 Estevan	RCAF
963/12950	12543	44	89	RR 12950 CAF	RCAF
964/12951	12411	44	72	ST CF-OOY Atlas Aviation	RCAF
965/-----	12876	44	69	ST OB-T-1043 Alpa Aero	RCAF
966/-----	12877	44	44	W/O 1944; 165 Sqd.	RCAF
967/-----	13086	44	46	W/O 27/09/46 Gander	RCAF
968/12952	13087	44	73	ST C-GXAU/C-GCTE Alt.Nt	RCAF
969/12953	13343	44	75	ST C-GWYX Ilford-River.	RCAF
970/12954	13342	44	71	ST CF-OOW Atlas Aviation	RCAF
971/-----	25370	44	66	WFU & Scrapped	RCAF
972/12955	25371	44	72	ST CF-BKT Maritime Aircraft	RCAF
973/12956	25368	44	75	ST C-GWMY NWT Air	RCAF
974/-----	25369	44	64	ST CF-AAC Austin A/W	RCAF
975/-----	26003	44	59	WFU & Scrapped	RCAF Europe

FLEET LISTING
CANADIAN ARMED FORCES

REG'N	C/N	IS	WFU	NOTES	AGENCY
C-47 Dakota (Continued)					
976/12957	26002	44	89	RR 12957 CAF 429 Sqd.	RCAF
977/12958	26005	44	72	ST CF-QHY NWT Air	RCAF
978/-----	26004	44	45	W/O 25/01/45 BigginHill	RCAF
979/12959	26641	44	89	NASARR; nose-"Pinocchio"	RCAF
980/-----	26644	44	52	W/O 06/05/52 Frobisher	RCAF
981/12960	26643	44	72	ST CF-QNF Sterling A/S	RCAF
982/-----	26642	44	49	WFU & Scrapped	RCAF
983/-----	27133	45	63	ST BJ912 Indian AF	RCAF
984/ A597	27135	45	52	W/O 28/07/52 St. Hubert to A597	RCAF
985/-----	32683	45	53	W/O 19/02/53	RCAF
986/-----	32681	45	46	W/O 29/03/46 Goose Bay	RCAF
987/-----	33115	45	49	W/O 27/01/49	RCAF
988/12961	33116	45	72	ST CF-BKU Maritime Aircraft	RCAF
989/-----	33466	45	62	ST BJ913 Indian AF	RCAF Europe
990/12962	33467	45	77	ST N99663 Basler	RCAF
991/-----	34219	45	54	W/O 27/12/54	RCAF
992/12963	12217	45	89	RR 12963 1970; 429 Sqd.	RCAF
993/12964	12483	45	75	ST C-GGNA Austin A/W	RCAF
994/-----	13476	45	62	ST BJ762 Indian AF	RCAF
1000/12965	33352	46	75	ST C-GSCC E.M.R.	RCAF/VIP 412 Sqd.
10910/-----	9862	51	70	ST CF-AAM Austin A/W	RCAF
10911/12966	9186	51	75	ST N46877 Basler	RCAF Europe
10912/12967	4441	51	72	ST CF-BKV Maritime Aircraft	RCAF
10913/12968	18986	51	75	ST C-GWYY Wilkinson	RCAF
10914/-----	32871	52	70	WFU & Scrapped	RCAF
10915/12969	33540	52	73	ST CF-ADB Air Dale	RCAF
10916/-----	32843	52	68	ST N6677/ CF-CTA NorCan	RCAF
10917/12970	27074	52	72	ST CF-BKZ Bot Construct	RCAF
10918/12971	12238	46	71	ST CF-OOX Atlas Aviation	RCAF
FL595/-----	12004	43	45	ST CF-TDM TCA	RCAF
FL598/-----	12007	44	46	ST CF-TDN TCA	RCAF
FL615/-----	12026	44	46	ST CF-TDO TCA	RCAF
FL616/-----	12027	44	45	ST CF-TDP TCA	RCAF
FL618/-----	12039	44	45	ST CF-TDQ TCA	RCAF
FL621/-----	12042	44	45	ST CF-TDR TCA	RCAF
FL636/-----	12063	43	46	WFU & Scrapped	RCAF
FL650/-----	12079	44	44	W/O 06/11/44	RCAF
FZ557/-----	12092	43	46	ST CF-TDS TCA	RCAF
FZ558/-----	12093	43	46	ST CF-TDT TCA	RCAF
FZ571/-----	12106	44	45	ST CF-TDU TCA	RCAF
FZ575/-----	12110	43	45	ST CF-TDV TCA	RCAF
FZ576/-----	12111	43	44	W/O 23/05/44-DD 12/43	RCAF
FZ581/-----	12116	44	44	W/O 26/02/44-DD 8/01/44	RCAF
FZ583/-----	12138	44	45	W/O 27/06/45; OB 6 OTU	RCAF
FZ584/-----	12139	44	46	ST CF-TDW TCA	RCAF
FZ586/-----	12141	44	45	ST CF-TDX TCA	RCAF
FZ596/-----	12151	44	44	W/O 22/08/44 at Sea	RCAF
FZ634/-----	12191	44	46	ST CF-TDY TCA	RCAF
FZ635/-----	12192	44	45	ST CF-TDZ TCA	RCAF
FZ669/12943	12254	46	75	ST C-GCXE Aero Trades	RCAF
FZ671/12944	12256	46	89	OB 429 Sqd.	RCAF
FZ678/-----	12273	46	49	WFU; OB 435/436 Sqd.	RCAF
FZ692/12945	12295	46	73	ST C-GRSB E.M.R.	RCAF
FZ694/-----	12300	44	68	ST CF-WTV Millardair	RCAF
FZ695/-----	12301	46	68	ST CF-YDH Norcanair	RCAF
KG312/12912	12307	46	75	ST C-GPOA Buffalo Air	RCAF
KG317/-----	12314	46	50	W/O 29/04/50 Summerside	RCAF
KG320/-----	12317	46	70	ST CF-BVF Wright Enter.	RCAF
KG330/12913	12327	46	76	ST C-GWZS Can-Air Service.	RCAF
KG337/12914	12344	46	72	ST CF-NTF NWT Air	RCAF
KG345/-----	12352	46	69	ST CF-XUS Ontario Central	RCAF
KG350/12915	12357	46	75	ST C-GWMX RC Wilkinson	RCAF
KG354/12916	12363	46	75	ST N59314 Basler F/S	RCAF
KG368/-----	12377	46	47	ST CF-GEI Eldorado	RCAF
KG382/-----	12412	44	46	ST CF-TEA TCA	RCAF Europe

FLEET LISTING
CANADIAN ARMED FORCES

REG'N	C/N	IS	WFU	NOTES	AGENCY
C-47 Dakota (Continued)					
KG389/-----	12419	46	67	ST CF-NWS NWT Air	RCAF
KG394/12918	12424	46	75	ST C-GUBT Bradley A/S	RCAF
KG395/12919	12425	46	77	ST C-GZCR & Sold in USA	RCAF
KG400/-----	12435	46	46	ST N6680 then CF-CTB	RCAF
KG403/12920	12438	46	72	ST N107AD Aerodyne	RCAF
KG414/-----	12449	46	62	ST BJ764 Indian AF	RCAF
KG416/-----	12451	46	52	W/O 18/04/52 Winnipeg	RCAF
KG423/-----	12458	46	69	ST N6619 then CF-NAG	RCAF
KG430/-----	12465	46	51	W/O 26/06/51 Summerside	RCAF
KG441/-----	12476	46	67	ST G-AVPW Hunting Sur.	RCAF Europe
KG455/12924	12490	46	89	OB 429 Sqd.	RCAF Europe
KG479/-----	12591	44	46	ST CF-TEB TCA	RCAF
KG485/-----	12597	44	46	ST CF-TEC TCA	RCAF
KG486/-----	12598	46	70	ST CF-TQW Reindeer A/S	RCAF
KG526/-----	12930	44	45	ST CF-TED TCA 1946	RCAF
KG545/12927	13028	46	80	ST C-GPNW Buffalo Air	RCAF
KG557/12928	13149	46	89	OB 429 Sqd.	RCAF
KG559/-----	13151	46	62	ST BJ767 Indian AF	RCAF
KG562/-----	13154	46	68	ST N6678 then CF-NAR	RCAF
KG563/-----	13155	46	69	ST CF-LFR St. Felicien	RCAF
KG568/-----	13160	46	62	ST BJ763 Indian AF	RCAF
KG577/12929	13300	46	72	ST CF-OOV Atlas Aviation	RCAF
KG580/12930	13303	46	71	W/O 03/11/71 Arctic	RCAF
KG587/12931	13310	46	72	ST C-GXAU/C-GRTM Buffalo Air	RCAF
KG600/ A601	13331	46	53	WFU to A601 Instuctional Airframe	RCAF
KG602/12932	13333	44	80	ST C-GPNR Buffalo Air	RCAF
KG623/12933	13383	46	89	OB 429 Sqd.	RCAF
KG632/12934	13392	46	71	ST CF-QHF NWT Air	RCAF
KG634/-----	13394	46	67	ST CF-WGM Millardair	RCAF
KG635/-----	13395	46	49	W/O 06/07/49	RCAF
KG641/12935	13453	46	72	ST CF-BJE Maritime Aircraft	RCAF
KG668/12942	13485	46	75	ST C-GRSA E.M.R.	RCAF
KG692/-----	13559	44	46	ST CF-TEE TCA	RCAF
KG693/-----	13560	44	46	ST CF-TEF TCA	RCAF
KG713/12946	13580	46	76	ST C-GJKM Buffalo Air	RCAF
KG769/-----	25313	44	46	ST CF-TEG TCA; CF-GXW	RCAF
KG808/12947	25485	46	72	ST CF-BKY Maritime Aircraft	RCAF
KJ827/-----	25611	44	70	ST CF-BYK Superior A/W	RCAF
KJ828/12948	25612	44	76	RR KG828 / 828 / 12948	RCAF
KJ936/-----	26109	44	50	WFU 06/45	RCAF
KJ956/12949	26248	51	89	OB 429 Sqd.	RCAF
KK101/-----	26440	44	47	WFU	RCAF
KK102/12901	26441	44	72	ST CF-BKQ Maritime Aircraft	RCAF
KK143/-----	26726	46	70	ST CF-AUQ Superior A/W	RCAF
KK160/-----	26744	44	68	ST N502PA Priority Air Transit	RCAF
KN200/12902	27004	45	72	ST CF-TVK Bradley A/S	RCAF
KN201/12903	27005	45	75	ST N46938 Basler F/S	RCAF
KN256/-----	27184	46	68	ST CF-KAH Kier Air	RCAF
KN258/12907	27187	46	83	ST ? not C-FPIK	RCAF
KN261/12908	27190	46	76	ST C-GSCA Skycraft Air Transport	RCAF
KN269/-----	27202	46	67	ST CF-PIK Northland A/L	RCAF
KN270/12909	27203	46	76	ST C-GCKE Ontario Central	RCAF
KN277/-----	27212	46	68	ST CF-XXT E. Bowhay	RCAF
KN278/-----	27214	46	63	W/O 08/08/63	RCAF
KN281/12910	27218	46	77	ST N64766 Sharvas Inv.	RCAF
KN291/12911	32540	46	72	RR 10291 64-67 Europe	RCAF Europe
KN392/12917	32813	51	72	ST CF-BKX Northward Avn	RCAF
KN427/12921	32855	46	72	ST CF-TVL Bradley A/S	RCAF
KN436/12922	32865	46	72	ST CF-BKS Maritime Acft	RCAF
KN443/12923	32873	46	75	ST N46950 Basler F/S	RCAF
KN448/-----	32918	46	68	WFU	RCAF
KN451/ 655B	32922	46	59	TO 655B Instruct. A/fr.	RCAF
KN485/12925	32963	52	76	ST C-GWUG Meridian Dev.	RCAF
KN511/12926	33046	46	76	ST C-GWUH Meridian Dev.	RCAF
KN665/-----	33368	46	67	ST CF-WGN Millardair	RCAF

FLEET LISTING
CANADIAN ARMED FORCES

REG'N	C/N	IS	WFU	NOTES	AGENCY
C-47 Dakota (Continued)					
KN666/-----	33369	46	62	ST BJ765 Indian AF	RCAF/UNEF; 115 Sqd
KN676/-----	33384	46	62	ST BJ766 Indian AF	RCAF
KP221/12904	33437	46	72	ST CF-BKR Maritime Acft	RCAF
KP224/12905	33441	46	75	ST C-GSCB Skycraft A/T	RCAF
KP227/12906	33445	46	77	ST N99665 Basler F/S	RCAF
TS422/-----	19345	46	67	ST CF-KAZ Kier Air Tran	RCAF
TS425/-----	19353	46	70	ST CF-AII Ilford-Rivert	RCAF
INSTRUCTIONAL AIRFRAMES					
Airf #/ RCAF#					
A508/650	9015	46	53	WFU	RCAF
A509/652	9108	46	55	ST CF-ITQ Abitibi	RCAF
A597/984	27135	52	82	WFU	RCAF
A601/KG600	13331	53	58	ST N96U Beldex Corp.	RCAF
A628/960	12267	59	62	ST CF-OVN Eldorado	RCAF
655B/KN451	32922	59	64	ST National Aero. Collect.	RCAF
CANADIAN ARMED FORCES CC-129 (C-47) DAKOTAS					
12901/KK102	26441	44	72	ST CF-BKQ Maritime Aircraft	CAF
12902/KN200	27004	44	72	ST CF-TVK Bradley A/S	CAF
12903/KN201	27005	45	75	ST N46938 Basler A/S	CAF
12904/KP221	33437	46	72	ST CF-BKR Maritime Aircraft	CAF
12905/KP224	33441	46	75	ST C-GSCB Skycraft A/T	CAF
12906/KP227	33445	46	77	ST N99665 Basler B/S	CAF
12907/KN258	27187	46	83	ST ? not C-FPIK	CAF
12908/KN261	27190	46	75	ST C-GSCA Skycraft Air Transport	CAF
12909/KN270	27203	46	76	ST C-GCKE Ontario Central	CAF
12910/KN281	27218	46	77	ST N64766 Shavis Investments	CAF
12911/KN291	32540	46	72	ST CF-BKW Maritime Aircraft	CAF
12912/KG312	12307	46	75	ST C-GPOA Buffalo Air	CAF
12913/KG330	12327	46	76	ST C-GWZS Can-Air Service	CAF
12914/KG337	12344	46	72	ST CF-NTF NWT Air	CAF
12915/KG350	12357	46	75	ST C-GWMX NWT Air	CAF
12916/KG354	12363	46	75	ST N59314 Basler A/S	CAF
12917/KN392	32813	51	72	ST CF-BKX Northward Aviation	CAF
12918/KG394	12424	46	75	ST C-GUBT Bradley A/S	CAF
12919/KG395	12425	46	77	ST USA	CAF
12920/KG403	12438	46	72	ST N107AD Aerodyne	CAF
12921/KN427	32855	46	72	ST CF-TVL Bradley A/S	CAF
12922/KN436	32865	46	72	ST CF-BKS Maritime Aircraft	CAF
12923/KN443	32873	46	75	ST N46950 Basler A/S	CAF
12924/KG455	12490	46	89	OB 429 Sqd.	CAF
12925/KN485	32963	52	76	ST C-GWUG Meridian Developments	CAF
12926/KN511	33046	46	76	ST C-GWUH Meridian Developments	CAF
12927/KG545	13028	46	80	ST C-GPNW Buffalo Air	CAF
12928/KG557	13149	46	75	WFU Saskatoon	CAF
12929/KG577	13300	46	72	ST CF-OOV Atlas Aviation	CAF
12930/KG580	13303	46	71	W/O 03/11/71 Arctic	CAF
12931/KG587	13310	46	72	ST C-GXAU/C-GRTM Buffalo Air	CAF
12932/KG602	13333	46	75	ST C-GPNR Buffalo Air	CAF
12933/KG623	13383	46	89	OB 429/402 Sqd.	CAF
12934/KG632	13392	46	71	ST CF-QHF NWT Air	CAF
12935/KG641	13453	46	72	ST CF-BJE Maritime Acft	CAF
12936/ 650	9290	43	75	ST N46949 Basler A/S	CAF
12937/ 653	9415	43	82	WFU for display Calgary	CAF
12938/ 656	9832	43	89	NASARR Nose	CAF
12939/ 657	9834	43	73	ST CF-IRW Ste. Felicien	CAF
12940/ 659	9833	43	74	ST N300ZZ Zoom Zoom Air	CAF
12941/ 660	10199	43	75	ST N64767 Sharvas Investments	CAF
12942/KG668	13485	46	75	ST C-GRSA E.M.R.	CAF
12943/FZ669	12254	46	76	ST C-GCXE Aero Trades	CAF
12944/FZ671	12256	46	89	OB 429 Sqd.	CAF
12945/FZ692	12295	46	73	ST C-GRSB E.M.R.	CAF
12946/KG713	13580	46	76	ST C-GJKM Buffalo Air	CAF
12947/KG808	25485	46	72	ST CF-BKY Maritime Aircraft	CAF
12948/KJ828	25612	44	72	ST C-GCXD Aero Trades	CAF

FLEET LISTING
CANADIAN ARMED FORCES

REG'N	C/N	IS	WFU	NOTES	AGENCY
CANADIAN ARMED FORCES CC-129 (C-47) DAKOTAS (Continued)					
12949/KG959	26248	51	89	OB 429 Sqd.	CAF
12950/963	12543	44	89	OB 429 Sqd.	CAF
12951/964	12411	44	72	ST CF-OOY Atlas Aviation	CAF
12953/969	13343	44	75	ST C-GWYX Ilford-River.	CAF
12954/970	13342	44	71	ST CF-OOW Atlas Aviation	CAF
12955/972	25371	44	72	ST CF-BKT Maritime Aircraft	CAF
12956/973	25368	44	75	ST C-GWMY NWT Air	CAF
12957/976	26002	44	89	OB 429 Sqd.	CAF
12958/977	26005	44	72	ST CF-QHY NWT Air	CAF
12959/979	26641	44	89	OB "Pinocchio" Cold Lake.	CAF
12960/981	26643	44	72	ST CF-QNF Sterling A/S	CAF
12961/988	33116	45	72	ST CF-BKU Maritime Aircraft	CAF
12962/990	33467	45	77	ST N99663 Basler A/S	CAF
12963/992	12217	45	89	OB 429 Sqd.	CAF
12964/993	12483	45	75	ST C-GGNA Austin A/W	CAF
12965/1000	33352	46	75	ST C-GSCC Skycraft	CAF
12966/10911	9186	51	75	ST N46877 Basler A/S	CAF
12967/10912	4441	51	72	ST CF-BKV Maritime Acft	CAF
12968/10913	18986	51	75	ST C-GWYY Wilkinson	CAF
12969/10915	33540	52	73	ST CF-ADB Air Dale	CAF
12970/10919	27074	52	72	ST CF-BKZ Bot Construct	CAF
12971/10920	12238	46	71	ST CF-OOX Atlas Avn.	CAF

C-45 Expeditor

REG'N					
1563	CA163	52	67	WFU	RCAF
1574	CA174	52	67	WFU	RCAF
1577	CA263	53	66	ON DISPLAY CFB Winnipeg	RCAF
1578	CA264	53	64	W/O 18/07/64 Summerside	RCAF
1589	CA275	53	67	WFU	RCAF
2307	CA180	52	67	ST CF-CKT Covlin et al	RCAF
2368	CA247	52	67	WFU	RCAF
2369	CA248	52	54	W/O 17/03/54 Grande Prairie	RCAF
2370	CA249	52	67	WFU	RCAF
2371	CA250	52	67	WFU	RCAF
2372	CA251	52	67	WFU	RCAF

NAE DHC-6 Twin Otter, CF-POK-X

DOT DHC-6 Twin Otter, C-FCSY

COAST GUARD

The Coast Guard operates a fleet consisting mainly of helicopters to service lighthouses and to operate from ice breaker ships. Bell Jet Rangers and Alouettes make up the bulk of the fleet. One Sikorsky S61N operates in BC. A single DC-3 was operated out of Ottawa on ice patrols along the St. Lawrence and for local transport, but has been replaced by a DOT DASH-7.

FLEET LISTING.

CANADIAN COAST GUARD

REG'N	C/N	IS	WFU	NOTES
DC-3				
C-FDTH*	12591	76	C	Based in Ottawa
Sikorsky S61N				
C-FDOH*	61704	73	C	Based on West Coast
Bell 206B				
C-FCGL*	25	67	86	Based in Victoria
Alouette III				
C-FCAW	1251	65	86	Based in Victoria
MBB BO-105				
C-GCHW	S-641	85	C	

DEPARTMENT OF ENERGY, MINES AND RESOURCES

Several aircraft are operated by *Innotech Aviation* on behalf of this branch of the federal government. A Convair, a former *Canadian Forces* Falcon jet and two former *Canadian Forces* Dakotas are based in Ottawa and operated by *Innotech*. A Short Skyvan and Beech Queen Air make up the current fleet.

FLEET LISTING

DEPARTMENT OF ENERGY, MINES AND RESOURCES

REG'N	C/N	IS	WFU	NOTES
DC-3				
C-GRSA	13485	75	C	OB Innotech; CF 12942
C-GRSB	12295	75	C	OB Innotech; CF 12945
Convair 580				
C-GRSC	72	74	C	OB Innotech; EX CF-BGY
Falcon 20C				
C-GRSD	157	72	C	OB Innotech; CF 117508
Shorts Skyvan				
C-FGSC*	1845	68	C	
Beech 65 B80				
C-FWZG	LD386	79	C	

DEPARTMENT OF TRANSPORT

The Department of Transport (DOT) has operated a wide variety of aircraft over the years, including helicopters. A large fleet of DC-3s has served with the department and three remained in service in 1988. Three Viscounts served as VIP aircraft through the 1960s and 1970s with the last phased out in 1983. In 1962 the first of four Jetstar executive jet aircraft was purchased. These were all retired when the Challenger jet became available. One Grumman Gulfstream II jet was purchased and used as a calibration aircraft until sold in 1987. This aircraft was replaced by the DASH-8 in 1987.

Twin Otters, including the eight former *Air Transit* aircraft, are used for general duties along with Beech 95s, and Beech 65s. One DASH-7 is used for ice reconnaissance work along the St. Lawrence and is operated by *Bradley Air Service* out of Ottawa.

All of the Challengers were turned over to the *Canadian Forces* early in 1985 to be operated as executive transport by 412 Squadron in Ottawa.

FLEET LISTING

DEPARTMENT OF TRANSPORT

REG'N	C/N	IS	WFU	NOTES
Dash-8				
C-GCFJ	020	86	C	Calibration a/c
C-GCFK	028	86	C	
Challenger CL600				
C-GBKC	1007	82	86	ST 144604 CF
C-GBEY	1008	81	86	ST 114605 CF
Challenger CL602				
C-GCFG	3022	84	C	Calibration a/c
C-GCFI	3020	84	C	Calibration a/c
Gulfstream II				
C-GCFB	28	76	87	ST N120EA EAF Aircraft
Jetstar				
C-FETN*	5021	70	86	EX CF-ETN Eatons
C-FDTF*	5088	67	86	
C-FDTM*	5052	72	86	
C-FDTX*	5018	62	8	
Viscount				
CF-DTA	229	58	82	WFU & Scrapped
CF-GXK	70	55	82	WFU & Scrapped
CF-TGP	53	64	70	WFU & Scrapped; EX TCA
DHC-6 Twin Otter				
C-FCST	351	76	C	EX CF-CST Air Transit
C-FCSU	352	76	C	EX CF-CSU Air Transit
C-FDTJ*	37	70	C	
DHC-2 Beaver				
C-FDTC*	34	49	C	
C-FDTI*	37	49	C	
DC-3				
C-FDOT*	4733	50	86	
C-FDTB*	12597	58	86	
C-FDTD*	12253	58	86	
C-FGXW*	25313	57	85	ST C-FGXW Odyssey 86
Lockheed 12A				
CF-CCT	1219	37	63	On display in Ottawa
DASH-7				
C-GCFR	102	86	C	OB Bradley A/S

NATIONAL AERONAUTICAL ESTABLISHMENT (NAE)

Based at Ottawa's Uplands Airport, the National Aeronautical Establishment is the aviation division of the National Research Council (NRC). NAE has several types of aircraft in its Flight Research Laboratory fleet, jet and piston fixed-wing aircraft and helicopters. A former RCAF North Star (CF-SUP-X) served for several years until replaced by a Convair 580. Former RCAF Beech Expeditors were used for much of the work in the 1960s and 1970s. A Harvard continues to serve in the fleet as do two T-33 Silver Stars jets. One T-33 is designed to achieve zero-g flight for up to 25 seconds to carry out micro-gravity experiments and the other has precise instrumentation for measuring speed and altitude. The Twin Otter carries instumentation to measure certain components of the atmosphere affecting agricultural crops. Current helicopters include a Bell 206 Jet Ranger and a Bell 205A. The first Buffalo aircraft produced was with the NRC in 1982 undergoing trials with jet engines before being returned to de Havilland.

NAE operates several wind tunnels for testing new aircraft designs and aircraft dynamics.

RCMP DHC-3 Otter, C-FMPK

RCMP Beech King Air, CF-VMH

FLEET LISTING
NATIONAL AERONAUTICAL ESTABLISHMENT

REG'N	C/N	IS	WFU	NOTES
North Star				
CF-SVP-X	121	65	79	ST N8022L Scrapped
Convair 580				
CF-NRC	473	73	C	
DHC-6 Twin Otter				
C-FPOK *	116	72	C	LT C-FPOK Kimba Air 82
T-33 Silver Star				
C-FSKH *	379	65	C	EX 21379 RCAF
C-FWIS *	590	67	C	EX 21590 RCN
Bell 205A				
C-FYZV *	30055	69	C	
Bell 206A				
C-FZUQ	629	71	C	
Beech 18				
CF-SKJ	CA138	65	80	EX 1538 RCAF
Harvard IV				
CF-PTP	CCF41	64	C	EX 20210 RCAF
Bell 47G				
C-FSCK	1213	64	80	WFU
DHC-5 Buffalo				
C-GFIU	1	82	82	ST C-GFIU de Havilland

ROYAL CANADIAN MOUNTED POLICE (RCMP)

Four deHavilland Dragaonfly aircraft were received by the force in 1937. The following year a Norseman was added but this aircraft was written off in the same year and replaced with another Norseman. Beech 18 aircraft and a Grumman Goose CF-MPG were added during 1946. The Beech 18s served for more than two decades and were sold or withdrawn due to cracked main trusses between 1968 and 1973. The Grumman Goose is still in operation. A Cornell and a Stinson Stationwagon were added in 1947 and a second Norseman in 1949. Late 1949 also saw the arrival of the Beaver aircraft. Twelve Beavers served with the Air Service over a period of thirty-seven years, half of them being written off in accidents.

The de Havilland Otter joined the fleet in 1954 with a total of eight being operated. One Otter remains in service in 1989. Several years passed before a new type of aircraft was added, during which Beavers and Otters made up the bulk of the fleet. In 1967 a Beechcraft King Air A90 was purchased and operated until involved in a wheels-up accident in 1987. In 1968 the first of three Turbo Beavers was added. The current mainstay of the fleet, the Twin Otter, joined the force in 1969 and ten remain in service in 1988.

The first helicopter used by the RCMP Air Service was a Bell 212 purchased in 1972 and sold in 1980. In 1973, the first of ten Bell 206 Jet Rangers was purchased. Two Jet Rangers have been destroyed in British Columbia, one by hitting an unmarked power wire near Ucluelet in December 1983.

A Beech 200 was added to the fleet in 1976 and is based at Victoria. A Cessna 182 was operated for only three years and was then replaced by a Cessna 206. The first jet in the RCMP Air Service, a Cessna Citation, was purchased new on 14 October 1987.

FLEET LISTING
ROYAL CANADIAN MOUNTED POLICE (RCMP)

REG'N	C/N	IS	WFU	NOTES
DH-90 Dragonfly				
CF-MPA	7530	37	40	ST 7530 RCAF
CF-MPB	7531	37	40	ST 7531 RCAF
CF-MPC	7522	37	40	ST 7522 RCAF
CF-MPD	7538	37	38	ST CF-BPD Noorduyn Aviation
Norseman IV				
CF-MPE	16	39	39	W/O 30/10/39 Sioux Lookout
CF-MPF	27	39	49	ST CF-MPF Hall's Air Service
Grumman Goose				
CF-MPG	37824	46	C	EX RCAF: based at Prince Rupert
Beech 18				
CF-MPA	5848	60	66	W/O 10/66 Edmonton hangar fire
CF-MPB	5964	60	68	WFU; EX RCAF
CF-MPC	A799	60	70	WFU; EX RCAF
CF-MPH	A-141	46	71	On Display Regina RCMP Museum
CF-MPI	A-142	46	73	WFU
Stinson 108-2				
CF-MPJ	2303	47	59	ST CF-MPJ Flight Investment
Fairchild M62A3				
CF-MPK	FV708	47	57	ST CF-MPK R.A. Hills
Norseman V				
CF-MPL	N2940	49	59	ST CF-MPL Bradley Air Service
DHC-2 Beaver				
CF-MPD	1510	62	84	ST CF-MPD Crown Assets
CF-MPE	1528	62	83	ST C-FPME Northwestern F/S
CF-MPM	62	49	78	ST CF-MPM Air Tiberiade
CF-MPN	335	52	78	ACC at Stephenville; Sold
CF-MPO	359	52	63	W/O 13/07/63 Carmacks, Yukon
CF-MPQ	837	56	59	W/O 04/11/59 Regina hangar fire
C-FMPQ*	1604	66	86	W/O 08/01/86 at Wallaston Lake

FLEET LISTING
ROYAL CANADIAN MOUNTED POLICE (RCMP)

REG'N	C/N	IS	WFU	NOTES
DHC-2 Beaver (Continued)				
CF-MPR	971	57	84	W/O 30/08/84 north Sept-Iles
CF-MPS	114	58	79	ST CF-MPS Northern Thunderbird
CF-MP	1260	59	79	ST CF-MPT Propair
CF-MPV	1304	60	79	ST CF-MPV Amos Aviation
CF-FHW	58	50	58	W/O 08/58 near Kamloops, B.C.
DHC-3 Otter				
CF-MPK	38	64	86	RR C-FEBX ST Brown's A/S 1986
C-FMPO*	52	64	C	Based Edmonton; EX 3686 RCAF
CF-MPP	42	54	83	ST C-FMPP Burrard Air
CF-MPU	44	58	61	LF 3683 RCAF; now C-GOFC
CF-MPW	271	59	76	W/O 18/08/76 Ile La Crosse, Sask.
CF-MPX	280	59	79	ST CF-MPX Bannock/Hyack
CF-MPY	324	59	79	ST CF-MPY Max Ward personal a/c
CF-MPZ	328	60	71	W/O 27/09/71 Deer Lake, Nfld.
DHC-6 Twin Otter				
C-FMPB*	276	70	C	Based at Yellowknife, N.W.T.
C-FMPC*	311	71	C	Based at Regina, Saskatchewan
C-FMPF*	312	71	C	Based at Frobisher Bay, N.W.T.
C-FMPH*	319	71	C	Based at Inuvik, N.W.T.
C-FMPL*	320	71	C	Based at Whitehorse, Yukon
C-FMPN*	321	71	C	Based at Edmonton, Alberta
C-FMPW	828	85	C	Based at Goose Bay, Labrador
C-GMPJ	534	77	C	Based at Prince Albert, Sask.
C-GMPK	471	76	C	Based at Thompson, Manitoba
C-GMPX	588	78	C	Based at Winnipeg, Manitoba
C-GMPY	796	82	C	Based at Peace River, Alberta
DHC-2 Turbo Beaver				
C-FCJB	TB-39	68	C	Based at Prince George, B.C.
C-FMPA	TB-53	68	C	Based at Calgary, Alberta
C-FOEX	TB-52	80	C	EX C-FOEX Air West/Ontario Govt.; Based at Kamloops, B.C.
Bell 212				
C-FMPZ	30528	72	80	ST C-FMPZ Bell Helicopters
Bell 206B				
C-FMPI*	978	73	84	ST C-FMPI Crown Assets
C-FMPQ	3512	86	C	
C-GDXB	1891	76	83	W/O 14/12/83 near Ucluelet, BC
C-GDXC	1901	76	C	Based at Fort McMurray, Alberta
C-GGRC	3623	82	C	Based at Kelowna, B.C.
C-GINB	3746	84	C	Based at Comox, B.C.
C-GMPS	2942	80	C	Based at St. John's, Nfld.
C-GRVM	2940	84	87	W/O 13/08/87 Cloudburst Mtn. BC
Bell 206L				
C-GMPM	45086	77	C	Based at Cornerbrook, Nfld.
C-GMPT	45149	78	C	Based at Fredericton, N.B.
C-GMPV	45414	80	C	Based at Gander, Newfoundland
Beech 65A90				
C-FVMH	LJ225	66	87	ACC at Ottawa, Ont.; Sold 2/88
Beech 200				
C-GPKK	BB181	76	C	Based at Victoria, B.C.
Cessna 182P				
C-GCZI	63693	82	85	Sold: EX N4692K
Cessna 208 Caravan				
C-GMPB	00082	86	C	EX N9521F: based at Montreal
C-GMPR	00116	87	C	
Cessna 210 Centurion				
C-FMOM	64924	85	C	
C-GTCT	64949	85	C	
Cessna 550				
C-FMPP	0411	87	C	Based at La Ronge; EX N200YM

Aircraft Statistics

The following statistics are taken from a variety of sources and are intended only as a guide. The number of passengers carried by an aircraft can vary considerably depending upon the number of first class, business class and economy class seats as well as the pitch of the seats. Cargo weights will vary with conditions, amount of fuel carried and desired range.

By reviewing this information, readers can compare the various aircraft flown by the airlines of Canada over the years.

Aircraft	Engine Type	No. of Engines	Length (Feet)	Span (Feet)	Cruise (MPH)	Range (Miles)	No. of Passengers	Cargo (Lbs.)
Boeing 767-200	J	2	159.2	156.1	530	3100	210	
Boeing 767-300	J	2	180.3	156.1	560	6600	260	
Boeing 747	J	4	232.0	196.0	555	5000	442	130,500
Boeing 737-300	J	2	109.5	94.8	495	2540	138	
Boeing 737-200	J	2	100.2	93.0	485	2200	117	
Boeing 727-200	J	3	153.2	108.0	530	2600	144	
Boeing 727-100	J	3	132.2	108.0	530	1500	118	46,000
Boeing 707-300	J	4	152.9	142.0	550	5700	189	55,000
Boeing 707-100	J	4	144.5	130.9	484	5400	179	47,450
Boeing 720	J	4	136.8	130.9	557	4155	167	
DC-10-30	J	3	182.0	165.0	540	5360	259	
DC-10-10	J	3	182.0	155.0	540	3220	259	
DC-9-32	J	2	119.3	93.3	520	1550	102	
DC-9-15	J	2	104.3	89.3	505	663	75	
DC-8-63	J	4	187.0	148.4	530	5000	227	98,000
DC-8-62	J	4	157.4	148.4	470	6000	189	52,000
DC-8-61	J	4	187.3	148.4	460	4800	151	85,000
DC-8-54F	J	4	150.5	142.3	530	2590	---	89,000
DC-8-21/43/50	J	4	150.2	142.3	530	4360	135	
Convair 990	J	4	139.2	120.0	555	3800	110	
L-1011-500	J	3	155.3	164.3	550	5500	244	
L-1011-100	J	3	178.7	155.3	570	3650	289	
L-1011-1	J	3	178.7	133.3	570	3000	289	
Airbus A300	J	2	175.9	147.1	530	3700	250	
Airbus A310	J	2	153.0	144.0	533	4370	196	
Airbus A320	J	2	123.3	111.3	525	2310	150	
BAC 1-11 (400)	J	2	93.5	93.5	460	2300	79	
Fokker F-28-1000	J	2	89.9	82.3	420	1600	65	
Fokker F-28-0100								
kBAe 146	J	4	85.8	85.5	435	1650	80	
Comet 1	J	4	93.1	114.8	460	2500	36	
Avro Jetliner	J	4	80.8	98.1	430	1100	50	
Vanguard	T	4	122.9	18.6	420	3100	108	
Viscount	T	4	81.2	93.9	315	1760	54	
Electra	T	4	104.5	99.0	375	2500	83	
Convair 640	T	2	81.5	105.3	300	1230	52	
Convair 580	T	2	79.1	105.3	340	1230	52	
Convair 540/CC109	T	2	81.5	105.3	310	1230	52	
Convair 440	P	2	81.5	105.3	289	1230	52	
Convair 240	P	2	74.7	91.8	272	900	40	
Nord 262	T	2	63.3	72.0	233	865	26	
Herald	T	2	75.5	94.8	230	1620	44	
YS-11A	T	2	86.3	105.0	280	2000	48	
HS-748	T	2	67.0	98.5	225	600	40	
SD-360	T	2	70.5	74.7	243	265	36	
SD-330	T	2	58.0	74.8	184	870	30	

Aircraft	Engine Type	No. of Engines	Length (Feet)	Span (Feet)	Cruise (MPH)	Range (Miles)	No. of Passengers	Cargo (Lbs.)
Shorts Skyvan	T	2	40.1	64.9	175	700	19	4,400
F-27	T	2	77.3	95.1	298	1200	40	
F-227	T	2	83.8	95.2	270	1580	52	
Cessna Citation I	J	2	47.2	51.7	443	1970	6	
Cessna Citation II	J	2	52.0	51.7	450	2000	10	
Challenger 600	J	2	68.4	61.9	488	3220	19	
Challenger 601	J	2	68.4	64.3	460	4364	19	
CC-106 Yukon	T	4	136.9	42.3	400	6700	134	52,000
Britannia	T	4	124.3	142.3	360	4270	114	
L-1049	P	4	113.6	123.0	330	4800	75	
North Star	P	4	93.9	117.5	225	3060	62	
C-5	P	4	97.3	117.5	320	2500	24	
DC-7	P	4	112.3	127.5	344	4600	105	
DC-6	P	4	105.6	117.5	315	3000	86	
DC-4	P	4	93.8	117.5	227	2500	62	
DC-3	P	2	64.5	95.0	165	2125	21	
ATR-42	T	2	74.4	80.6	300	740	48	
Metro II	T	2	59.1	45.9	285	350	16	
BAe 3100 Jetstream	T	2	47.2	52.0	269	455	19	
Dash-8	T	2	75.5	84.0	300	690	36	7,820
Dash-7	T	4	80.7	93.0	230	855	50	11,400
DHC-6 Twin Otter	T	2	51.8	65.0	210	810	18	5,000
DHC-4 Caribou	P	2	72.6	95.6	180	600	30	8,600
DHC-3 Otter	P	1	41.8	58.0	138	875	10	3,600
DHC-2 Beaver	P	1	30.2	48.0	130	450	7	1,900
DHC-2 Turbo Beaver	T	1	35.2	48.0	151	600	7	2.600
Grumman Mallard	P	2	48.3	66.8	180	1380	10	
Turbo Mallard	T	2	48.3	66.8	220	1600	10	
Grumman Goose	P	2	39.6	50.8	200	800	7	
Turbo Goose	T	2	39.6	50.8	240	1200	7	
Beech 18	P	2	35.2	49.8	185	1530	7	
Gulfstream I	T	2	64.8	78.3	300	2300	12	
MU-2	T	2	39.4	39.2	340	1600	9	
BN Islander	T	2	35.8	49.0	150	870	9	
Hercules	T	4	106.0	132.5	322	2400	---	45,000
Carvair	P	4	102.6	117.5	213	2300	---	32,000
Argosy	T	4	86.8	115.0	280	2000	---	23,000
Bristol 170	P	2	73.3	108.0	163	2000	32	8,000
Curtiss C-46	P	2	76.3	108.0	235	1800	36	13,000
Boeing 247D	P	2	51.6	74.0	189	750	10	
Avro York	P	4	102.0	78.5	240	2700	24	
Cessna Cran	P	2	32.8	41.9	175	750	4	
Avro Anson	P	2	42.3	56.5	158	790	8	
Norseman	P	1	31.8	51.8	150	1150	8	1,690
PBY Canso	P	2	64.8	104.3	120	4000	17	
Stearman	P	1	24.0	32.2	107	440	0	
Lockheed 10A	P	2	38.6	55.0	190	700	10	
Lockheed 12A	P	2	35.0	50.0	200	700	6	
Lockheed 14	P	2	44.2	65.5	201	800	10	
Lockheed 18	P	2	49.8	65.5	190	750	17	
Lancastrian	P	4	75.0	102.0	230	3100	10	

Bibliography

BAIN, D.M., *Canadian Pacific Airlines - Its History and Aircraft,* Kishorn Publications, Calgary, 1987

BLATHERWICK, F.J., *Airlines of Canada,* FJB Air Publication, New Westminster, 1978

COLLINS, DAVID H.,*Wings Across Time - The Story of Air Canada,* Griffin Press Limited, Toronto, 1978.

CONDIT, JOHN, *Wings Over The West - Russ Baker And The Rise Of Pacific Western Airlines,* Harbour Publishing company, Madeira Park, B.C., 1984.

ELLIS, JOHN R., *Canadian Civil Aircraft Registry,* Canadian Aviation Historical Society, Toronto.

ENDERS, GUNTER E., *World Airline Fleets 1987 (and Other Years),* Aviation Data Centre, Feltham, Middlesex, 1987.

FULLER, G.A., GRIFFIN, J.A., MOLSON, K.M., *125 Years Of Canadian Aeronautics - A chronology 1840-1965,* Canadian Aviation Historical Society, 1983

GRADIDGE, J.M.G., *The Douglas Dc-3,* Air Britain Publications, 1984.

GRIFFIN, J.A., *Canadian Military Aircraft, Serials and Photographs,* Canadian War Museum, Ottawa, 1969.

HAYES, KARL E., *De Havilland Canada DHC-3 Otter,* Irish Air Letter, Dublin, Ireland, 1982.

HOTSON, FRED W., *The De Havilland Canada Story,* Canav Books, Toronto, 1983

KEITH, RONALD A., *Bush Pilot With A Brief Case,* Doubleday, Toronto, 1972. (Story of Grant McConachie and Canadian Pacific Airlines.).

KILLION, G.L., *The Convair Twins 240 To 640,* Macdonald & Jane Airline Publications, 1979.

MAIN, J.R.K., *Voyageurs of the Air, a History of Civil Aviation in Canada 1858-1967,* The Queen's Printer, Ottawa, 1967.

MILBERRY, LARRY, *Aviation In Canada,* McGraw-Hill Ryerson Limited, Toronto, 1979.

MILBERRY, LARRY, *The Canadair North Star, Canav Books, Toronto, 1982.*

TOMKINS, NIGEL, *Airliner Production List 1986/87 (and Other Years),* Aviation Data Centre, Feltham, 1987.

OTHER RESEARCH SOURCES

Air Britain Publications
  Curtiss C-46 Commando, the Boeing 707, 727, The Douglas DC-6 and DC-7 Series, The McDonnell-douglas DC-8

Air Britain News
  published by Air-Britain (Historians) Limited, 1 East Street, Tonbridge, Kent, England.

Airline Publication & Sales Ltd.,
  Douglas DC-6 and Douglas DC-7 books.

Aviation Letter
  Lundkvist Avition Reserarch Inc.,
  P.O. Box 8946, Coral Springs, Florida, 33075-8946, USA (published monthly)

Canadian
  Airstream Inflight Marketing Inc. (published monthly)

Canadian Aviation Magazine

Canadian Aviation Historical Society Journals

Canadian Civil Aircraft Registry

En Route
  Airmedia Sales (published monthly)

North American Aviation News (NAAN)
  6540 Hayvenhurst Avenue, #6, Van Nuys, California, USA, 91406.

Westflight
  P.O. Box 23374, Vancouver A.M.F., B.C., V7B 1W1. ($27.00 per year).

Wings